The

·Elde   ·ies·

The Elderberries.

A Cartoon Collection

IL FRANK and JOE TROISE

Andrews McMeel
Publishing, LLC
Kansas City

The Elderberries is distributed internationally by Universal Press Syndicate.

08 09 10 11 12 TWP 10 9 8 7 6 5 4 3 2 1

ISBN-13: 978-0-7407-7368-6
ISBN-10: 0-7407-7368-2

Library of Congress Control Number: 2008924877

www.andrewsmcmeel.com

Dedicated to Phil Frank . . . the character he was
and the characters he created

Foreword

When a cartoonist creates a new comic strip, he or she is actually creating a fantasy world. The artist has to populate it with one, two, or maybe, in an act of daring, up to six recognizable characters, while keeping in mind that it's a small world, after all—only a few inches long—so it can't be too crowded. It also needs geography, which can be as simple as someone's backyard, as surreal as an unidentified desert landscape, or as complex as the solar system. Furniture, buildings, and even doghouses are useful, as it gets a bit boring to watch little figures standing around in empty space. It's not as easy as it looks.

Phil Frank was unique among cartoonists in that he created a number of worlds in his long career as a cartoonist—some all his own, and others in collaboration. There was the reporter named Farley, who traveled across America, at least until he settled in San Francisco for the duration. Another world, one of animals, contained a traveling dog named Miles. There was the realm of Nigel Shiftright, Automotive Anachronism, an anglophile who lived in his own mind most of the time—the world of imagination. And finally, *The Elderberries*, represented by a pen-and-ink universe called Elderpark, written and drawn in collaboration with yours truly.

So how is this particular cartoon world different from all the others? I don't know what Phil's answer would have been, but mine is this—it was the first cartoon strip I ever worked on with Phil where the characters told us who they really wanted to be. Some, whom we had great plans for, faded into the background within a few months; others, who we thought might be merely decorative, grabbed the spotlight.

When you meet Dusty, the quintessential American individualist; the General, a war hero; Boone, the wise commentator; Evelyn, the older person we'd all like to be; Mr. Johnson, a man still young at heart; the Professor, whom you never want to play Scrabble with; and Ludmilla, with her heart of gold and her bicep of iron—please notice how beautifully they are drawn and how alive they seem. Within their creation lies the magic of a unique art form, and a very demanding one—a type of art that Phil Frank mastered as well as any person who possessed the extraordinary gift of squeezing humor out of the tip of a pen.

Joe Troise
Santa Cruz, California, 2008

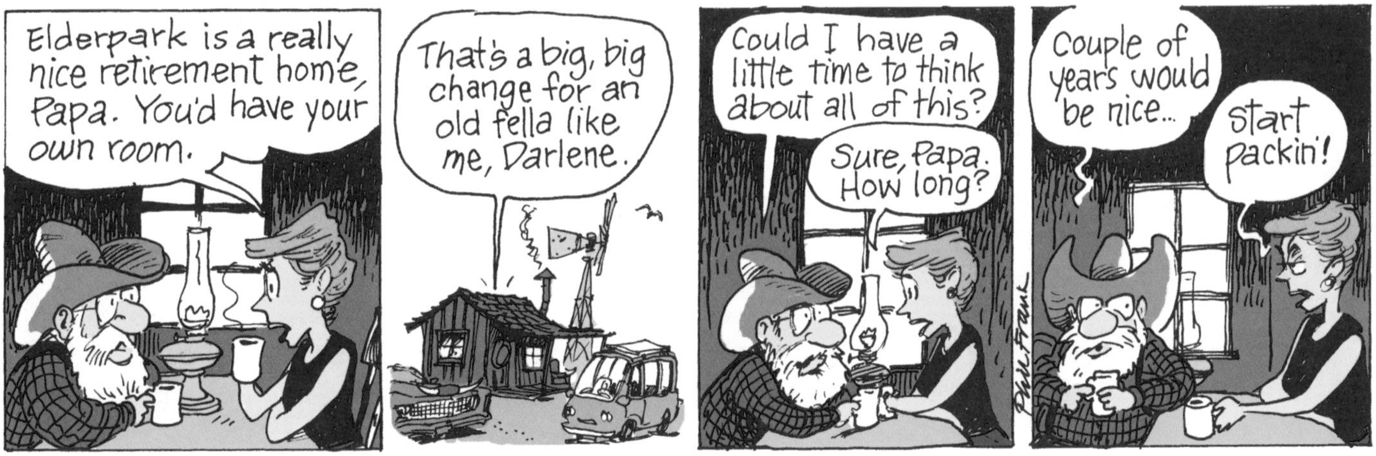
Elderpark is a really nice retirement home, Papa. You'd have your own room.
That's a big, big change for an old fella like me, Darlene.
Could I have a little time to think about all of this?
Sure, Papa. How long?
Couple of years would be nice...
Start packin'!
Phil Frank

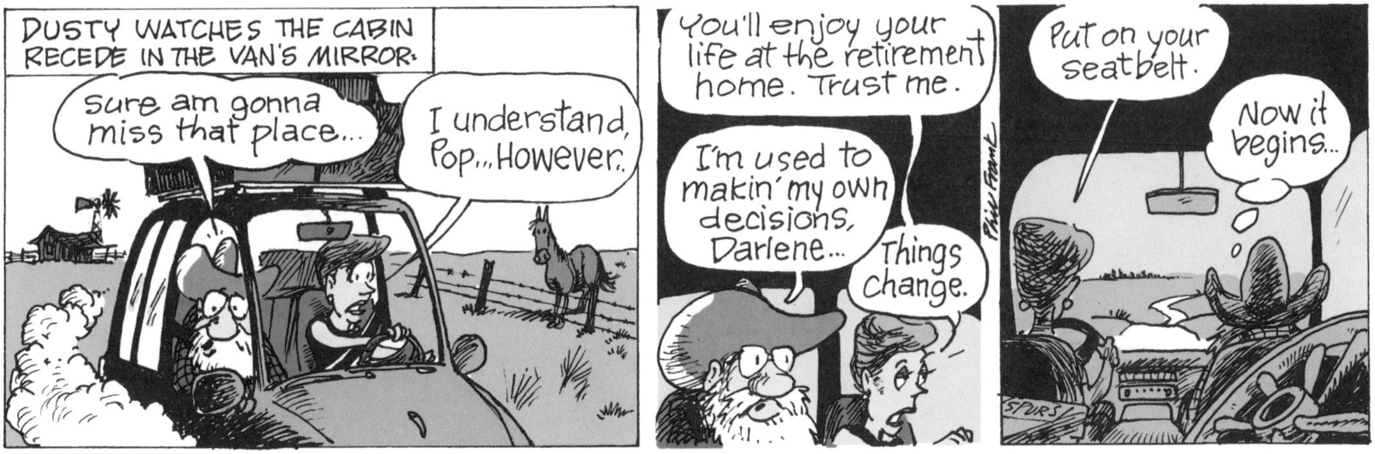
DUSTY WATCHES THE CABIN RECEDE IN THE VAN'S MIRROR.
Sure am gonna miss that place...
I understand, Pop... However...
You'll enjoy your life at the retirement home. Trust me.
I'm used to makin' my own decisions, Darlene...
Things change.
Phil Frank
Put on your seatbelt.
Now it begins...
SPURS

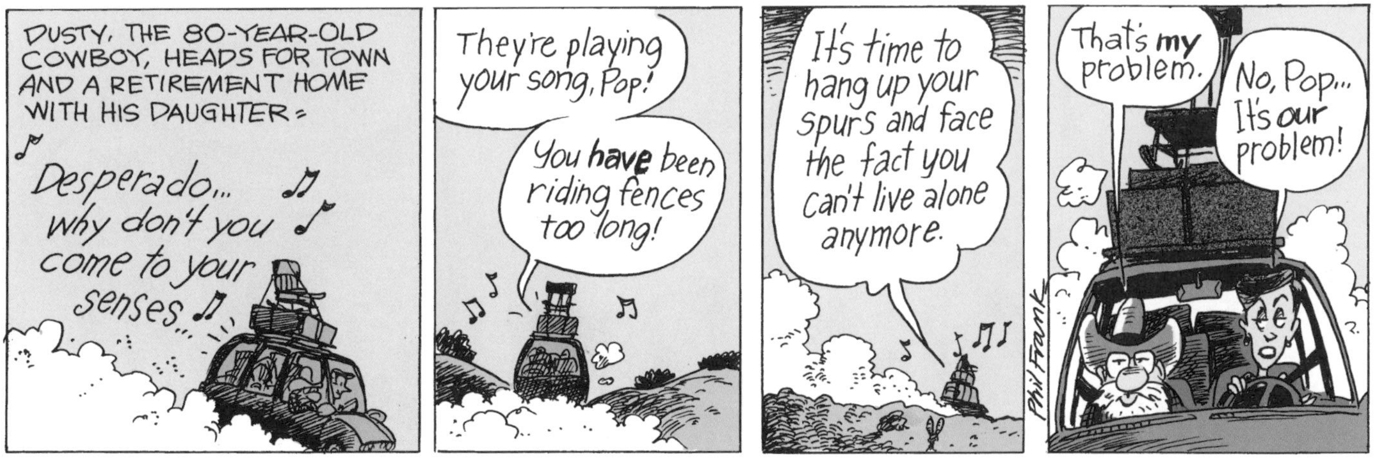
DUSTY, THE 80-YEAR-OLD COWBOY, HEADS FOR TOWN AND A RETIREMENT HOME WITH HIS DAUGHTER.
Desperado... why don't you come to your senses...
They're playing your song, Pop!
You **have** been riding fences too long!
It's time to hang up your spurs and face the fact you can't live alone anymore.
Phil Frank
That's **my** problem.
No, Pop... It's **our** problem!

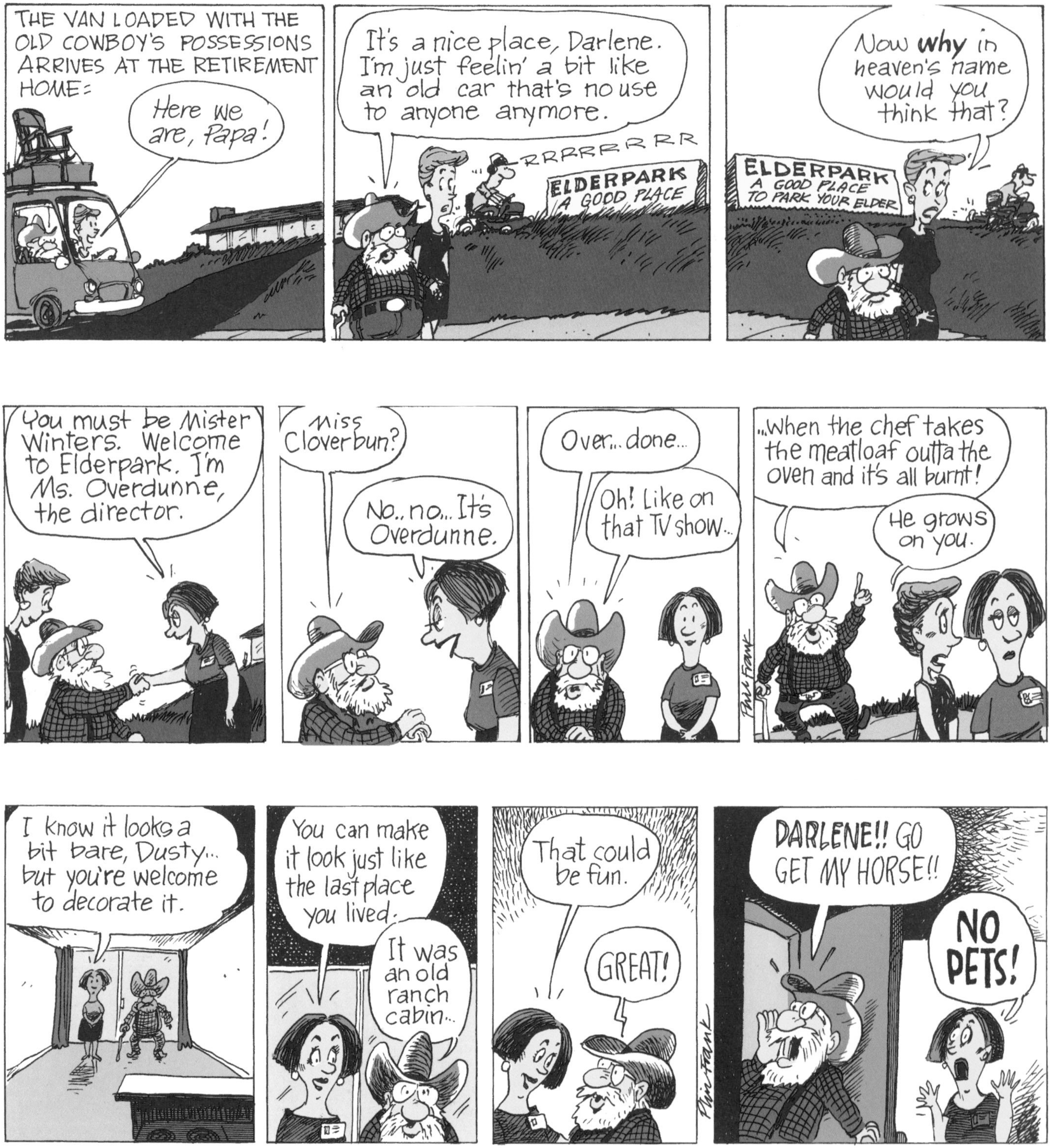
THE VAN LOADED WITH THE OLD COWBOY'S POSSESSIONS ARRIVES AT THE RETIREMENT HOME:
Here we are, Papa!
It's a nice place, Darlene. I'm just feelin' a bit like an old car that's no use to anyone anymore.
RRRRRRRRRR
ELDERPARK A GOOD PLACE
Now why in heaven's name would you think that?
ELDERPARK A GOOD PLACE TO PARK YOUR ELDER
You must be Mister Winters. Welcome to Elderpark. I'm Ms. Overdunne, the director.
Miss Cloverbun?
No.. no... It's Overdunne.
Over... done...
Oh! Like on that TV show...
...When the chef takes the meatloaf outta the oven and it's all burnt!
He grows on you.
I know it looks a bit bare, Dusty... but you're welcome to decorate it.
You can make it look just like the last place you lived.
It was an old ranch cabin...
That could be fun.
GREAT!
DARLENE!! GO GET MY HORSE!!
NO PETS!

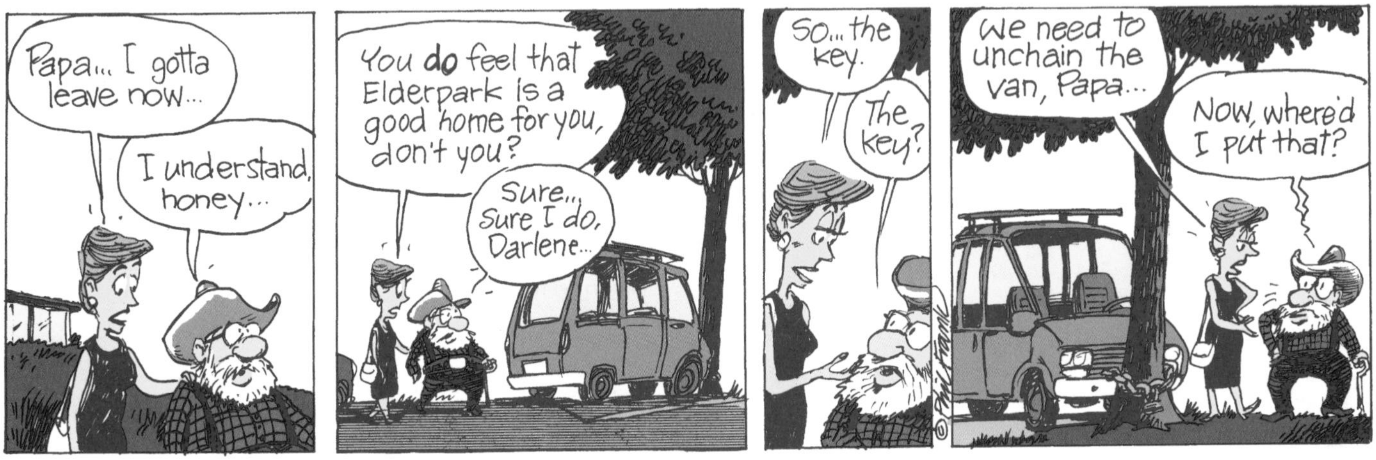
Papa... I gotta leave now...
I understand, honey...
You **do** feel that Elderpark is a good home for you, don't you?
Sure... Sure I do, Darlene...
So... the key.
The key?
We need to unchain the van, Papa...
Now, where'd I put that?

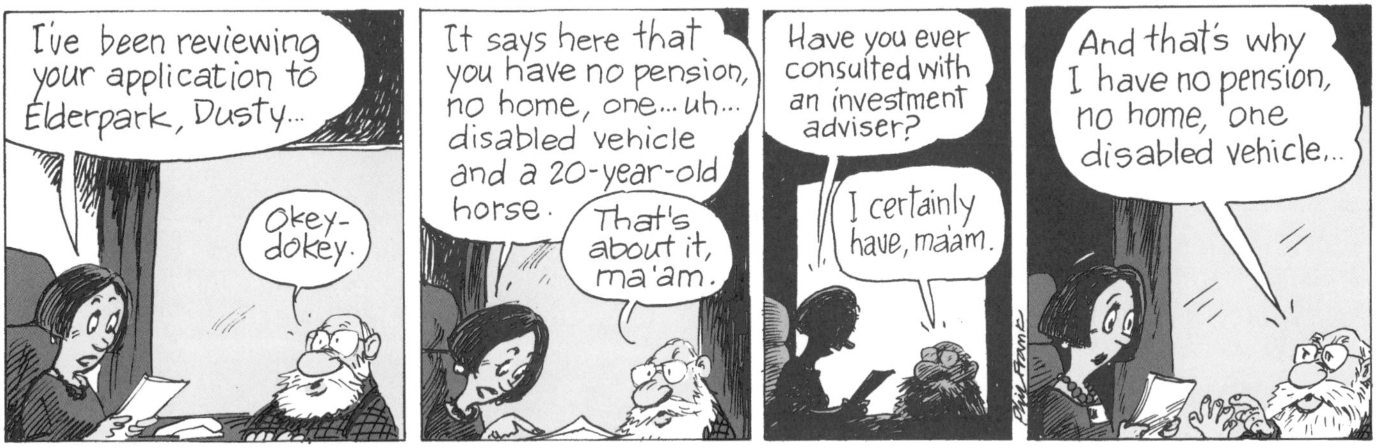
I've been reviewing your application to Elderpark, Dusty...
Okey-dokey.
It says here that you have no pension, no home, one... uh... disabled vehicle and a 20-year-old horse.
That's about it, ma'am.
Have you ever consulted with an investment adviser?
I certainly have, ma'am.
And that's why I have no pension, no home, one disabled vehicle...

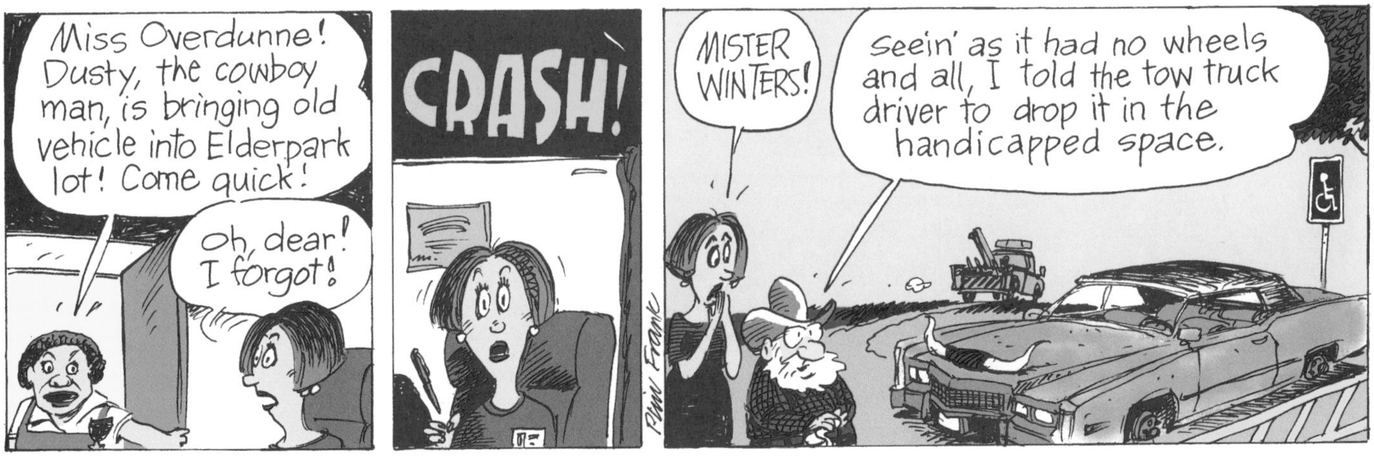
Miss Overdunne! Dusty, the cowboy man, is bringing old vehicle into Elderpark lot! Come quick!
Oh, dear! I forgot!
CRASH!
MISTER WINTERS!
Seein' as it had no wheels and all, I told the tow truck driver to drop it in the handicapped space.

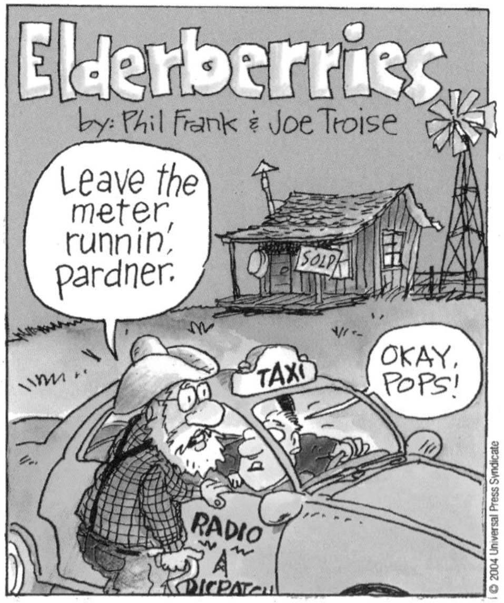
Elderberries
by: Phil Frank & Joe Troise
Leave the meter, runnin', pardner.
SOLD
TAXI
OKAY, POPS!
RADIO
© 2004 Universal Press Syndicate

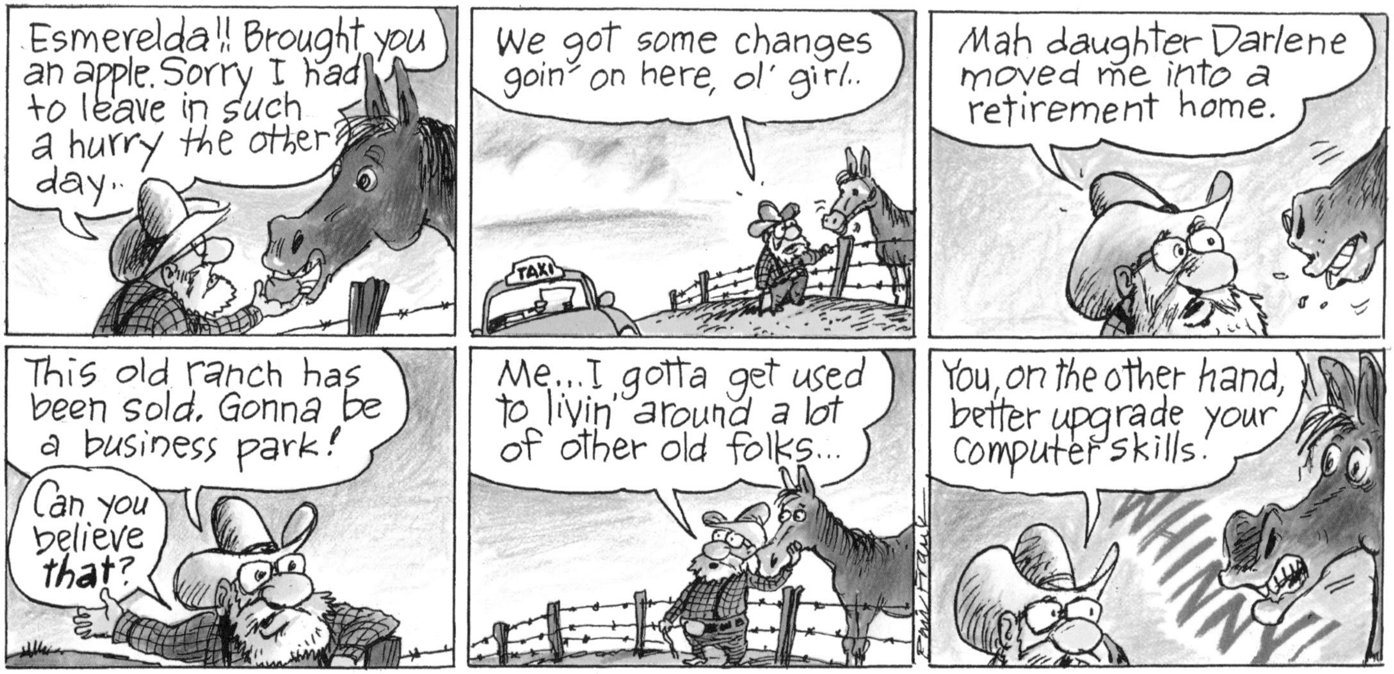
Esmerelda!! Brought you an apple. Sorry I had to leave in such a hurry the other day..
We got some changes goin' on here, ol' girl..
TAXI
Mah daughter Darlene moved me into a retirement home.
This old ranch has been sold. Gonna be a business park!
Can you believe that?
Me...I gotta get used to livin' around a lot of other old folks...
Phil Frank
You, on the other hand, better upgrade your computer skills.
WHINNY

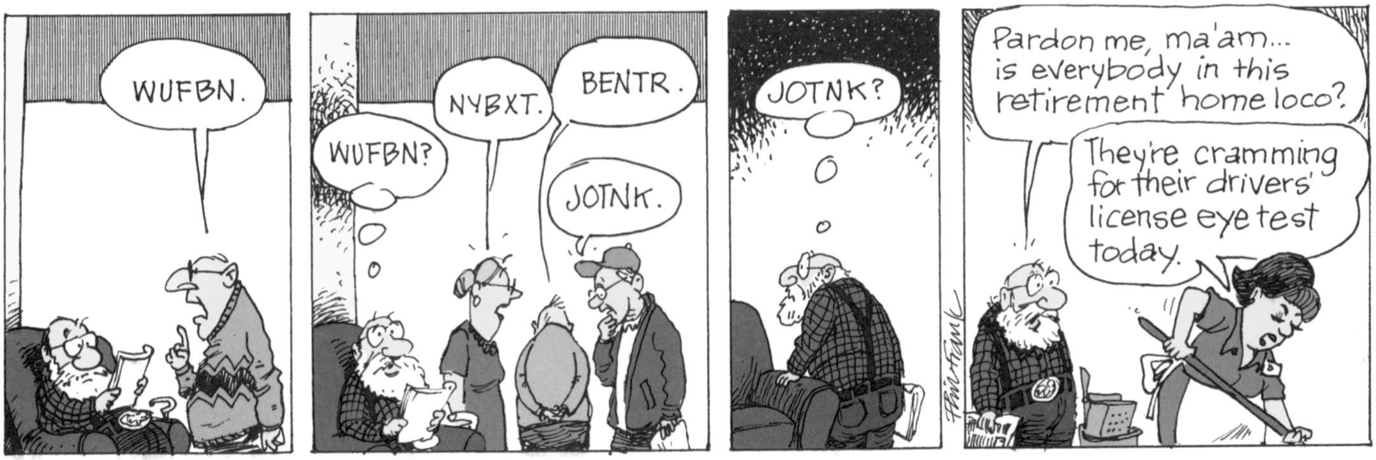
WUFBN.
WUFBN?
NYBXT.
BENTR.
JOTNK.
JOTNK?
Pardon me, ma'am... is everybody in this retirement home loco?
They're cramming for their drivers' license eye test today.

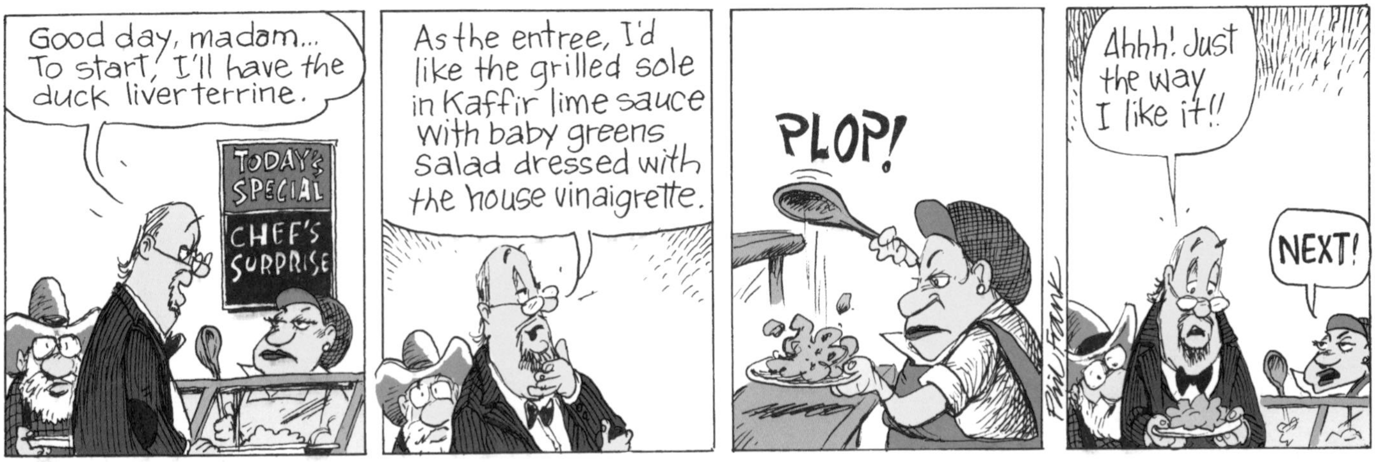
Good day, madam... To start, I'll have the duck liver terrine.
TODAY'S SPECIAL
CHEF'S SURPRISE
As the entree, I'd like the grilled sole in Kaffir lime sauce with baby greens salad dressed with the house vinaigrette.
PLOP!
Ahhh! Just the way I like it!!
NEXT!

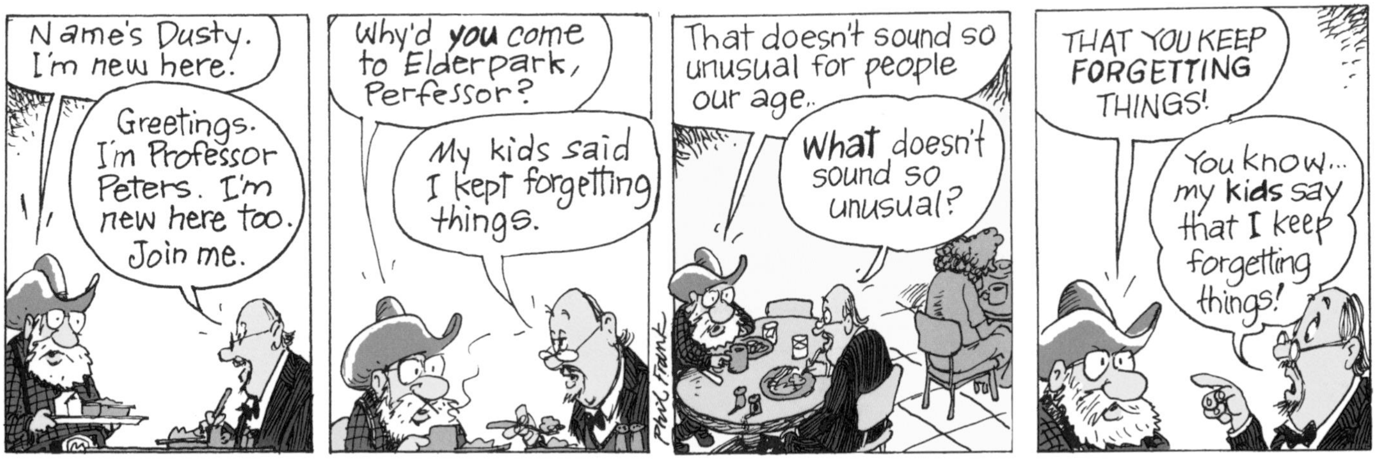
Name's Dusty. I'm new here.
Greetings. I'm Professor Peters. I'm new here too. Join me.
Why'd you come to Elderpark, Perfessor?
My kids said I kept forgetting things.
That doesn't sound so unusual for people our age..
What doesn't sound so unusual?
THAT YOU KEEP FORGETTING THINGS!
You know... my kids say that I keep forgetting things!

Elderberries
·by·
Phil Frank and Joe Troise
I think Dusty's apartment is down this corridor..

KNOCK! KNOCK!
Hello, Dusty... are we intruding?
No! Come on in, ladies!!
ELDERPARK
A GOOD PLACE TO PARK YOUR ELDER
This is Gladys. I wanted her to see what you've done with your space.
How do! I'm still gettin' my place all put together..
I'm settin' it up just like the ranch cabin I lived in...
It's **so** quaint, Dusty!
Got mah saddle and spurs and mah lariat...
...mah telephone and a place for some vittles...
Dusty... I just **have** to say..
SLAM!
"What a nice bunch of antiques!?"
How was I to know he bought them all new?

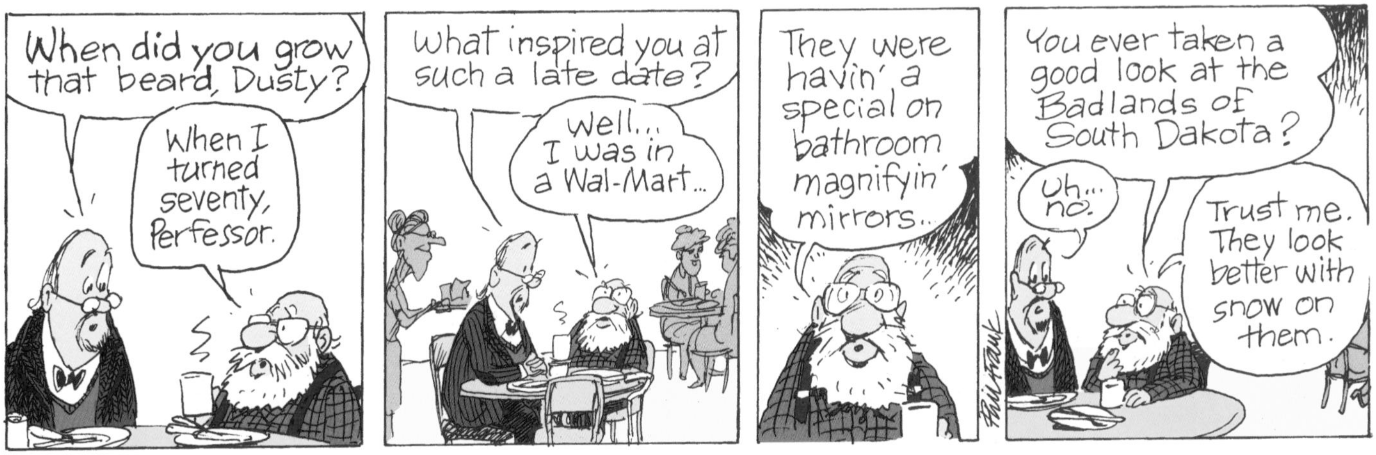
When did you grow that beard, Dusty?
When I turned seventy, Perfessor.
What inspired you at such a late date?
Well... I was in a Wal-Mart...
They were havin' a special on bathroom magnifyin' mirrors...
You ever taken a good look at the Badlands of South Dakota?
Uh... no.
Trust me. They look better with snow on them.

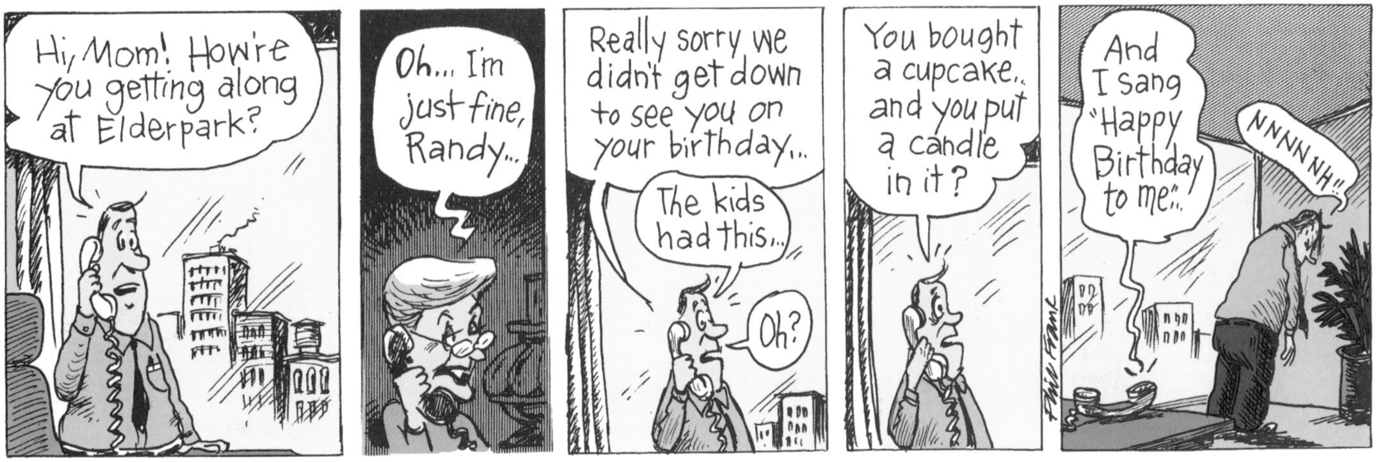
Hi, Mom! How're you getting along at Elderpark?
Oh... I'm just fine, Randy...
Really sorry we didn't get down to see you on your birthday...
The kids had this...
Oh?
You bought a cupcake... and you put a candle in it?
And I sang "Happy Birthday to me"...
NNNNNH!!

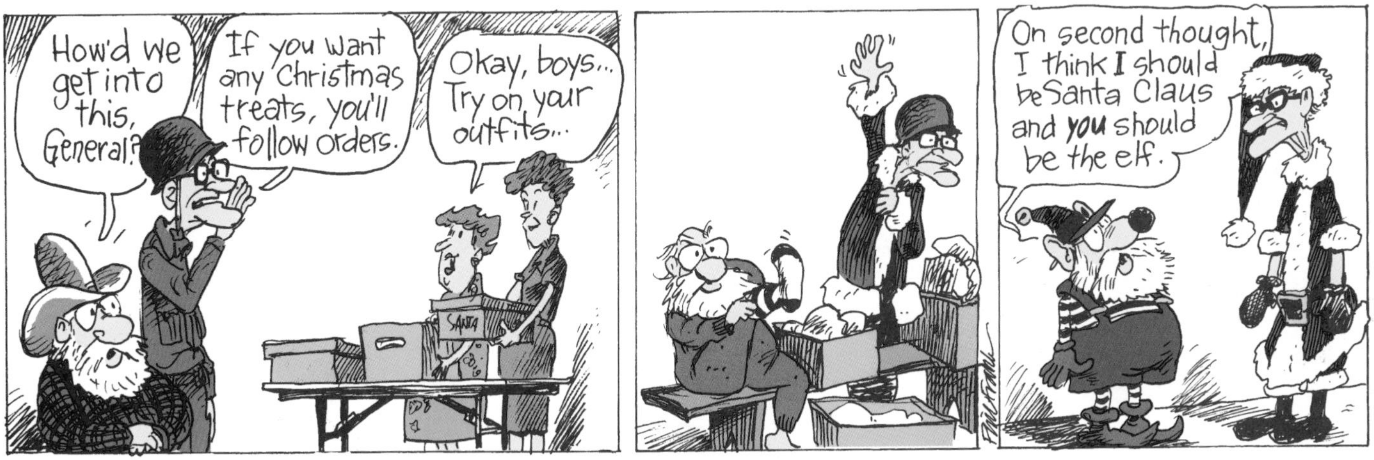
How'd we get into this, General?
If you want any Christmas treats, you'll follow orders.
Okay, boys... Try on your outfits...
SANTA
On second thought, I think I should be Santa Claus and you should be the elf.

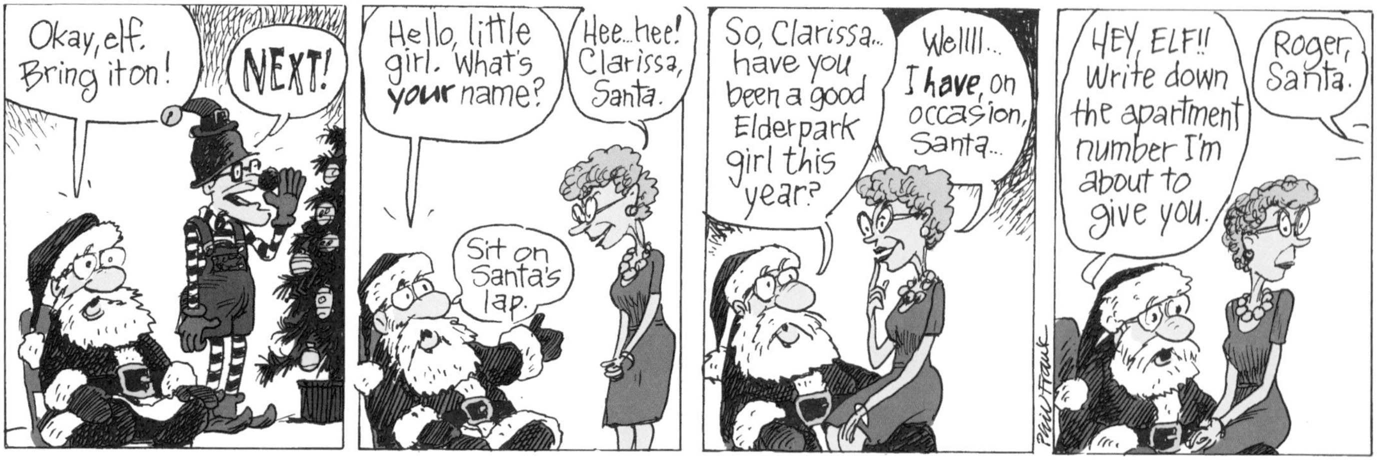
Okay, elf. Bring it on!
NEXT!
Hello, little girl. What's **your** name?
Hee...hee! Clarissa, Santa.
Sit on Santa's lap.
So, Clarissa... have you been a good Elderpark girl this year?
Wellll... I **have**, on occasion, Santa...
HEY, ELF!! Write down the apartment number I'm about to give you.
Roger, Santa.

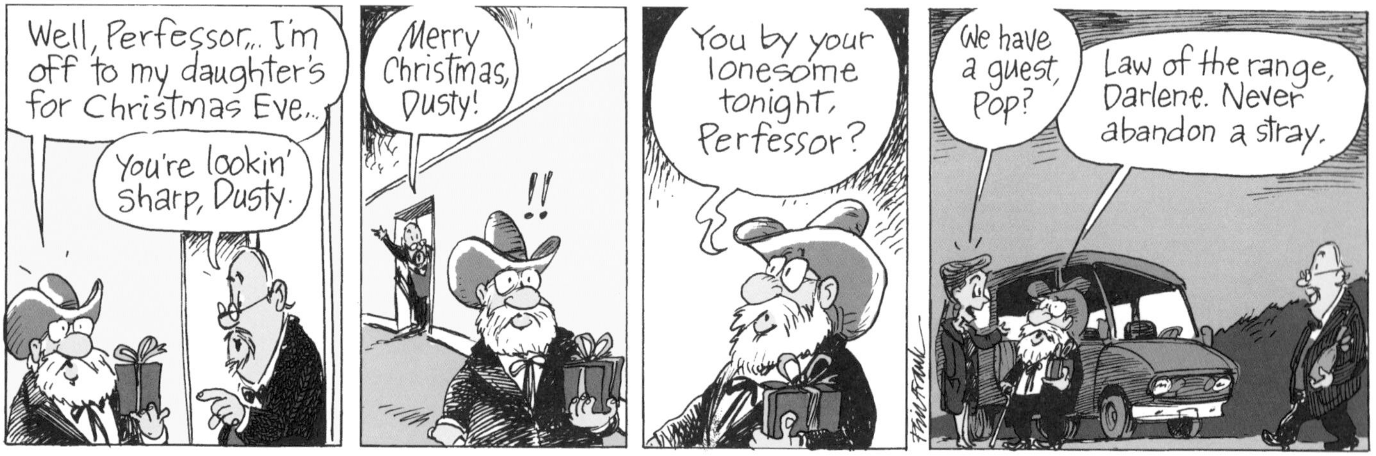
Well, Perfessor... I'm off to my daughter's for Christmas Eve...
You're lookin' sharp, Dusty.
Merry Christmas, Dusty!
!!
You by your lonesome tonight, Perfessor?
We have a guest, Pop?
Law of the range, Darlene. Never abandon a stray.

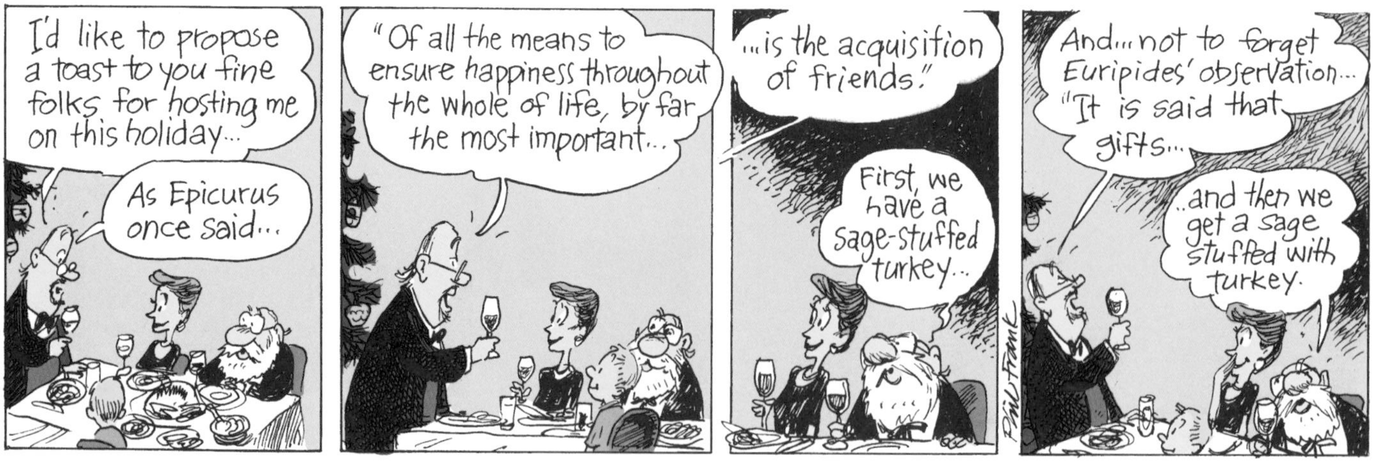
I'd like to propose a toast to you fine folks for hosting me on this holiday...
As Epicurus once said...
"Of all the means to ensure happiness throughout the whole of life, by far the most important...
...is the acquisition of friends."
First, we have a sage-stuffed turkey...
And... not to forget Euripides' observation... "It is said that gifts...
...and then we get a sage stuffed with turkey.

Elderberries
Phil Frank & Joe Troise
OKAY, singers... PRESENT PRESENTS!!

The Elderpark Carolers are singing, Ludmilla!
How lovely!
Christmas Day is over with The gifts they are abounding The huge amount of useless junk, It really is astounding.
I see you have a DVD to take into the shower..
And I myself have just received a phone shaped like a flower!
Oh, would you care to swap those socks for my ceramic kitten?
Or maybe cookies dyed bright green, that I have hardly bitten?
FA-LA-LA and FA-LA-LEE! Let's pile this stuff up higher, and dance around like we were kids,.. and light it all afire.
Ludmilla... do you smell smoke?
SNIFF!
Give me Department of Fire.

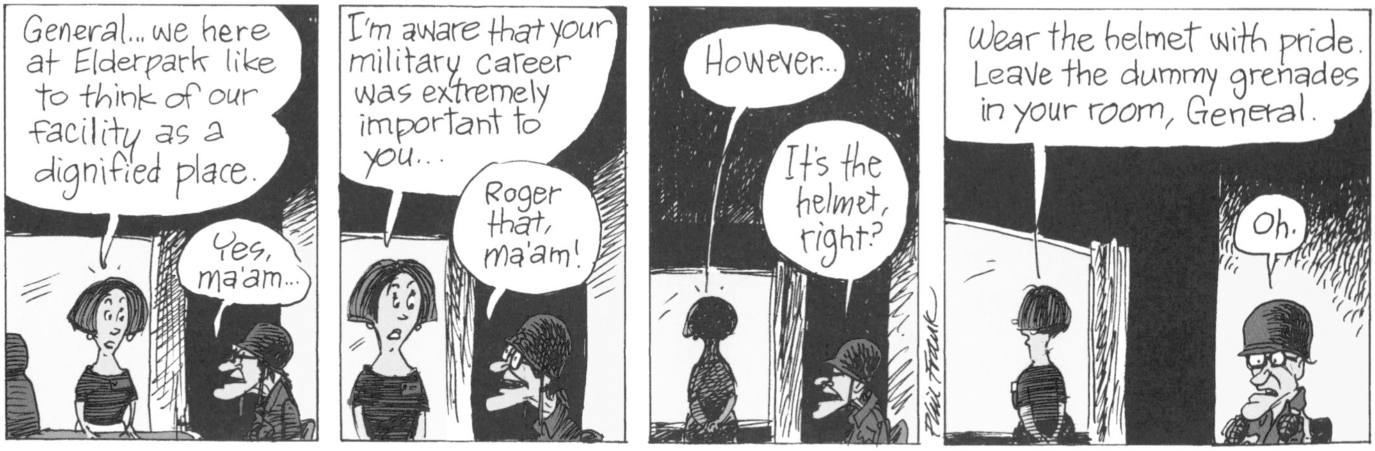
General... we here at Elderpark like to think of our facility as a dignified place.
Yes, ma'am...
I'm aware that your military career was extremely important to you...
Roger that, ma'am!
However...
It's the helmet, right?
Wear the helmet with pride. Leave the dummy grenades in your room, General.
Oh.

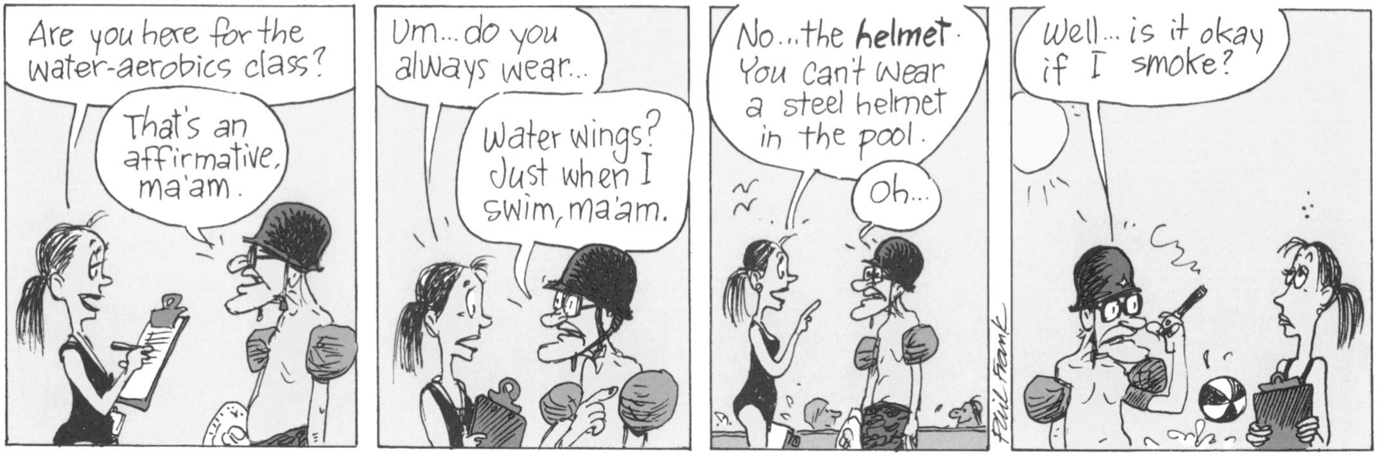
Are you here for the water-aerobics class?
That's an affirmative, ma'am.
Um... do you always wear...
Water wings? Just when I swim, ma'am.
No... the **helmet**. You can't wear a steel helmet in the pool.
Oh...
Well... is it okay if I smoke?

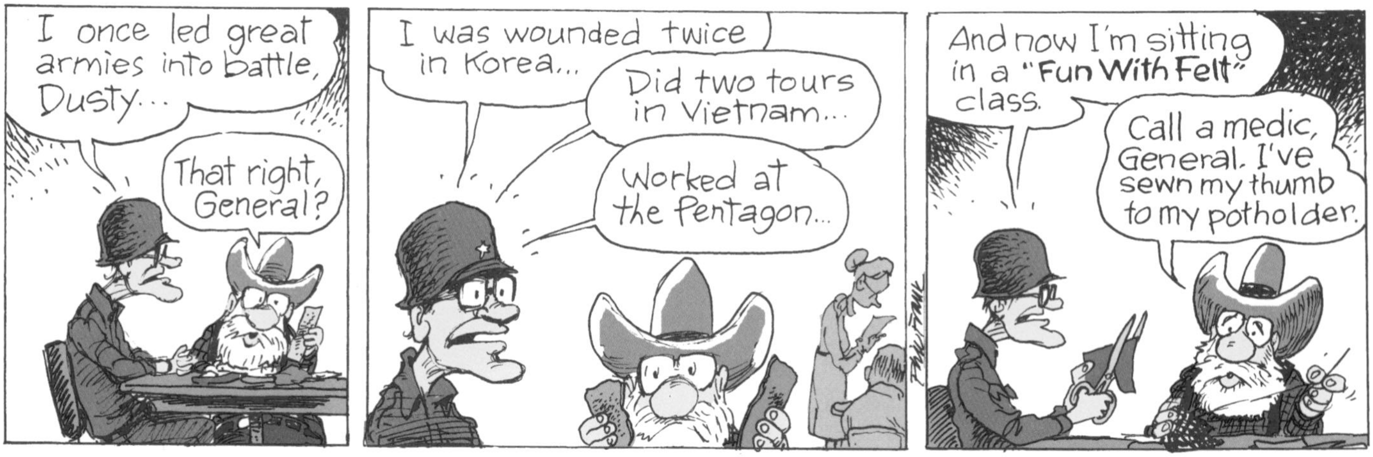
I once led great armies into battle, Dusty...
That right, General?
I was wounded twice in Korea...
Did two tours in Vietnam...
Worked at the Pentagon...
And now I'm sitting in a "**Fun With Felt**" class.
Call a medic, General. I've sewn my thumb to my potholder.

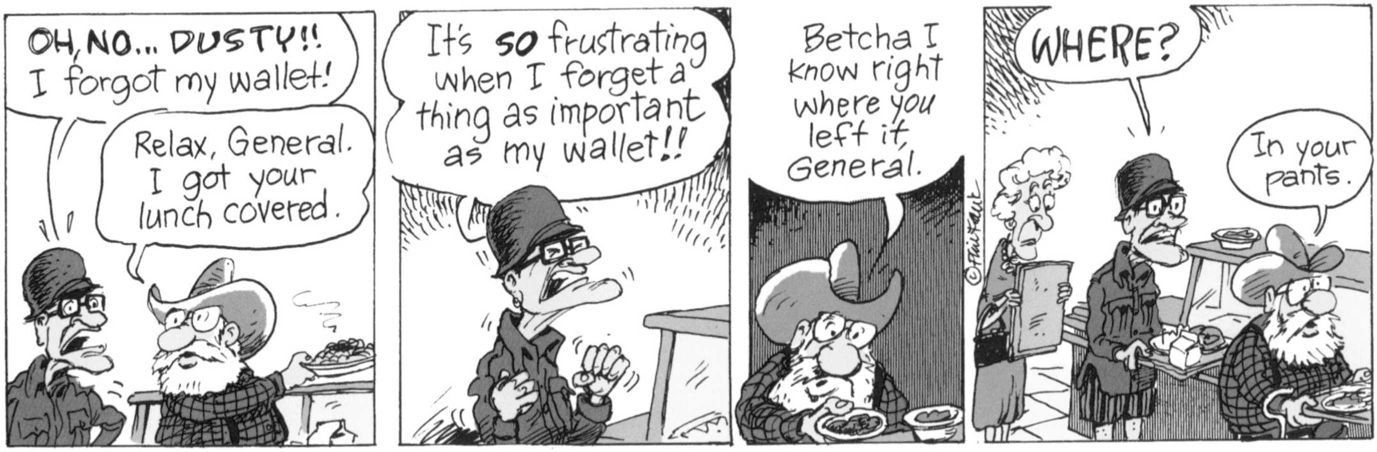
OH, NO... DUSTY!! I forgot my wallet!
Relax, General. I got your lunch covered.
It's **SO** frustrating when I forget a thing as important as my wallet!!
Betcha I know right where you left it, General.
©Phil Frank
WHERE?
In your pants.

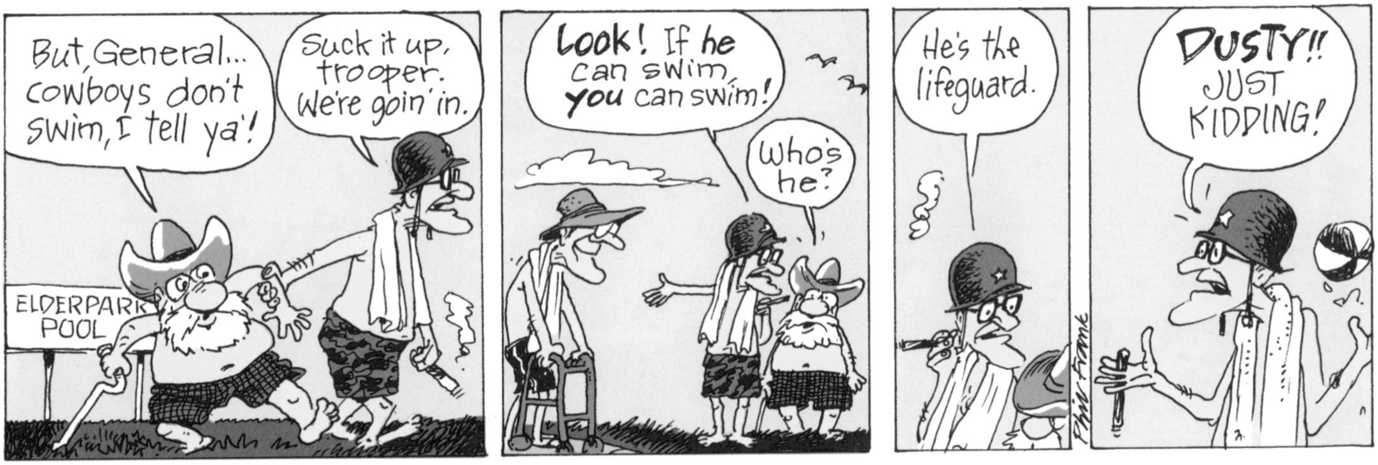
But, General... cowboys don't swim, I tell ya'!
Suck it up, trooper. We're goin' in.
ELDERPARK POOL
LOOK! If **he** can swim, **you** can swim!
Who's he?
He's the lifeguard.
Phil Frank
DUSTY!! JUST KIDDING!

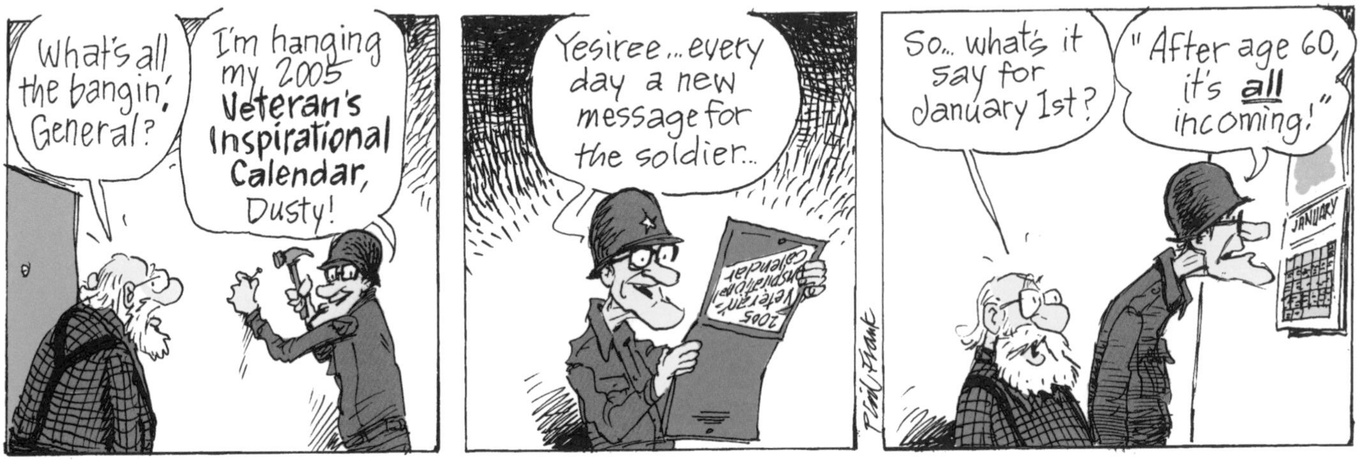
What's all the bangin', General?
I'm hanging my 2005 **Veteran's Inspirational Calendar**, Dusty!
Yesiree... every day a new message for the soldier...
Phil Frank
So... what's it say for January 1st?
"After age 60, it's <u>all</u> incoming!"
JANUARY

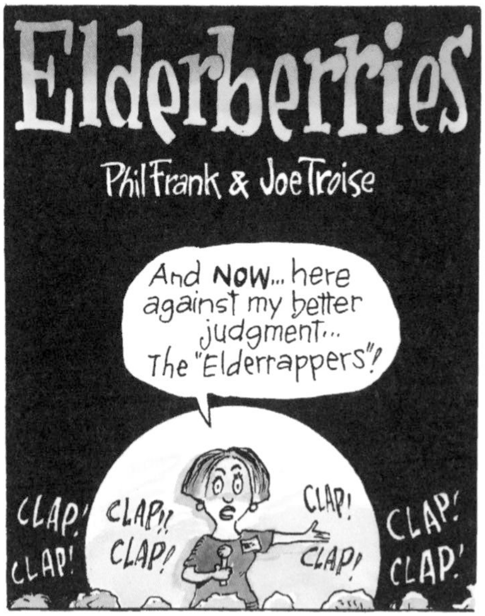

Elderberries
Phil Frank & Joe Troise
And NOW... here against my better judgment... The "Elderrappers"!
CLAP! CLAP!
CLAP!! CLAP!
CLAP! CLAP!
CLAP! CLAP!

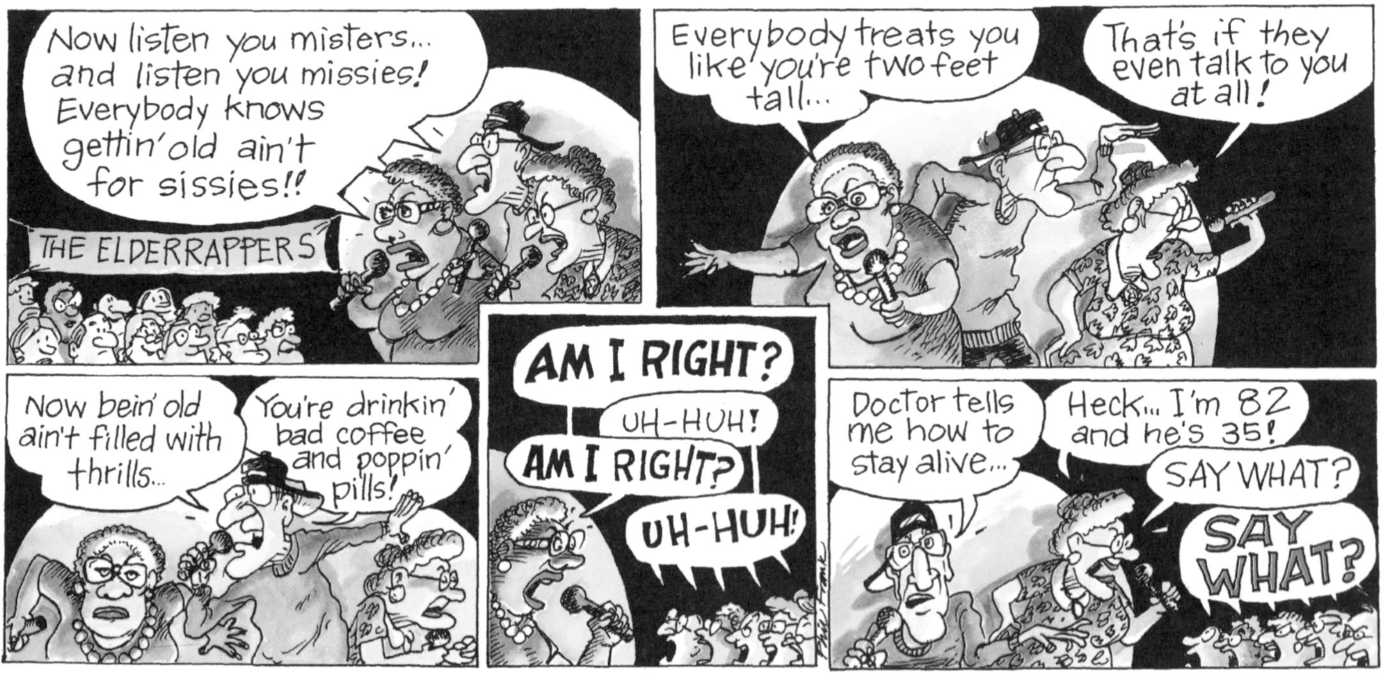

Now listen you misters... and listen you missies! Everybody knows gettin' old ain't for sissies!!
THE ELDERRAPPERS
Everybody treats you like you're two feet tall...
That's if they even talk to you at all!
Now bein' old ain't filled with thrills...
You're drinkin' bad coffee and poppin' pills!
AM I RIGHT?
UH-HUH!
AM I RIGHT?
UH-HUH!
Doctor tells me how to stay alive...
Heck... I'm 82 and he's 35!
SAY WHAT?
SAY WHAT?

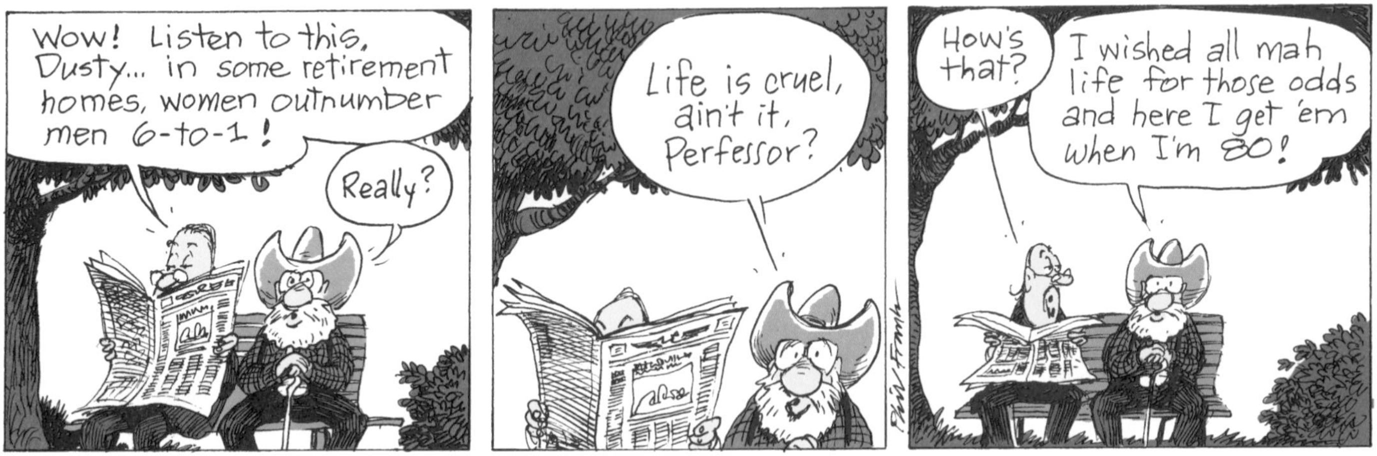
Wow! Listen to this, Dusty... in some retirement homes, women outnumber men 6-to-1!
Really?
Life is cruel, ain't it, Perfessor?
How's that?
I wished all mah life for those odds and here I get 'em when I'm 80!

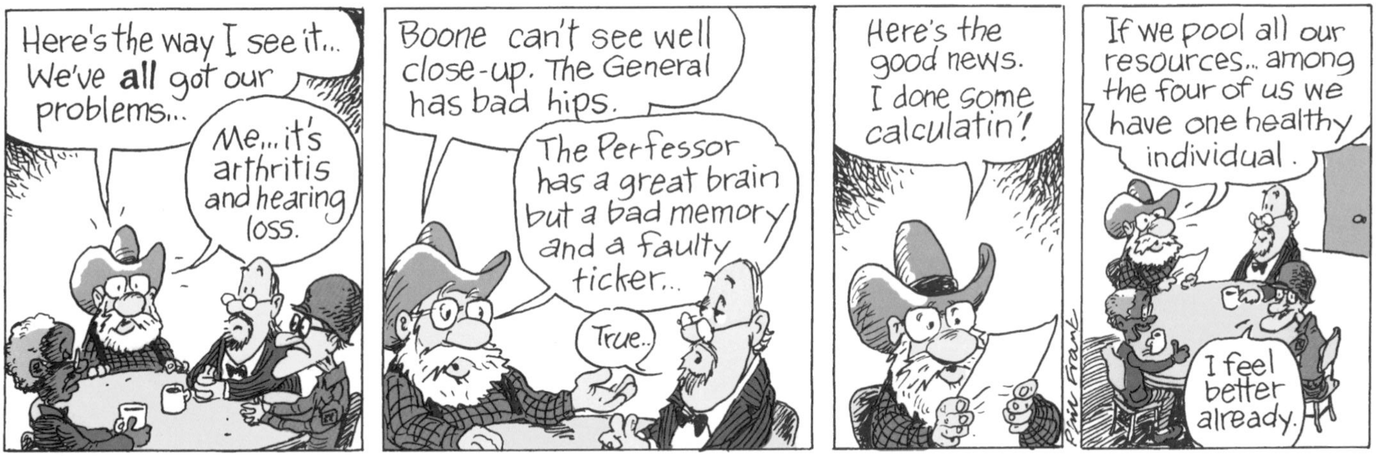
Here's the way I see it... We've **all** got our problems...
Me... it's arthritis and hearing loss.
Boone can't see well close-up. The General has bad hips.
The Perfessor has a great brain but a bad memory and a faulty ticker...
True...
Here's the good news. I done some calculatin'!
If we pool all our resources... among the four of us we have one healthy individual.
I feel better already.

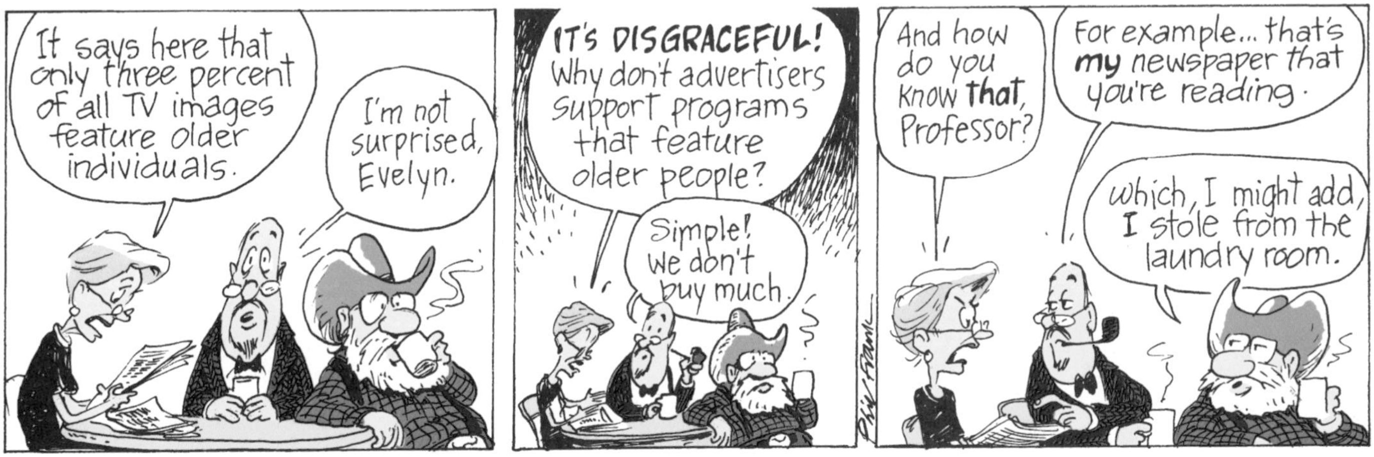
It says here that only three percent of all TV images feature older individuals.
I'm not surprised, Evelyn.
IT'S DISGRACEFUL! Why don't advertisers support programs that feature older people?
Simple! We don't buy much.
And how do you know **that**, Professor?
For example... that's **my** newspaper that you're reading.
Which, I might add, I stole from the laundry room.

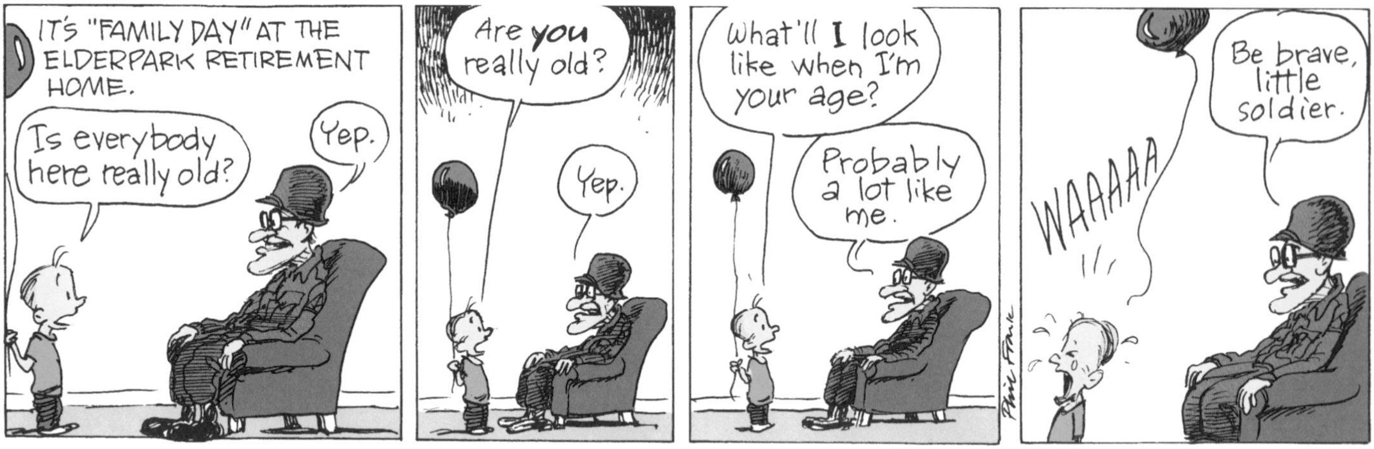
IT'S "FAMILY DAY" AT THE ELDERPARK RETIREMENT HOME.
Is everybody here really old?
Yep.
Are you really old?
Yep.
What'll I look like when I'm your age?
Probably a lot like me.
WAAAAA
Be brave, little soldier.

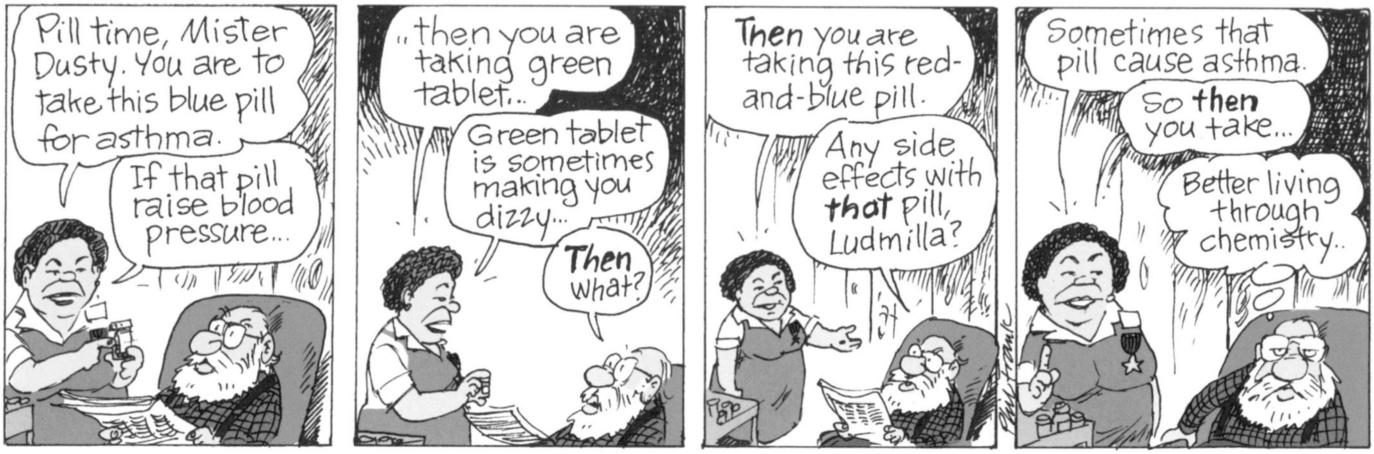
Pill time, Mister Dusty. You are to take this blue pill for asthma.
If that pill raise blood pressure...
..then you are taking green tablet...
Green tablet is sometimes making you dizzy...
Then what?
Then you are taking this red-and-blue pill.
Any side effects with that pill, Ludmilla?
Sometimes that pill cause asthma.
So then you take...
Better living through chemistry..

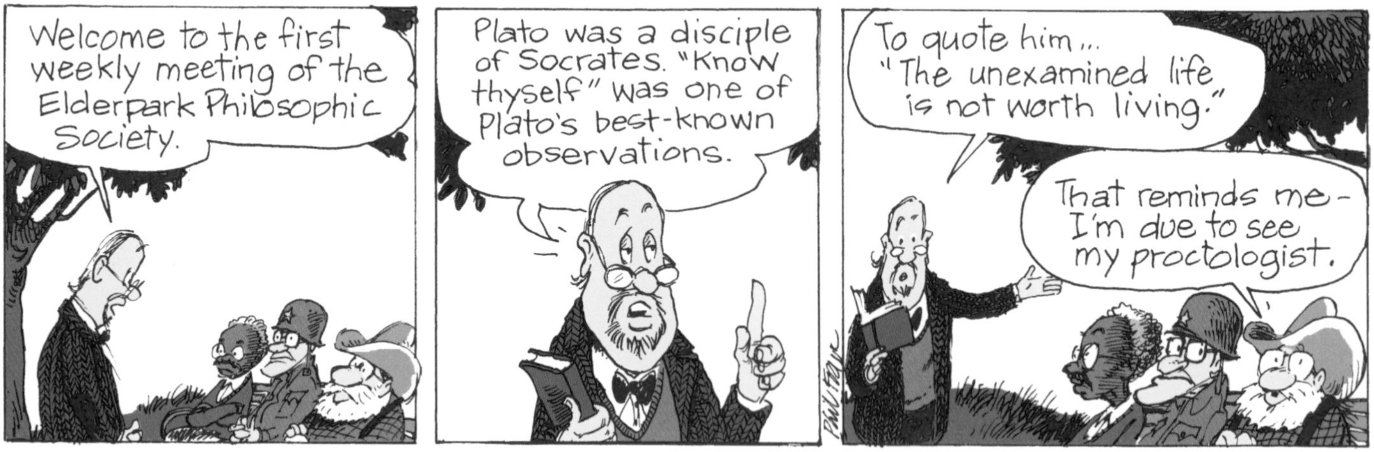
Welcome to the first weekly meeting of the Elderpark Philosophic Society.
Plato was a disciple of Socrates. "Know thyself" was one of Plato's best-known observations.
To quote him... "The unexamined life is not worth living."
That reminds me - I'm due to see my proctologist.

Elderberries
by Phil Frank and Joe Troise
ONE FALSE STEP AND YOU'RE ROADKILL!

So there I was on this cattle drive near Pecos 'bout fifty years ago...
We're all bedded down for the night. It's real quiet...
I'm just dozin' off when I hear this sound that about curled my boots...
Dusty's telling us a **great** story, ma'am.
Sure enough... it was a Texas Night-singing Chickadee! About as sweet a sound as I...
Carry on...
...ever...did... hear...
Sure enough... it was a big ol' rattlesnake coiled up on my canteen...
Slowly I raised my Winchester...

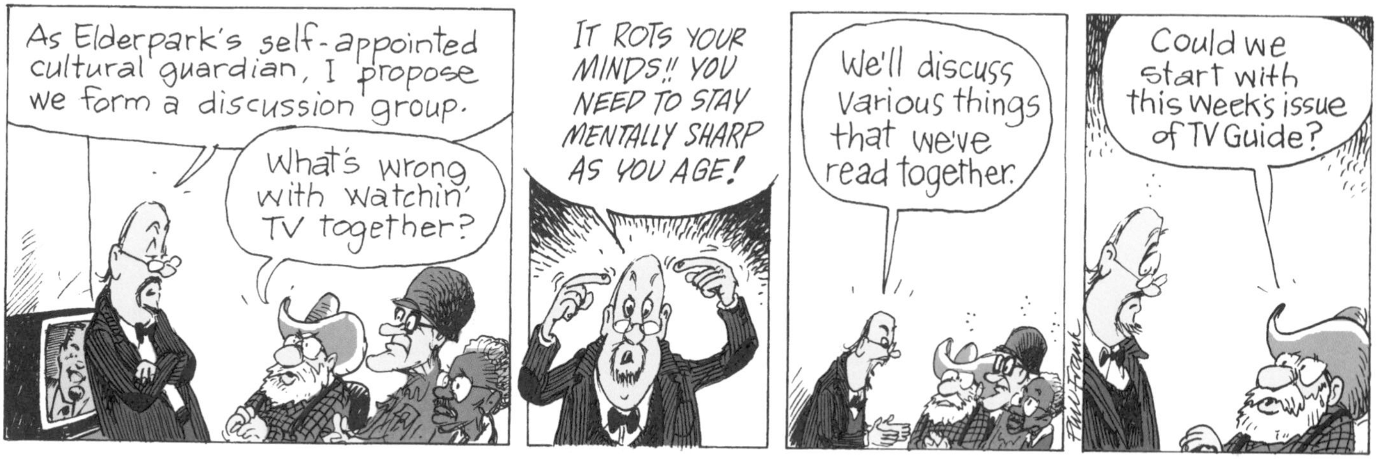
As Elderpark's self-appointed cultural guardian, I propose we form a discussion group.
What's wrong with watchin' TV together?
IT ROTS YOUR MINDS!! YOU NEED TO STAY MENTALLY SHARP AS YOU AGE!
We'll discuss various things that we've read together.
Could we start with this week's issue of TV Guide?

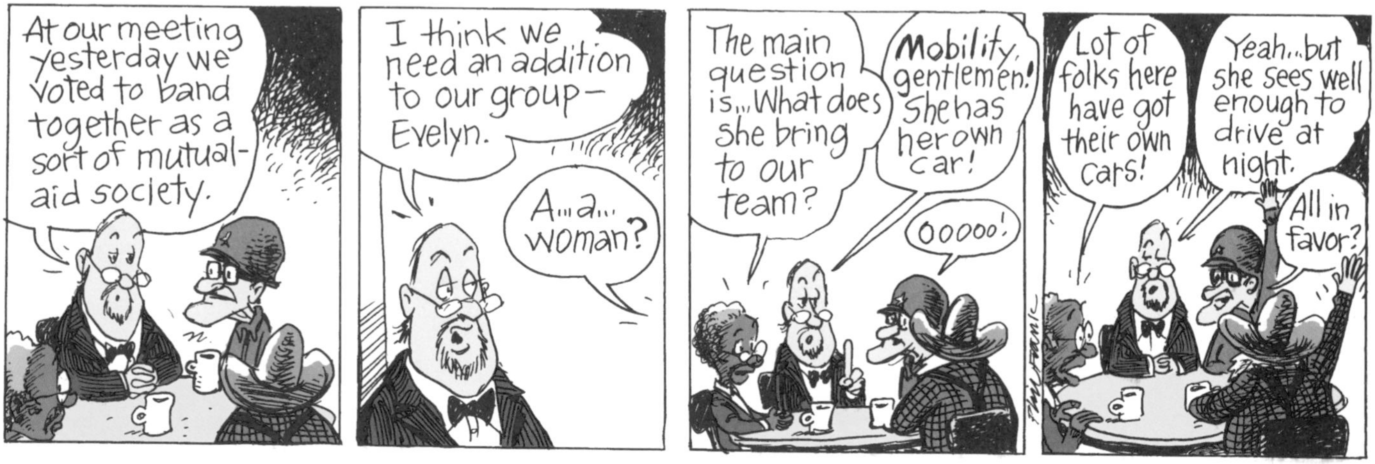
At our meeting yesterday we voted to band together as a sort of mutual-aid society.
I think we need an addition to our group— Evelyn.
A...a... woman?
The main question is... What does she bring to our team?
Mobility, gentlemen! She has her own car!
Ooooo!
Lot of folks here have got their own cars!
Yeah...but she sees well enough to drive at night.
All in favor?

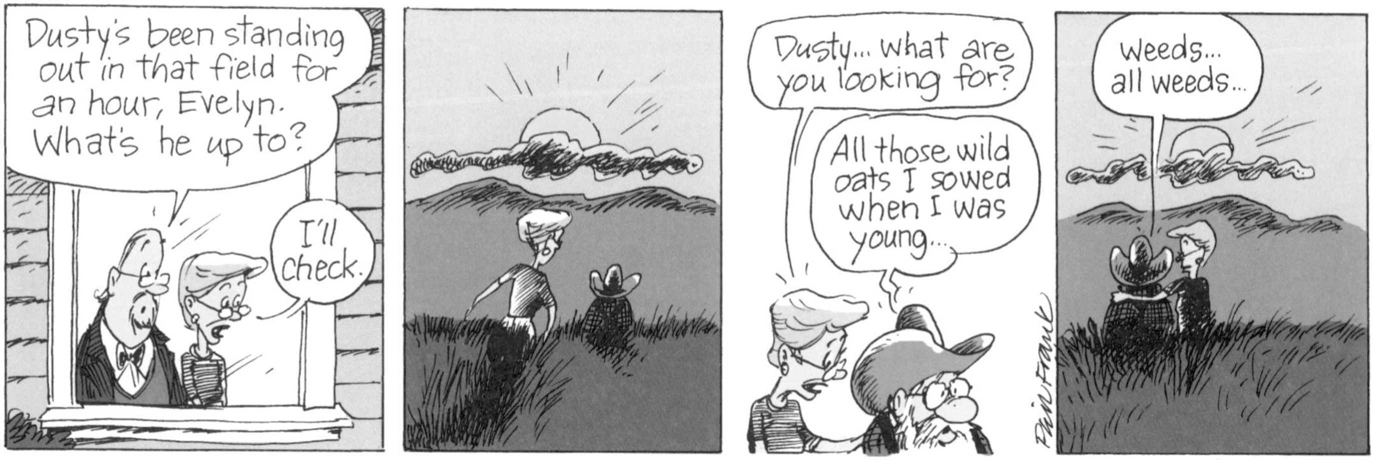
Dusty's been standing out in that field for an hour, Evelyn. What's he up to?
I'll check.
Dusty... what are you looking for?
All those wild oats I sowed when I was young...
Weeds... all weeds...

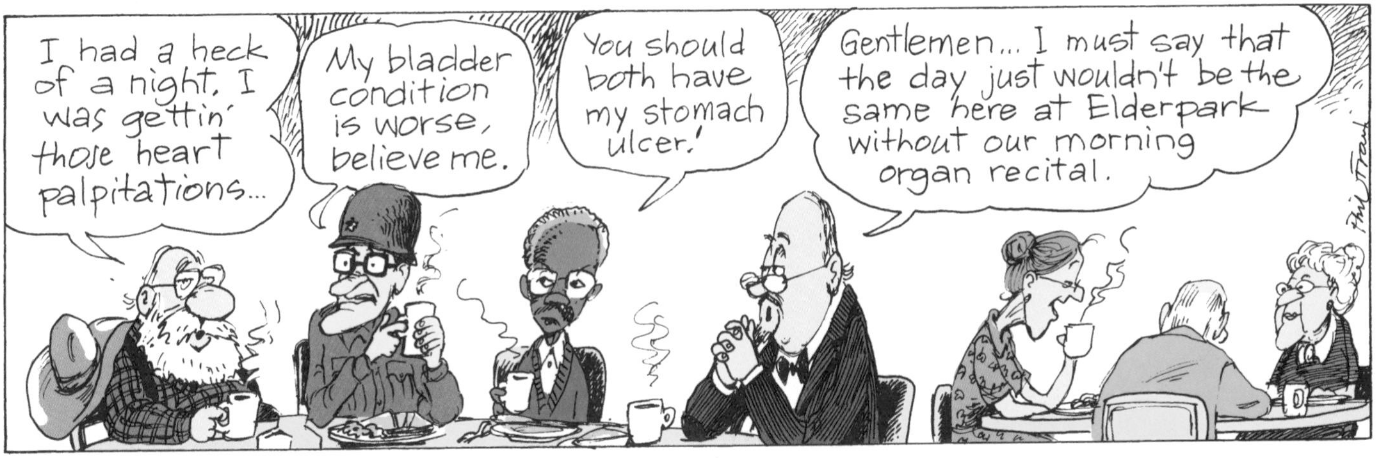
I had a heck of a night, I was gettin' those heart palpitations...
My bladder condition is worse, believe me.
You should both have my stomach ulcer!
Gentlemen... I must say that the day just wouldn't be the same here at Elderpark without our morning organ recital.
Phil Frank

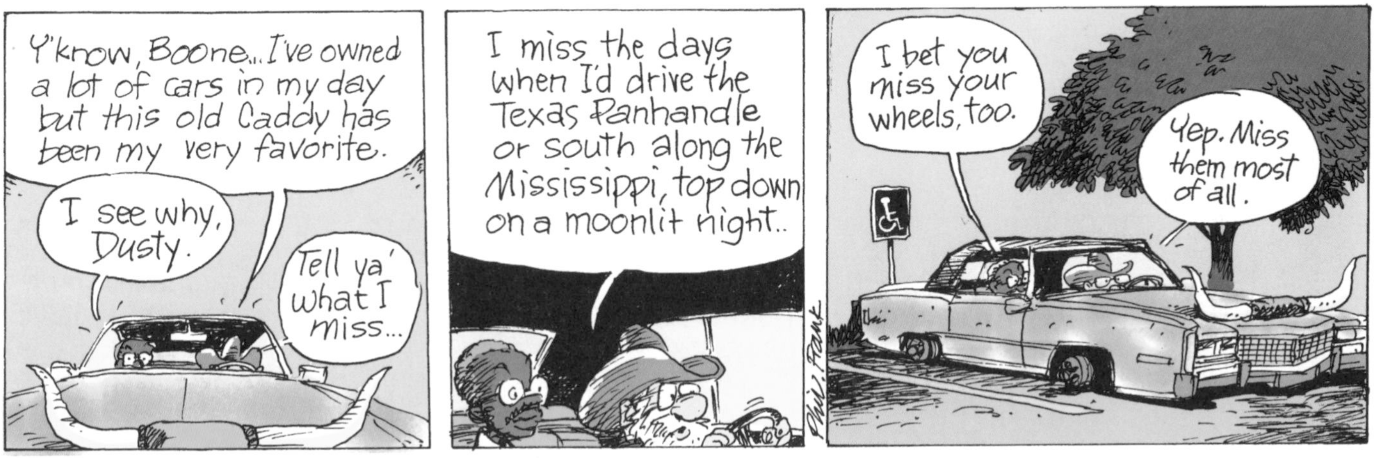
Y'know, Boone... I've owned a lot of cars in my day but this old Caddy has been my very favorite.
I see why, Dusty.
Tell ya' what I miss...
I miss the days when I'd drive the Texas Panhandle or south along the Mississippi, top down on a moonlit night..
Phil Frank
I bet you miss your wheels, too.
Yep. Miss them most of all.

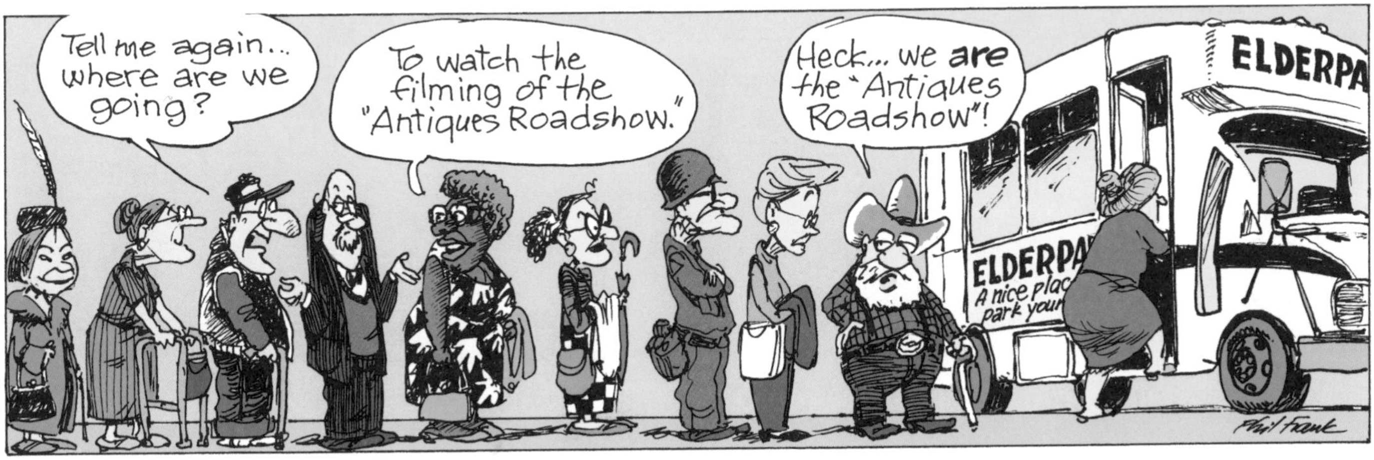
Tell me again... where are we going?
To watch the filming of the "Antiques Roadshow."
Heck... we **are** the "Antiques Roadshow"!
ELDERPA
Phil Frank

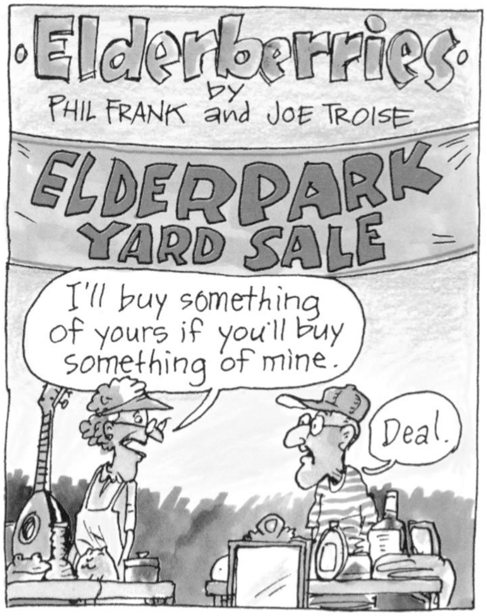
Elderberries
by
PHIL FRANK and JOE TROISE
ELDERPARK YARD SALE
I'll buy something of yours if you'll buy something of mine.
Deal.

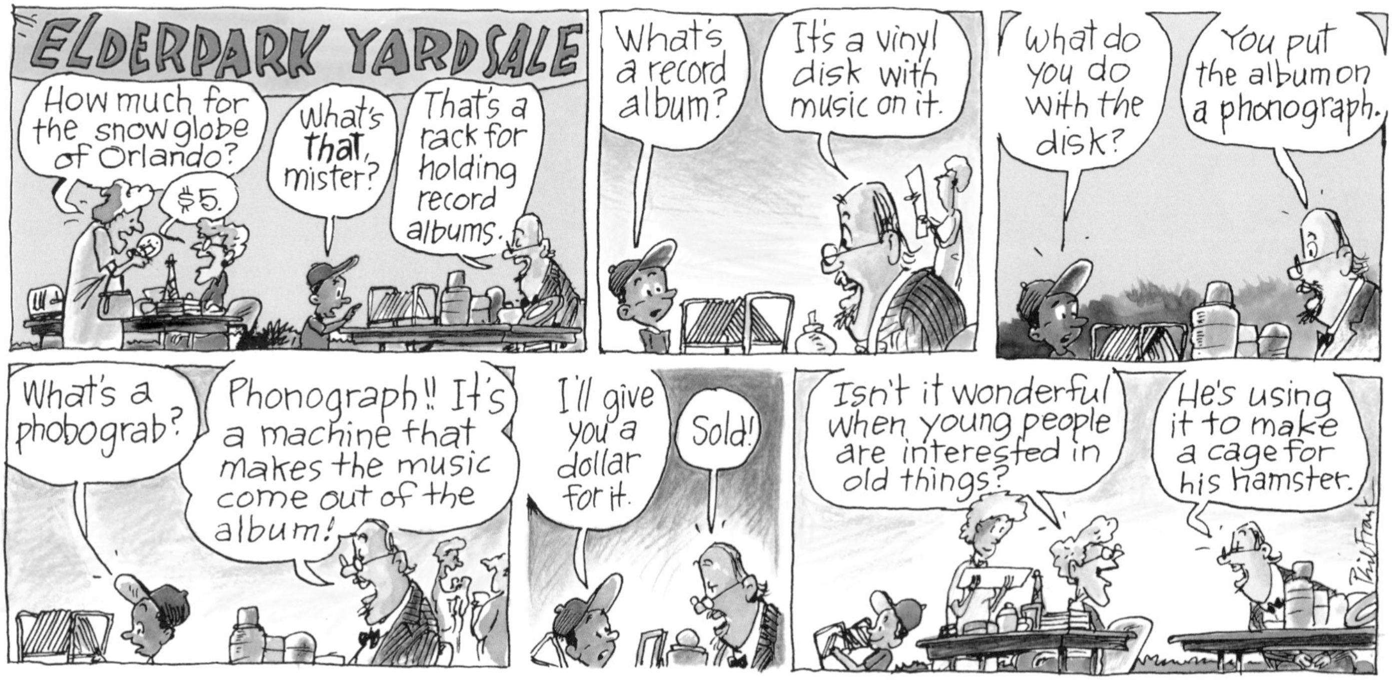
ELDERPARK YARDSALE
How much for the snowglobe of Orlando?
$5.
What's that, mister?
That's a rack for holding record albums.
What's a record album?
It's a vinyl disk with music on it.
What do you do with the disk?
You put the album on a phonograph.
What's a phobograb?
Phonograph!! It's a machine that makes the music come out of the album!
I'll give you a dollar for it.
Sold!
Isn't it wonderful when young people are interested in old things?
He's using it to make a cage for his hamster.

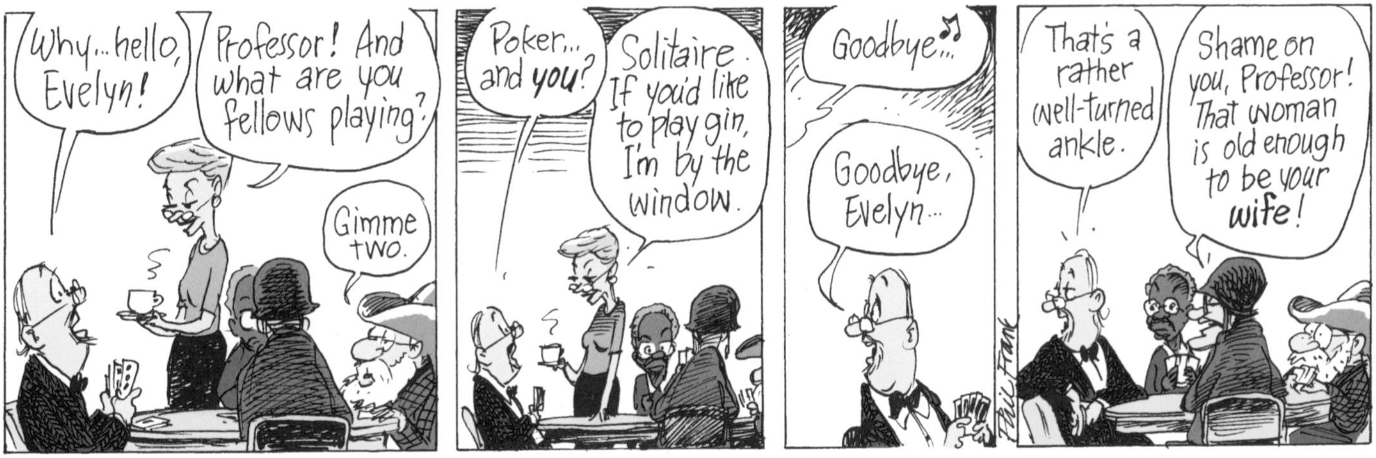
Why... hello, Evelyn!
Professor! And what are you fellows playing?
Gimme two.
Poker... and you?
Solitaire. If you'd like to play gin, I'm by the window.
Goodbye...
Goodbye, Evelyn...
That's a rather well-turned ankle.
Shame on you, Professor! That woman is old enough to be your wife!

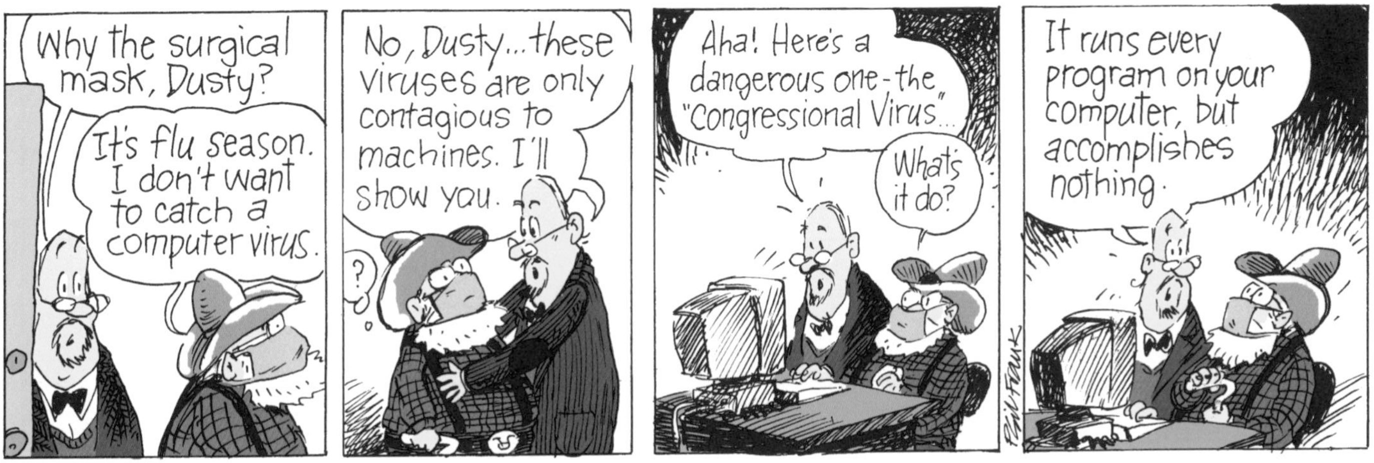
Why the surgical mask, Dusty?
It's flu season. I don't want to catch a computer virus.
No, Dusty... these viruses are only contagious to machines. I'll show you.
?
Aha! Here's a dangerous one - the "Congressional Virus"...
What's it do?
It runs every program on your computer, but accomplishes nothing.

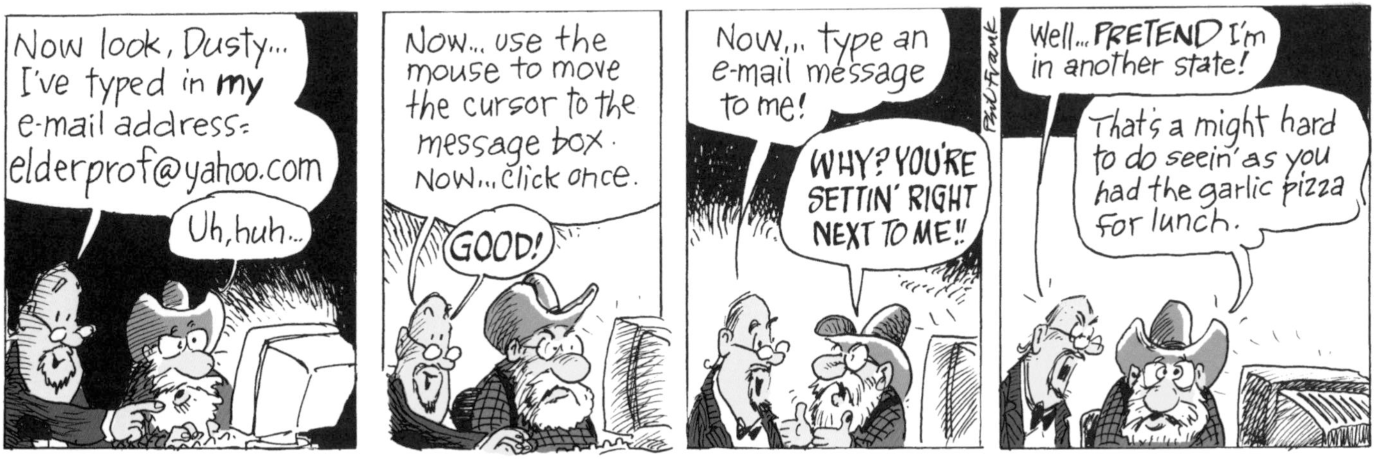
Now look, Dusty... I've typed in my e-mail address: elderprof@yahoo.com
Uh, huh...
Now... use the mouse to move the cursor to the message box. Now... click once.
GOOD!
Now... type an e-mail message to me!
WHY? YOU'RE SETTIN' RIGHT NEXT TO ME!!
Well... PRETEND I'm in another state!
That's a might hard to do seein' as you had the garlic pizza for lunch.

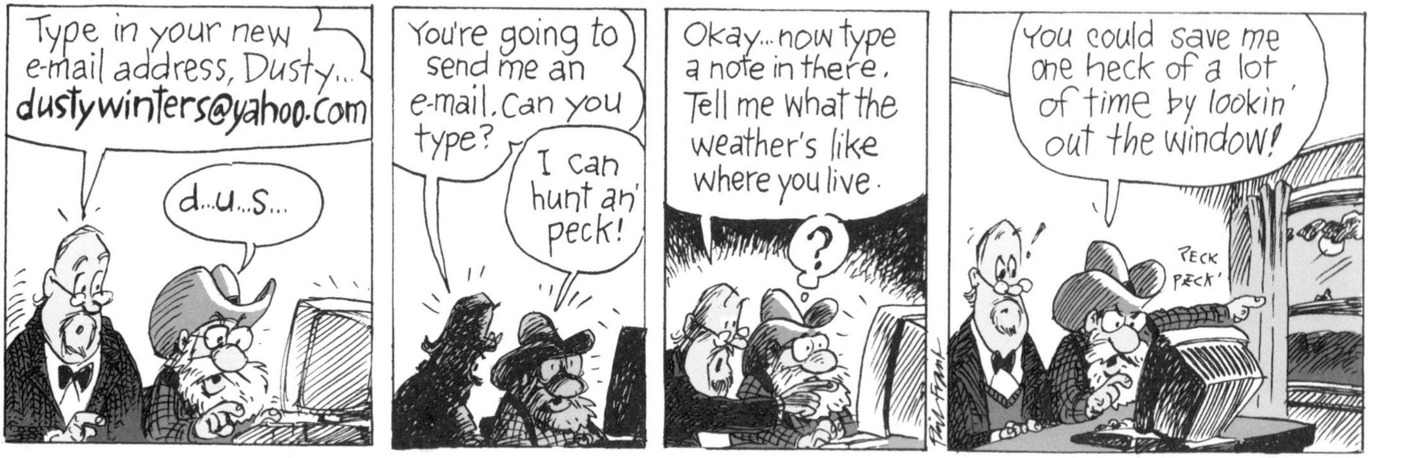
Type in your new e-mail address, Dusty... dustywinters@yahoo.com
d...u...s...
You're going to send me an e-mail. Can you type?
I can hunt an' peck!
Okay... now type a note in there. Tell me what the weather's like where you live.
?
You could save me one heck of a lot of time by lookin' out the window!
PECK PECK

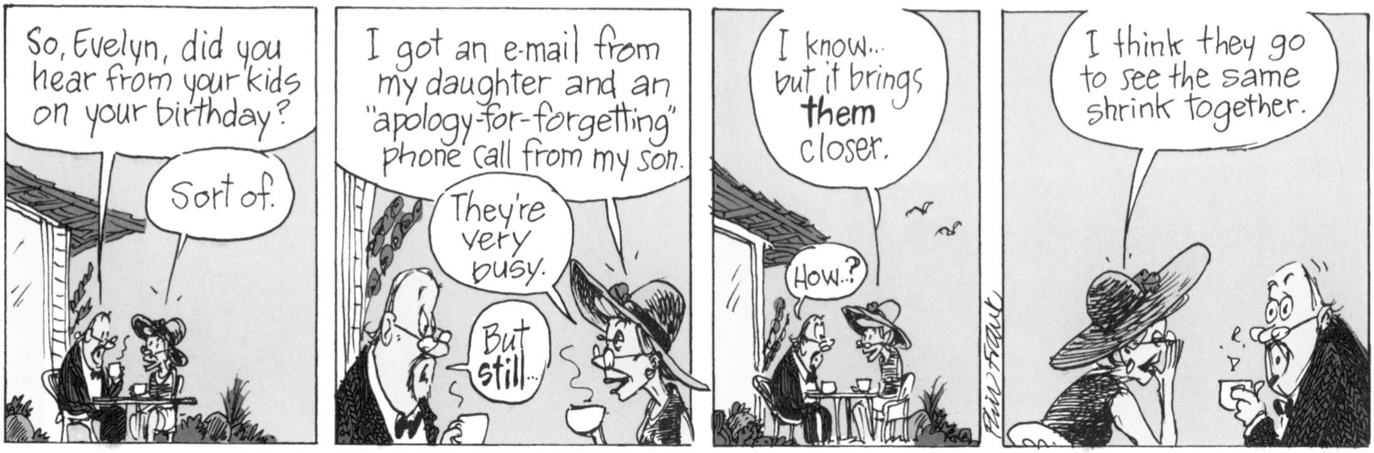
So, Evelyn, did you hear from your kids on your birthday?
Sort of.
I got an e-mail from my daughter and an "apology-for-forgetting" phone call from my son.
They're very busy.
But still...
I know... but it brings them closer.
How..?
I think they go to see the same shrink together.

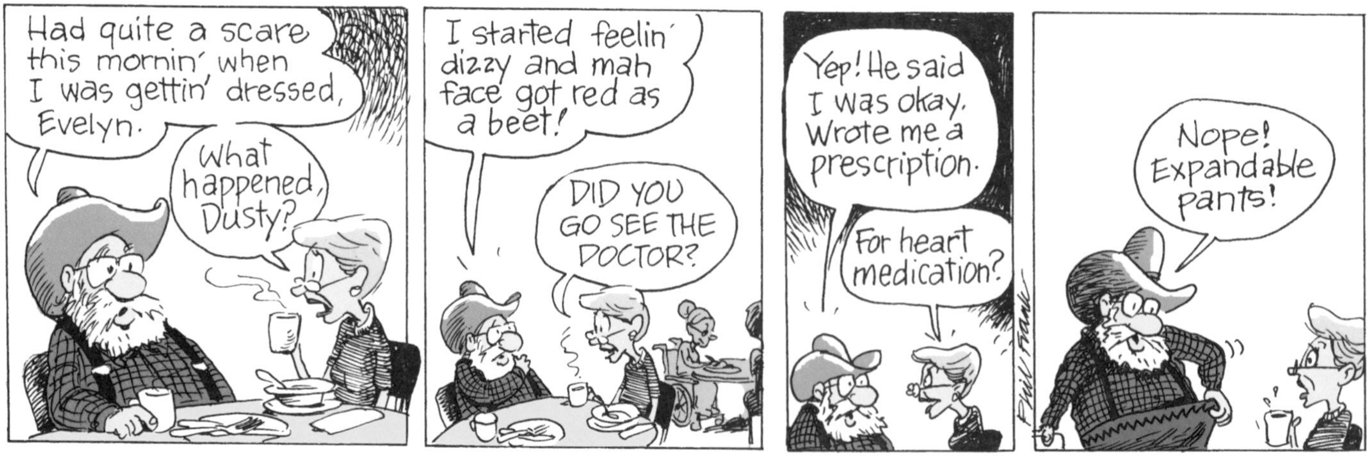
Had quite a scare this mornin' when I was gettin' dressed, Evelyn.
What happened, Dusty?
I started feelin' dizzy and mah face got red as a beet!
DID YOU GO SEE THE DOCTOR?
Yep! He said I was okay. Wrote me a prescription.
For heart medication?
Nope! Expandable pants!

Elderberries
by
Phil Frank & Joe Troise
You've got mail!!
Now What?

Well... look at **that**, Dusty... you got your first e-mail at dustywinters@yahoo.com
Somebody wrote to **me**?
Click on that icon and the letter will open...
Stand back! Here goes!
WHAT'S THIS? Magumbe Obada?? A **NIGERIAN PRINCE** with access to **$** 14,000,000 has written to **me**!
And..., and... he wants **me** to have half the money!!
THAT'S $7,000,000! I'M RICH! I'M RICH!
All Magumbe needs to get access to all that money is my credit card number!
WHERE'S MY WALLET?
Phil Frank ©
YEE-HAW!
I DON'T NEED MY CANE ANYMORE! I CAN WALK!!
Maybe this wasn't such a good idea...

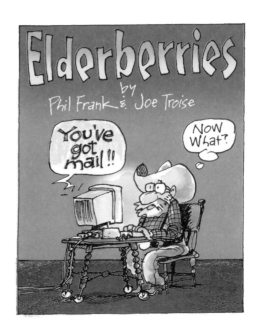

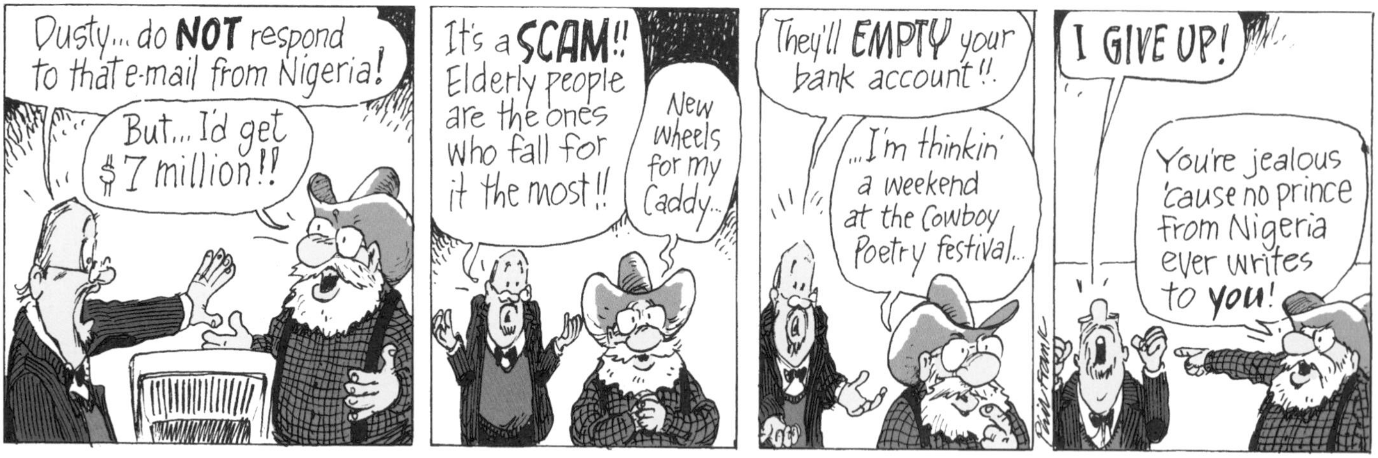
Dusty... do NOT respond to that e-mail from Nigeria!
But... I'd get $7 million!!
It's a SCAM!! Elderly people are the ones who fall for it the most!!
New wheels for my Caddy...
They'll EMPTY your bank account!!
...I'm thinkin' a weekend at the Cowboy Poetry festival...
I GIVE UP!
You're jealous 'cause no prince from Nigeria ever writes to you!

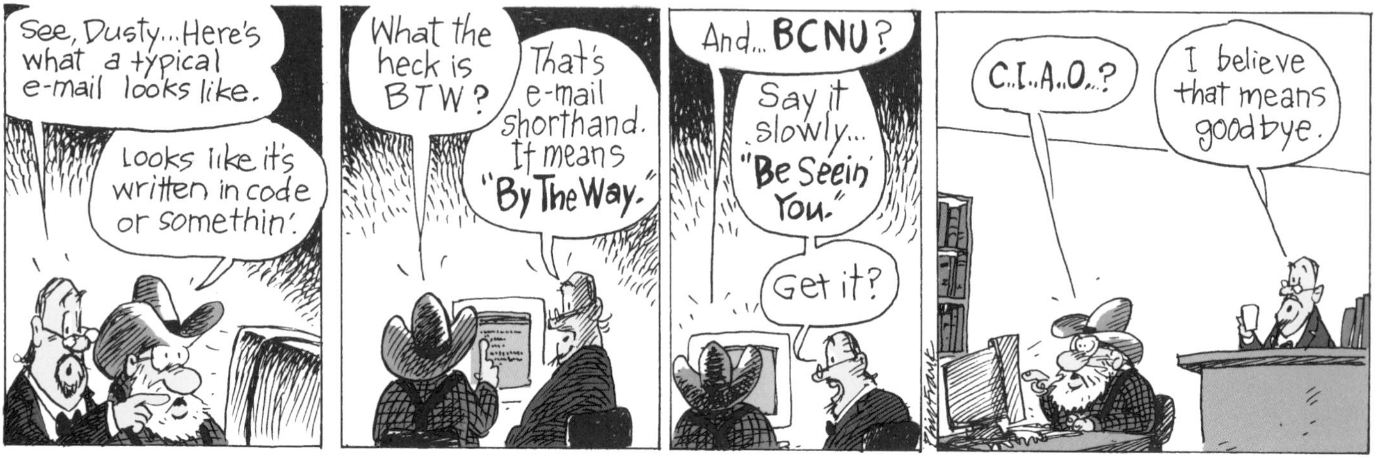
See, Dusty... Here's what a typical e-mail looks like.
Looks like it's written in code or somethin'.
What the heck is BTW?
That's e-mail shorthand. It means "By The Way."
And... BCNU?
Say it slowly... "Be Seein' You."
Get it?
C.I.A.O.?
I believe that means goodbye.

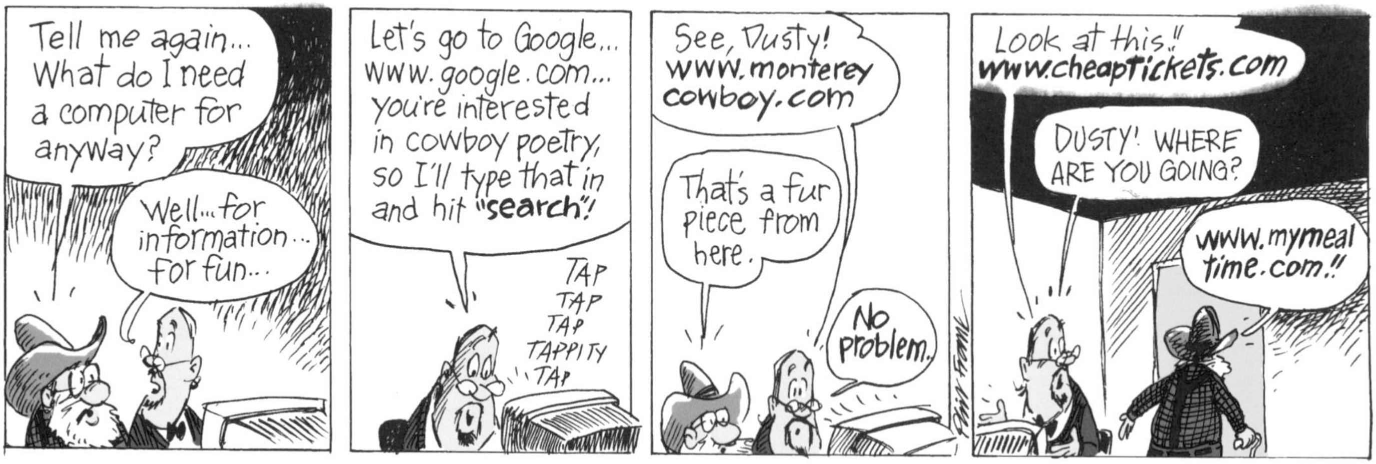
Tell me again... What do I need a computer for anyway?
Well... for information... for fun...
Let's go to Google... www.google.com... you're interested in cowboy poetry, so I'll type that in and hit "search"!
TAP TAP TAP TAPPITY TAP
See, Dusty! www.montereycowboy.com
That's a fur piece from here.
No problem.
Look at this!! www.cheaptickets.com
DUSTY! WHERE ARE YOU GOING?
www.mymealtime.com!!

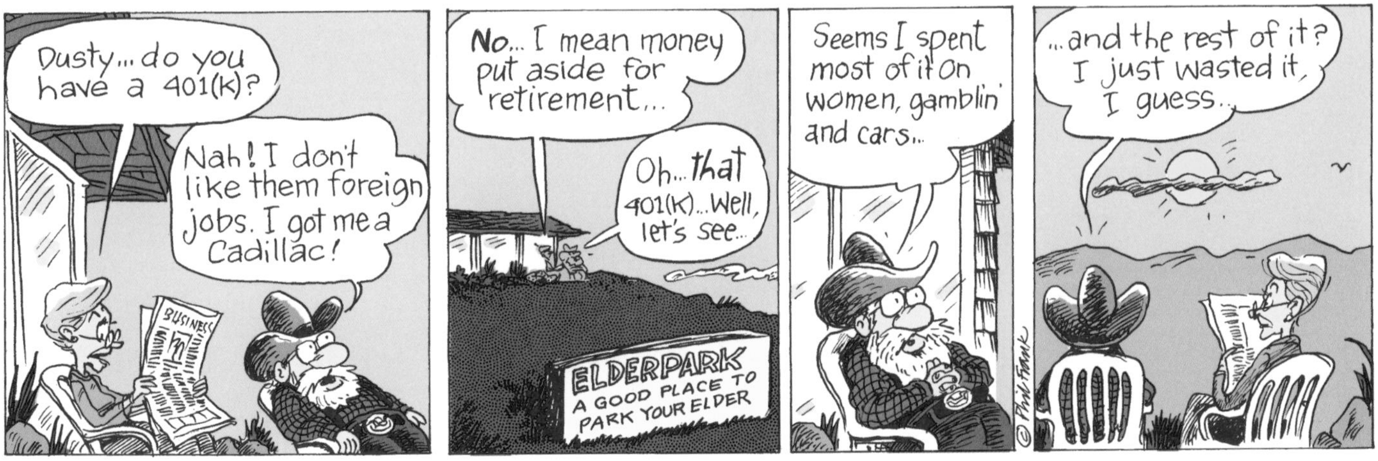
Dusty... do you have a 401(k)?
Nah! I don't like them foreign jobs. I got me a Cadillac!
BUSINESS
No... I mean money put aside for retirement...
Oh... that 401(k)... Well, let's see...
ELDERPARK
A GOOD PLACE TO PARK YOUR ELDER
Seems I spent most of it on women, gamblin' and cars...
© Phil Frank
...and the rest of it? I just wasted it, I guess...

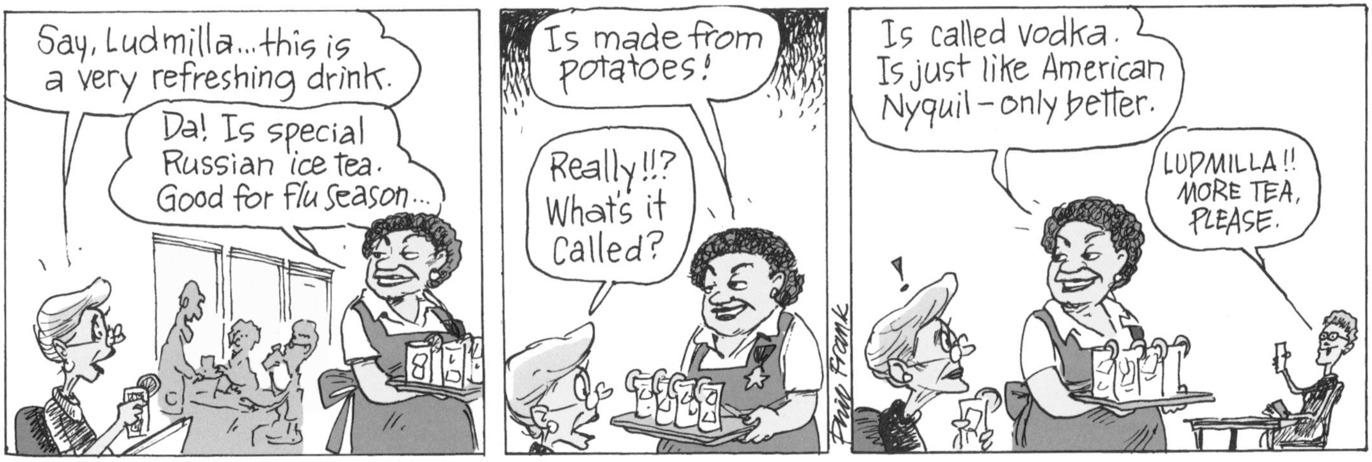
Say, Ludmilla... this is a very refreshing drink.
Da! Is special Russian ice tea. Good for flu season...
Is made from potatoes!
Really!!? What's it called?
Phil Frank
Is called vodka. Is just like American Nyquil – only better.
!
LUDMILLA!! MORE TEA, PLEASE.

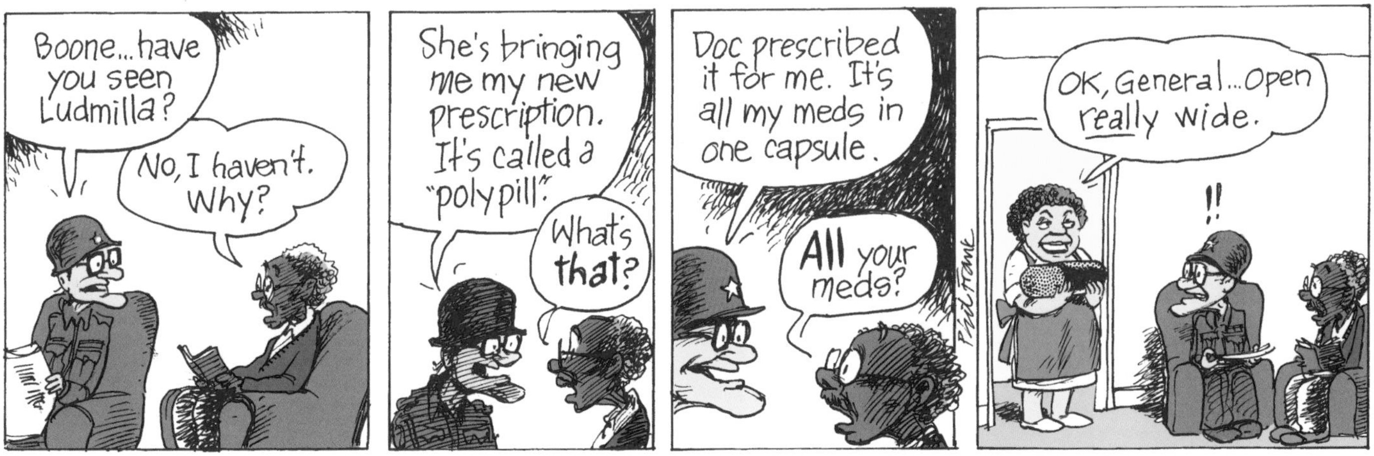
Boone... have you seen Ludmilla?
No, I haven't. Why?
She's bringing me my new prescription. It's called a "polypill."
What's that?
Doc prescribed it for me. It's all my meds in one capsule.
All your meds?
Phil Frank
OK, General... Open really wide.
!!

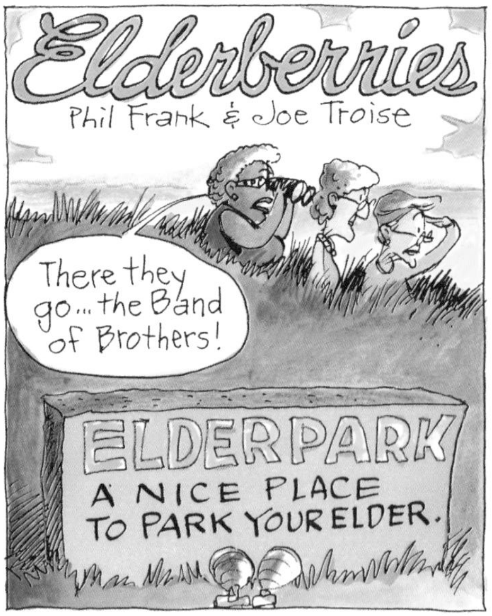
Elderberries
Phil Frank & Joe Troise
There they go... the Band of Brothers!
ELDERPARK
A NICE PLACE TO PARK YOUR ELDER.

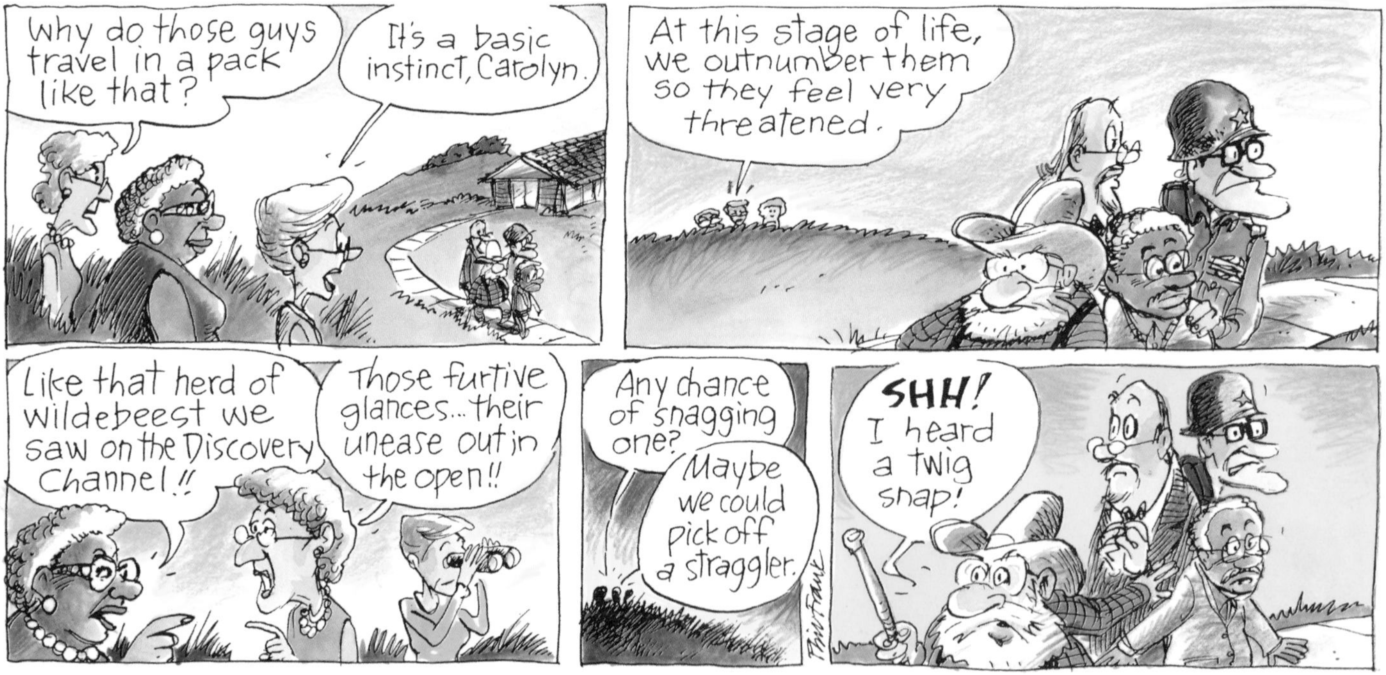
Why do those guys travel in a pack like that?
It's a basic instinct, Carolyn.
At this stage of life, we outnumber them so they feel very threatened.
Like that herd of wildebeest we saw on the Discovery Channel!!
Those furtive glances... their unease out in the open!!
Any chance of snagging one?
Maybe we could pick off a straggler.
Phil Frank
SHH! I heard a twig snap!

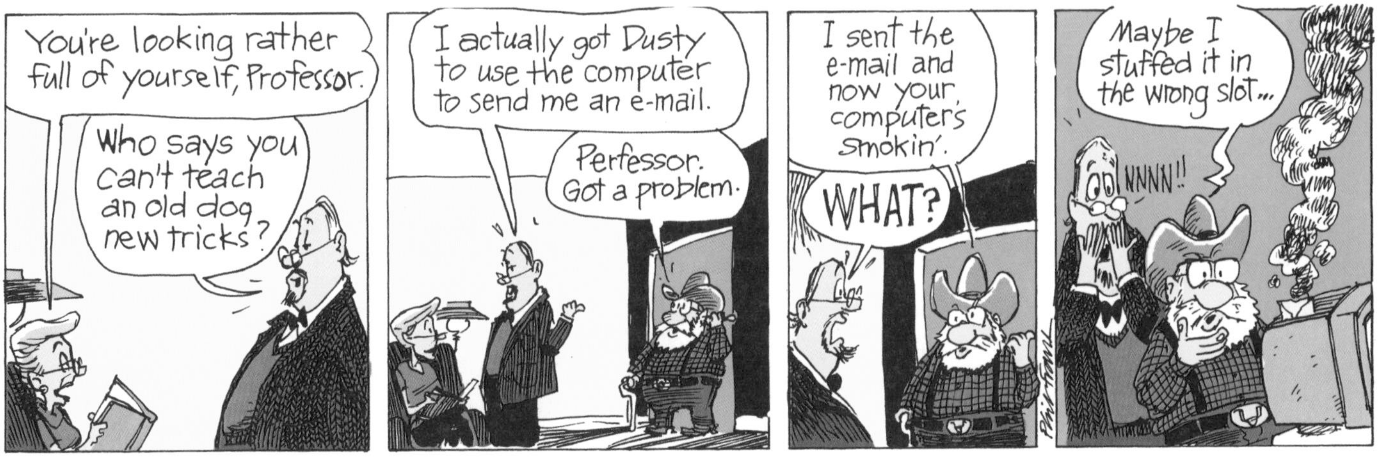
You're looking rather full of yourself, Professor.
Who says you can't teach an old dog new tricks?
I actually got Dusty to use the computer to send me an e-mail.
Perfessor. Got a problem.
I sent the e-mail and now your computer's smokin'.
WHAT?
Maybe I stuffed it in the wrong slot...
NNNN!!

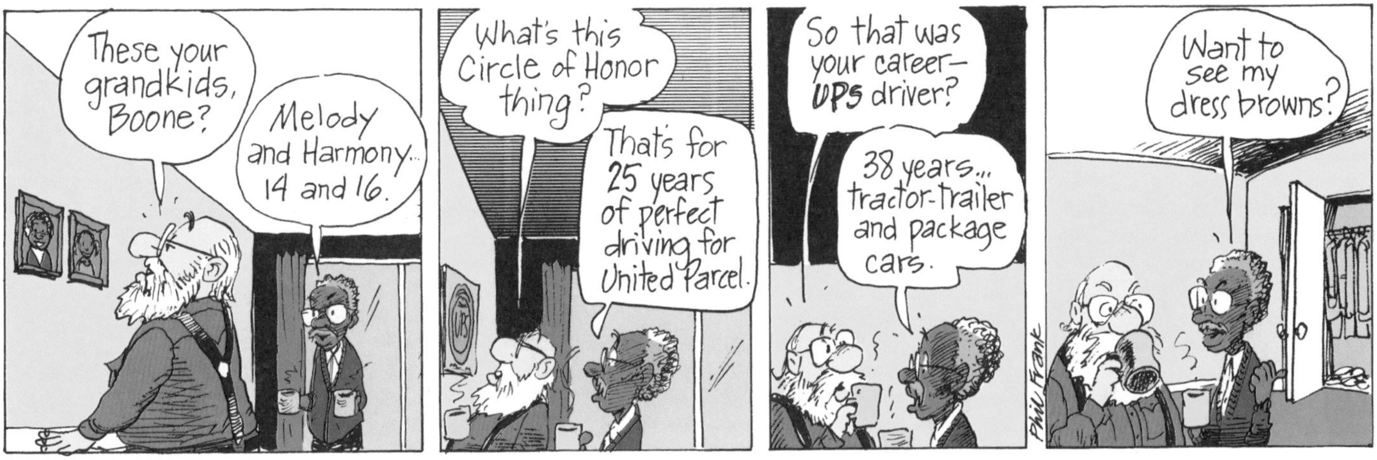
These your grandkids, Boone?
Melody and Harmony... 14 and 16.
What's this Circle of Honor thing?
That's for 25 years of perfect driving for United Parcel.
So that was your career— UPS driver?
38 years... tractor-trailer and package cars.
Want to see my dress browns?

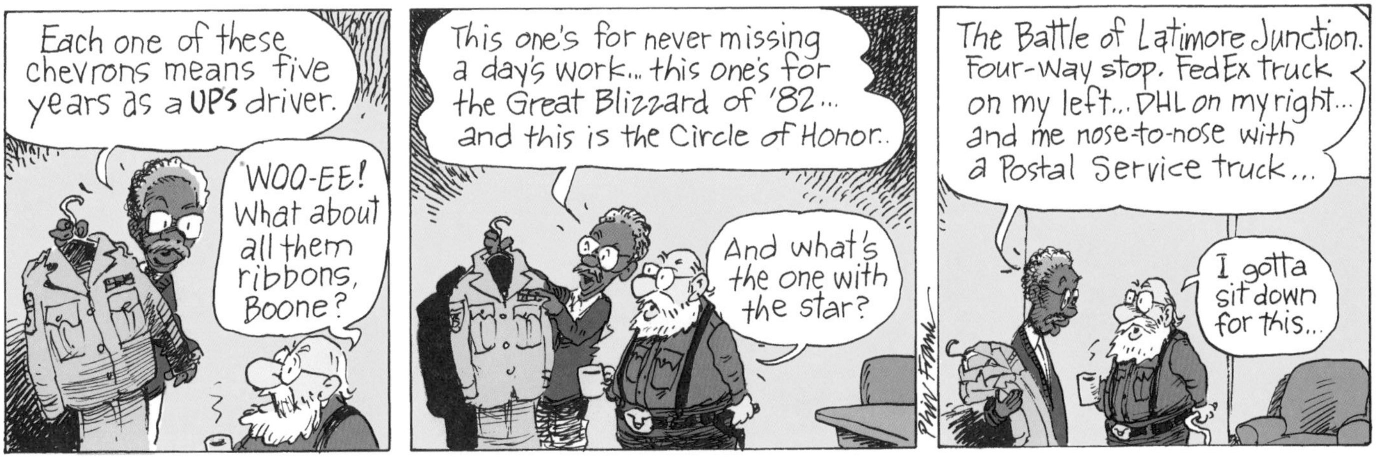
Each one of these chevrons means five years as a UPS driver.
WOO-EE! What about all them ribbons, Boone?
This one's for never missing a day's work... this one's for the Great Blizzard of '82... and this is the Circle of Honor.
And what's the one with the star?
The Battle of Latimore Junction. Four-Way stop. FedEx truck on my left... DHL on my right... and me nose-to-nose with a Postal Service truck...
I gotta sit down for this...

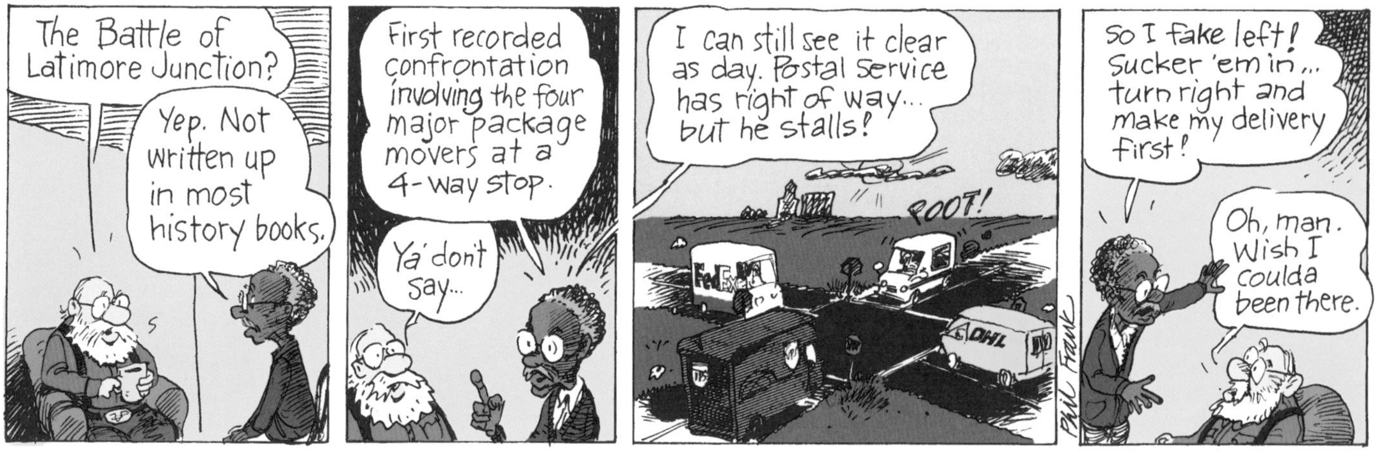
The Battle of Latimore Junction?
Yep. Not written up in most history books.
First recorded confrontation involving the four major package movers at a 4-way stop.
Ya' don't say...
I can still see it clear as day. Postal Service has right of way... but he stalls!
POOT!
So I fake left! Sucker 'em in... turn right and make my delivery first!
Oh, man. Wish I coulda been there.

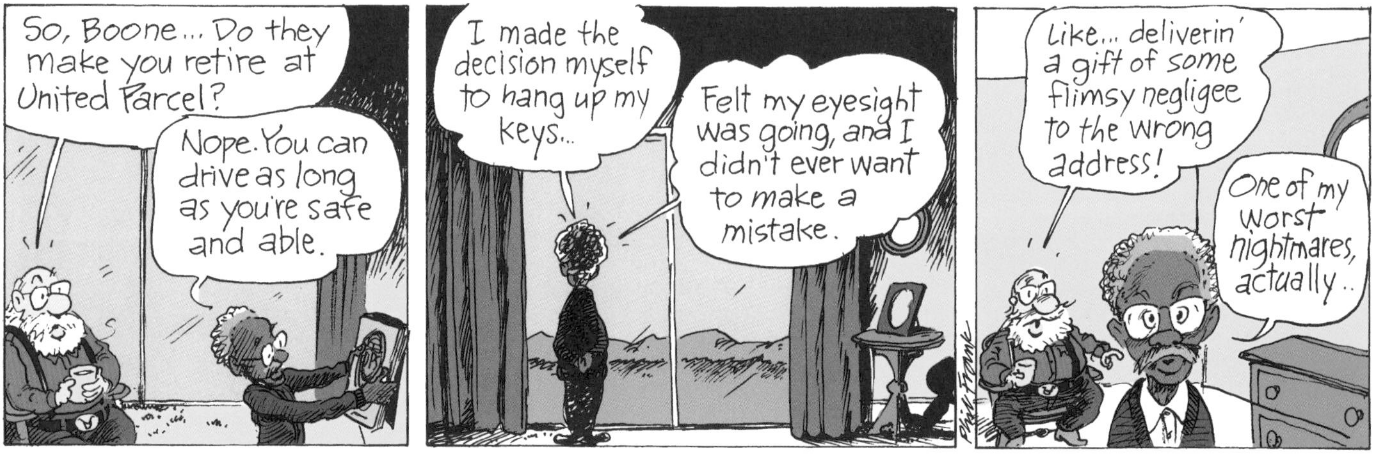
So, Boone... Do they make you retire at United Parcel?
Nope. You can drive as long as you're safe and able.
I made the decision myself to hang up my keys...
Felt my eyesight was going, and I didn't ever want to make a mistake.
Like... deliverin' a gift of some flimsy negligee to the wrong address!
One of my worst nightmares, actually..

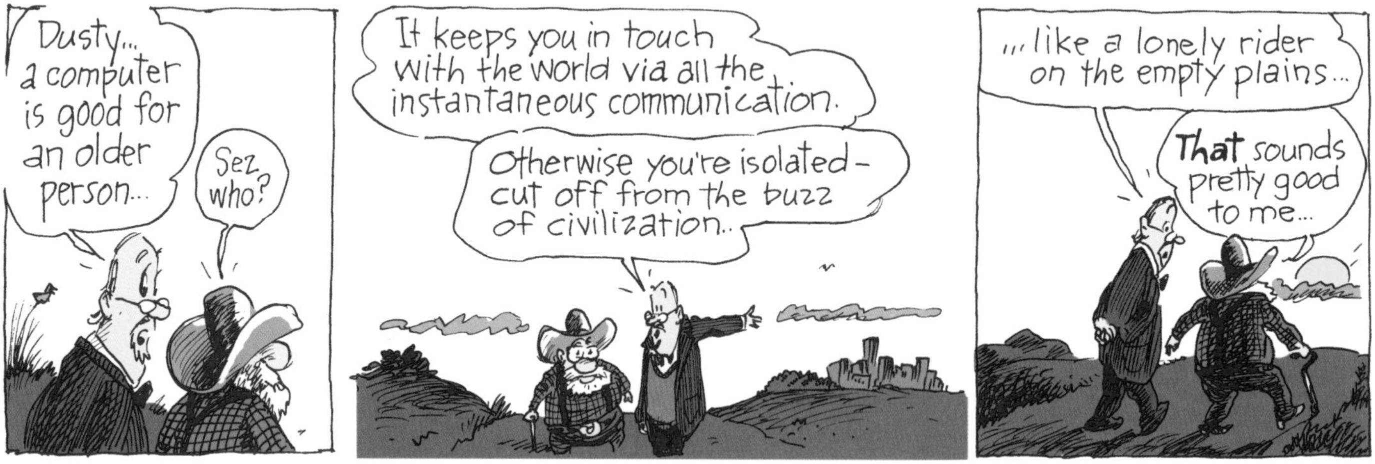
Dusty... a computer is good for an older person...
Sez who?
It keeps you in touch with the world via all the instantaneous communication.
Otherwise you're isolated - cut off from the buzz of civilization..
...like a lonely rider on the empty plains...
That sounds pretty good to me...

ELDER
BERRIES
BY PHIL FRANK AND JOE TROISE
What's a three-letter word for a mother's anger?
Hmm...

OK... so you were leaving your mother Evelyn at Elderpark for the first time, and?
I said... "Mom, even though you're in this retirement home now"...
"...I'll never ever let **anything** come between us!!"
And what was her response?
Actually...
OH, NO!! Don't tell me! You answered your cell phone again?
I wasn't thinking... I... I...
It was the dry cleaners! I needed those drapes by 5 o'clock! We were having a dinner party...
NEXT!

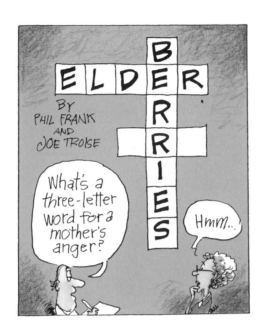

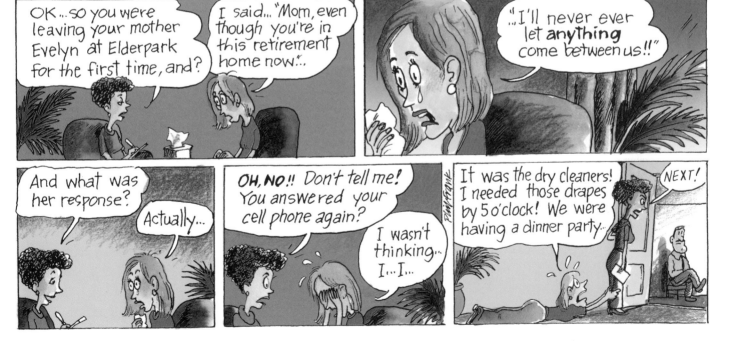

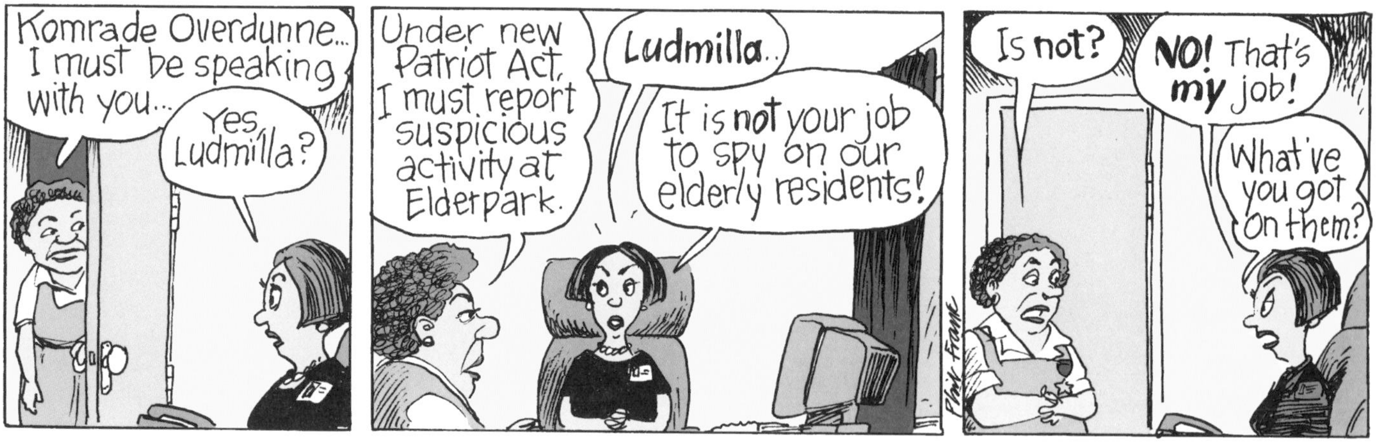
Komrade Overdunne... I must be speaking with you...
Yes, Ludmilla?
Under new Patriot Act, I must report suspicious activity at Elderpark.
Ludmilla..
It is **not** your job to spy on our elderly residents!
Is **not?**
NO! That's **my** job!
What've you got on them?
Phil Frank

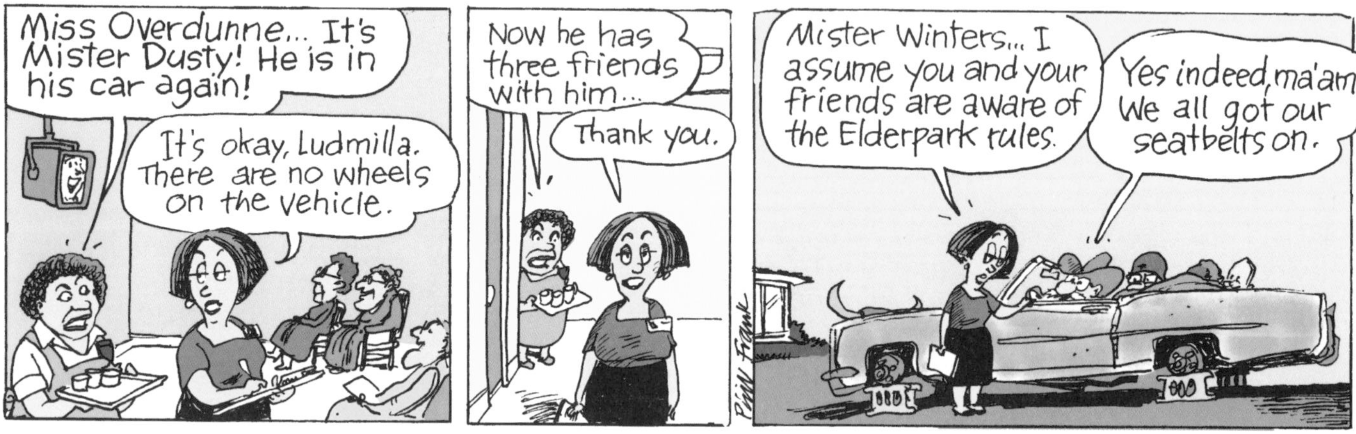
Miss Overdunne... It's Mister Dusty! He is in his car again!
It's okay, Ludmilla. There are no wheels on the vehicle.
Now he has three friends with him...
Thank you.
Mister Winters... I assume you and your friends are aware of the Elderpark rules.
Yes indeed, ma'am. We all got our seatbelts on.
Phil Frank

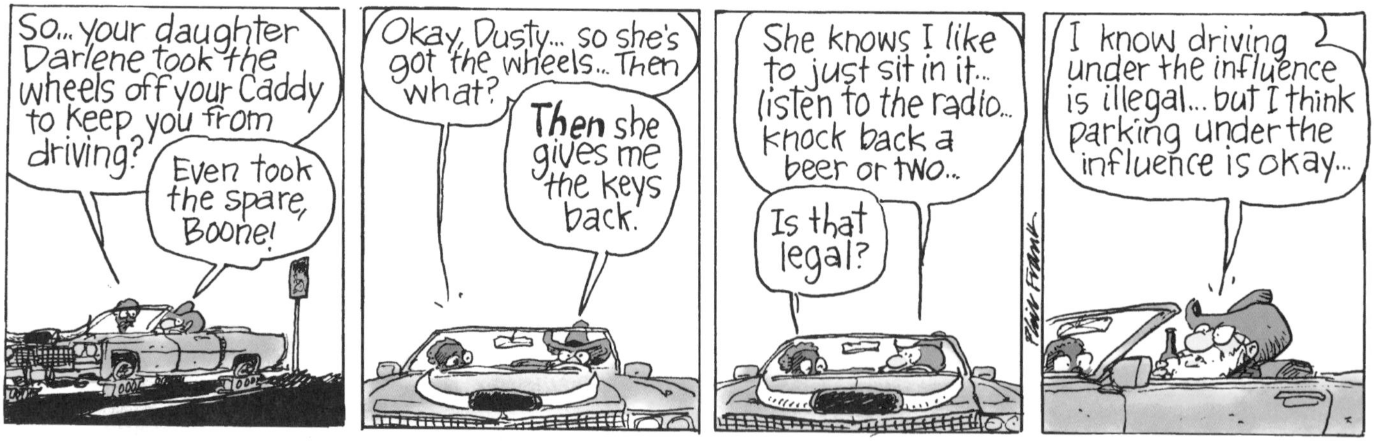
So... your daughter Darlene took the wheels off your Caddy to keep you from driving?
Even took the spare, Boone!
Okay, Dusty... so she's got the wheels... Then what?
Then she gives me the keys back.
She knows I like to just sit in it... listen to the radio... knock back a beer or two...
Is that legal?
I know driving under the influence is illegal... but I think parking under the influence is okay...
Phil Frank

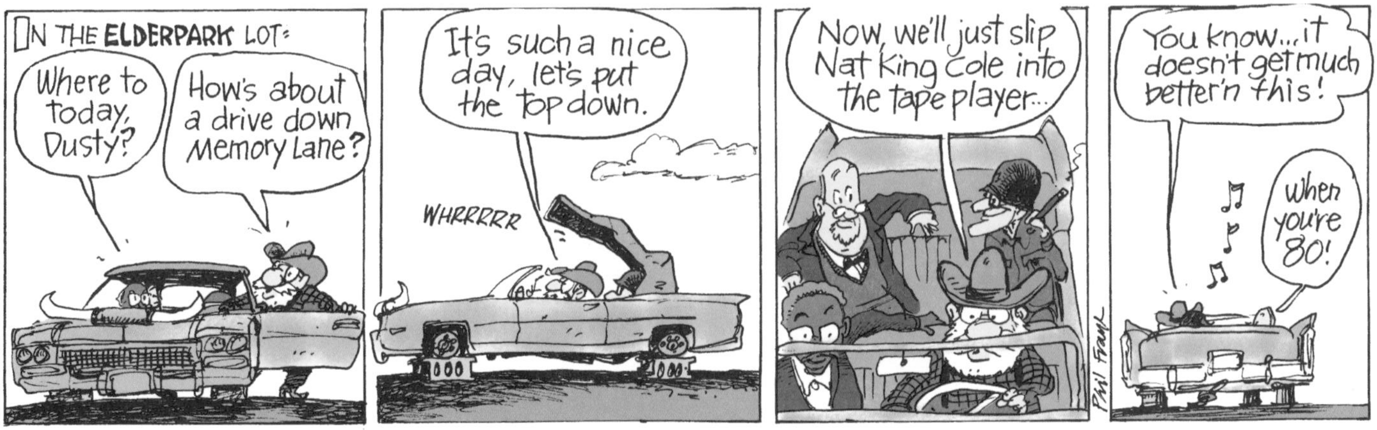
ON THE ELDERPARK LOT:
Where to today, Dusty?
How's about a drive down Memory Lane?
It's such a nice day, let's put the top down.
WHRRRRR
Now, we'll just slip Nat King Cole into the tape player...
Phil Frank
You know... it doesn't get much better'n this!
When you're 80!

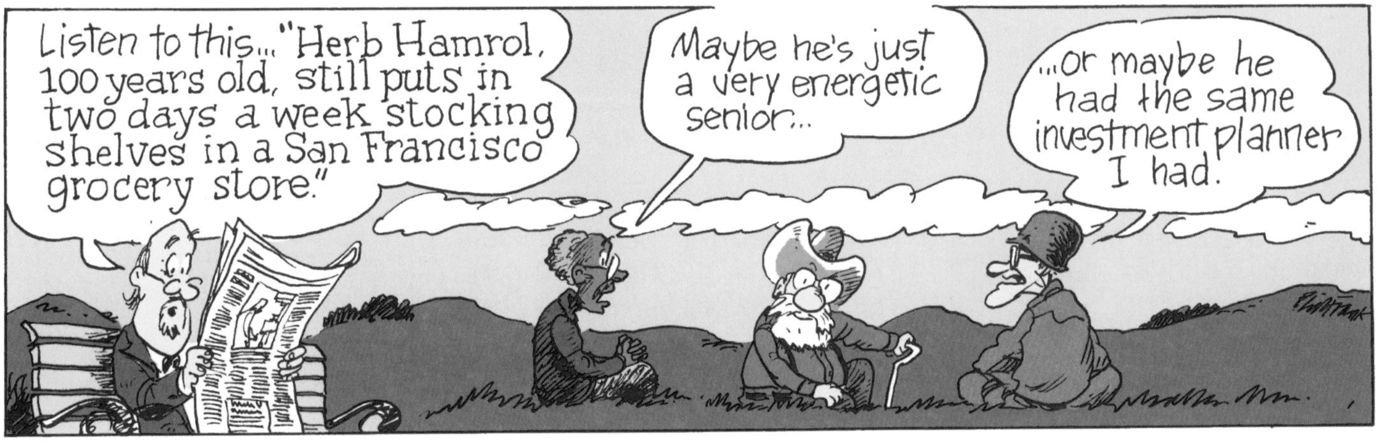
Listen to this... "Herb Hamrol, 100 years old, still puts in two days a week stocking shelves in a San Francisco grocery store."
Maybe he's just a very energetic senior...
...or maybe he had the same investment planner I had.

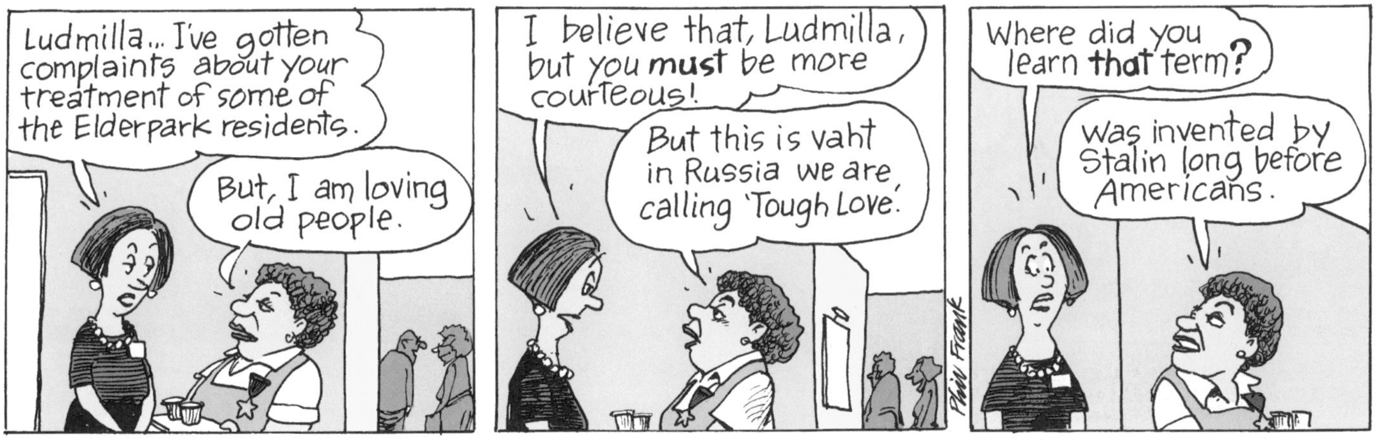
Ludmilla... I've gotten complaints about your treatment of some of the Elderpark residents.
But, I am loving old people.
I believe that, Ludmilla, but you **must** be more courteous!
But this is vaht in Russia we are calling 'Tough Love'.
Phil Frank
Where did you learn **that** term?
Was invented by Stalin long before Americans.

Elderberries
by Phil Frank & Joe Troise

Evelyn... here's a little somethin' I whittled for you.
Oh, Dusty!! How thoughtful!
You've caught me completely off guard, giving me a gift the day **before** Valentine's Day!
Uh...
?
SMEK!
It's **so** sweet! I've got to go get something for **you**!
WHOA, EVELYN!! REIN IT IN, GAL!!
What was **that** about, Dusty?
Perfessor! I'm in trouble! Evelyn thinks I got her a Valentine's Day gift!
What did you give her?
Phil Frank
I just carved her a horny toad settin' on a rock.
Oh... you're in trouble, all right!

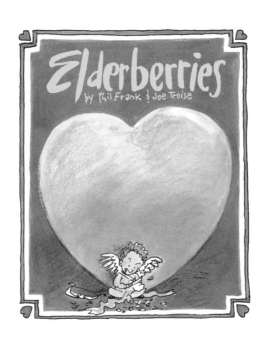

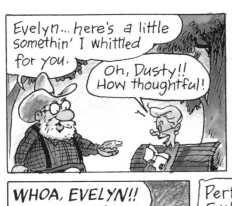

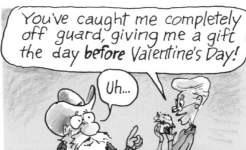

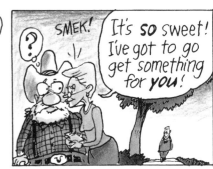

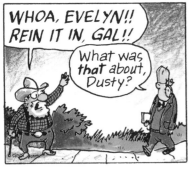

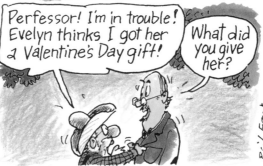

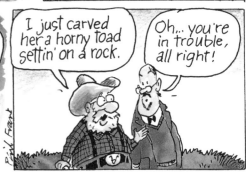

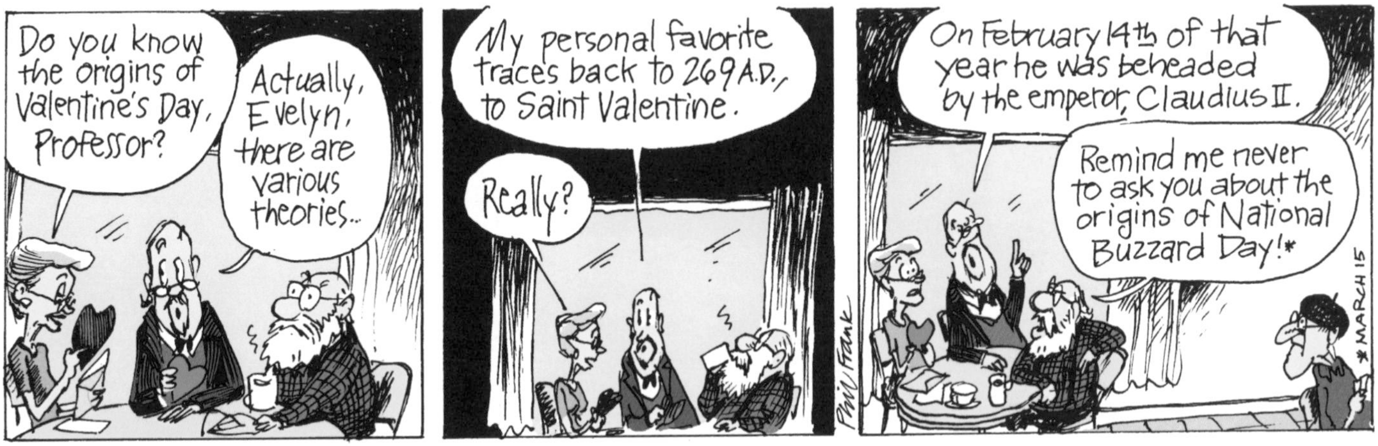
Do you know the origins of Valentine's Day, Professor?
Actually, Evelyn, there are various theories...
My personal favorite traces back to 269 A.D., to Saint Valentine.
Really?
On February 14th of that year he was beheaded by the emperor, Claudius II.
Remind me never to ask you about the origins of National Buzzard Day!*
*MARCH 15

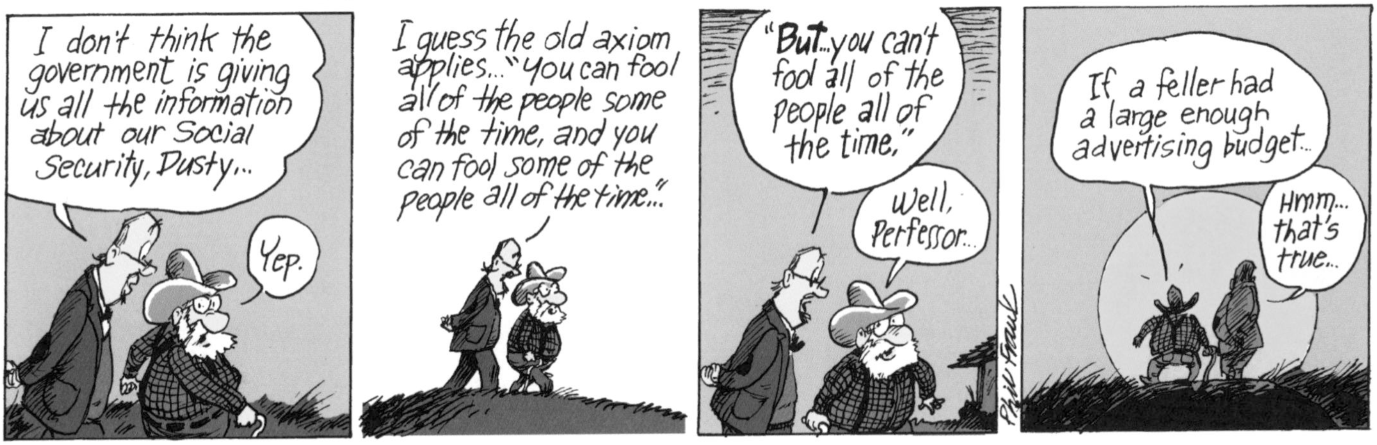
I don't think the government is giving us all the information about our Social Security, Dusty...
Yep.
I guess the old axiom applies... "You can fool all of the people some of the time, and you can fool some of the people all of the time..."
"But...you can't fool all of the people all of the time."
Well, Perfessor...
If a feller had a large enough advertising budget...
Hmm... that's true...

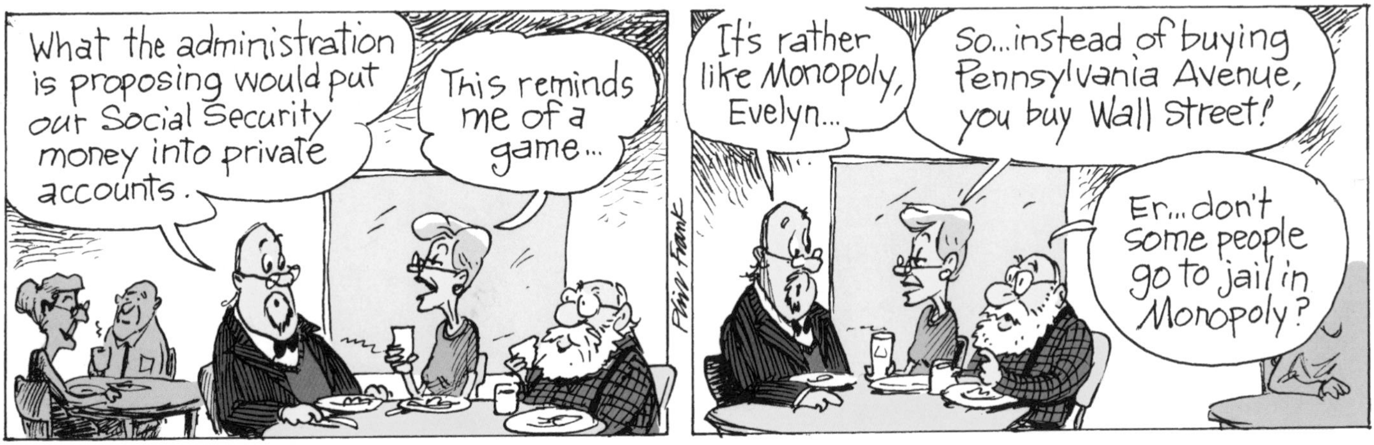
What the administration is proposing would put our Social Security money into private accounts.
This reminds me of a game...
It's rather like Monopoly, Evelyn...
So...instead of buying Pennsylvania Avenue, you buy Wall Street!
Er...don't some people go to jail in Monopoly?

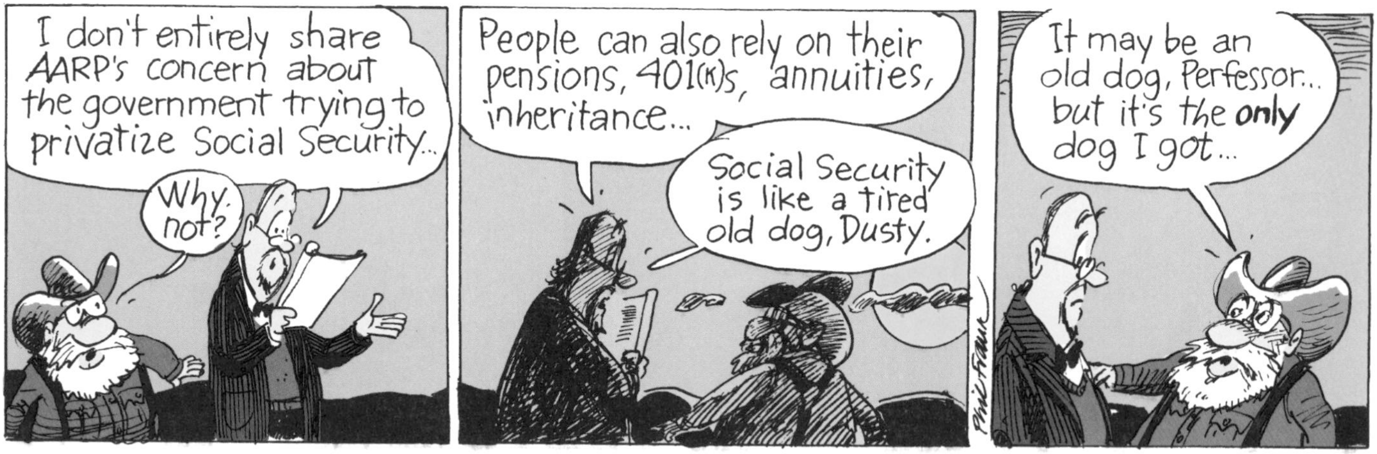
I don't entirely share AARP's concern about the government trying to privatize Social Security...
Why not?
People can also rely on their pensions, 401(k)s, annuities, inheritance...
Social Security is like a tired old dog, Dusty.
It may be an old dog, Perfessor... but it's the **only** dog I got...
Phil Frank

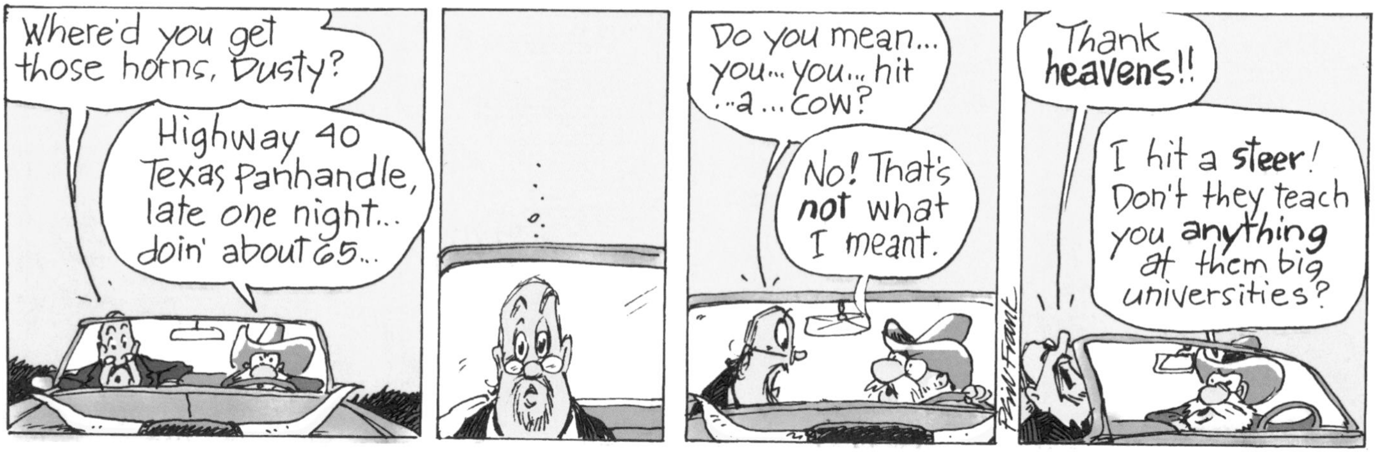
Where'd you get those horns, Dusty?
Highway 40 Texas Panhandle, late one night... doin' about 65...
Do you mean... you... you... hit ...a... cow?
No! That's **not** what I meant.
Thank **heavens**!!
I hit a **steer**! Don't they teach you **anything** at them big universities?
Phil Frank

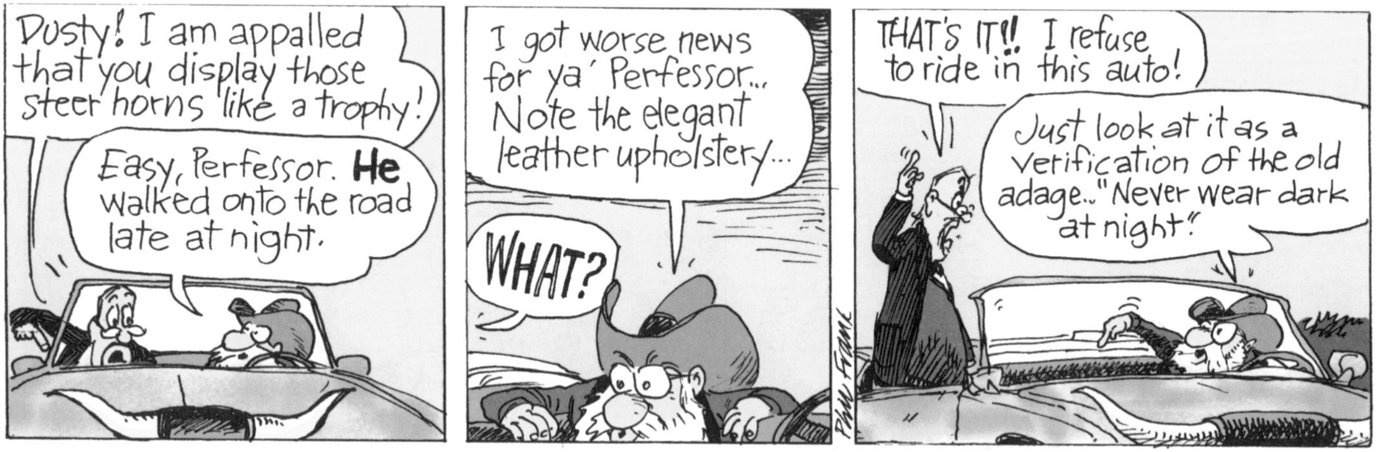
Dusty! I am appalled that you display those steer horns like a trophy!
Easy, Perfessor. **He** walked onto the road late at night.
I got worse news for ya' Perfessor... Note the elegant leather upholstery...
WHAT?
THAT'S IT!! I refuse to ride in this auto!
Just look at it as a verification of the old adage.."Never wear dark at night"
Phil Frank

Elderberries
by
Phil Frank & Joe Troise
What rhymes with "Medicare"?
Nostril hair.

Back by popular demand and against my better judgment...
Theeee Elderrappers!
YEAH!
CLAP!
CLAP!
Hey!! We're back! Shook off some flak...
From those people in power...
Livin in an ivory tower.
They don't like us sayin'... that we don't like grayin'...
They'd rather we just pay and stay outta the way
WHADDYA SAY?
NO WAY! NO WAY!
So, no more jive about quiet recreation. We're buildin' ourselves an older nation!
Better get used to hearin' us squawkin'
This ain't some nice ol' grandma talkin'!
YOU GO, GIRL!

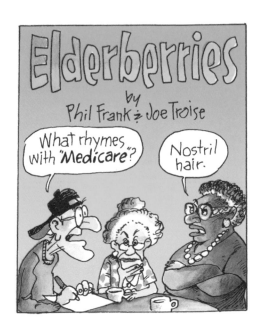

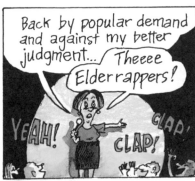

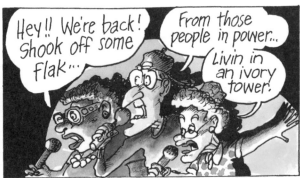

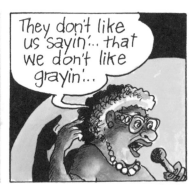

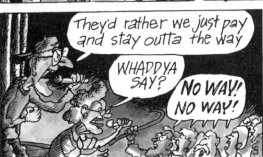

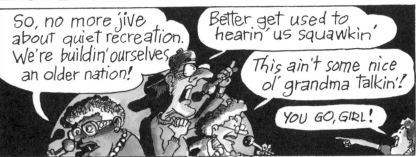

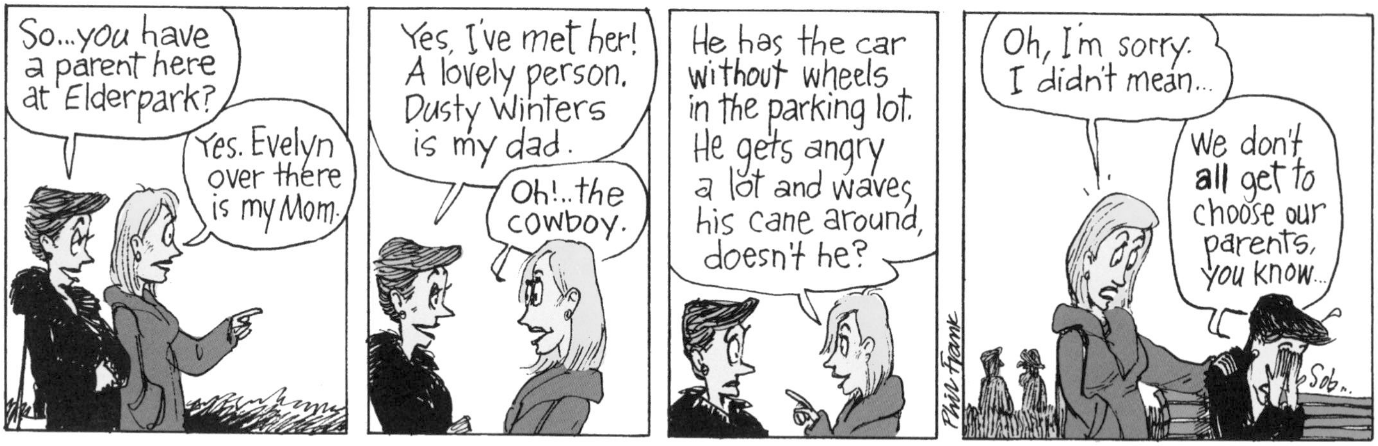
So...you have a parent here at Elderpark?
Yes. Evelyn over there is my Mom.
Yes, I've met her! A lovely person. Dusty Winters is my dad.
Oh!..the cowboy.
He has the car **without** wheels in the parking lot. He gets angry a lot and waves his cane around, doesn't he?
Phil Frank
Oh, I'm sorry. I didn't mean...
We don't **all** get to choose our parents, you know...
Sob..

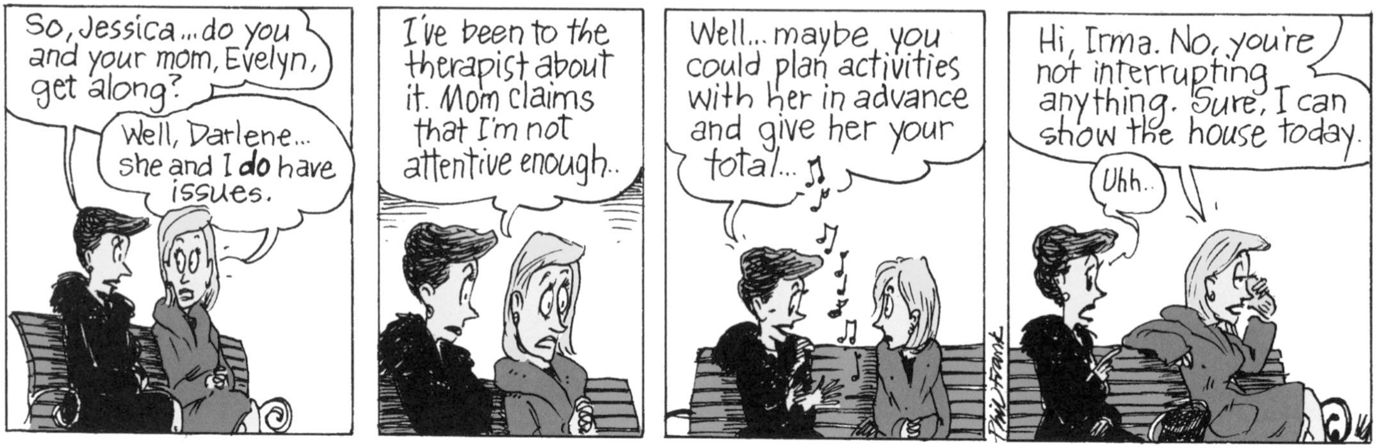
So, Jessica...do you and your mom, Evelyn, get along?
Well, Darlene... she and I **do** have issues.
I've been to the therapist about it. Mom claims that I'm not attentive enough..
Well... maybe you could plan activities with her in advance and give her your total...
Phil Frank
Hi, Irma. No, you're not interrupting anything. Sure, I can show the house today.
Uhh..

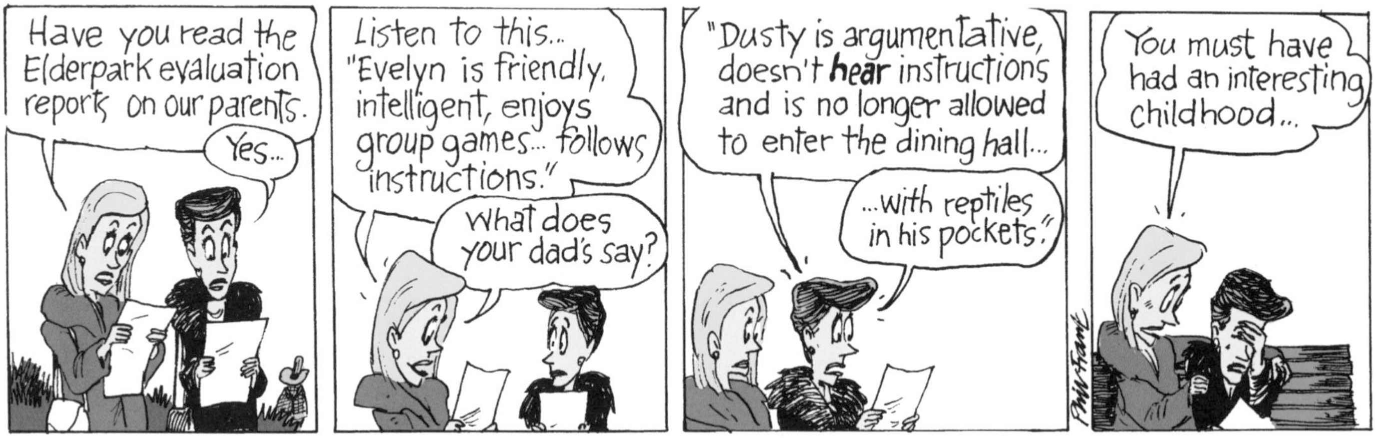
Have you read the Elderpark evaluation reports on our parents.
Yes...
Listen to this... "Evelyn is friendly, intelligent, enjoys group games... follows instructions."
What does your dad's say?
"Dusty is argumentative, doesn't **hear** instructions and is no longer allowed to enter the dining hall...
...with reptiles in his pockets."
Phil Frank
You must have had an interesting childhood...

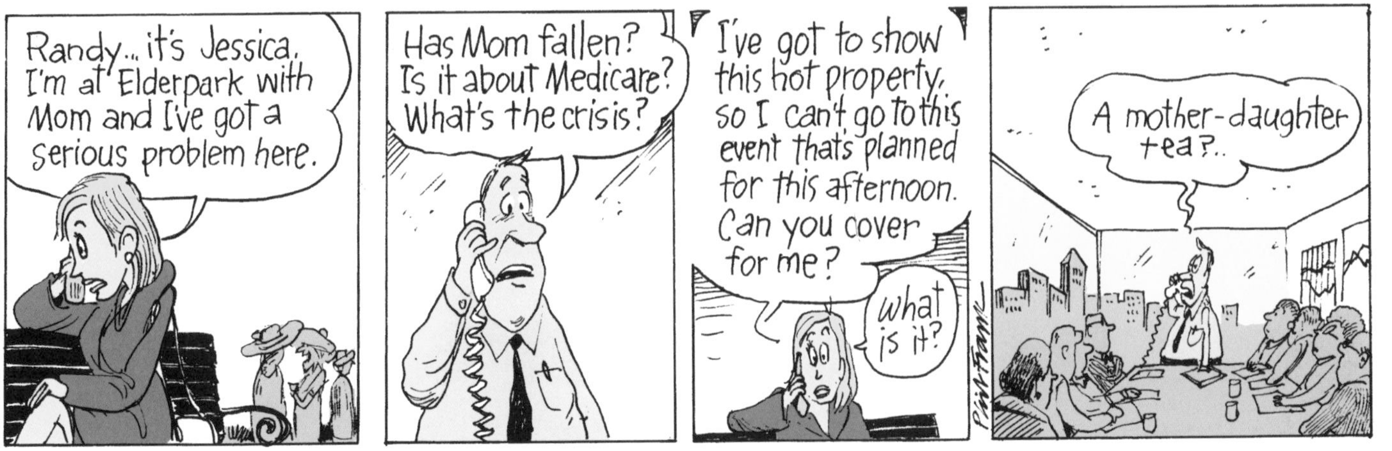
Randy... it's Jessica. I'm at Elderpark with Mom and I've got a serious problem here.
Has Mom fallen? Is it about Medicare? What's the crisis?
I've got to show this hot property, so I can't go to this event that's planned for this afternoon. Can you cover for me?
What is it?
A mother-daughter tea?..

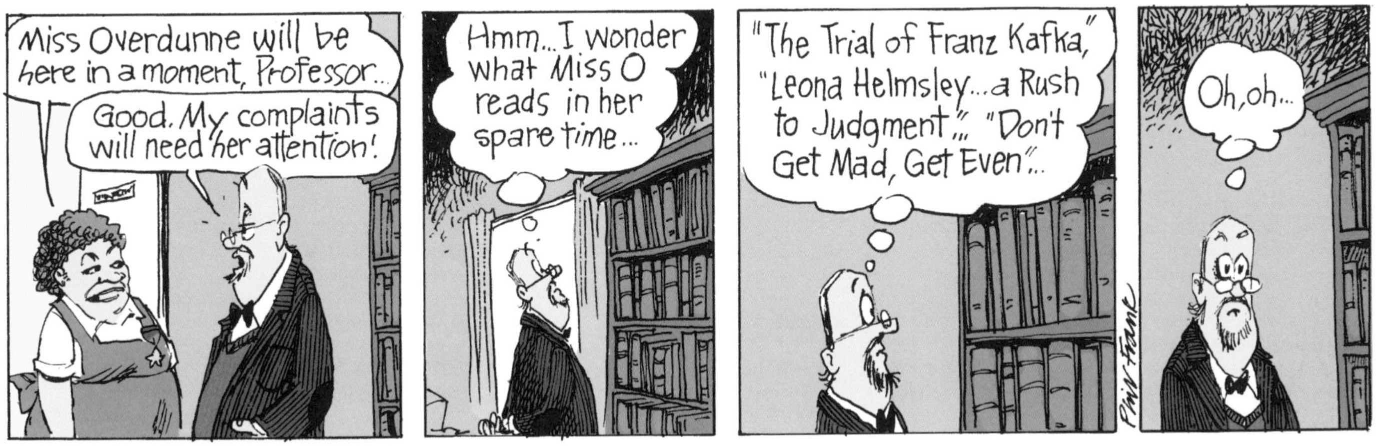
Miss Overdunne will be here in a moment, Professor...
Good. My complaints will need her attention!
Hmm...I wonder what Miss O reads in her spare time...
"The Trial of Franz Kafka," "Leona Helmsley...a Rush to Judgment"... "Don't Get Mad, Get Even"...
Oh, oh...

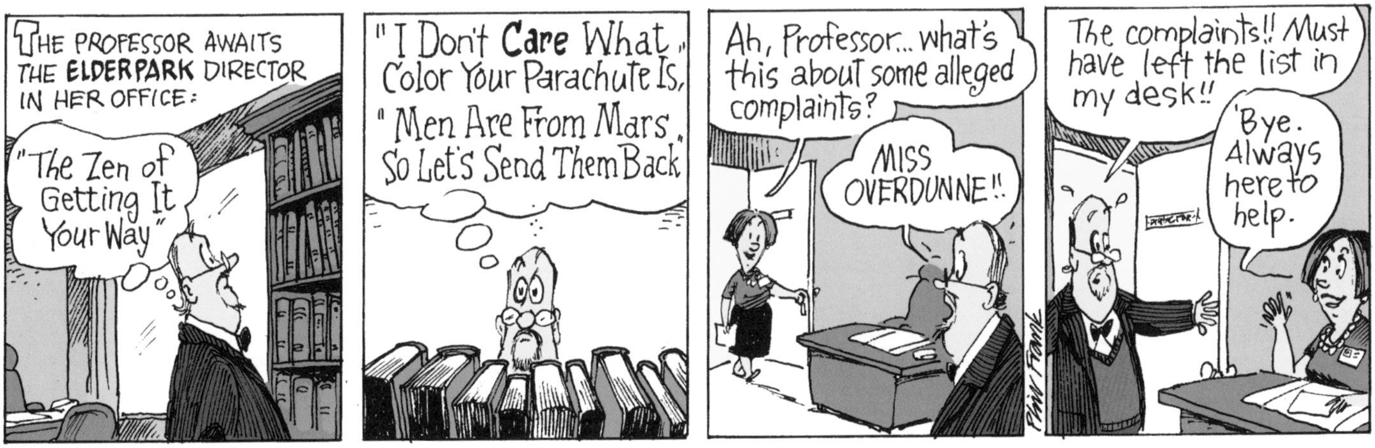
THE PROFESSOR AWAITS THE ELDERPARK DIRECTOR IN HER OFFICE:
"The Zen of Getting It Your Way"
"I Don't Care What Color Your Parachute Is," "Men Are From Mars, So Let's Send Them Back"
Ah, Professor... what's this about some alleged complaints?
MISS OVERDUNNE!!
The complaints!! Must have left the list in my desk!!
'Bye. Always here to help.

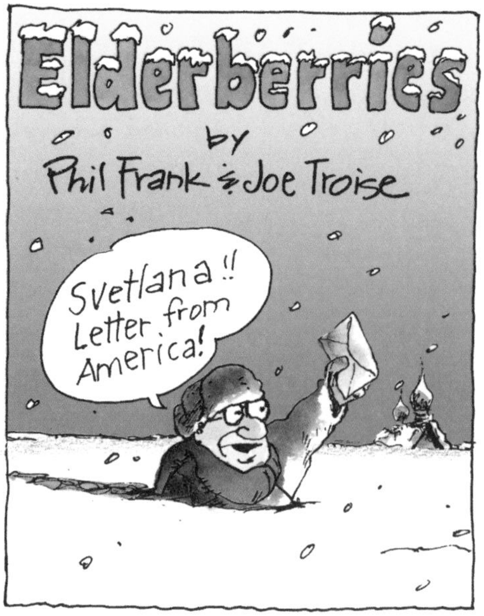
Elderberries
by
Phil Frank & Joe Troise
Svetlana!! Letter from America!

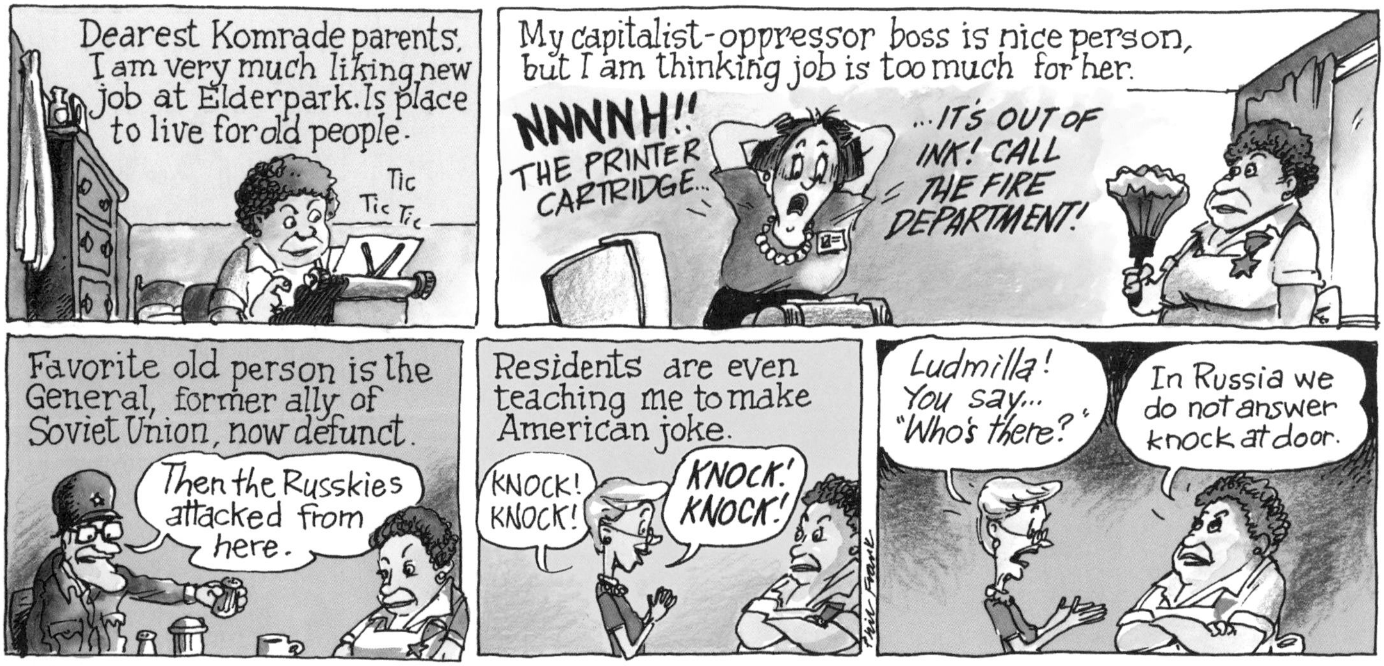
Dearest Komrade parents, I am very much liking new job at Elderpark. Is place to live for old people.
Tic Tic Tic
My capitalist-oppressor boss is nice person, but I am thinking job is too much for her.
NNNNH!! THE PRINTER CARTRIDGE...
...IT'S OUT OF INK! CALL THE FIRE DEPARTMENT!
Favorite old person is the General, former ally of Soviet Union, now defunct.
Then the Russkies attacked from here.
Residents are even teaching me to make American joke.
KNOCK! KNOCK!
KNOCK! KNOCK!
Ludmilla! You say... "Who's there?"
In Russia we do not answer knock at door.

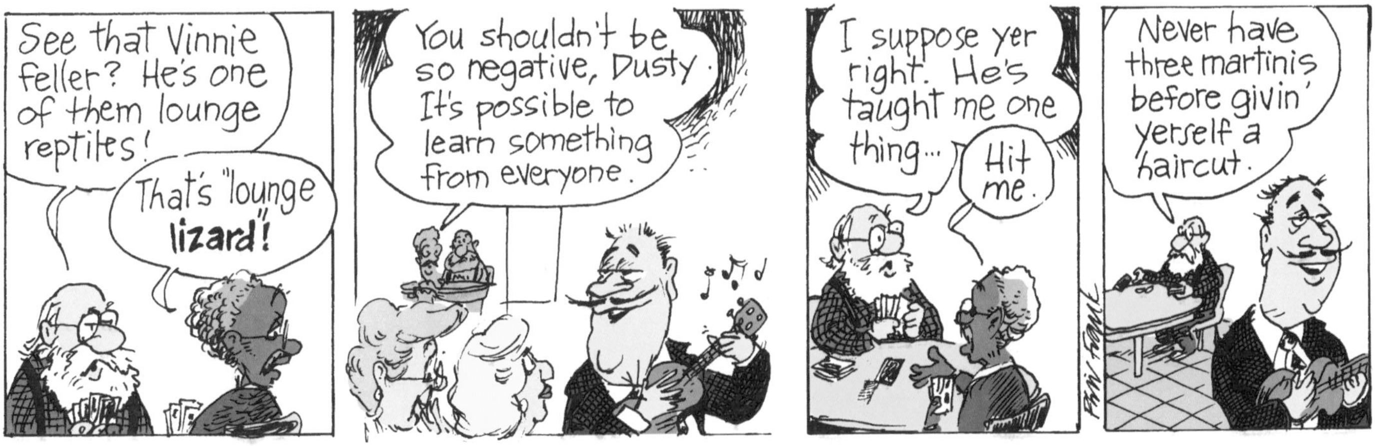
See that Vinnie feller? He's one of them lounge reptiles!
That's "lounge lizard"!
You shouldn't be so negative, Dusty. It's possible to learn something from everyone.
I suppose yer right. He's taught me one thing...
Hit me.
Never have three martinis before givin' yerself a haircut.
Phil Frank

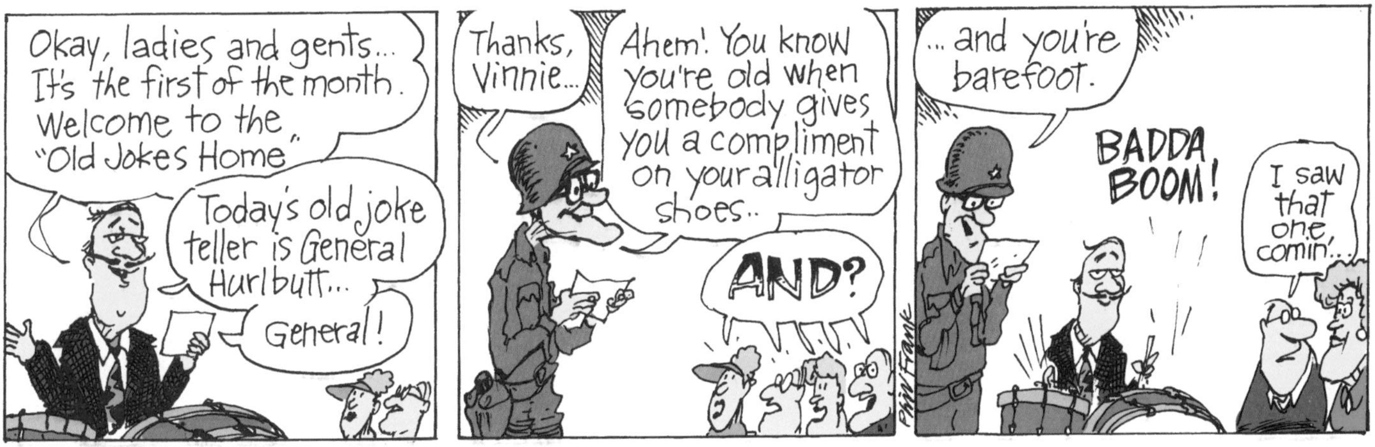
Okay, ladies and gents... It's the first of the month. Welcome to the "Old Jokes Home"
Today's old joke teller is General Hurlbutt...
General!
Thanks, Vinnie...
Ahem! You know you're old when somebody gives you a compliment on your alligator shoes..
AND?
... and you're barefoot.
BADDA BOOM!
I saw that one comin'...
Phil Frank

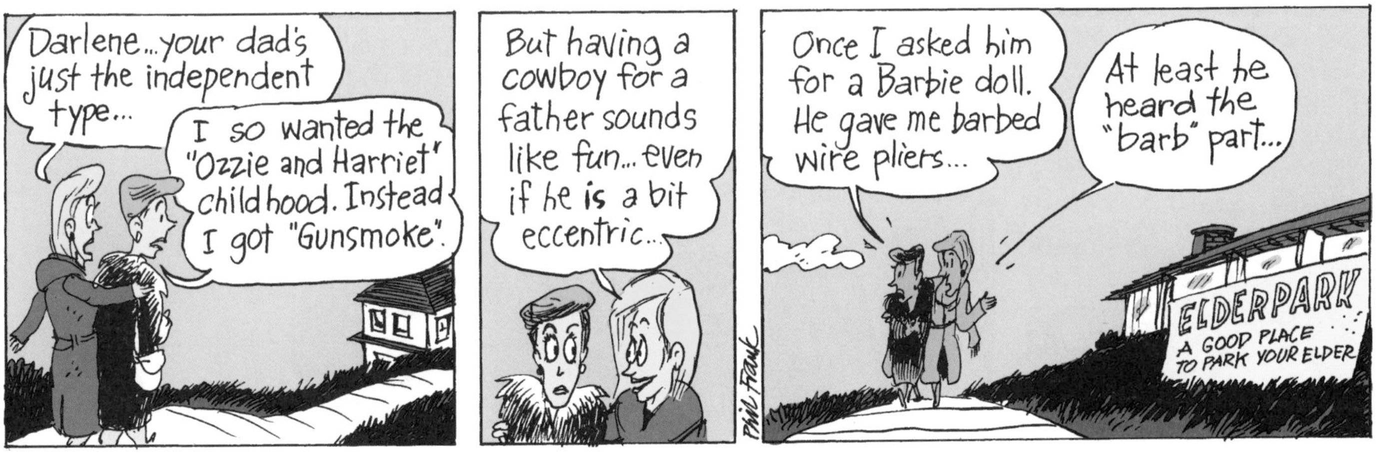
Darlene...your dad's just the independent type...
I so wanted the "Ozzie and Harriet" childhood. Instead I got "Gunsmoke".
But having a cowboy for a father sounds like fun... even if he is a bit eccentric..
Once I asked him for a Barbie doll. He gave me barbed wire pliers...
At least he heard the "barb" part...
ELDERPARK
A GOOD PLACE TO PARK YOUR ELDER
Phil Frank

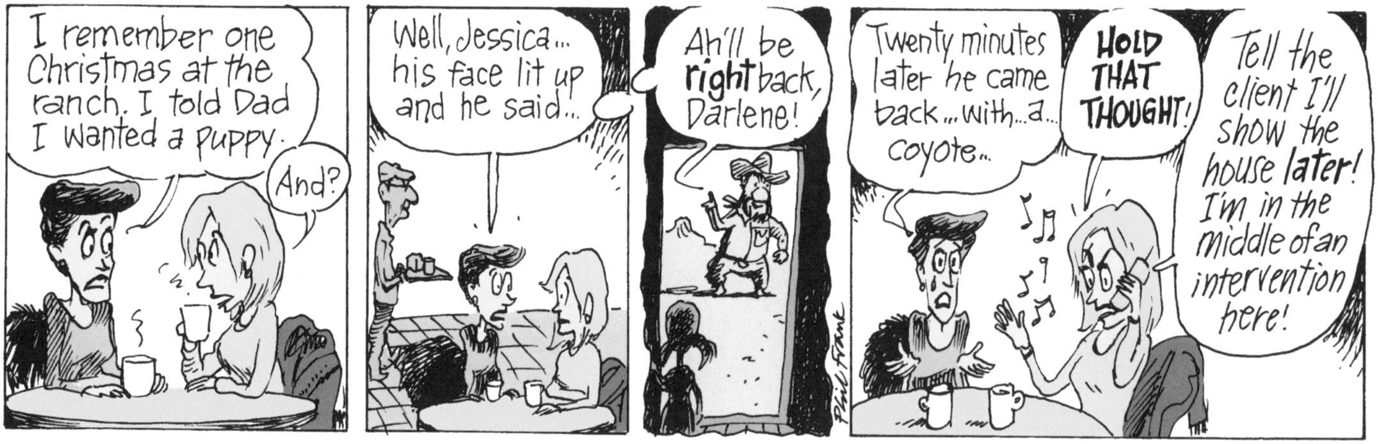
I remember one Christmas at the ranch. I told Dad I wanted a puppy.
And?
Well, Jessica... his face lit up and he said...
Ah'll be **right** back, Darlene!
Twenty minutes later he came back... with... a... coyote...
HOLD THAT THOUGHT!
Tell the client I'll show the house **later**! I'm in the middle of an intervention here!

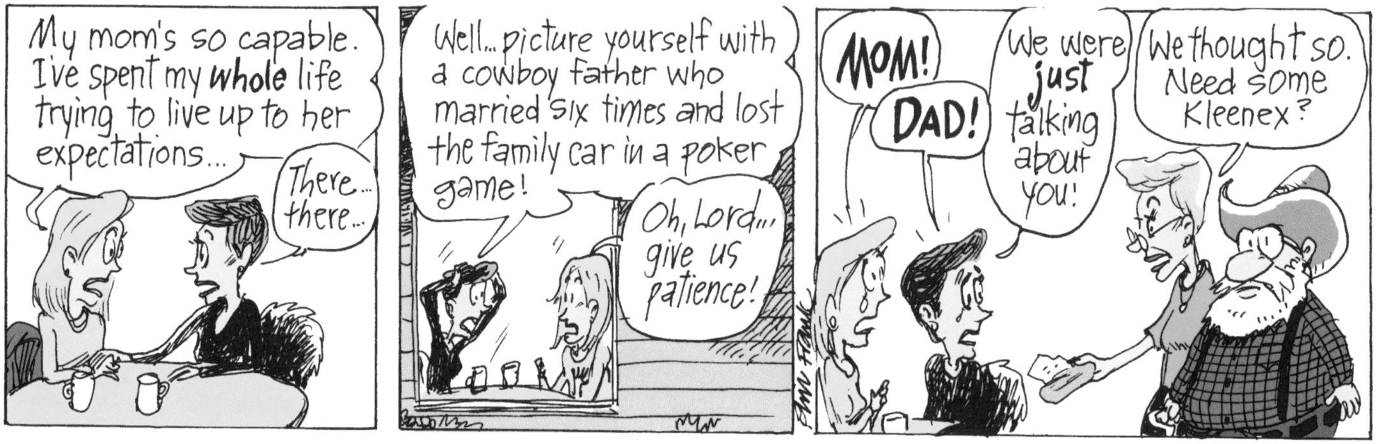
My mom's so capable. I've spent my **whole** life trying to live up to her expectations...
There... there...
Well... picture yourself with a cowboy father who married six times and lost the family car in a poker game!
Oh, Lord... give us patience!
MOM!
DAD!
We were **just** talking about you!
We thought so. Need some Kleenex?

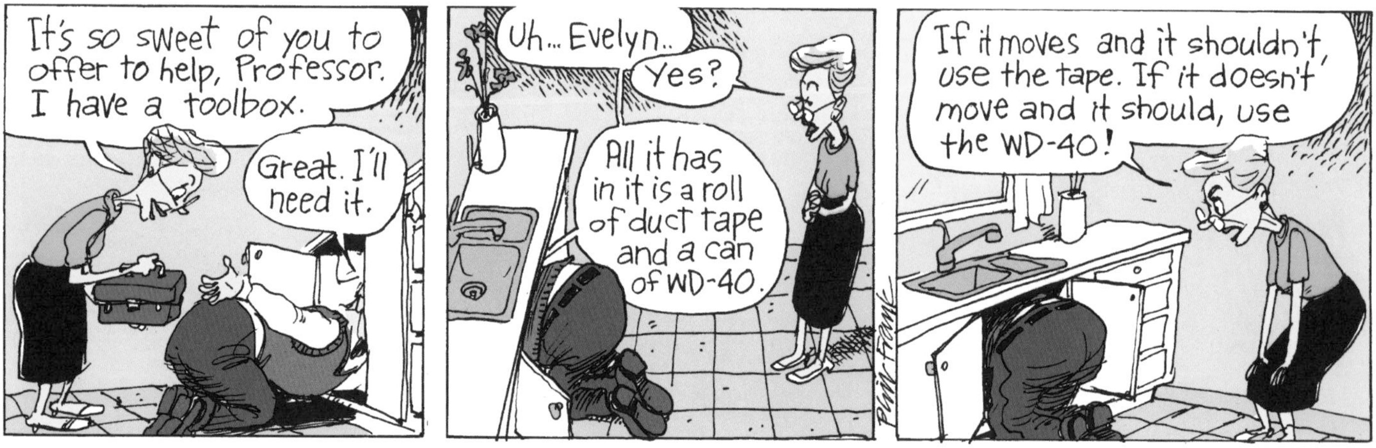
It's so sweet of you to offer to help, Professor. I have a toolbox.
Great. I'll need it.
Uh... Evelyn..
Yes?
All it has in it is a roll of duct tape and a can of WD-40.
If it moves and it shouldn't, use the tape. If it doesn't move and it should, use the WD-40!

Elderberries

by Phil Frank and Joe Troise

Funny...I never noticed that trademark symbol before today...

ELDERPARK™
A GOOD PLACE TO PARK YOUR ELDER

WHOA!! LOOK AT **THIS**, DUSTY!

What is it, Perfessor?

When I did a search for "Elderpark" on the Internet, I got this elaborate flow chart.

A flow chart? Maybe we can finally fix the plumbing around here.

No! It's about corporate business connections... who owns what... fascinating...

What's it say?

For one thing, there are 35 Elderparks!

You mean we're a chain, like Wal-Mart?

The company that owns the retirement home also leases shipping containers and warehouse space.

"Elderpark, Inc., a subsidiary of Jujitsu Heavy Industries... your global storage specialist!"

Hmm... is that the director on a forklift?

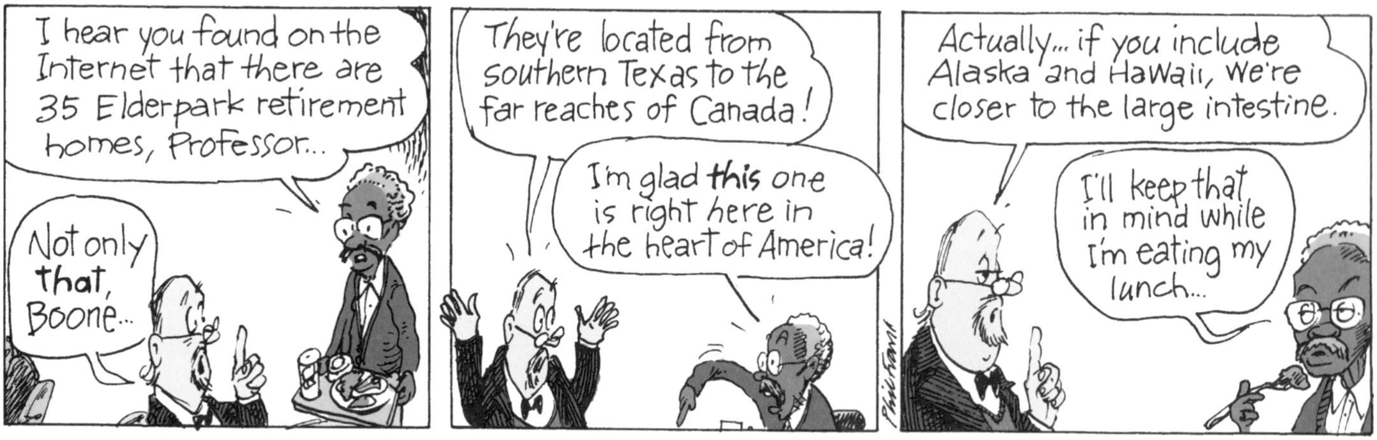
I hear you found on the Internet that there are 35 Elderpark retirement homes, Professor...
Not only **that**, Boone...
They're located from southern Texas to the far reaches of Canada!
I'm glad **this** one is right here in the heart of America!
Actually... if you include Alaska and Hawaii, we're closer to the large intestine.
I'll keep that in mind while I'm eating my lunch...
Phil Frank

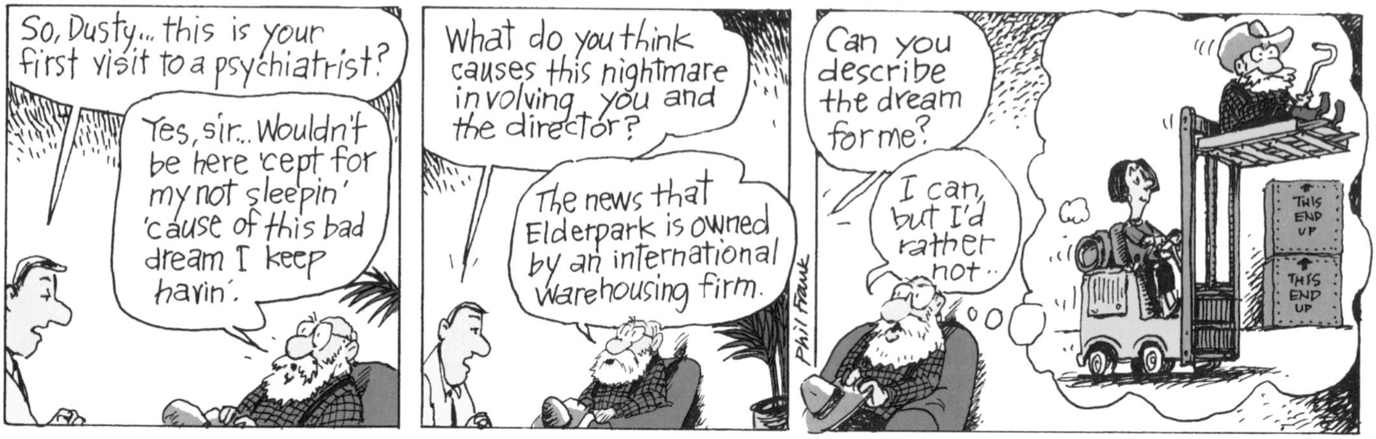
So, Dusty... this is your first visit to a psychiatrist?
Yes, sir... Wouldn't be here 'cept for my not sleepin' 'cause of this bad dream I keep havin'.
What do you think causes this nightmare involving you and the director?
The news that Elderpark is owned by an international warehousing firm.
Phil Frank
Can you describe the dream for me?
I can, but I'd rather not...
THIS END UP
THIS END UP

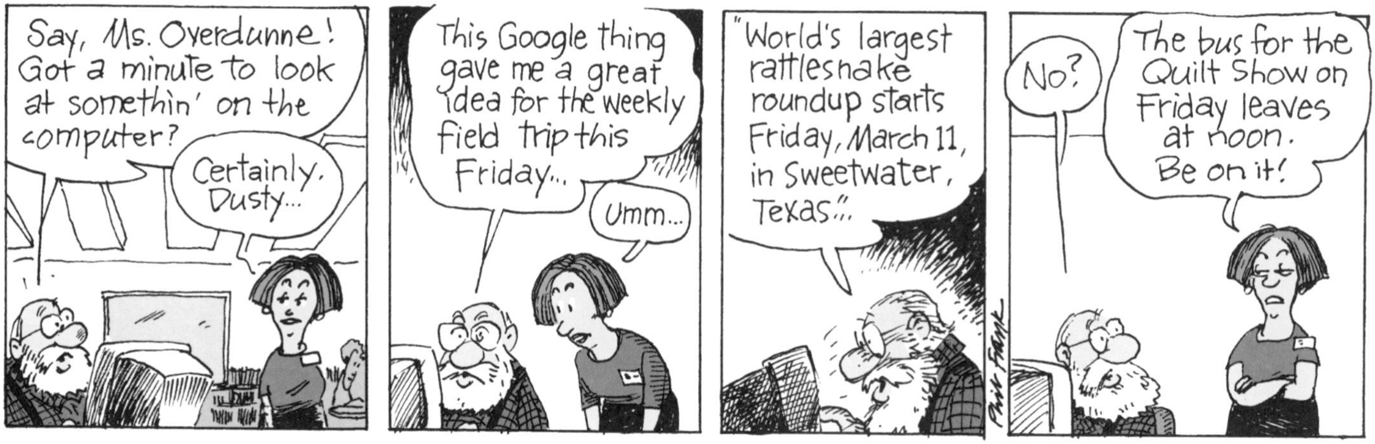
Say, Ms. Overdunne! Got a minute to look at somethin' on the computer?
Certainly, Dusty...
This Google thing gave me a great idea for the weekly field trip this Friday...
Umm...
"World's largest rattlesnake roundup starts Friday, March 11, in Sweetwater, Texas."
Phil Frank
No?
The bus for the Quilt Show on Friday leaves at noon. Be on it!

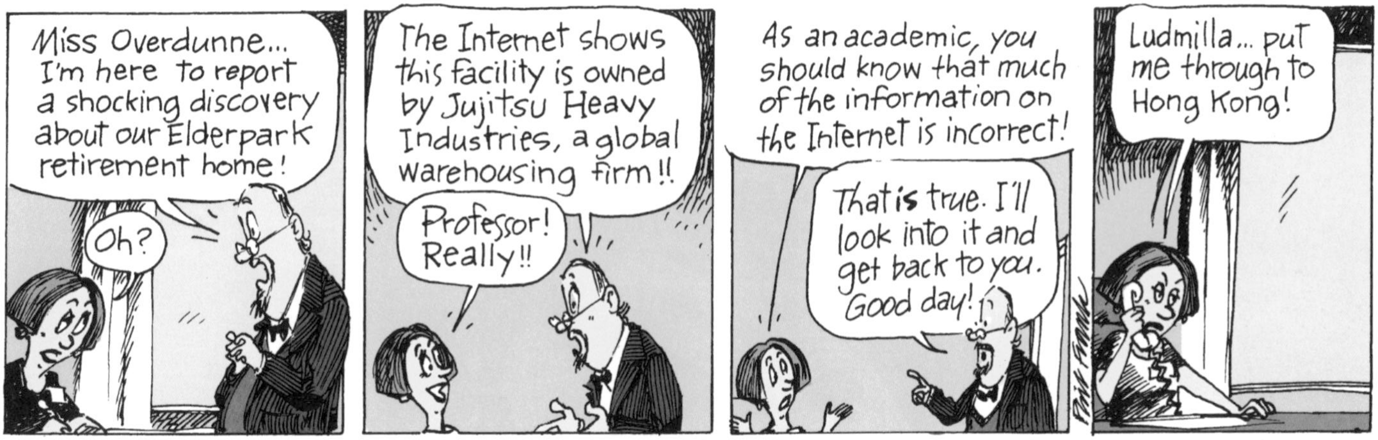
Miss Overdunne... I'm here to report a shocking discovery about our Elderpark retirement home!
Oh?
The Internet shows this facility is owned by Jujitsu Heavy Industries, a global warehousing firm!!
Professor! Really!!
As an academic, you should know that much of the information on the Internet is incorrect!
That **is** true. I'll look into it and get back to you. Good day!
Ludmilla... put me through to Hong Kong!

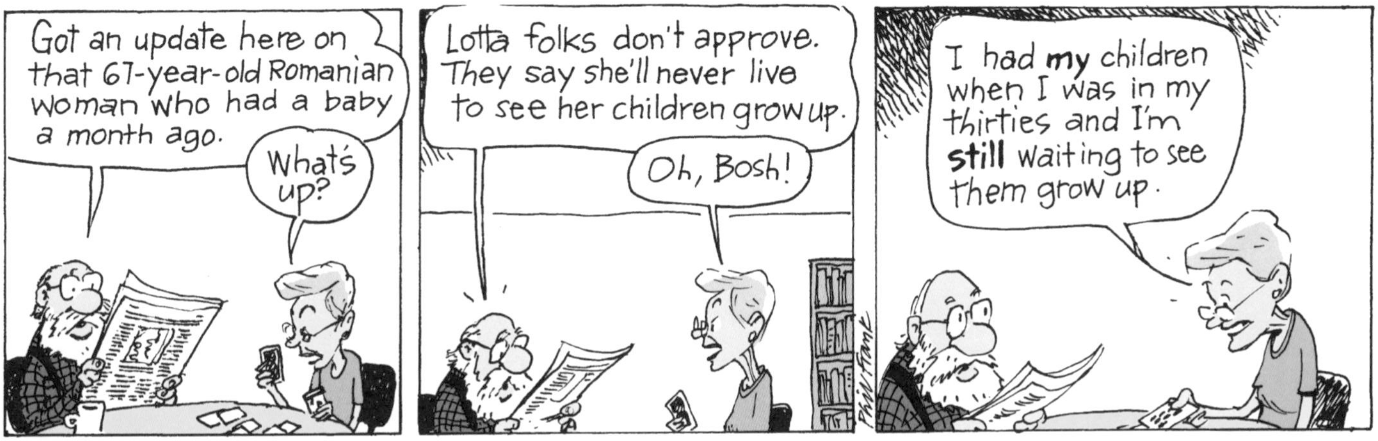
Got an update here on that 67-year-old Romanian woman who had a baby a month ago.
What's up?
Lotta folks don't approve. They say she'll never live to see her children grow up.
Oh, Bosh!
I had **my** children when I was in my thirties and I'm **still** waiting to see them grow up.

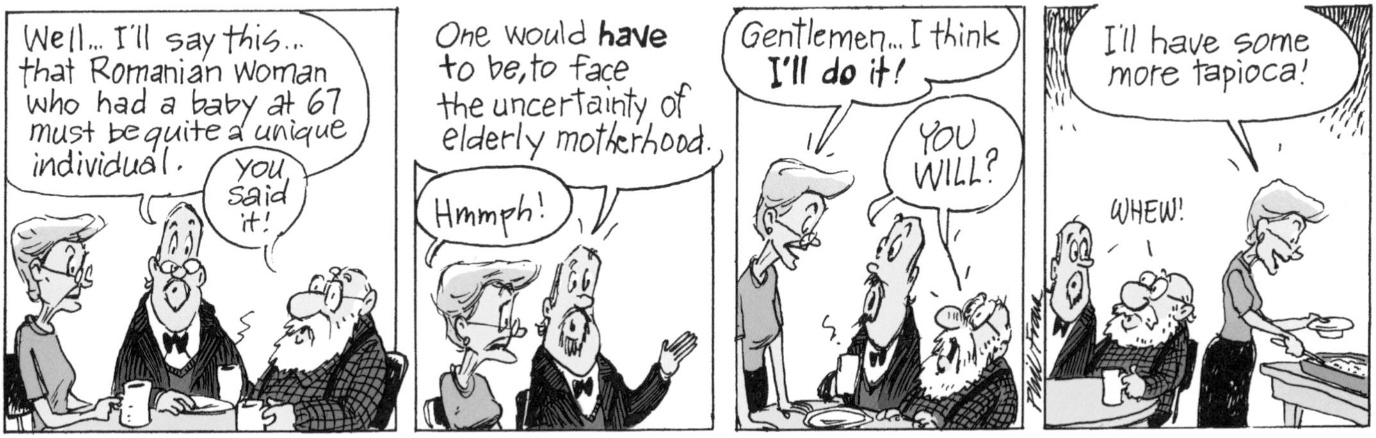
Well... I'll say this... that Romanian woman who had a baby at 67 must be quite a unique individual.
You said it!
One would **have** to be, to face the uncertainty of elderly motherhood.
Hmmph!
Gentlemen... I think **I'll do it!**
YOU WILL?
WHEW!
I'll have some more tapioca!

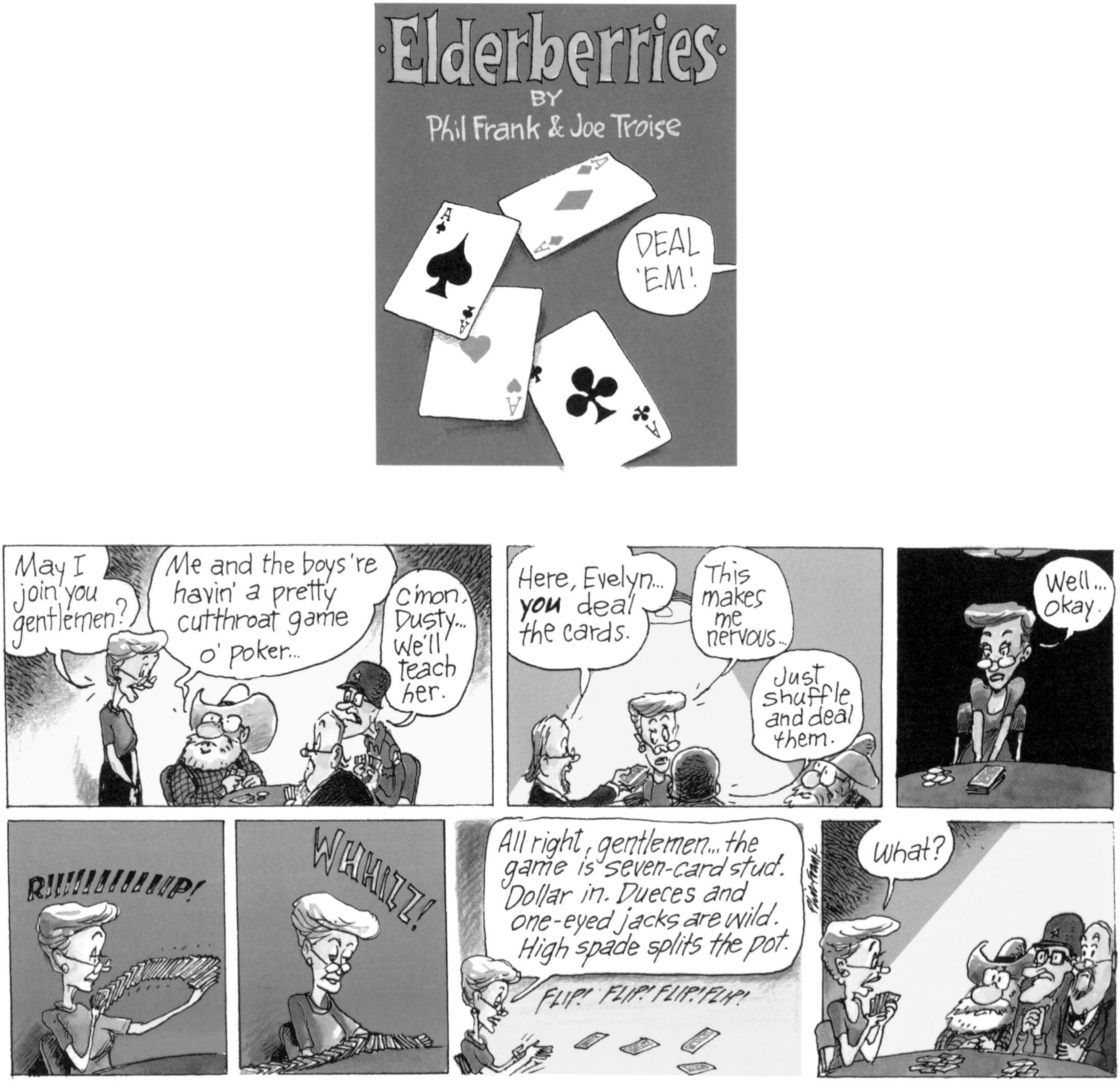

Elderberries
BY
Phil Frank & Joe Troise
DEAL 'EM!
May I join you gentlemen?
Me and the boys're havin' a pretty cutthroat game o' poker...
C'mon, Dusty... we'll teach her.
Here, Evelyn... **you** deal the cards.
This makes me nervous...
Just shuffle and deal them.
Well... okay.
RIIIIIIIIIIIIP!
WHHIZZ!
All right, gentlemen... the game is seven-card stud. Dollar in. Dueces and one-eyed jacks are wild. High spade splits the pot.
FLIP! FLIP! FLIP! FLIP!
What?

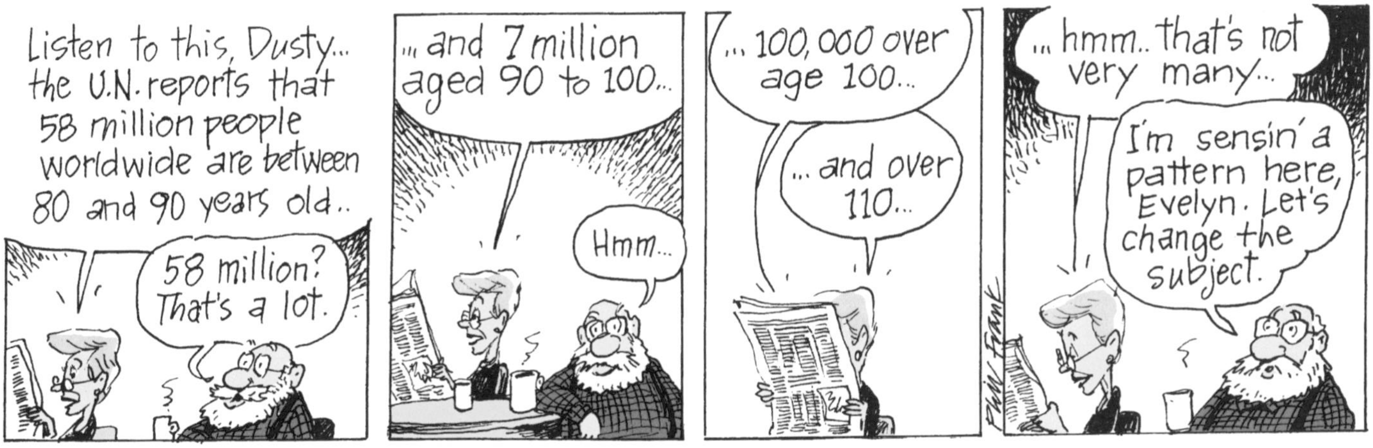
Listen to this, Dusty... the U.N. reports that 58 million people worldwide are between 80 and 90 years old..
58 million? That's a lot.
... and 7 million aged 90 to 100...
Hmm...
... 100,000 over age 100...
... and over 110...
... hmm.. that's not very many...
I'm sensin' a pattern here, Evelyn. Let's change the subject.
Phil Frank

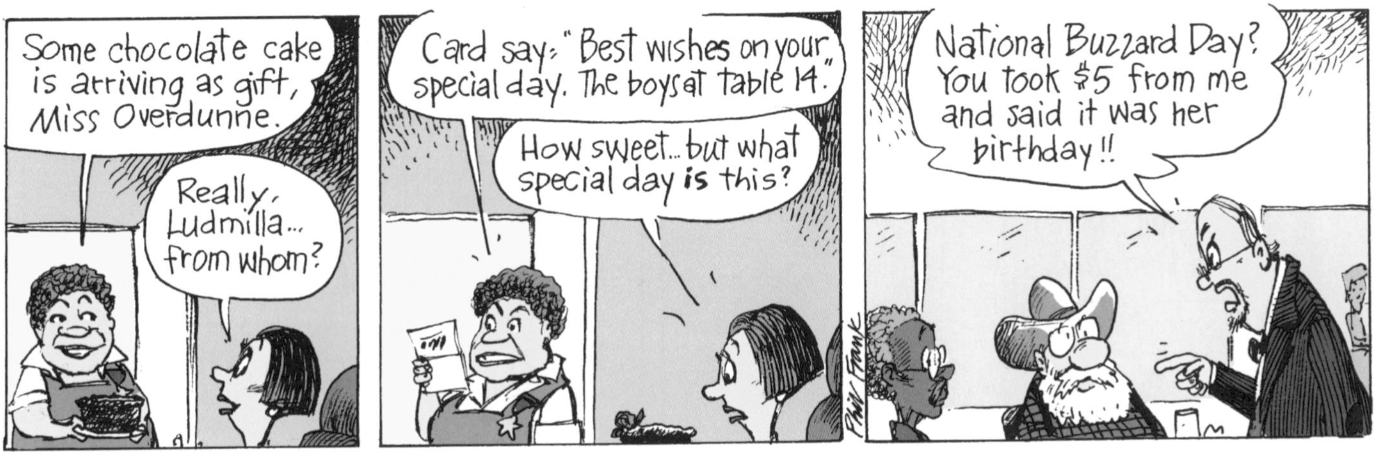
Some chocolate cake is arriving as gift, Miss Overdunne.
Really, Ludmilla... from whom?
Card say: "Best wishes on your special day. The boys at table 14."
How sweet... but what special day **is** this?
National Buzzard Day? You took $5 from me and said it was her birthday!!
Phil Frank

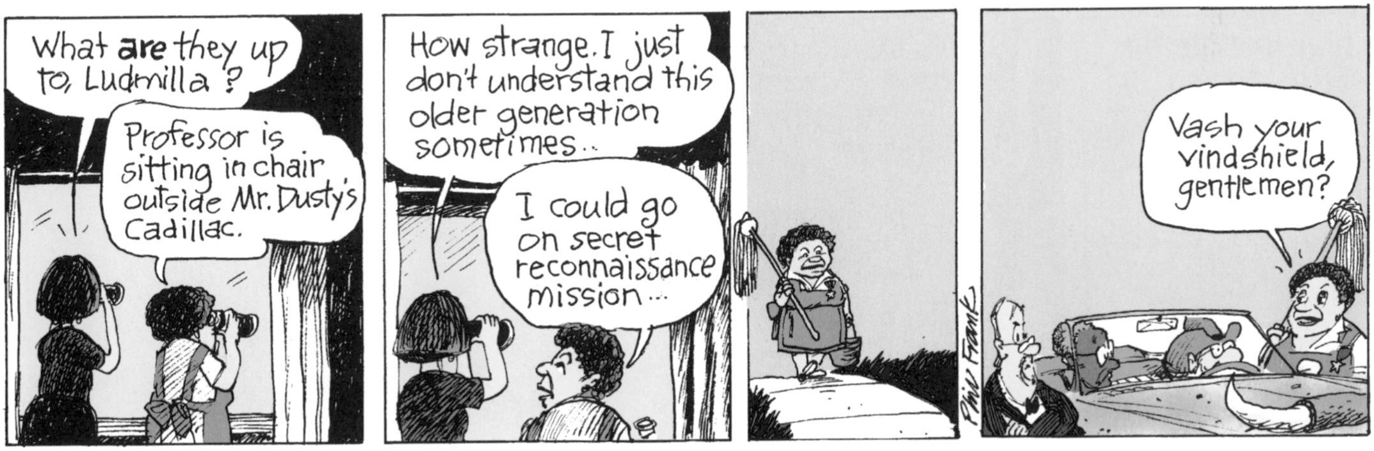
What **are** they up to, Ludmilla?
Professor is sitting in chair outside Mr. Dusty's Cadillac.
How strange. I just don't understand this older generation sometimes..
I could go on secret reconnaissance mission...
Vash your vindshield, gentlemen?
Phil Frank

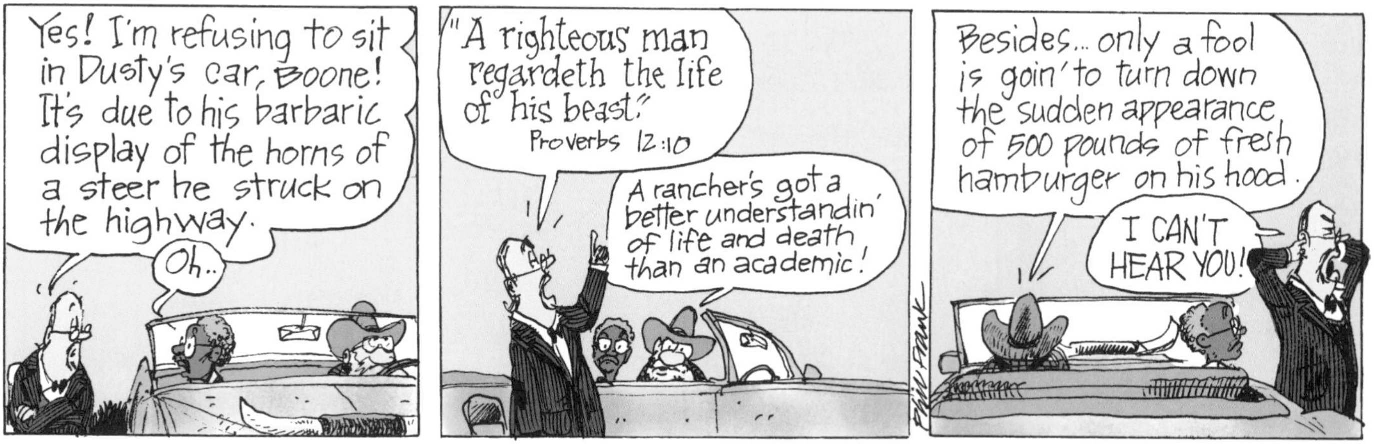
Yes! I'm refusing to sit in Dusty's car, Boone! It's due to his barbaric display of the horns of a steer he struck on the highway.
Oh..
"A righteous man regardeth the life of his beast." Proverbs 12:10
A rancher's got a better understandin' of life and death than an academic!
Besides... only a fool is goin' to turn down the sudden appearance of 500 pounds of fresh hamburger on his hood.
I CAN'T HEAR YOU!

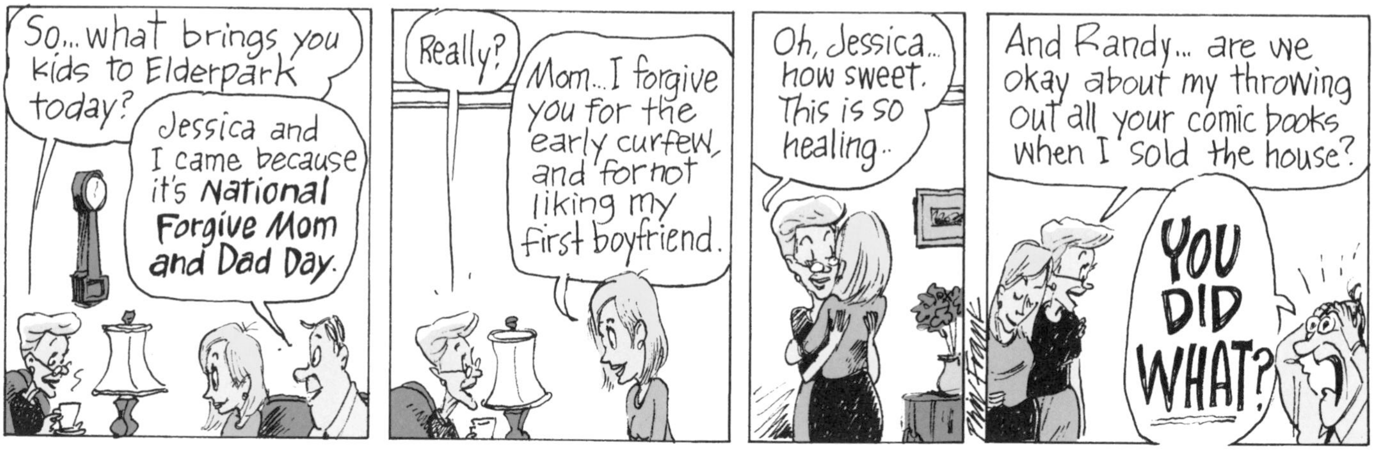
So... what brings you kids to Elderpark today?
Jessica and I came because it's **National Forgive Mom and Dad Day**.
Really?
Mom... I forgive you for the early curfew, and for not liking my first boyfriend.
Oh, Jessica... how sweet. This is so healing..
And Randy... are we okay about my throwing out all your comic books when I sold the house?
YOU DID WHAT?

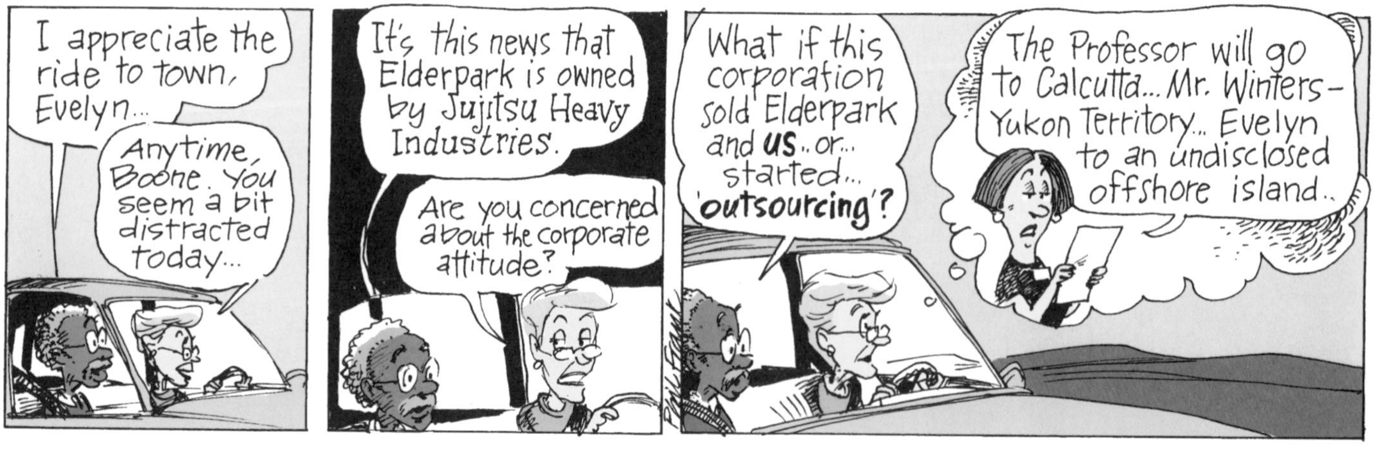
I appreciate the ride to town, Evelyn...
Anytime, Boone. You seem a bit distracted today...
It's this news that Elderpark is owned by Jujitsu Heavy Industries.
Are you concerned about the corporate attitude?
What if this corporation sold Elderpark and **US**.. or... started... '**outsourcing**'?
The Professor will go to Calcutta... Mr. Winters - Yukon Territory... Evelyn to an undisclosed offshore island..

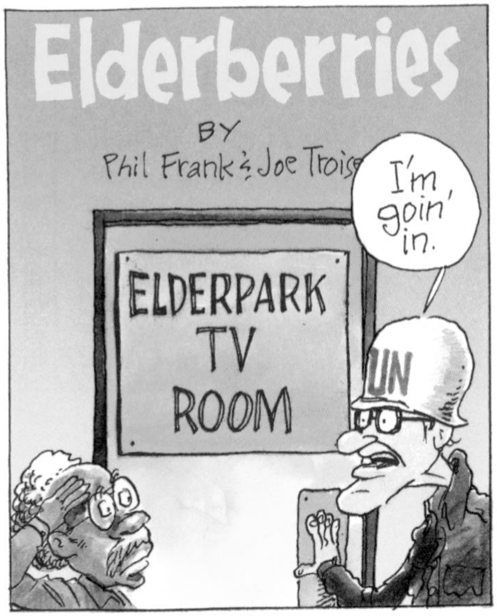
Elderberries
BY
Phil Frank & Joe Trois
I'm goin' in.
ELDERPARK TV ROOM
UN

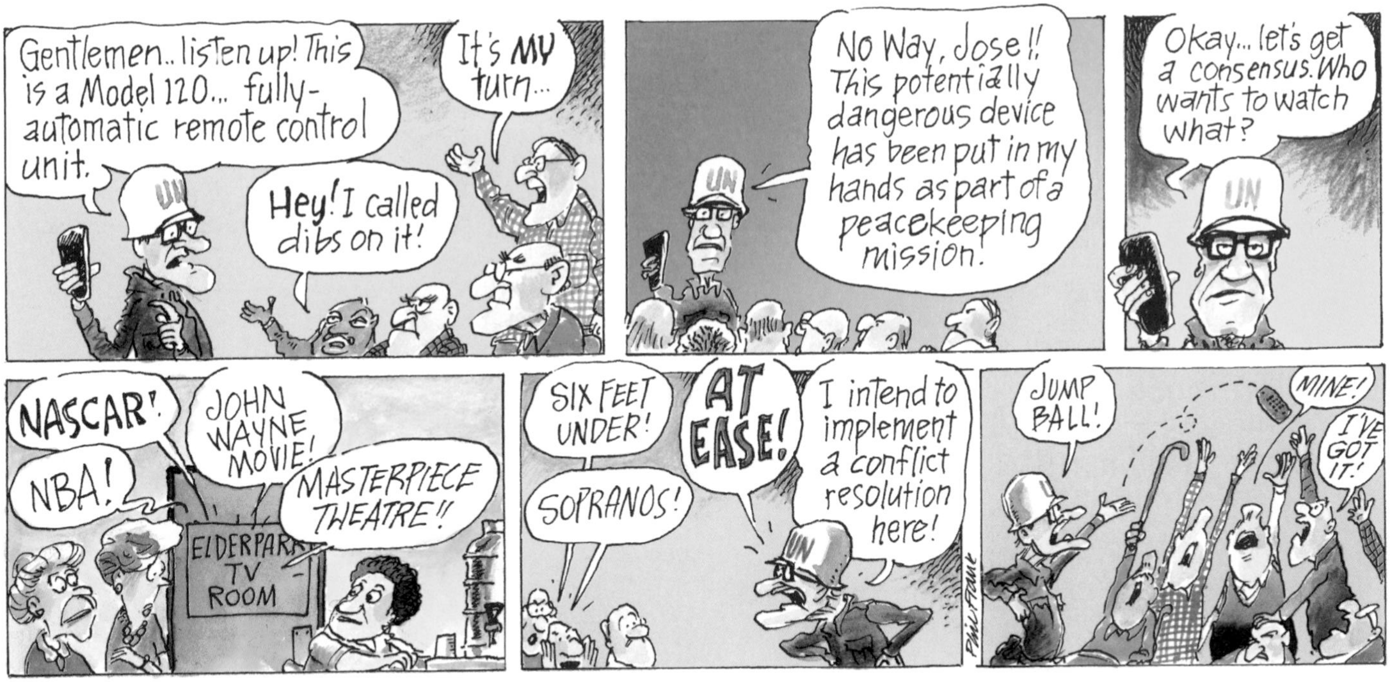
Gentlemen.. listen up! This is a Model 120... fully-automatic remote control unit.
It's MY turn...
Hey! I called dibs on it!
No Way, Jose!! This potentially dangerous device has been put in my hands as part of a peacekeeping mission!
Okay... let's get a consensus. Who wants to watch what?
NASCAR!
NBA!
JOHN WAYNE MOVIE!
MASTERPIECE THEATRE!!
ELDERPARK TV ROOM
SIX FEET UNDER!
SOPRANOS!
AT EASE!
I intend to implement a conflict resolution here!
JUMP BALL!
MINE!
I'VE GOT IT!

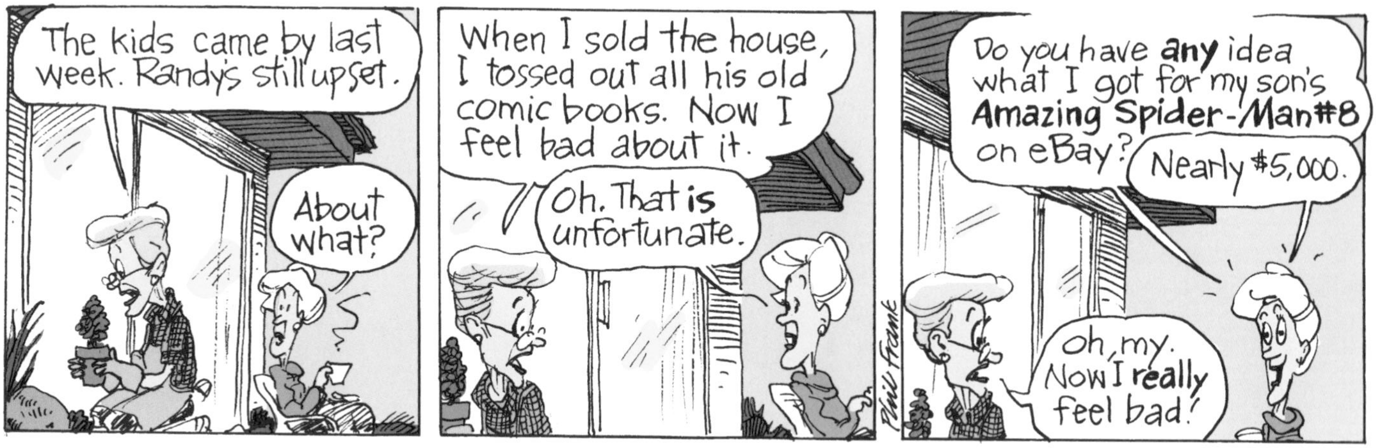
The kids came by last week. Randy's still upset.
About what?
When I sold the house, I tossed out all his old comic books. Now I feel bad about it.
Oh. That **is** unfortunate.
Do you have **any** idea what I got for my son's **Amazing Spider-Man #8** on eBay?
Nearly $5,000.
Oh, my. Now I **really** feel bad!
Phil Frank

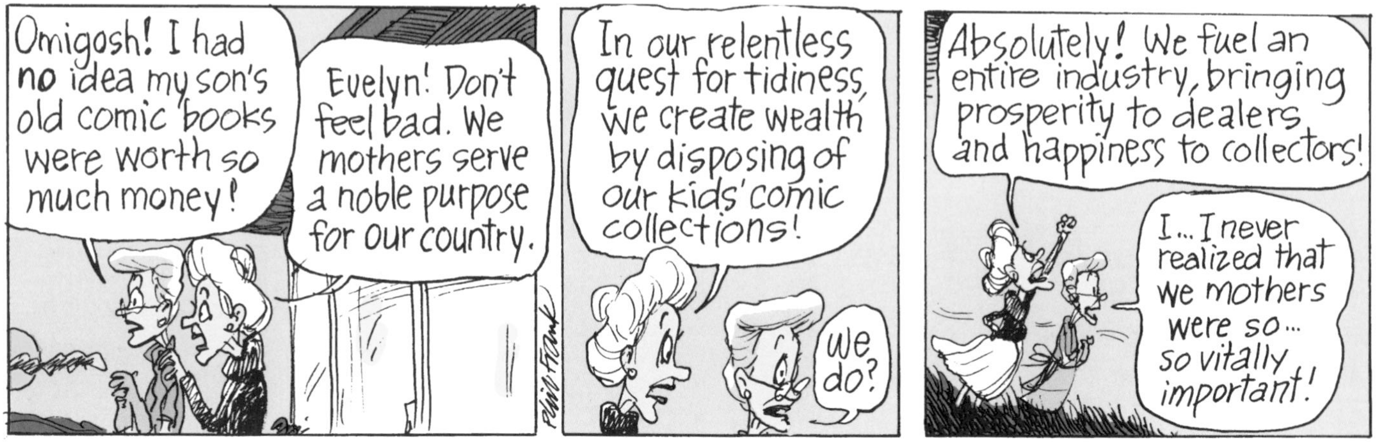
Omigosh! I had **no** idea my son's old comic books were worth so much money!
Evelyn! Don't feel bad. We mothers serve a noble purpose for our country.
Phil Frank
In our relentless quest for tidiness, we create wealth by disposing of our kids' comic collections!
We do?
Absolutely! We fuel an entire industry, bringing prosperity to dealers and happiness to collectors!
I... I never realized that we mothers were so... so vitally important!

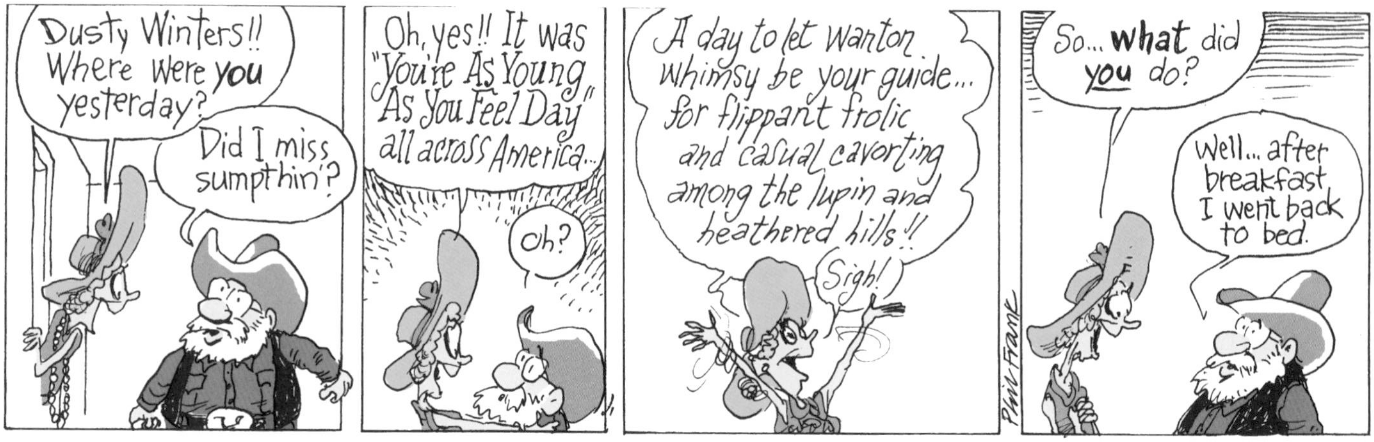
Dusty Winters!! Where were **you** yesterday?
Did I miss sumpthin'?
Oh, yes!! It was "You're As Young As You Feel Day" all across America...
Oh?
A day to let wanton whimsy be your guide... for flippant frolic and casual cavorting among the lupin and heathered hills!!
Sigh!
Phil Frank
So... **what** did **you** do?
Well... after breakfast I went back to bed.

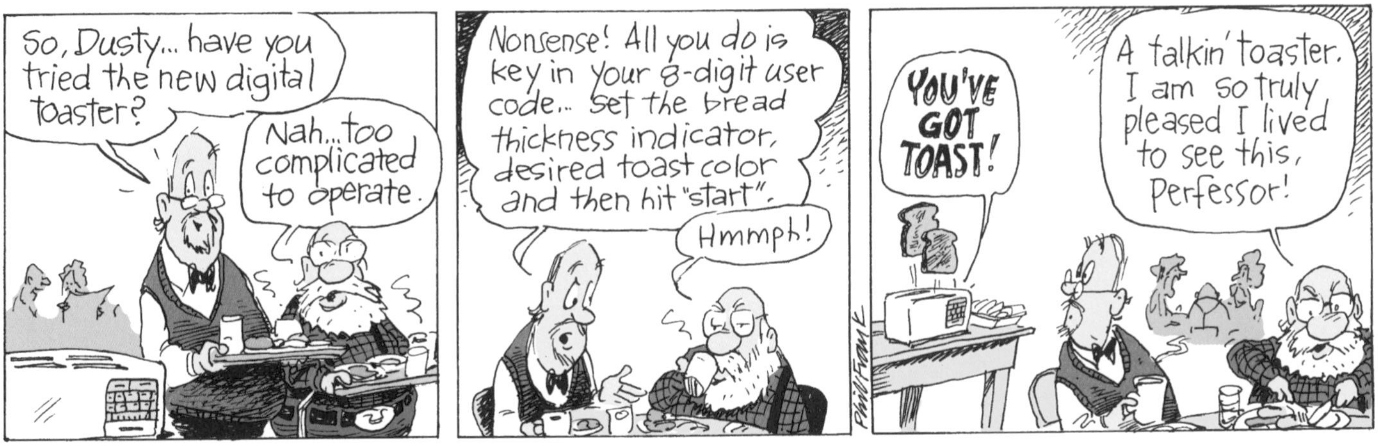
So, Dusty... have you tried the new digital toaster?
Nah...too complicated to operate.
Nonsense! All you do is key in your 8-digit user code... set the bread thickness indicator, desired toast color and then hit "start".
Hmmph!
YOU'VE GOT TOAST!
A talkin' toaster. I am so truly pleased I lived to see this, Perfessor!

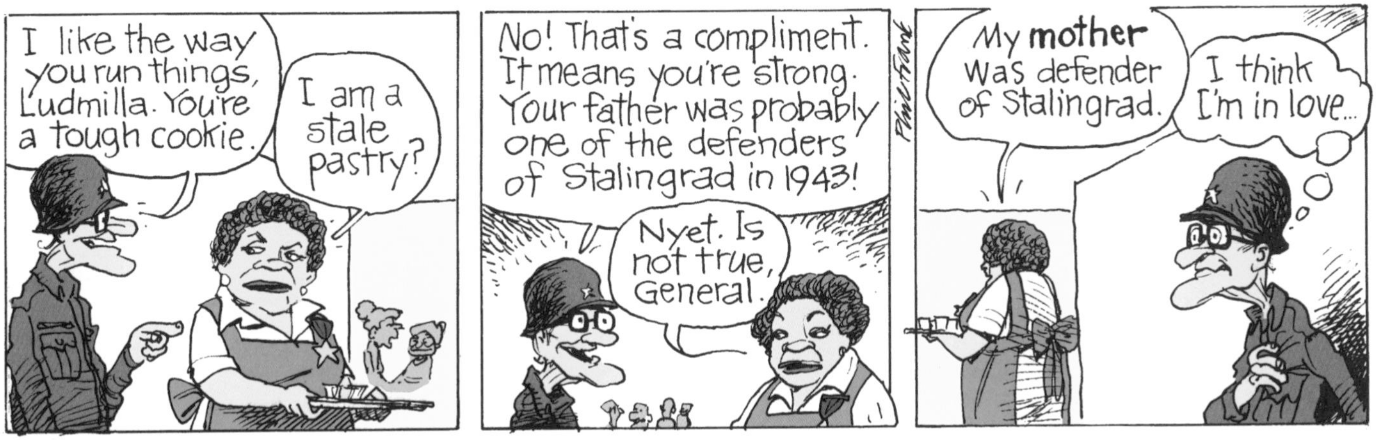
I like the way you run things, Ludmilla. You're a tough cookie.
I am a stale pastry?
No! That's a compliment. It means you're strong. Your father was probably one of the defenders of Stalingrad in 1943!
Nyet. Is not true, General.
My **mother** was defender of Stalingrad.
I think I'm in love...

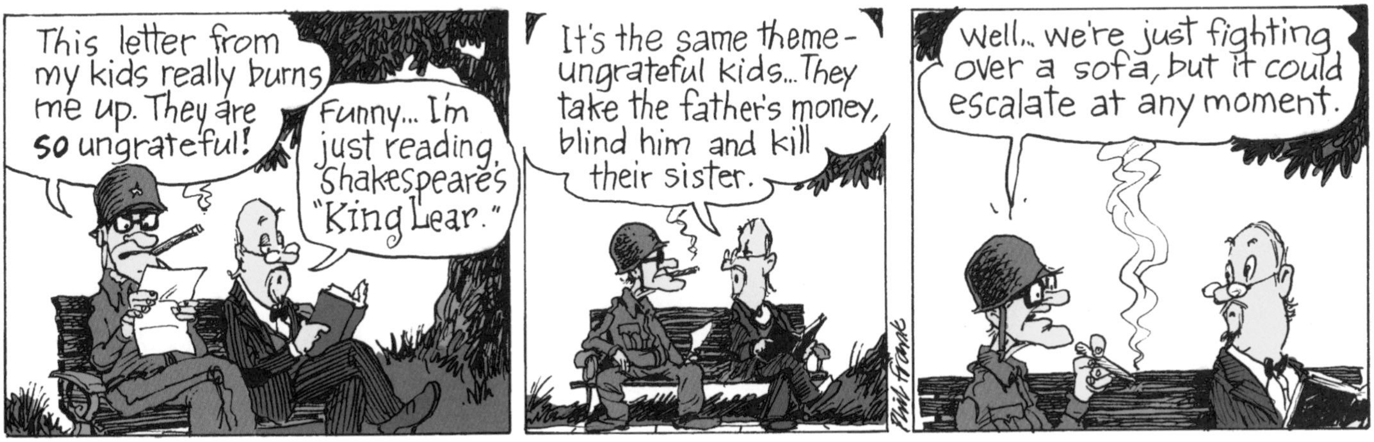
This letter from my kids really burns me up. They are **so** ungrateful!
Funny... I'm just reading Shakespeare's "King Lear."
It's the same theme - ungrateful kids... They take the father's money, blind him and kill their sister.
Well... we're just fighting over a sofa, but it could escalate at any moment.

The Elderberries
by
Phil Frank
and
Joe Troise
QUIET PLEASE!
ELDERPARK PHILOSOPHICAL SOCIETY MEETING

So... the question before the Elderpark Philosophical Society today...
"What is a guiding principle in your life?"
General?
An eye for an eye... a tooth for a tooth.
Boone?
If there is no wind, row!
Evelyn?
Do unto others as you would have them do unto you.
Dusty?
Never squat with your spurs on!
Phil Frank

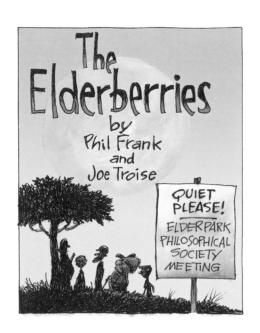

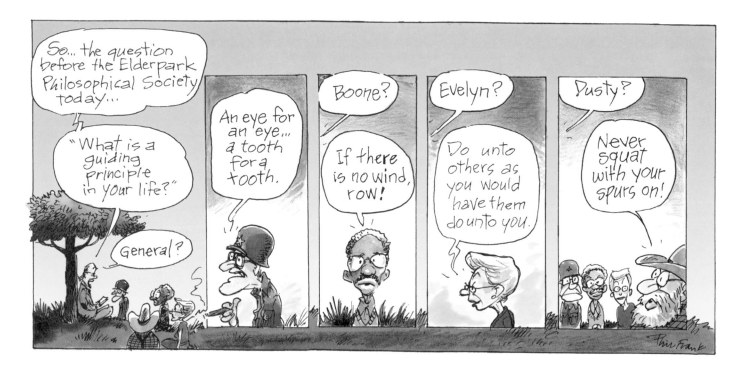

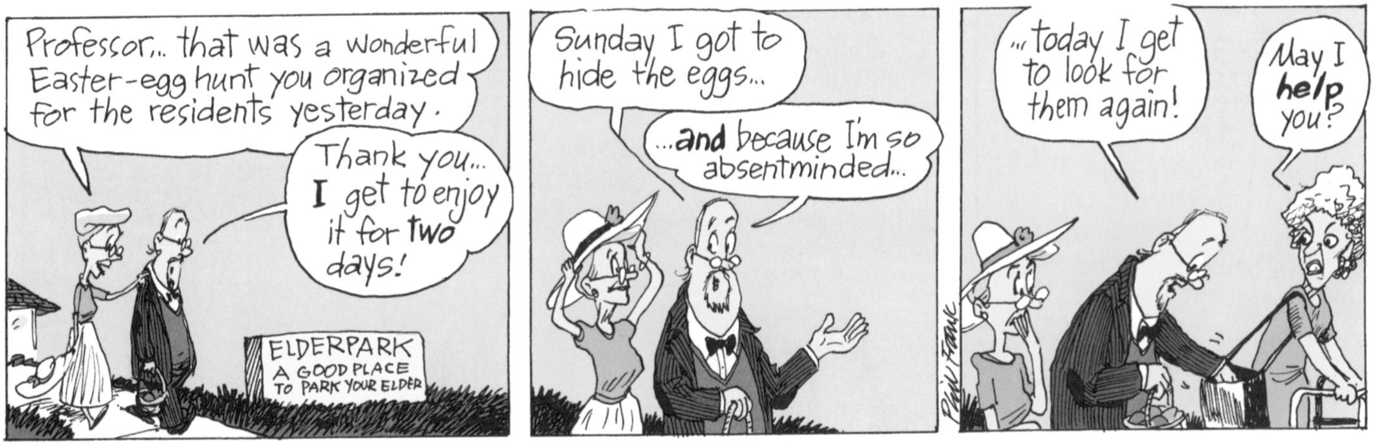
Professor.. that was a wonderful Easter-egg hunt you organized for the residents yesterday.
Thank you... I get to enjoy it for two days!
ELDERPARK
A GOOD PLACE TO PARK YOUR ELDER
Sunday I got to hide the eggs...
...and because I'm so absentminded...
...today I get to look for them again!
May I help you?

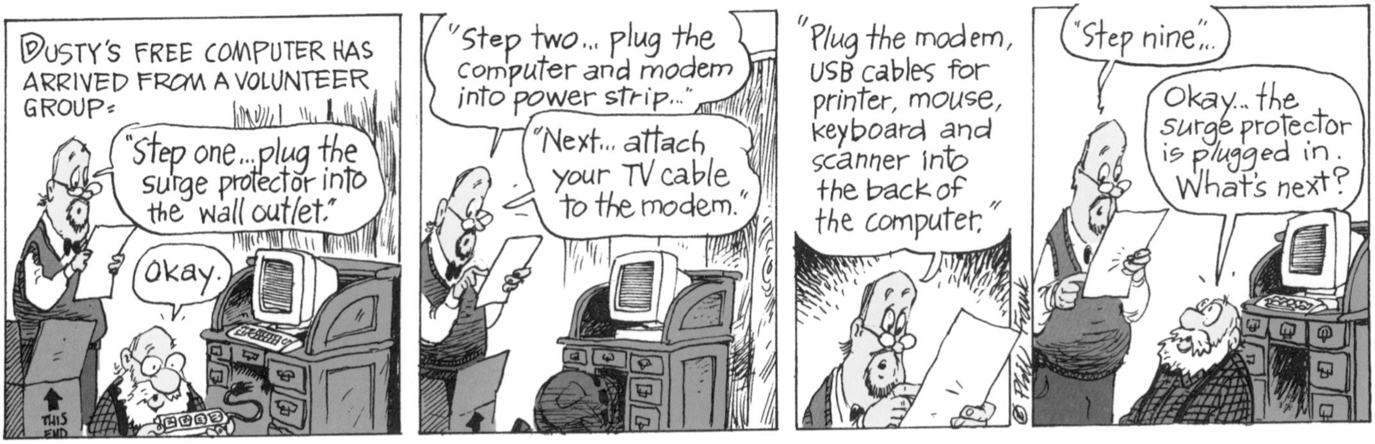
DUSTY'S FREE COMPUTER HAS ARRIVED FROM A VOLUNTEER GROUP=
"Step one... plug the surge protector into the wall outlet."
Okay.
THIS END
"Step two... plug the computer and modem into power strip..."
"Next... attach your TV cable to the modem."
"Plug the modem, USB cables for printer, mouse, keyboard and scanner into the back of the computer."
"Step nine"...
Okay... the surge protector is plugged in. What's next?

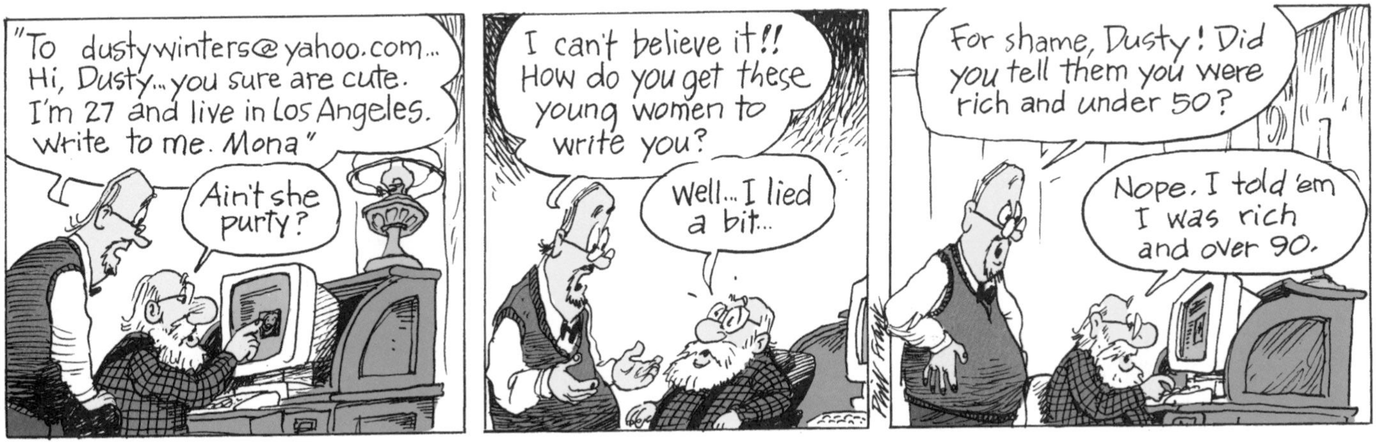
"To dustywinters@yahoo.com... Hi, Dusty... you sure are cute. I'm 27 and live in Los Angeles. Write to me. Mona"
Ain't she purty?
I can't believe it!! How do you get these young women to write you?
Well... I lied a bit...
For shame, Dusty! Did you tell them you were rich and under 50?
Nope. I told 'em I was rich and over 90.

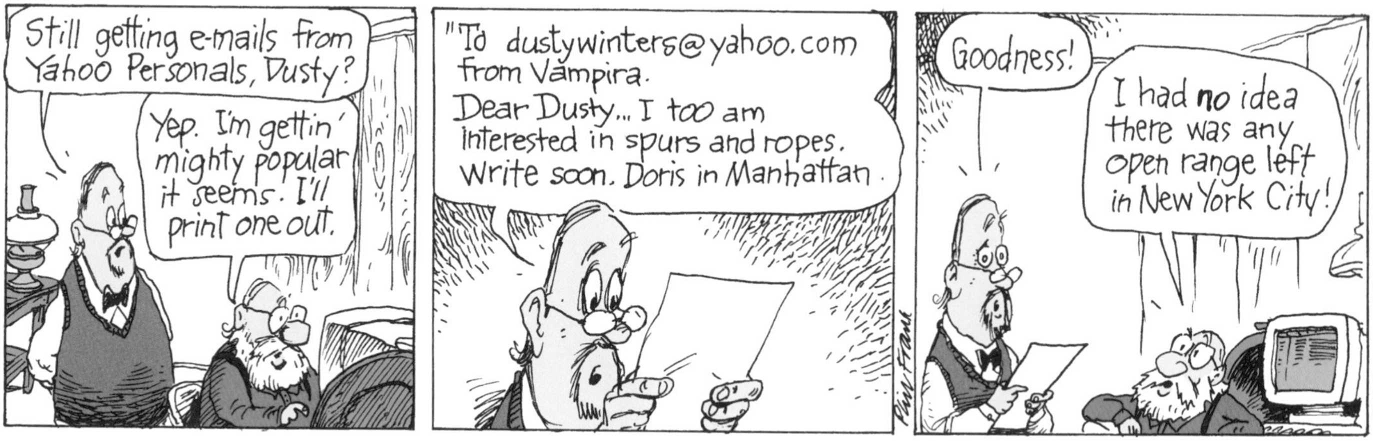
Still getting e-mails from Yahoo Personals, Dusty?
Yep. I'm gettin' mighty popular it seems. I'll print one out.
"To dustywinters@yahoo.com from Vampira.
Dear Dusty... I too am interested in spurs and ropes. Write soon. Doris in Manhattan.
Goodness!
I had **no** idea there was any open range left in New York City!

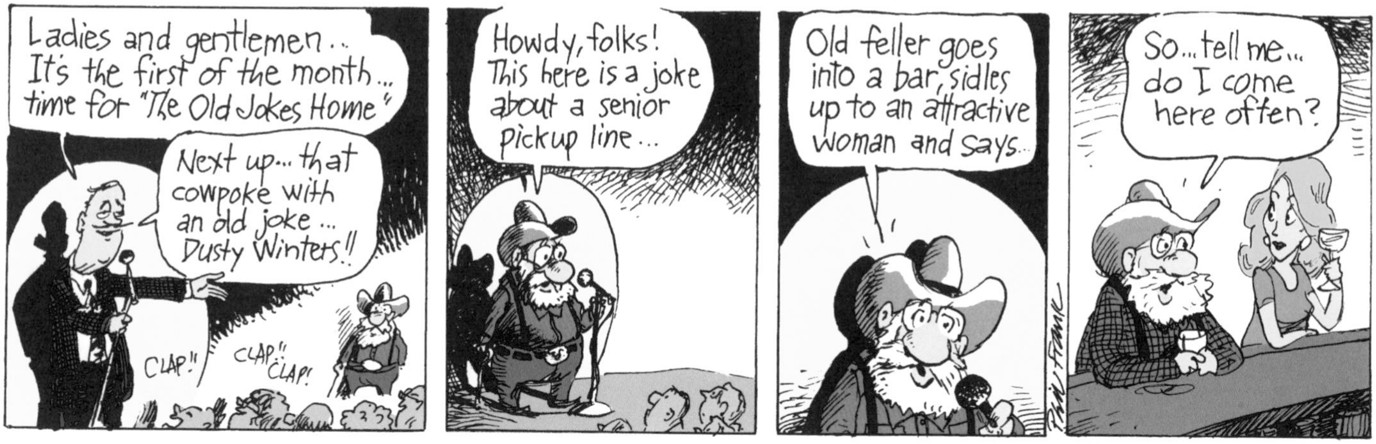
Ladies and gentlemen... It's the first of the month... time for "The Old Jokes Home"
Next up... that cowpoke with an old joke... Dusty Winters!!
CLAP!! CLAP!! CLAP!
Howdy, folks! This here is a joke about a senior pickup line...
Old feller goes into a bar, sidles up to an attractive woman and says...
So... tell me... do I come here often?

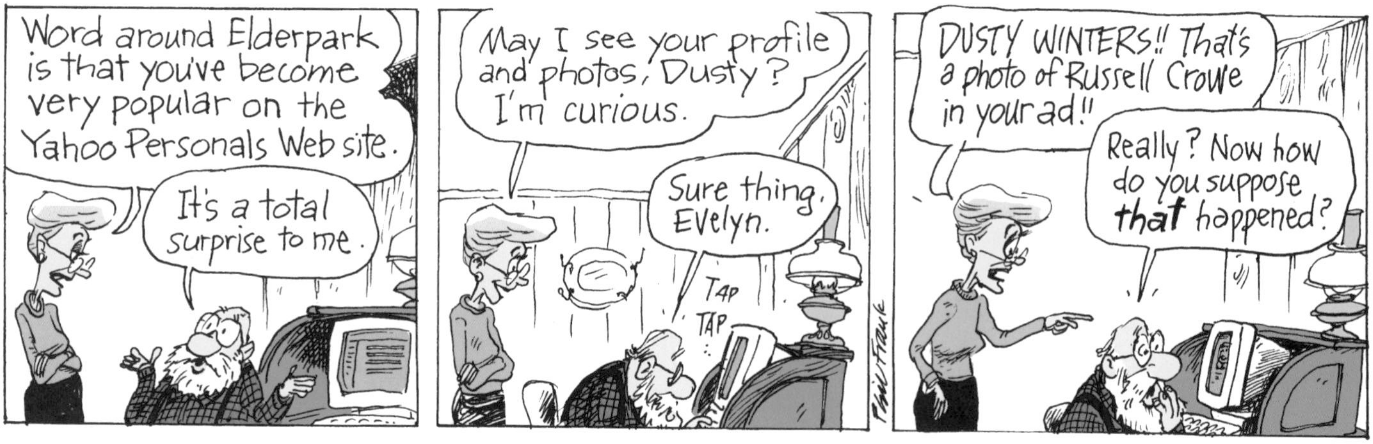
Word around Elderpark is that you've become very popular on the Yahoo Personals Web site.
It's a total surprise to me.
May I see your profile and photos, Dusty? I'm curious.
Sure thing, Evelyn.
TAP TAP
DUSTY WINTERS!! That's a photo of Russell Crowe in your ad!!
Really? Now how do you suppose **that** happened?

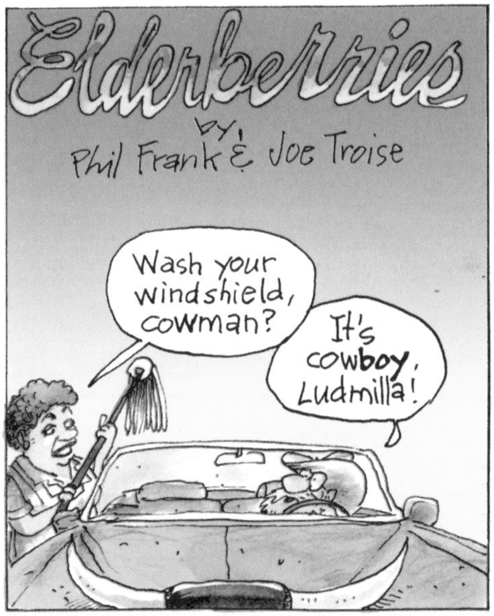
Elderberries
by
Phil Frank & Joe Troise
Wash your windshield, cowman?
It's cowboy, Ludmilla!

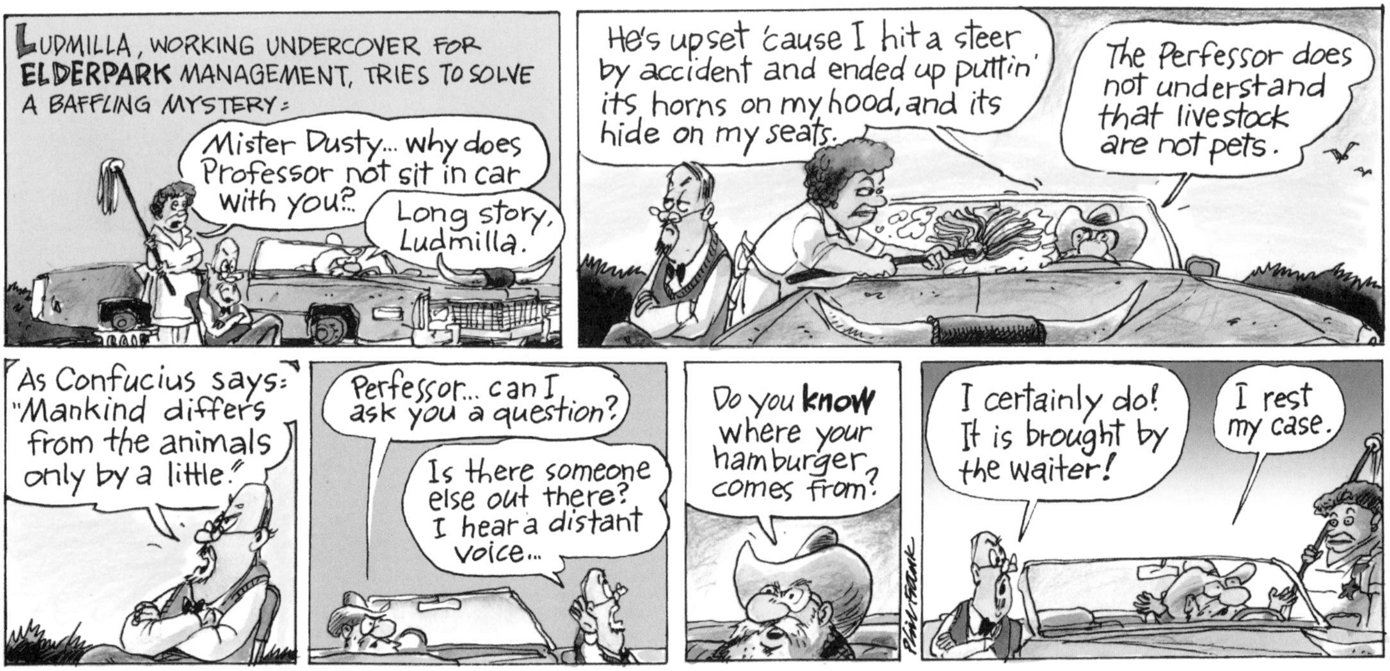
LUDMILLA, WORKING UNDERCOVER FOR ELDERPARK MANAGEMENT, TRIES TO SOLVE A BAFFLING MYSTERY:
Mister Dusty... why does Professor not sit in car with you?..
Long story, Ludmilla.
He's upset 'cause I hit a steer by accident and ended up puttin' its horns on my hood, and its hide on my seats.
The Perfessor does not understand that livestock are not pets.
As Confucius says: "Mankind differs from the animals only by a little."
Perfessor... can I ask you a question?
Is there someone else out there? I hear a distant voice...
Do you know where your hamburger comes from?
I certainly do! It is brought by the waiter!
I rest my case.
PHIL FRANK

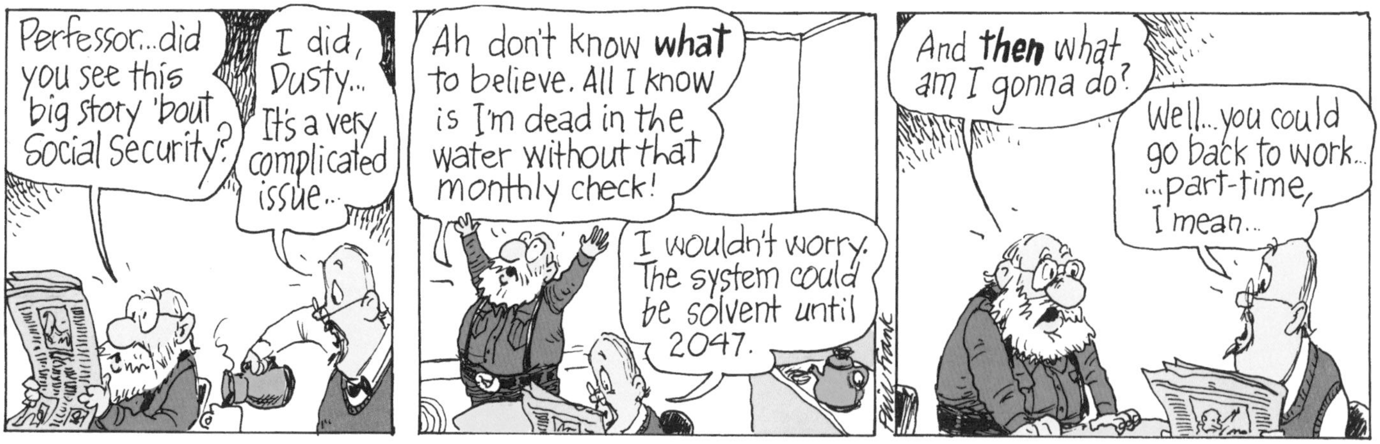
Perfessor...did you see this big story 'bout Social Security?
I did, Dusty... It's a very complicated issue...
Ah don't know **what** to believe. All I know is I'm dead in the water without that monthly check!
I wouldn't worry. The system could be solvent until 2047.
And **then** what am I gonna do?
Well...you could go back to work... ...part-time, I mean...

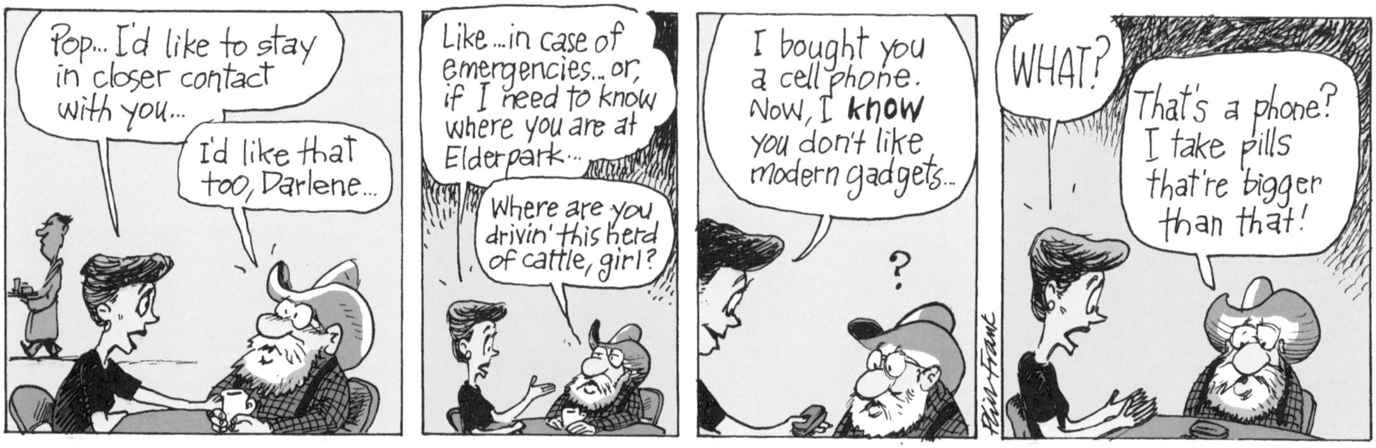
Pop... I'd like to stay in closer contact with you...
I'd like that too, Darlene...
Like...in case of emergencies...or, if I need to know where you are at Elderpark...
Where are you drivin' this herd of cattle, girl?
I bought you a cell phone. Now, I **know** you don't like modern gadgets...
?
WHAT?
That's a phone? I take pills that're bigger than that!

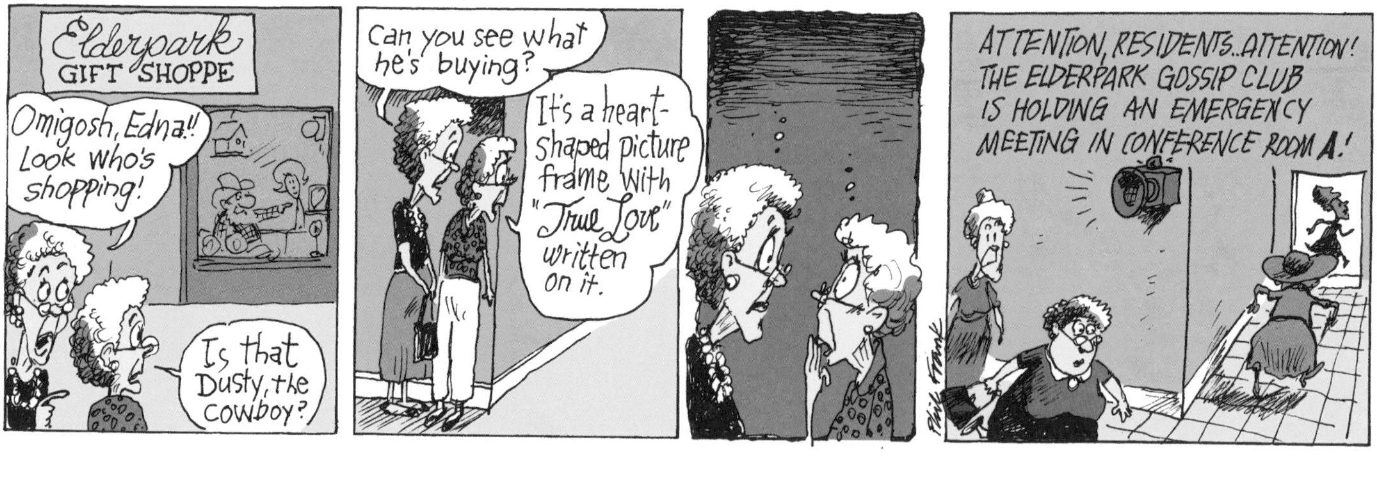
Elderpark GIFT SHOPPE
Omigosh, Edna!! Look who's shopping!
Is that Dusty, the cowboy?
Can you see what he's buying?
It's a heart-shaped picture frame with "True Love" written on it.
ATTENTION, RESIDENTS...ATTENTION! THE ELDERPARK GOSSIP CLUB IS HOLDING AN EMERGENCY MEETING IN CONFERENCE ROOM **A**!

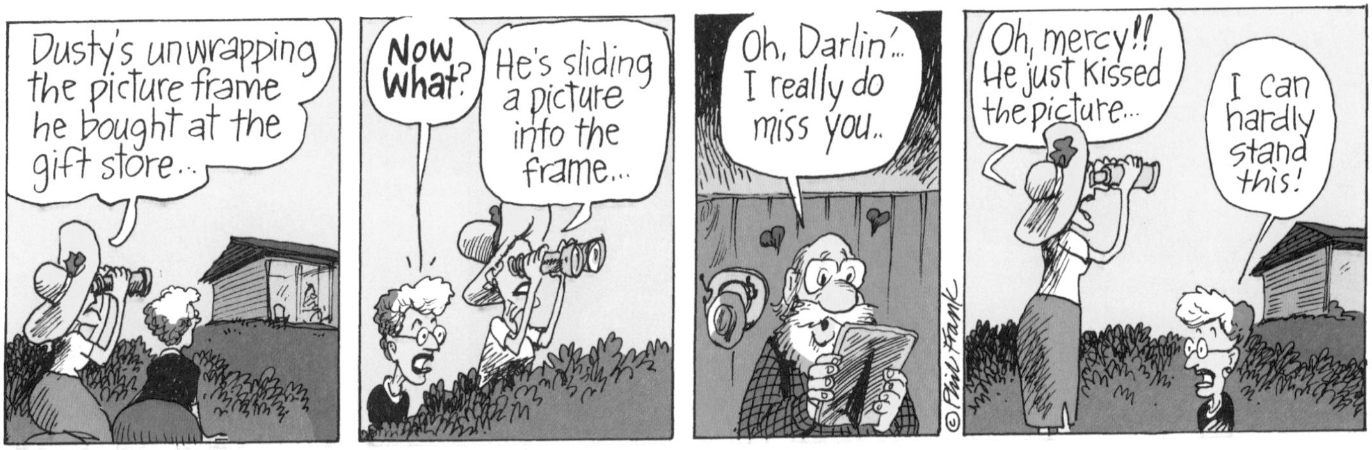
Dusty's unwrapping the picture frame he bought at the gift store...
Now What?
He's sliding a picture into the frame...
Oh, Darlin'... I really do miss you..
Oh, mercy!! He just kissed the picture...
I can hardly stand this!
© Phil Frank

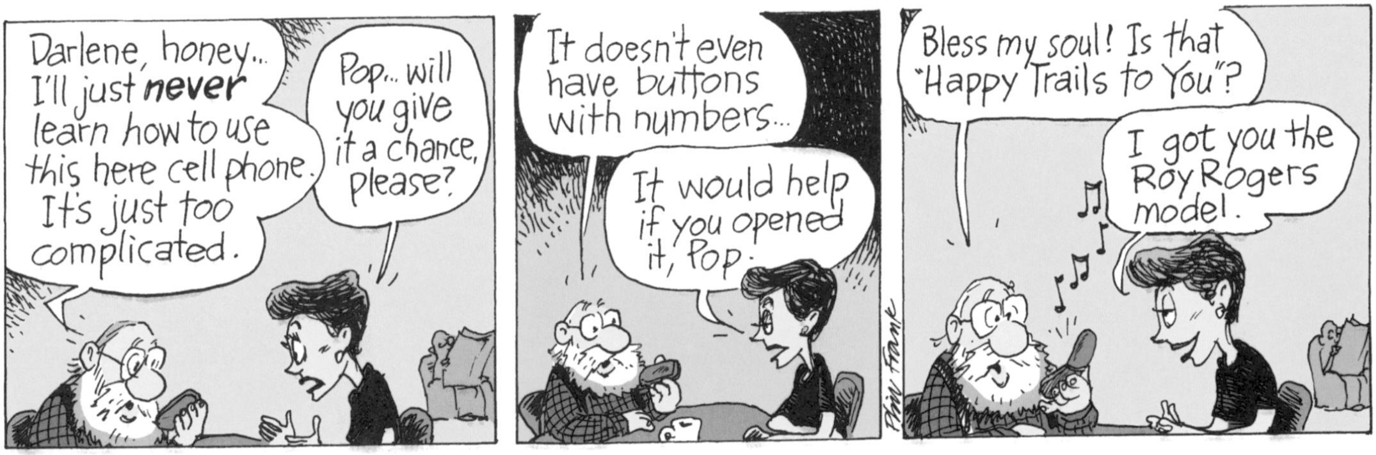
Darlene, honey... I'll just **never** learn how to use this here cell phone. It's just too complicated.
Pop... will you give it a chance, please?
It doesn't even have buttons with numbers...
It would help if you opened it, Pop.
Phil Frank
Bless my soul! Is that "Happy Trails to You"?
I got you the Roy Rogers model.

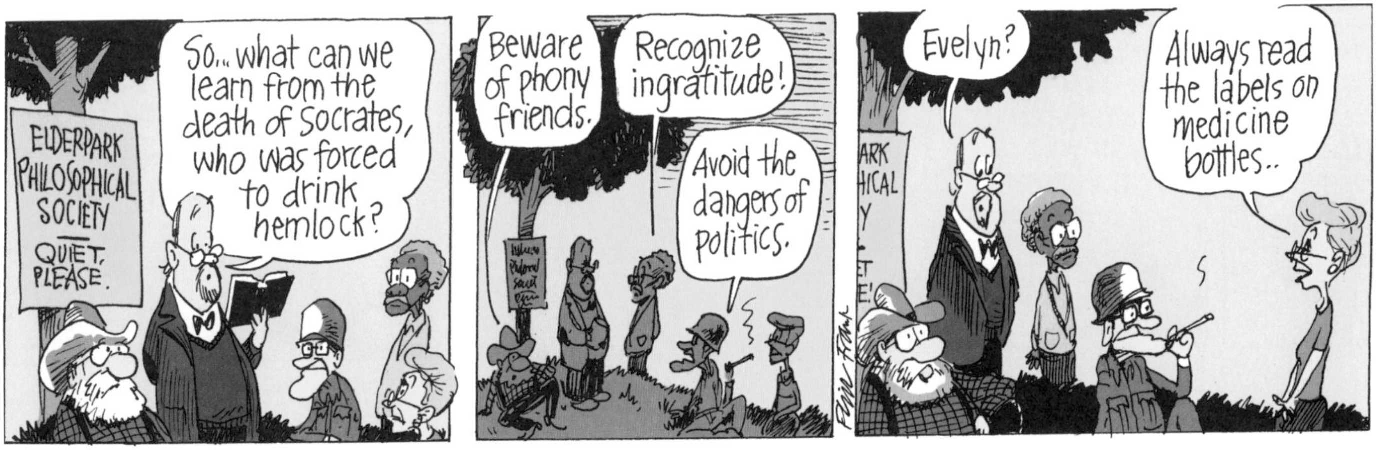
ELDERPARK PHILOSOPHICAL SOCIETY
QUIET, PLEASE.
So... what can we learn from the death of Socrates, who was forced to drink hemlock?
Beware of phony friends.
Recognize ingratitude!
Avoid the dangers of politics.
Phil Frank
Evelyn?
Always read the labels on medicine bottles..

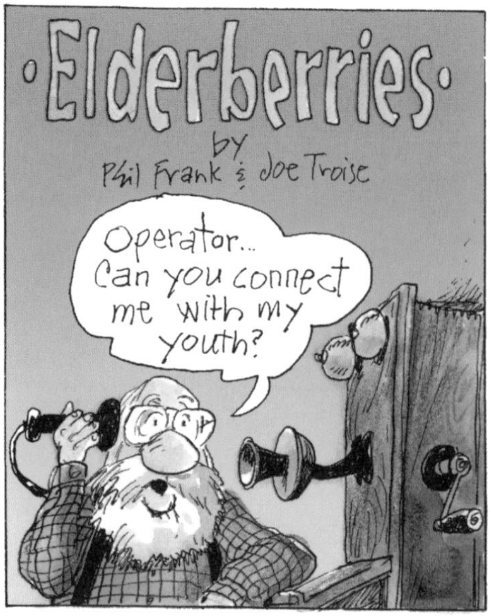
·Elderberries·
by
Phil Frank & Joe Troise
Operator... Can you connect me with my youth?

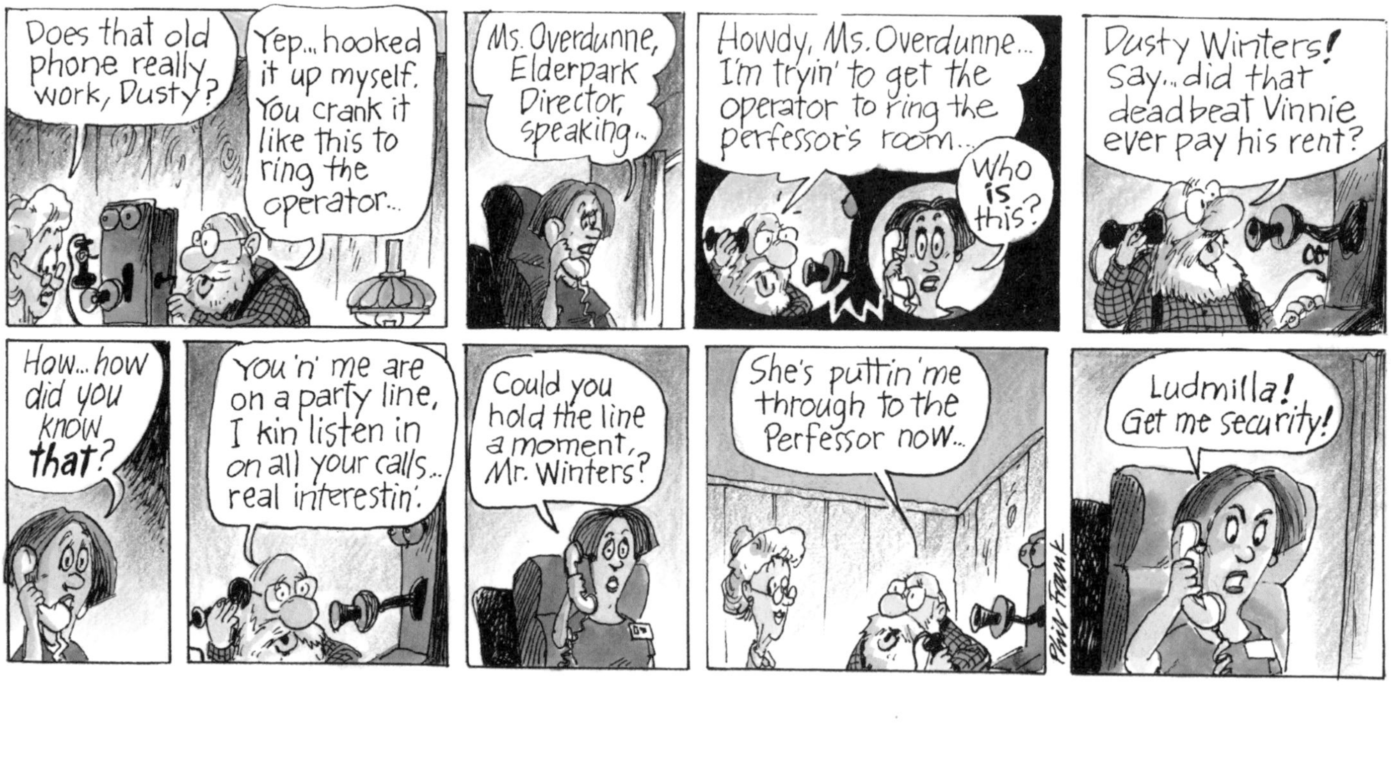
Does that old phone really work, Dusty?
Yep... hooked it up myself. You crank it like this to ring the operator...
Ms. Overdunne, Elderpark Director, speaking...
Howdy, Ms. Overdunne... I'm tryin' to get the operator to ring the perfessor's room...
Who **is** this?
Dusty Winters! Say... did that deadbeat Vinnie ever pay his rent?
How... how did you know **that**?
You 'n' me are on a party line, I kin listen in on all your calls... real interestin'.
Could you hold the line a moment, Mr. Winters?
She's puttin' me through to the Perfessor now...
Phil Frank
Ludmilla! Get me security!

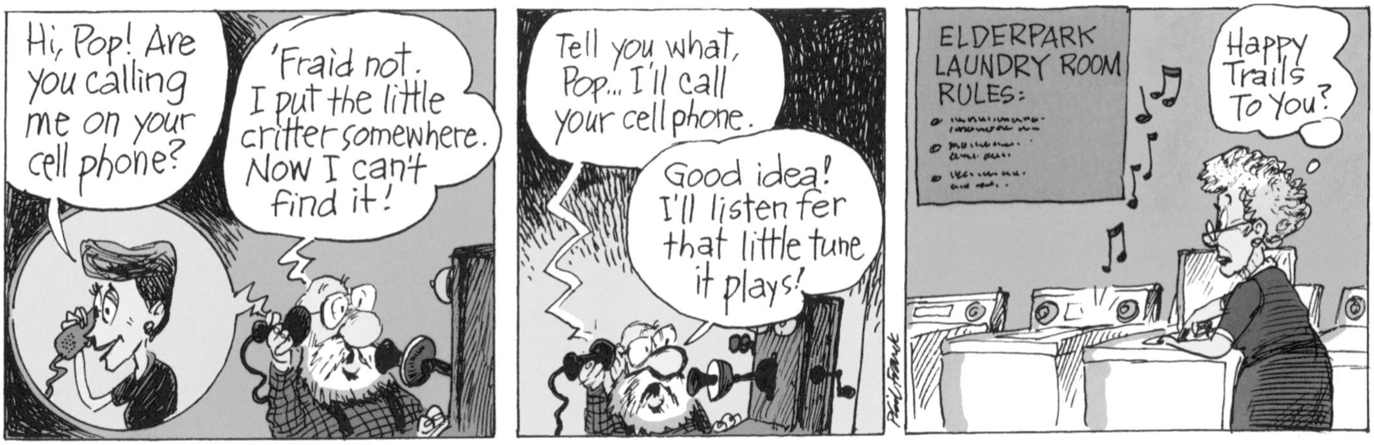
Hi, Pop! Are you calling me on your cell phone?
'Fraid not. I put the little critter somewhere. Now I can't find it!
Tell you what, Pop... I'll call your cell phone.
Good idea! I'll listen fer that little tune it plays!
ELDERPARK LAUNDRY ROOM RULES:
Happy Trails To You?

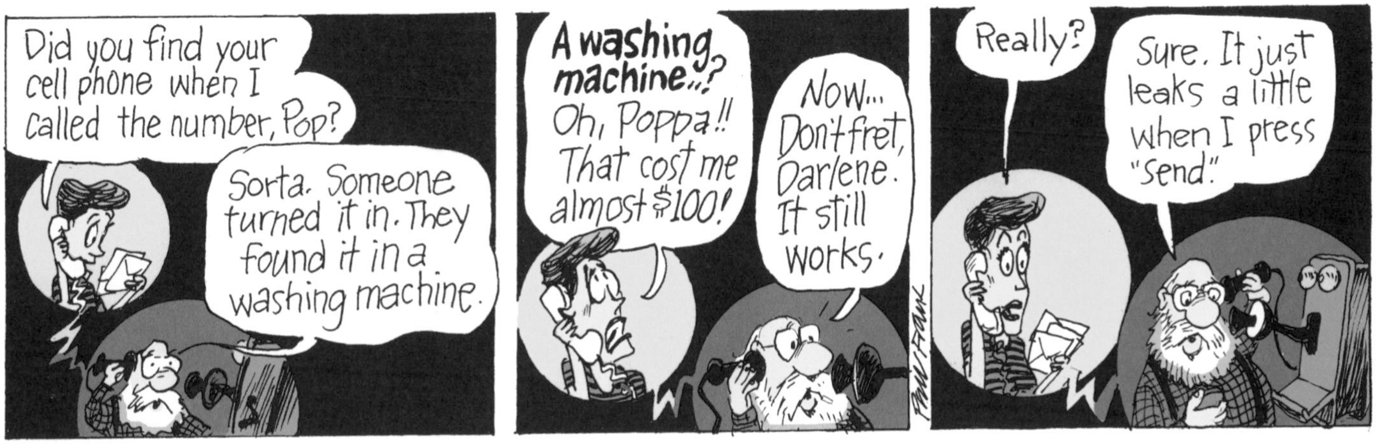
Did you find your cell phone when I called the number, Pop?
Sorta. Someone turned it in. They found it in a washing machine.
A washing machine...? Oh, Poppa!! That cost me almost $100!
Now... Don't fret, Darlene. It still works.
Really?
Sure. It just leaks a little when I press "send."

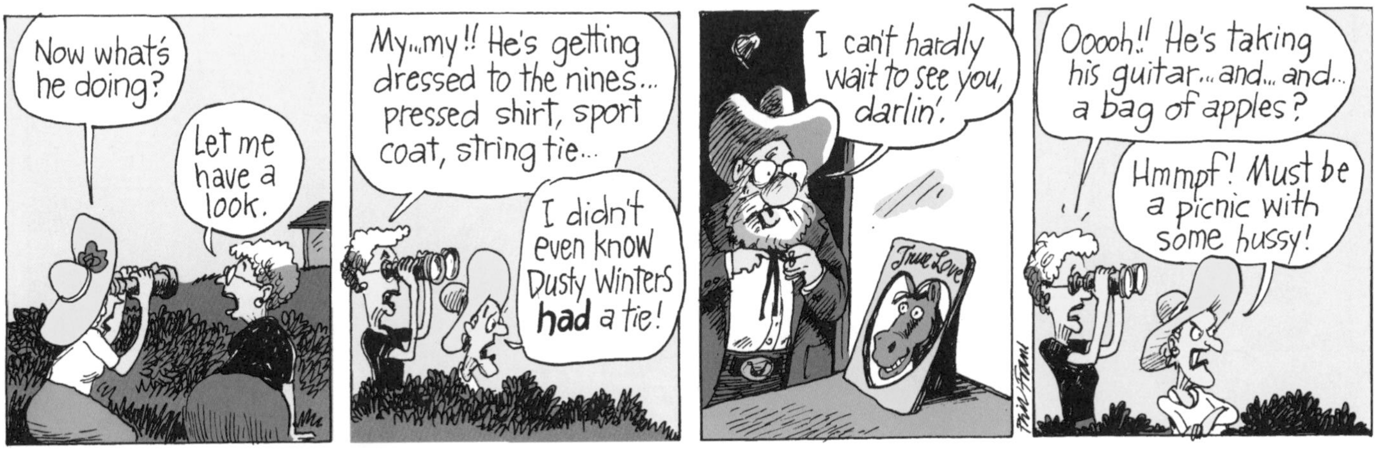
Now what's he doing?
Let me have a look.
My...my!! He's getting dressed to the nines... pressed shirt, sport coat, string tie...
I didn't even know Dusty Winters had a tie!
I can't hardly wait to see you, darlin'.
True Love
Ooooh!! He's taking his guitar... and... and... a bag of apples?
Hmmpf! Must be a picnic with some hussy!

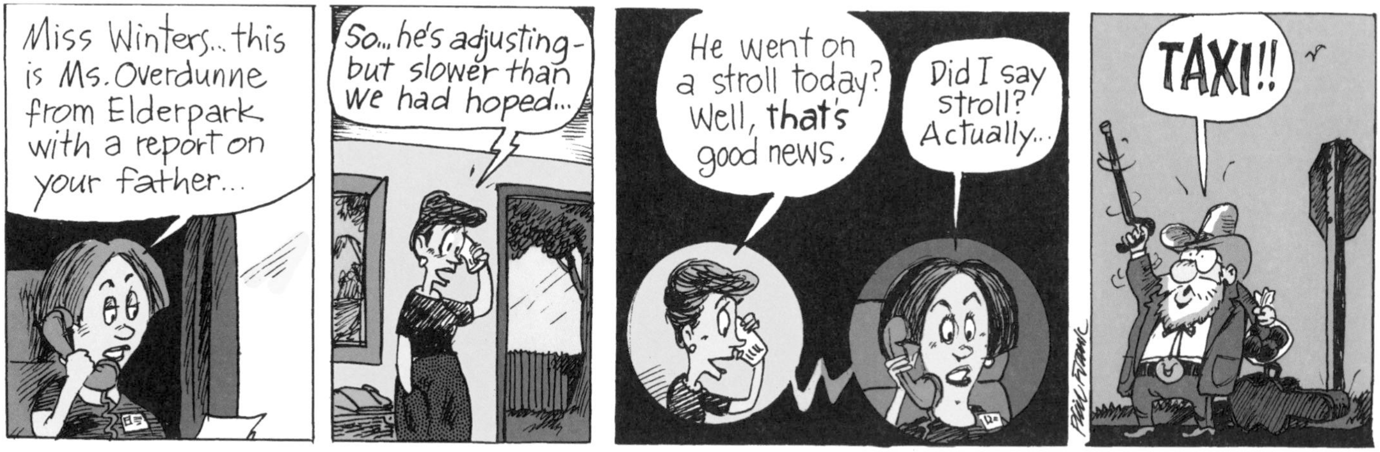
Miss Winters... this is Ms. Overdunne from Elderpark with a report on your father...
So... he's adjusting - but slower than we had hoped...
He went on a stroll today? Well, that's good news.
Did I say stroll? Actually...
TAXI!!

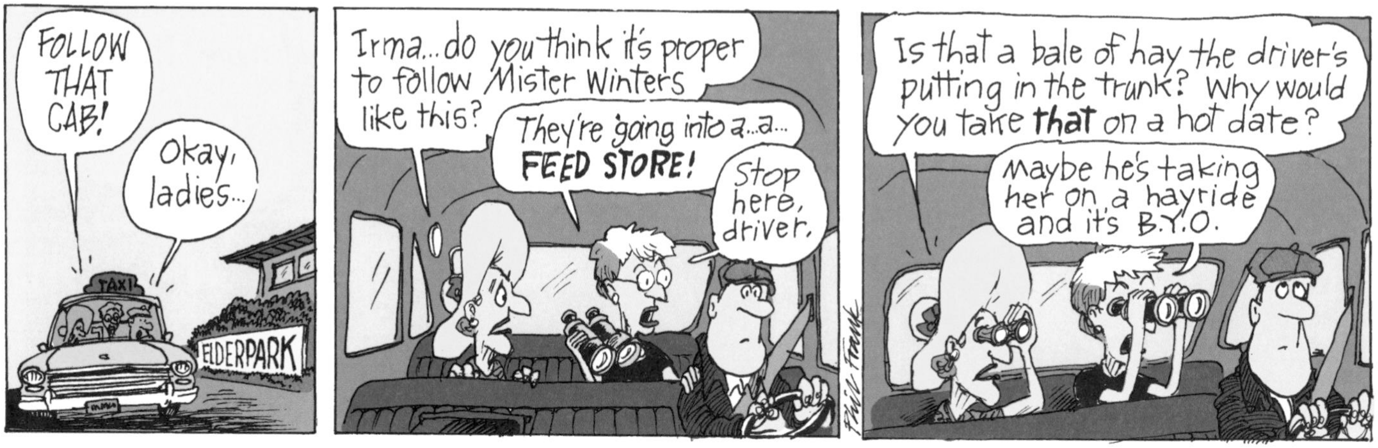
FOLLOW THAT CAB!
Okay, ladies...
ELDERPARK
Irma... do you think it's proper to follow Mister Winters like this?
They're going into a... a... FEED STORE!
Stop here, driver.
Is that a bale of hay the driver's putting in the trunk? Why would you take that on a hot date?
Maybe he's taking her on a hayride and it's B.Y.O.

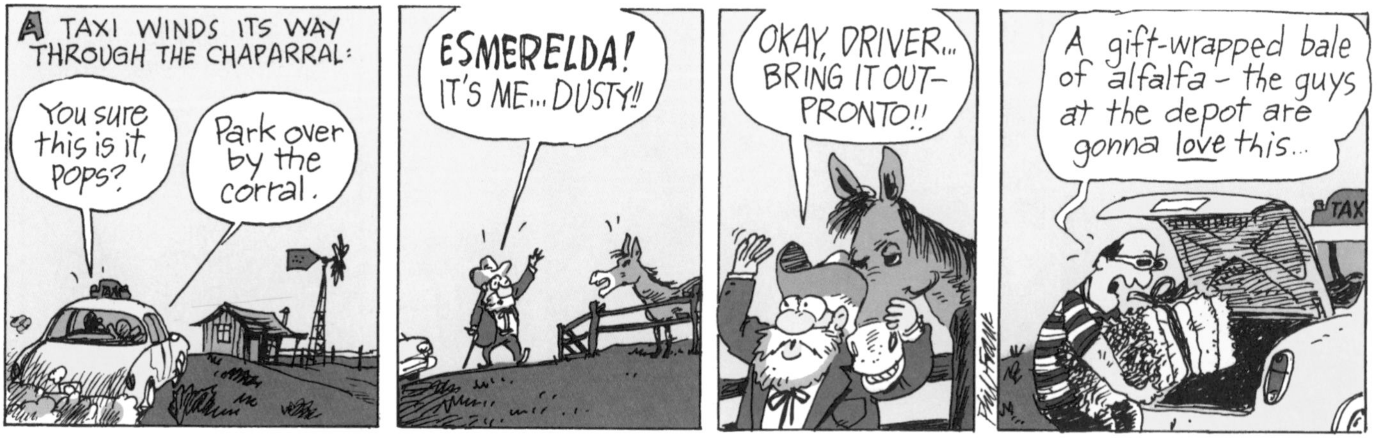
A TAXI WINDS ITS WAY THROUGH THE CHAPARRAL:
You sure this is it, pops?
Park over by the corral.
ESMERELDA! IT'S ME... DUSTY!!
OKAY, DRIVER... BRING IT OUT - PRONTO!!
A gift-wrapped bale of alfalfa - the guys at the depot are gonna love this...

ELDERBERRIES
by Phil Frank & Joe Troise
I need a minute with my horse, pardner...
TAXI
OK, Pops.

I brought you some apples, too, Esmerelda.
You know, girl... I don't think retirement is doin' either of us much good...
I'm so tired these days I need two beds to sleep in...
... and you're about as thin as a bar of soap after wash day...
CHOMP!
TAXI
Between my bad back, my failin' eyesight and my poor hearin'...
CHOMP!
CHOMP
Are you even listenin' to what I'm sayin'?
Six failed marriages... and now **this**...
CHOMP! CHOMP!

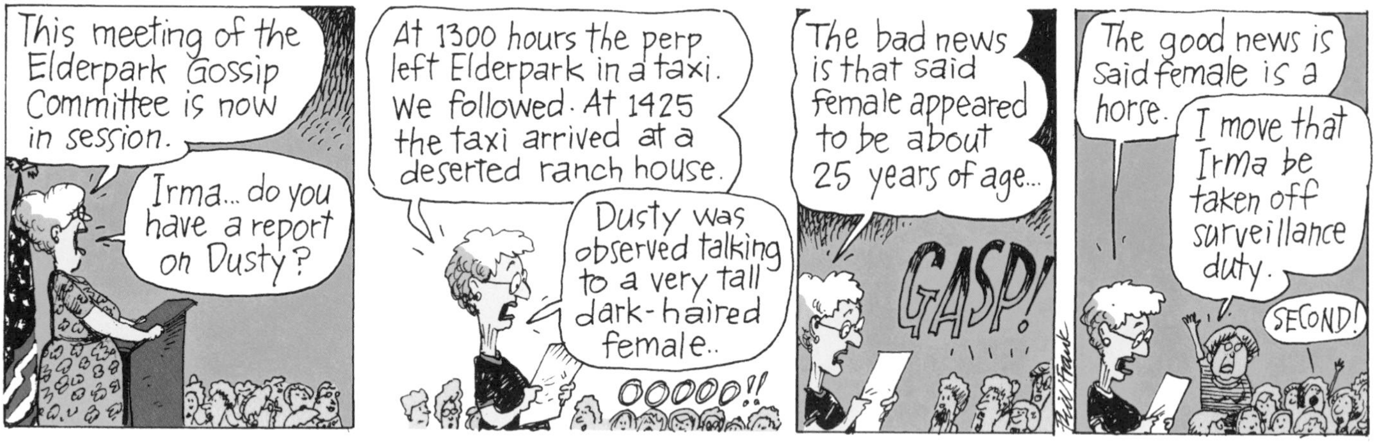
This meeting of the Elderpark Gossip Committee is now in session.
Irma... do you have a report on Dusty?
At 1300 hours the perp left Elderpark in a taxi. We followed. At 1425 the taxi arrived at a deserted ranch house.
Dusty was observed talking to a very tall dark-haired female..
OOOOO!!
The bad news is that said female appeared to be about 25 years of age...
GASP!
The good news is said female is a horse.
I move that Irma be taken off surveillance duty.
SECOND!

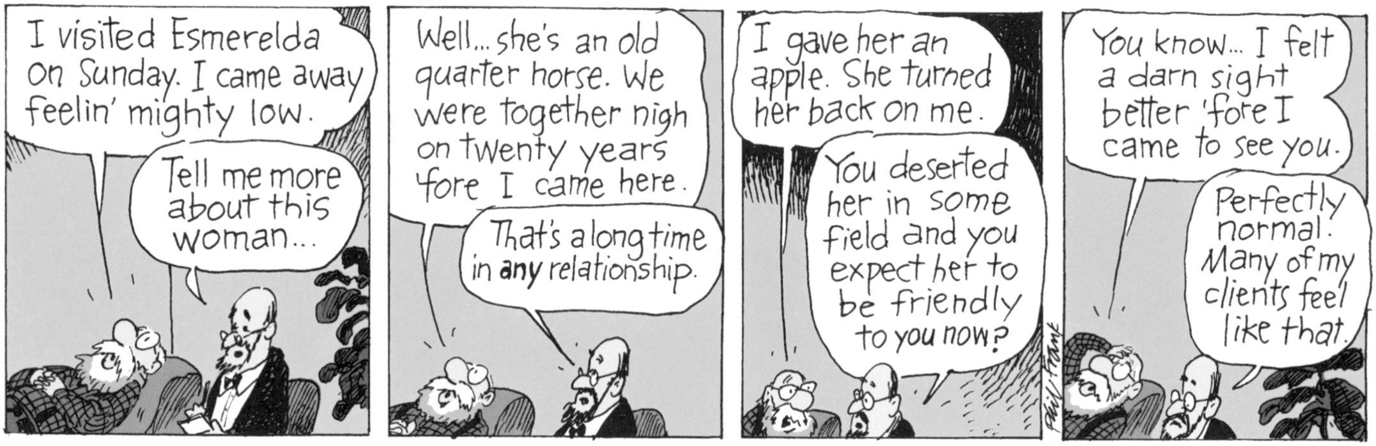
I visited Esmerelda on Sunday. I came away feelin' mighty low.
Tell me more about this woman...
Well... she's an old quarter horse. We were together nigh on twenty years 'fore I came here.
That's a long time in **any** relationship.
I gave her an apple. She turned her back on me.
You deserted her in some field and you expect her to be friendly to you now?
You know... I felt a darn sight better 'fore I came to see you.
Perfectly normal. Many of my clients feel like that.

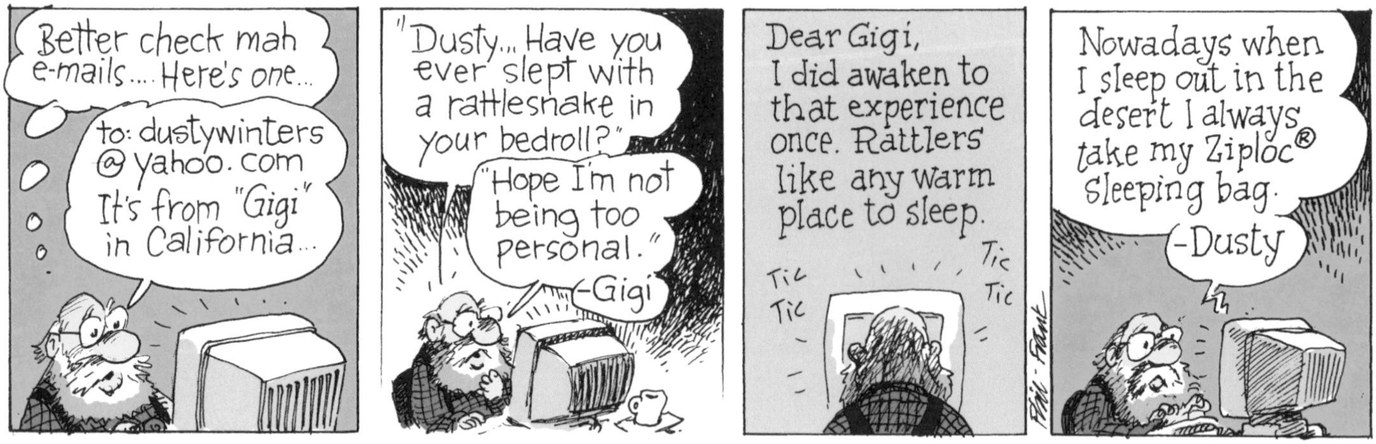
Better check mah e-mails.... Here's one...
to: dustywinters @yahoo.com It's from "Gigi" in California...
"Dusty... Have you ever slept with a rattlesnake in your bedroll?"
"Hope I'm not being too personal."
-Gigi
Dear Gigi, I did awaken to that experience once. Rattlers like any warm place to sleep.
Tic Tic Tic Tic
Nowadays when I sleep out in the desert I always take my Ziploc® sleeping bag.
-Dusty

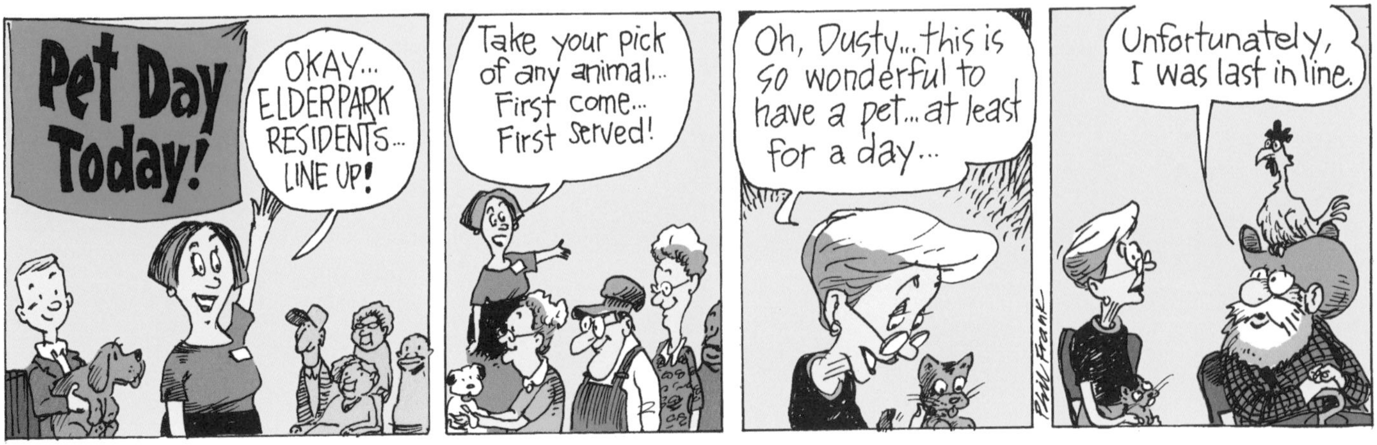
Pet Day Today!
OKAY... ELDERPARK RESIDENTS... LINE UP!
Take your pick of any animal... First come... First served!
Oh, Dusty... this is so wonderful to have a pet... at least for a day...
Unfortunately, I was last in line.
Phil Frank

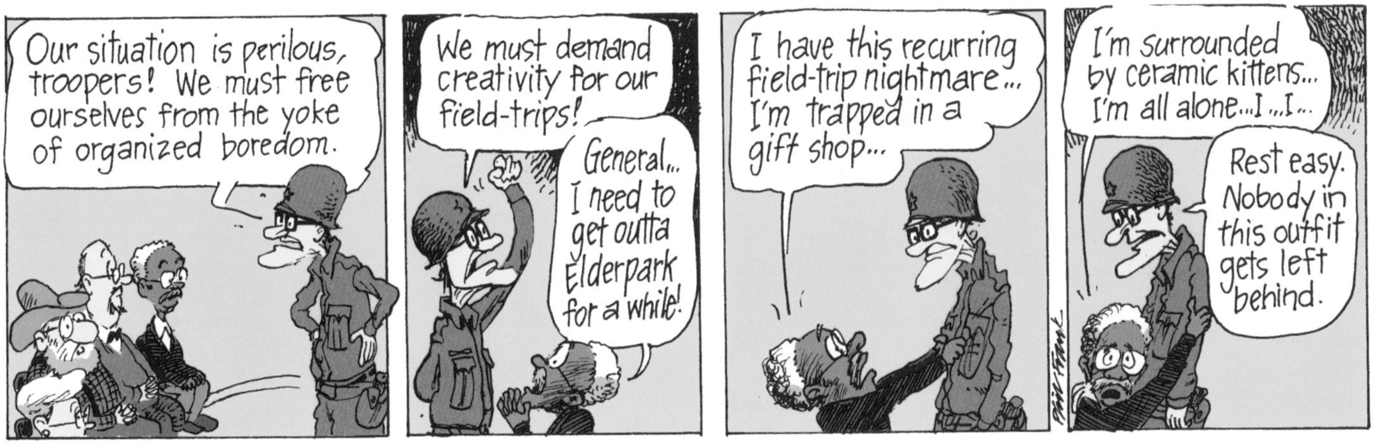
Our situation is perilous, troopers! We must free ourselves from the yoke of organized boredom.
We must demand creativity for our field-trips!
General... I need to get outta Elderpark for a while!
I have this recurring field-trip nightmare... I'm trapped in a gift shop...
I'm surrounded by ceramic kittens... I'm all alone... I... I...
Rest easy. Nobody in this outfit gets left behind.
Phil Frank

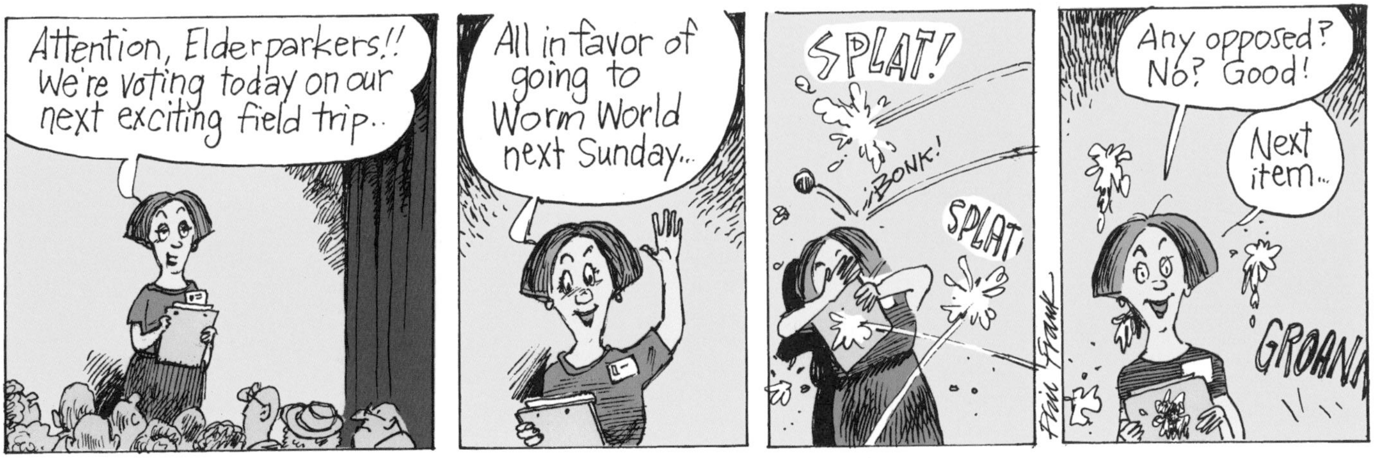
Attention, Elderparkers!! We're voting today on our next exciting field trip..
All in favor of going to Worm World next Sunday...
SPLAT!
BONK!
SPLAT!
Phil Frank
Any opposed? No? Good!
Next item...
GROAN

Elderberries
by
Phil Frank and Joe Troise
Worm World
this exit

Attention, Elderparkers!! Welcome to **Worm World**!
ELDERPARK
WORM WORLD
Stay with the group! Don't wander off, please..
All right... now... All aboard the Worm Train!
?
A WORM FARM! Who plans these stupid outings?
Got me!
HERE WE GO!!
CLINK!
Well, General... looks like our worm done lost its tail.
I hear they grow back. Let's go get a beer.

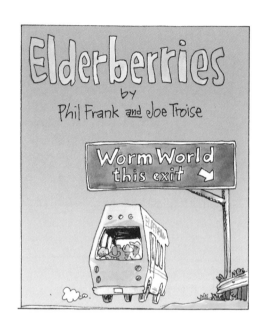

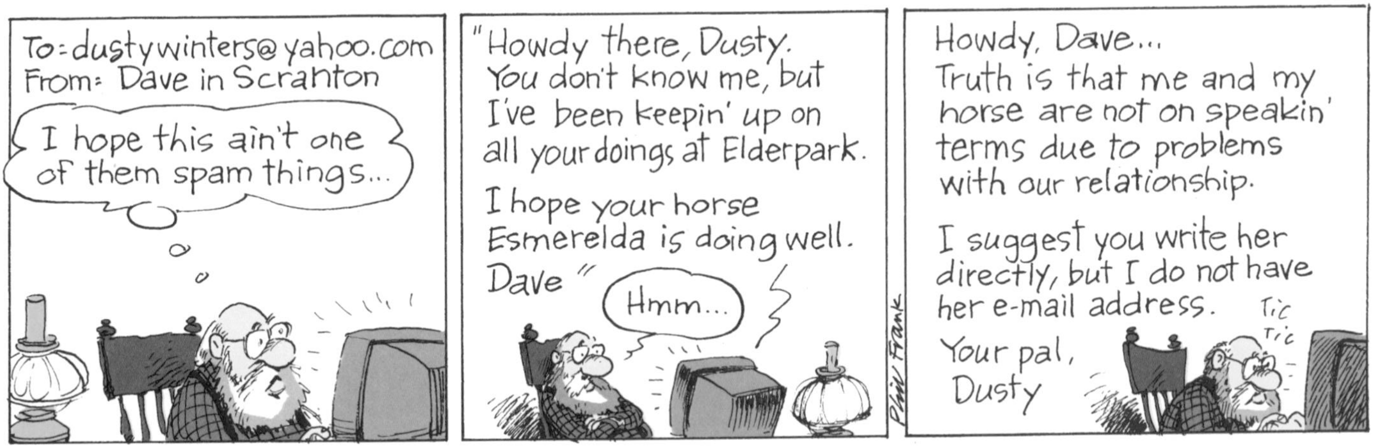
To: dustywinters@yahoo.com
From: Dave in Scranton
I hope this ain't one of them spam things...
"Howdy there, Dusty. You don't know me, but I've been keepin' up on all your doings at Elderpark.
I hope your horse Esmerelda is doing well.
Dave"
Hmm...
Howdy, Dave...
Truth is that me and my horse are not on speakin' terms due to problems with our relationship.
I suggest you write her directly, but I do not have her e-mail address.
Your pal,
Dusty
Tic
Tic
Phil Frank

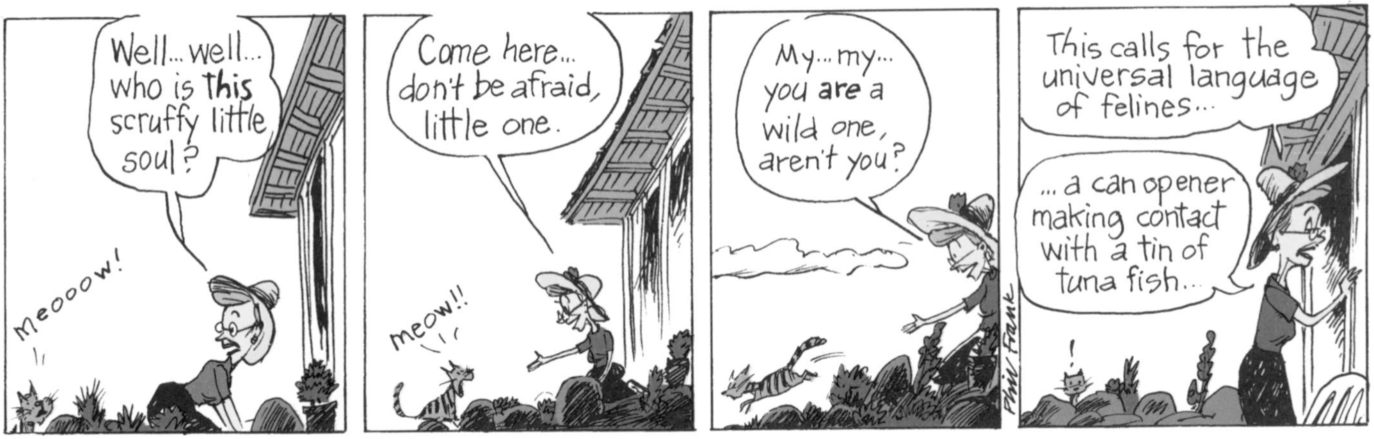
Well... well... who is **this** scruffy little soul?
meooow!
Come here... don't be afraid, little one.
meow!!
My... my... you **are** a wild one, aren't you?
This calls for the universal language of felines...
...a can opener making contact with a tin of tuna fish...
!
Phil Frank

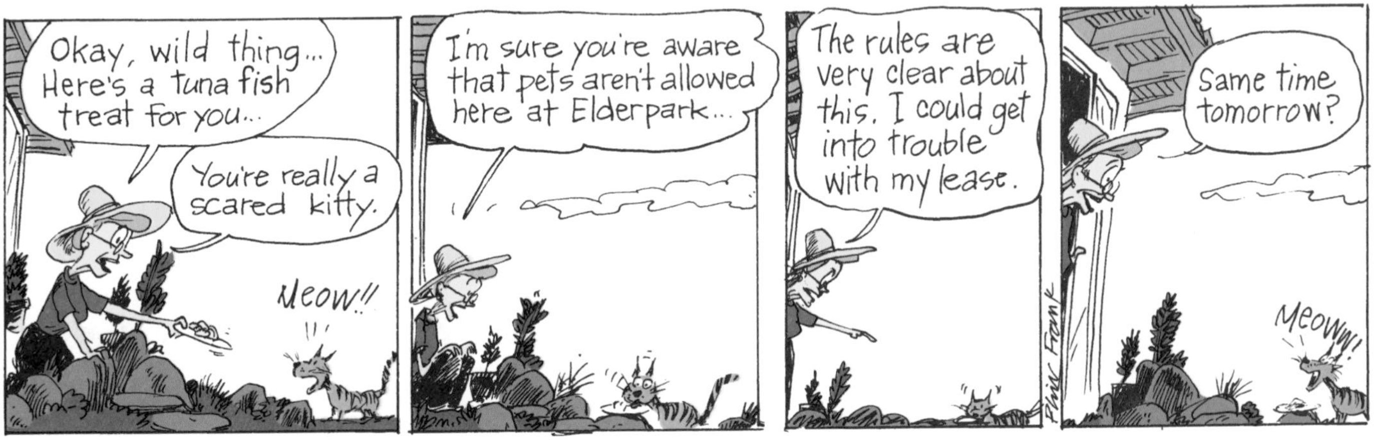
Okay, wild thing... Here's a tuna fish treat for you...
You're really a scared kitty.
Meow!!
I'm sure you're aware that pets aren't allowed here at Elderpark...
The rules are very clear about this. I could get into trouble with my lease.
Same time tomorrow?
Meoww!
Phil Frank

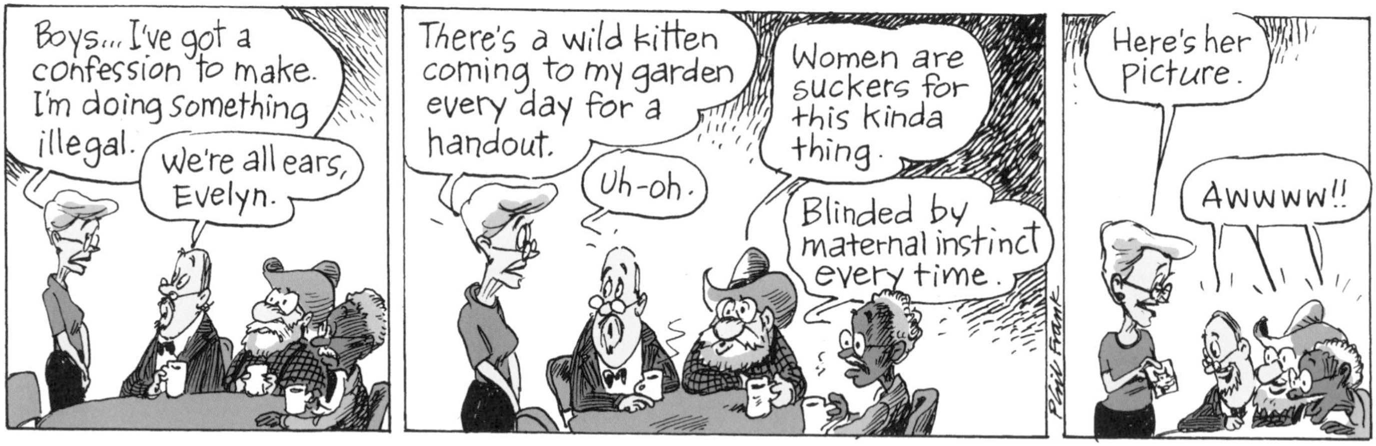
Boys... I've got a confession to make. I'm doing something illegal.
We're all ears, Evelyn.
There's a wild kitten coming to my garden every day for a handout.
Uh-oh.
Women are suckers for this kinda thing.
Blinded by maternal instinct every time.
Here's her picture.
AWWWW!!

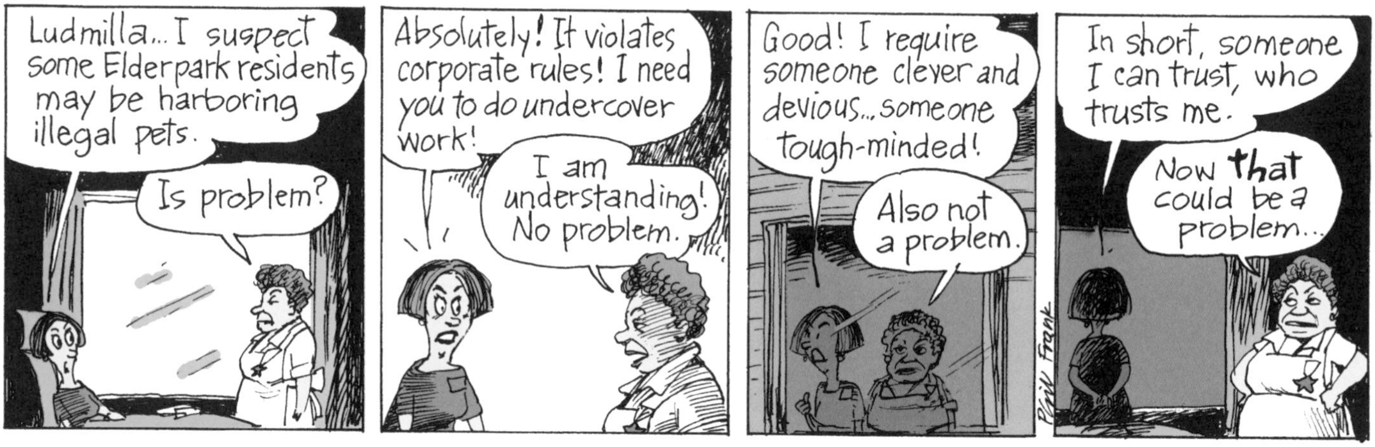
Ludmilla... I suspect some Elderpark residents may be harboring illegal pets.
Is problem?
Absolutely! It violates corporate rules! I need you to do undercover work!
I am understanding! No problem.
Good! I require someone clever and devious... someone tough-minded!
Also not a problem.
In short, someone I can trust, who trusts me.
Now that could be a problem...

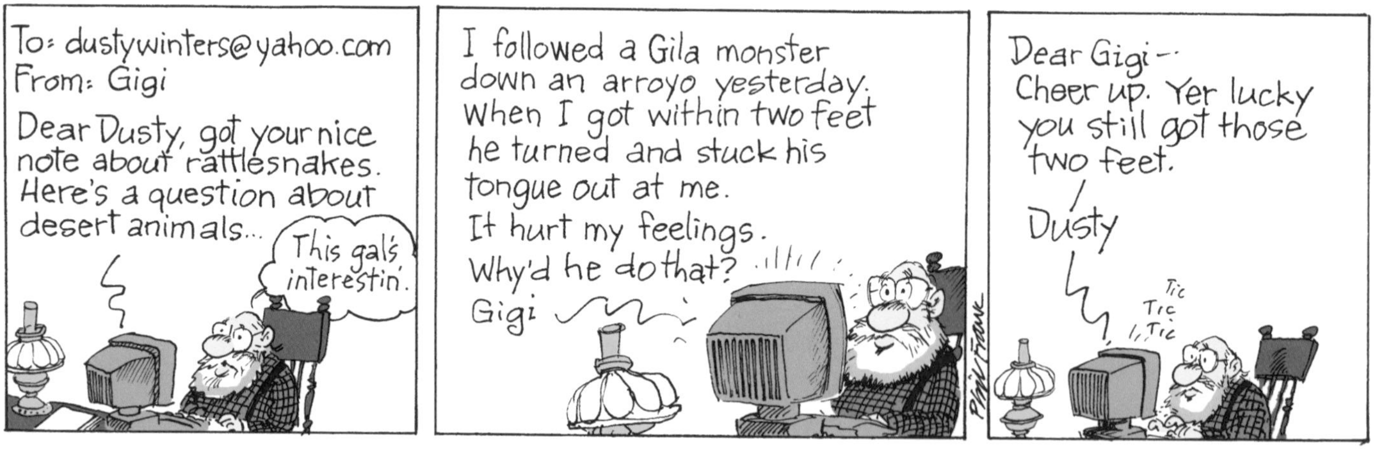
To: dustywinters@yahoo.com
From: Gigi
Dear Dusty, got your nice note about rattlesnakes. Here's a question about desert animals...
This gal's interestin'.
I followed a Gila monster down an arroyo yesterday. When I got within two feet he turned and stuck his tongue out at me.
It hurt my feelings.
Why'd he do that?
Gigi
Dear Gigi --
Cheer up. Yer lucky you still got those two feet.
Dusty
Tic
Tic
Tic

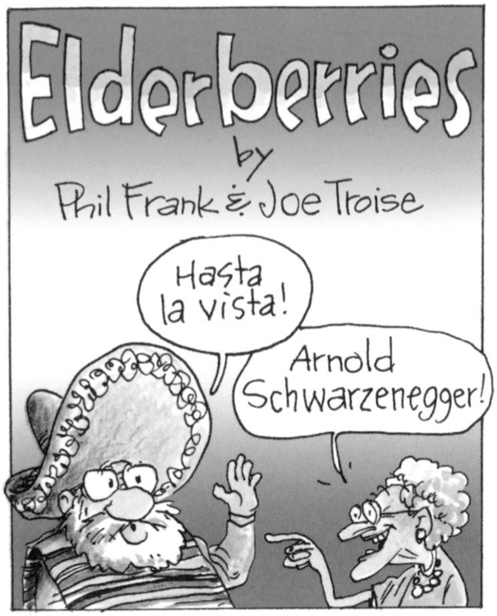
Elderberries
by
Phil Frank & Joe Troise
Hasta la vista!
Arnold Schwarzenegger!

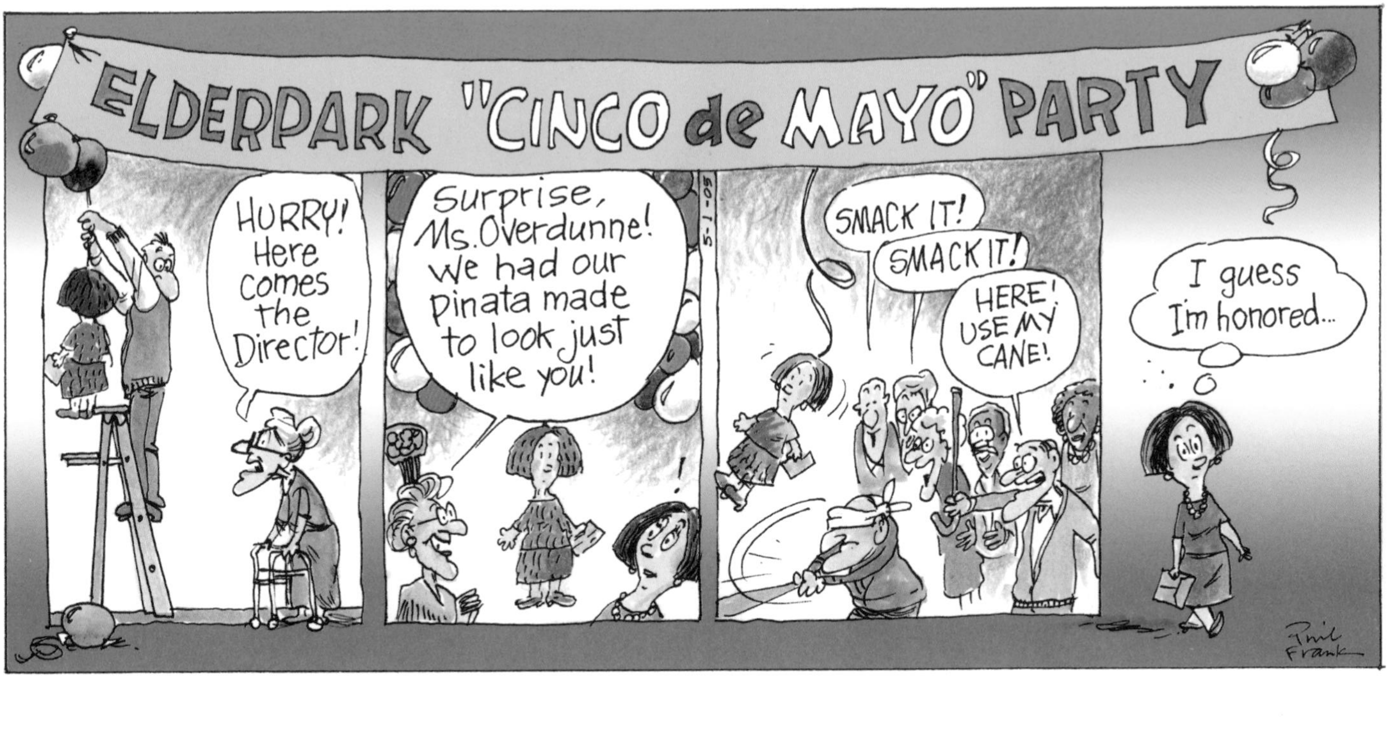
ELDERPARK "CINCO de MAYO" PARTY
HURRY! Here comes the Director!
Surprise, Ms. Overdunne! We had our pinata made to look just like you!
SMACK IT!
SMACK IT!
HERE! USE MY CANE!
I guess I'm honored...

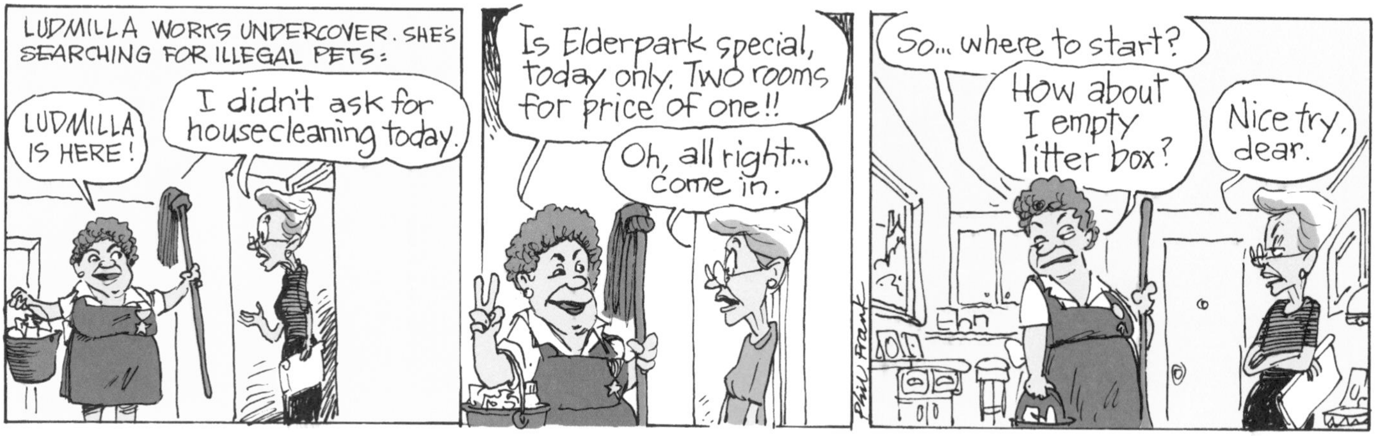
LUDMILLA WORKS UNDERCOVER. SHE'S SEARCHING FOR ILLEGAL PETS:
LUDMILLA IS HERE!
I didn't ask for housecleaning today.
Is Elderpark special, today only. Two rooms for price of one!!
Oh, all right... come in.
So... where to start?
How about I empty litter box?
Nice try, dear.

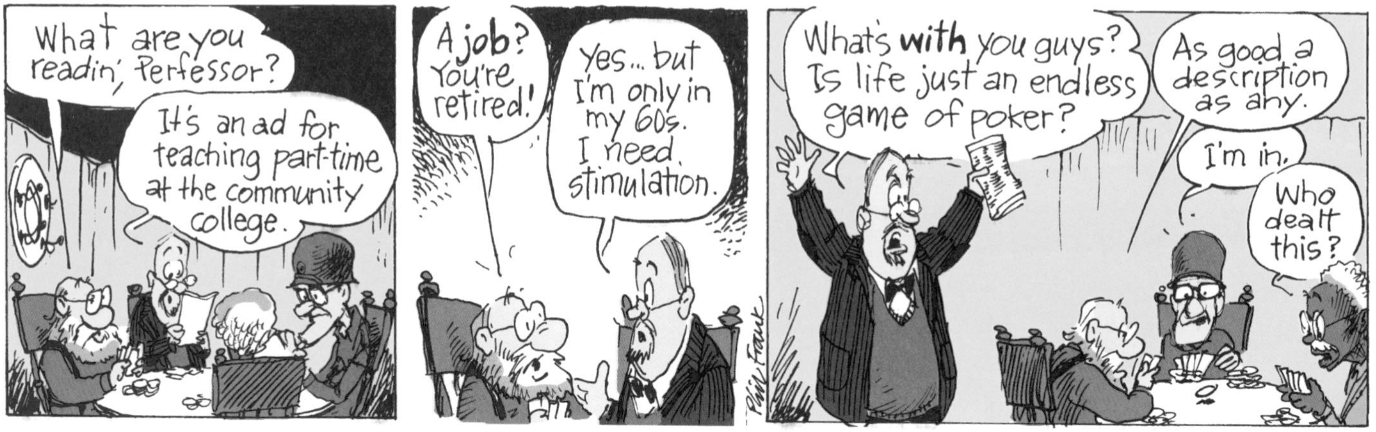
What are you readin', Perfessor?
It's an ad for teaching part-time at the community college.
A **job**? You're retired!
Yes... but I'm only in my 60s. I need stimulation.
What's **with** you guys? Is life just an endless game of poker?
As good a description as any.
I'm in.
Who dealt this?

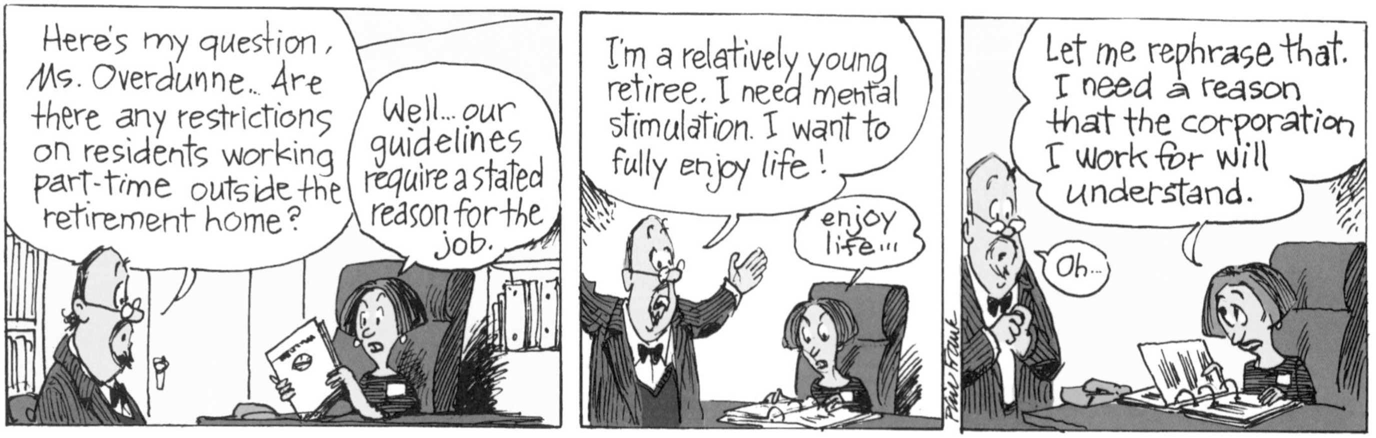
Here's my question, Ms. Overdunne.. Are there any restrictions on residents working part-time outside the retirement home?
Well... our guidelines require a stated reason for the job.
I'm a relatively young retiree. I need mental stimulation. I want to fully enjoy life!
enjoy life...
Let me rephrase that. I need a reason that the corporation I work for will understand.
Oh...

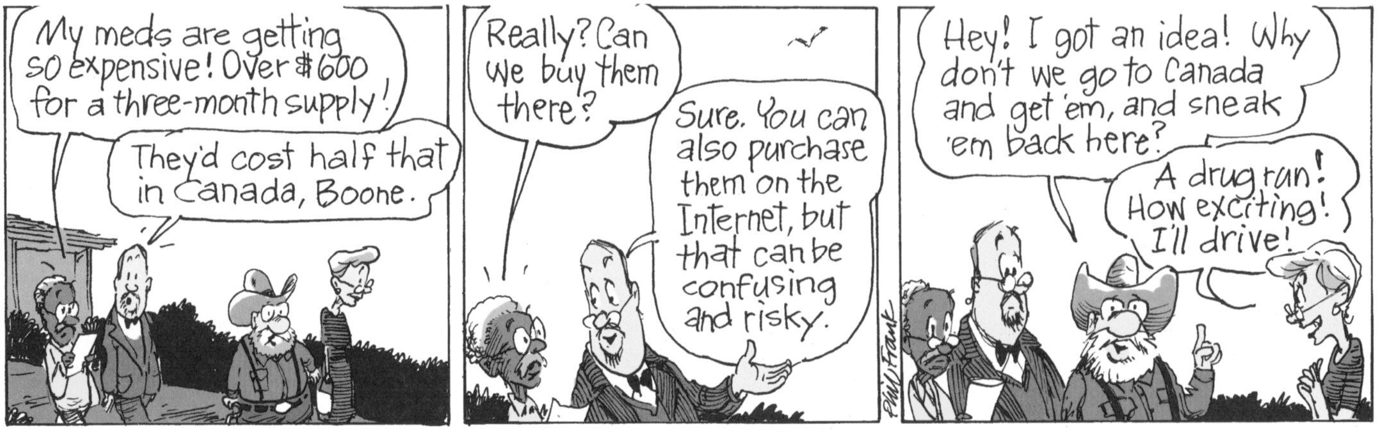
My meds are getting so expensive! Over $600 for a three-month supply!
They'd cost half that in Canada, Boone.
Really? Can we buy them there?
Sure. You can also purchase them on the Internet, but that can be confusing and risky.
Hey! I got an idea! Why don't we go to Canada and get 'em, and sneak 'em back here?
A drug run! How exciting! I'll drive!

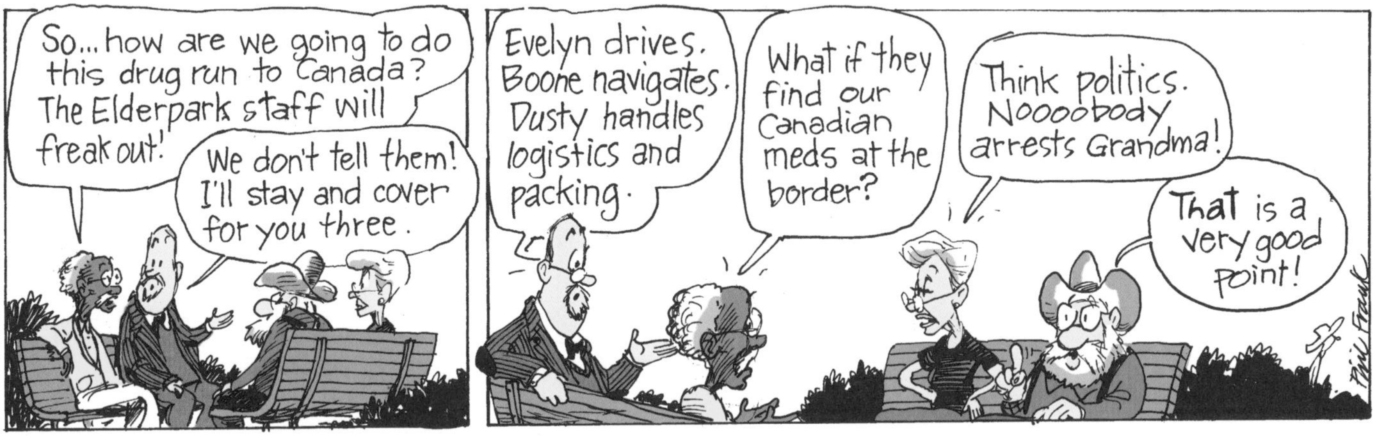
So... how are we going to do this drug run to Canada? The Elderpark staff will freak out!
We don't tell them! I'll stay and cover for you three.
Evelyn drives. Boone navigates. Dusty handles logistics and packing.
What if they find our Canadian meds at the border?
Think politics. Nooooobody arrests Grandma!
That is a very good point!

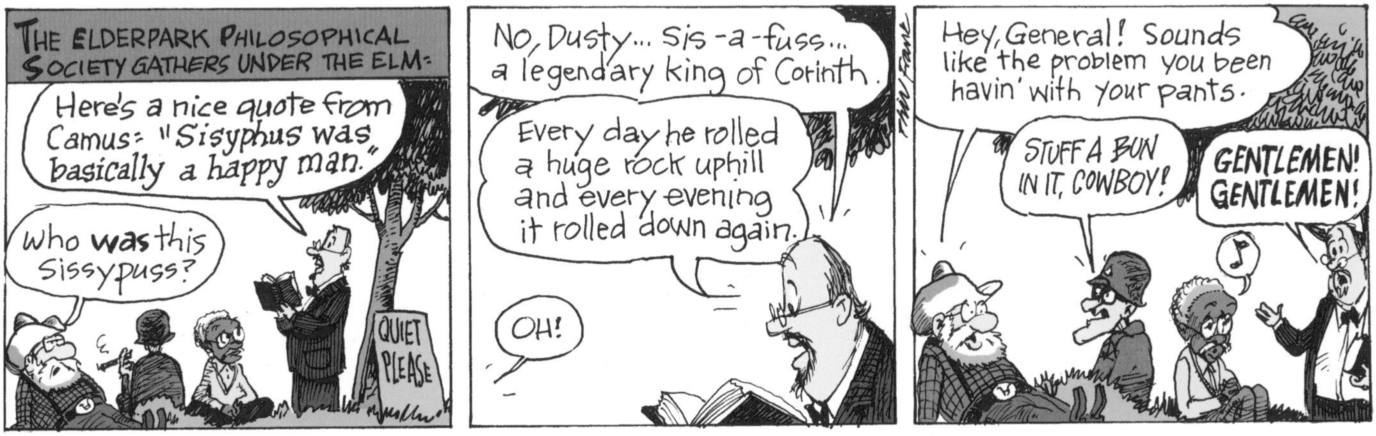
THE ELDERPARK PHILOSOPHICAL SOCIETY GATHERS UNDER THE ELM.
Here's a nice quote from Camus: "Sisyphus was basically a happy man."
Who was this Sissypuss?
QUIET PLEASE
No, Dusty... Sis-a-fuss... a legendary king of Corinth.
Every day he rolled a huge rock uphill and every evening it rolled down again.
OH!
Hey, General! Sounds like the problem you been havin' with your pants.
STUFF A BUN IN IT, COWBOY!
GENTLEMEN! GENTLEMEN!

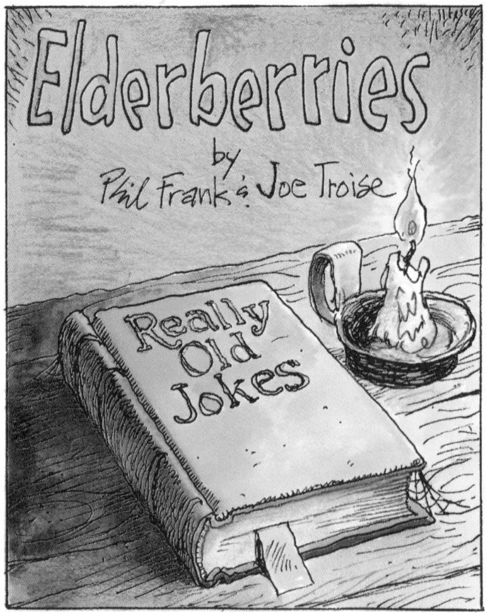
Elderberries
by Phil Frank & Joe Troise
Really Old Jokes

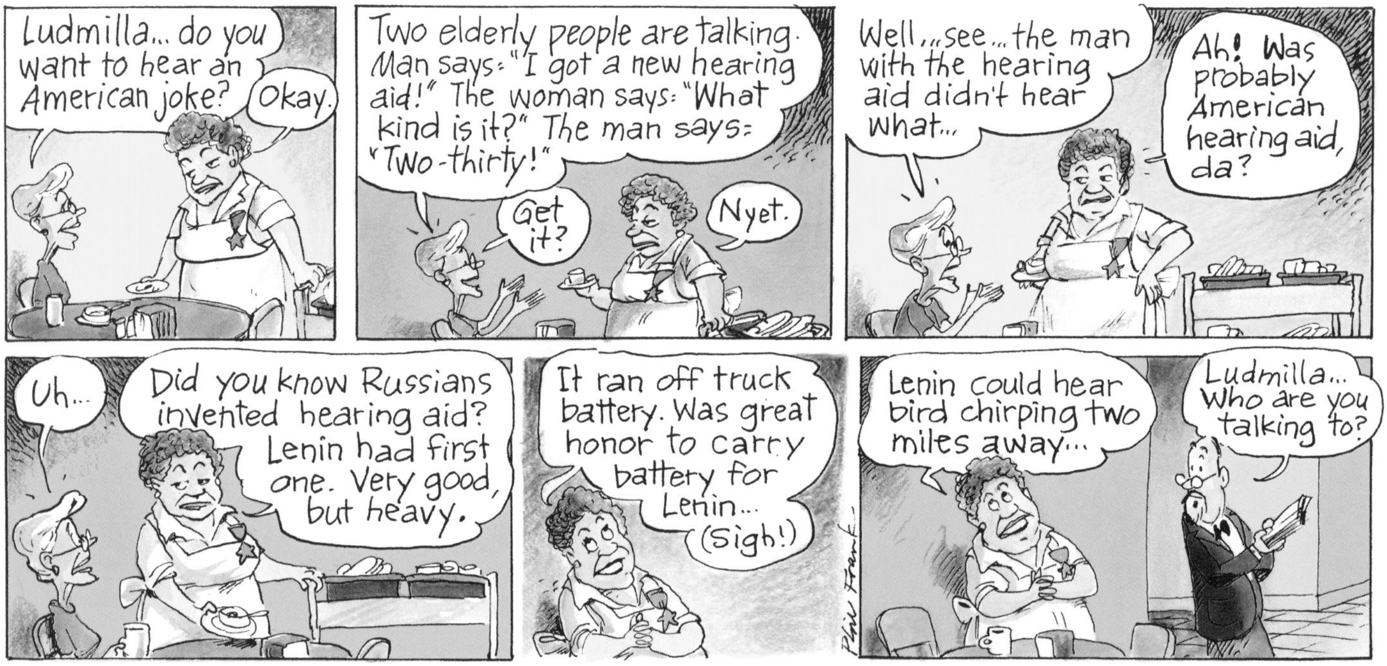
Ludmilla... do you want to hear an American joke?
Okay.
Two elderly people are talking. Man says: "I got a new hearing aid!" The woman says: "What kind is it?" The man says: "Two-thirty!"
Get it?
Nyet.
Well,.,see... the man with the hearing aid didn't hear what...
Ah! Was probably American hearing aid, da?
Uh...
Did you know Russians invented hearing aid? Lenin had first one. Very good, but heavy.
It ran off truck battery. Was great honor to carry battery for Lenin...
(Sigh!)
Lenin could hear bird chirping two miles away...
Ludmilla... Who are you talking to?
Phil Frank

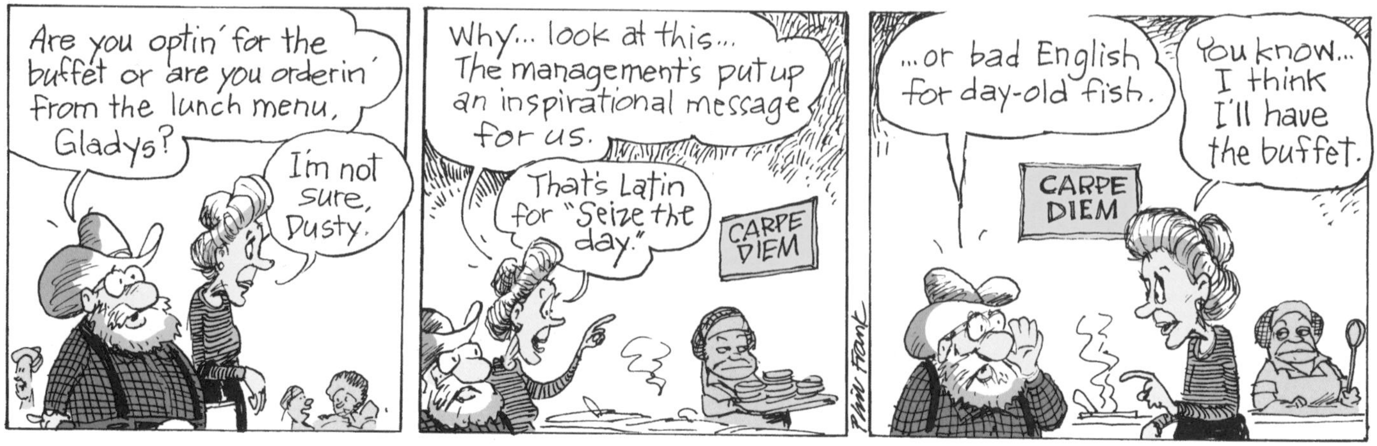
Are you optin' for the buffet or are you orderin' from the lunch menu, Gladys?
I'm not sure, Dusty.
Why... look at this... The management's put up an inspirational message for us.
That's Latin for "Seize the day."
CARPE DIEM
...or bad English for day-old fish.
CARPE DIEM
You know... I think I'll have the buffet.

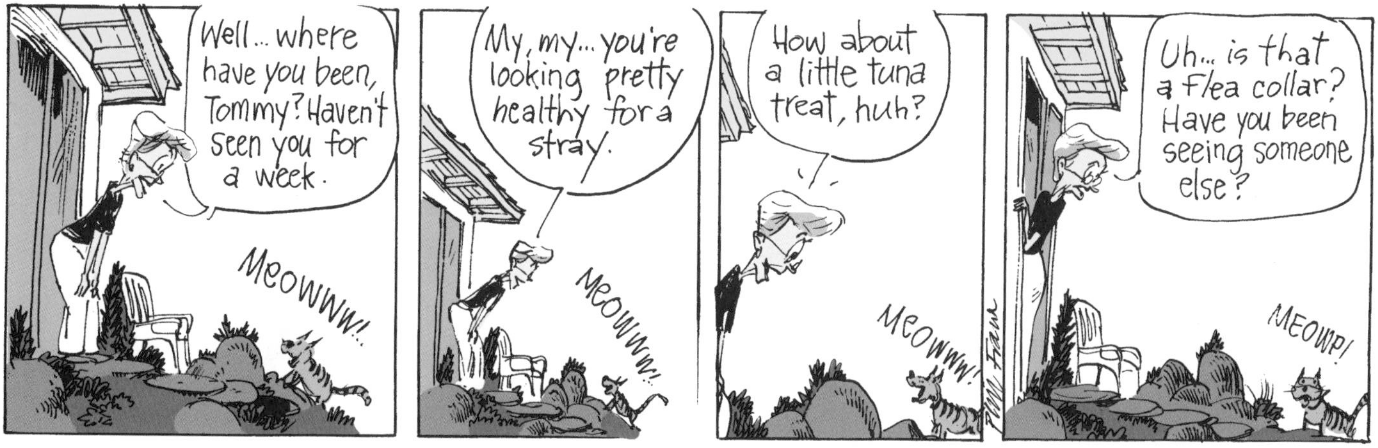
Well... where have you been, Tommy? Haven't seen you for a week.
MEOWWW!!
My, my... you're looking pretty healthy for a stray.
MEOWWW!!
How about a little tuna treat, huh?
MEOWWW!
Uh... is that a flea collar? Have you been seeing someone else?
MEOWP!

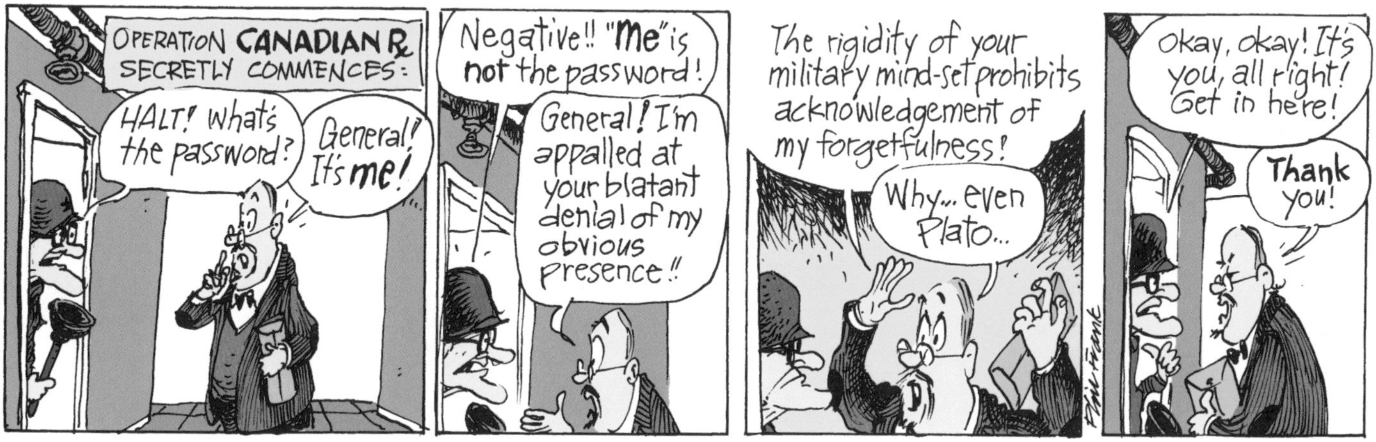
OPERATION CANADIAN Rx SECRETLY COMMENCES:
HALT! What's the password?
General! It's me!
Negative!! "Me" is not the password!
General! I'm appalled at your blatant denial of my obvious presence!!
The rigidity of your military mind-set prohibits acknowledgement of my forgetfulness!
Why... even Plato...
Okay, okay! It's you, all right! Get in here!
Thank you!

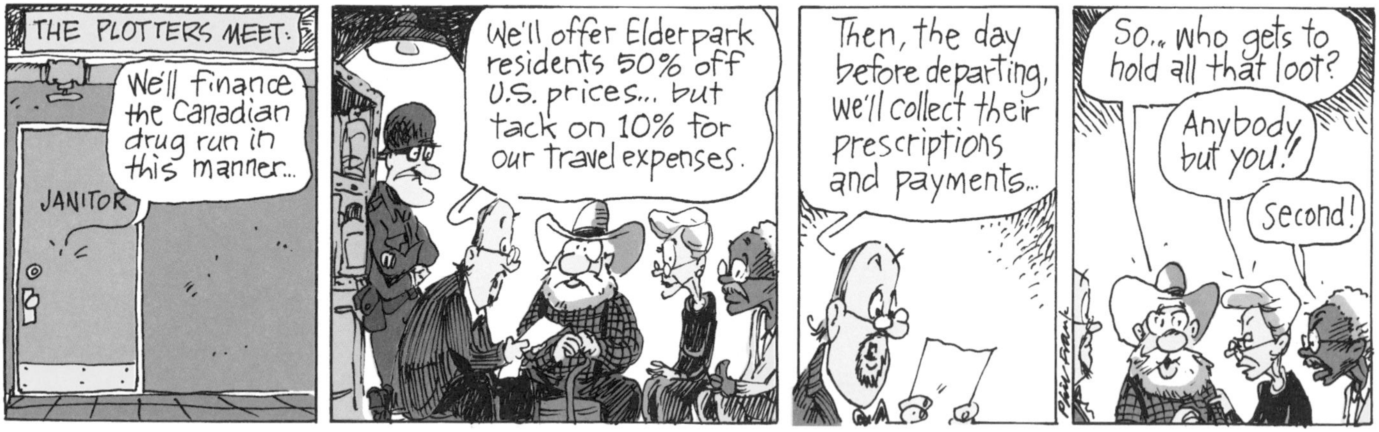
THE PLOTTERS MEET:
We'll finance the Canadian drug run in this manner...
JANITOR
We'll offer Elderpark residents 50% off U.S. prices... but tack on 10% for our travel expenses.
Then, the day before departing, we'll collect their prescriptions and payments...
So... who gets to hold all that loot?
Anybody but you!
Second!

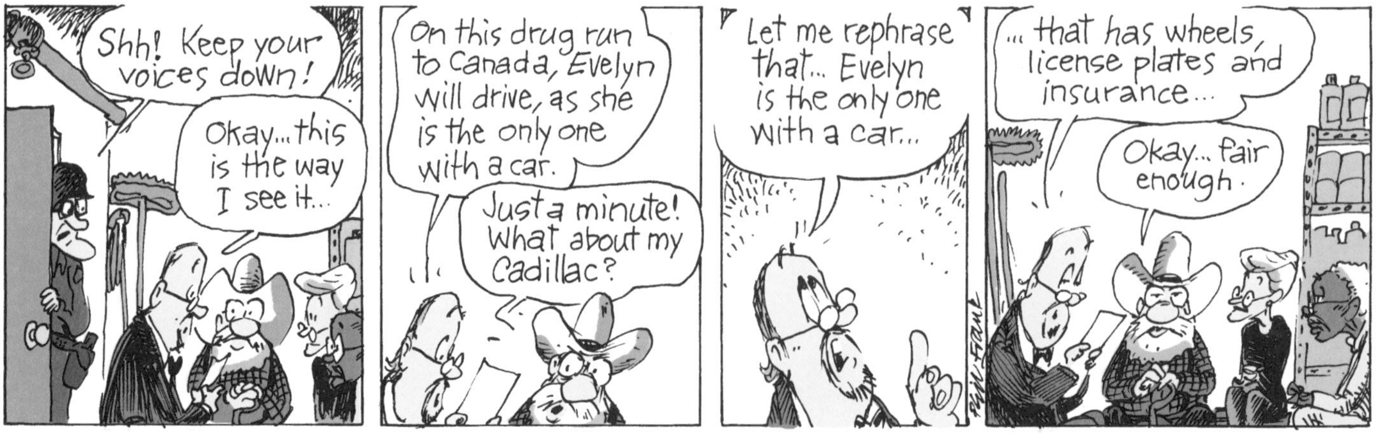
Shh! Keep your voices down!
Okay... this is the way I see it...
On this drug run to Canada, Evelyn will drive, as she is the only one with a car.
Just a minute! What about my Cadillac?
Let me rephrase that... Evelyn is the only one with a car...
... that has wheels, license plates and insurance...
Okay... fair enough.

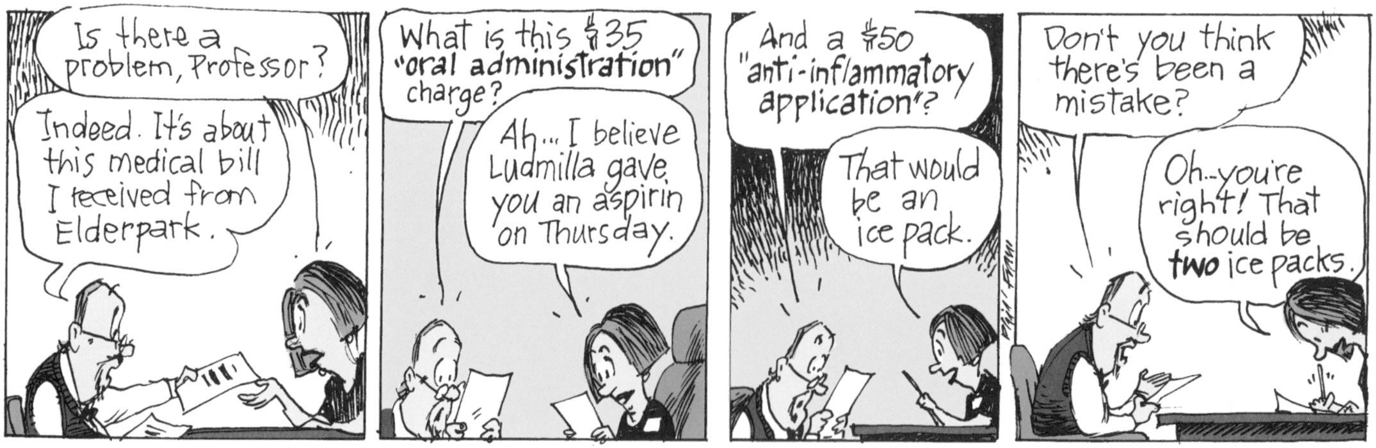
Is there a problem, Professor?
Indeed. It's about this medical bill I received from Elderpark.
What is this $35 "oral administration" charge?
Ah... I believe Ludmilla gave you an aspirin on Thursday.
And a $50 "anti-inflammatory application"?
That would be an ice pack.
Don't you think there's been a mistake?
Oh... you're right! That should be two ice packs.

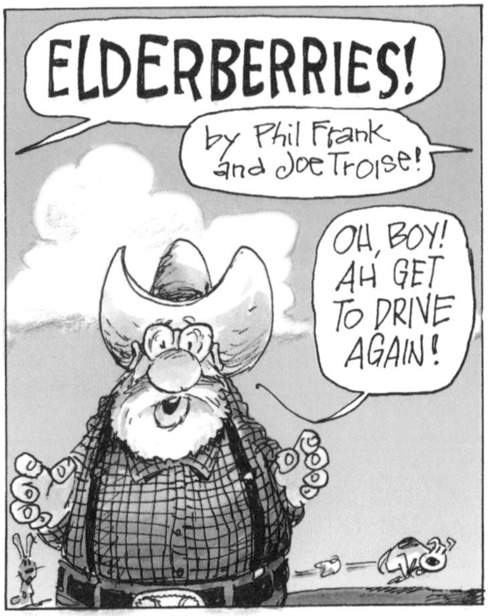
ELDERBERRIES!
by Phil Frank and Joe Troise!
OH, BOY! AH GET TO DRIVE AGAIN!

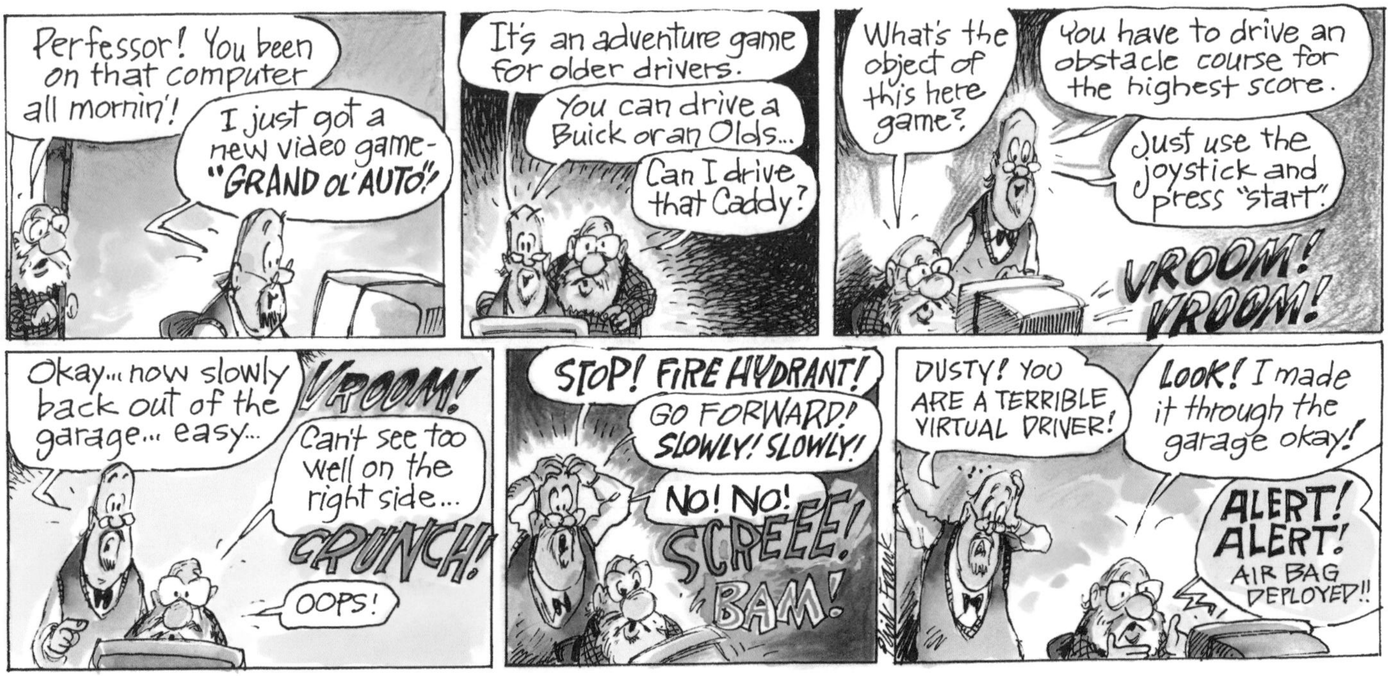
Perfessor! You been on that computer all mornin'!
I just got a new video game- "GRAND OL' AUTO"!
It's an adventure game for older drivers.
You can drive a Buick or an Olds...
Can I drive that Caddy?
What's the object of this here game?
You have to drive an obstacle course for the highest score.
Just use the joystick and press "start".
VROOM! VROOM!
Okay... now slowly back out of the garage... easy...
VROOM!
Can't see too well on the right side...
CRUNCH!
OOPS!
STOP! FIRE HYDRANT!
GO FORWARD! SLOWLY! SLOWLY!
NO! NO!
SCREEE!
BAM!
DUSTY! YOU ARE A TERRIBLE VIRTUAL DRIVER!
LOOK! I made it through the garage okay!
ALERT! ALERT! AIR BAG DEPLOYED!!

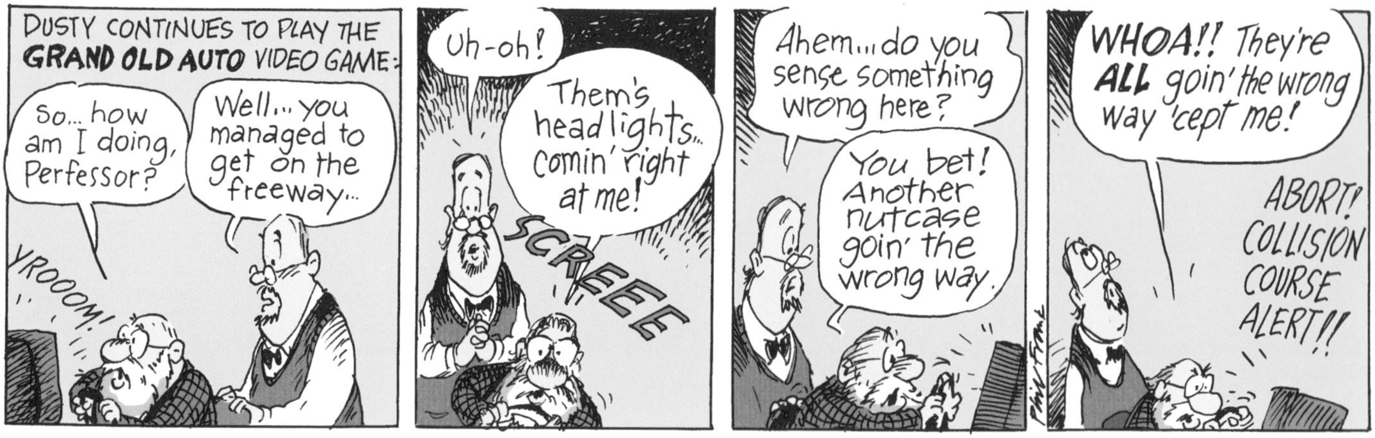
DUSTY CONTINUES TO PLAY THE GRAND OLD AUTO VIDEO GAME:
So... how am I doing, Perfessor?
Well... you managed to get on the freeway...
VROOOM!
Uh-oh!
Them's headlights... comin' right at me!
SCREEEE
Ahem... do you sense something wrong here?
You bet! Another nutcase goin' the wrong way.
WHOA!! They're ALL goin' the wrong way 'cept me!
ABORT! COLLISION COURSE ALERT!!

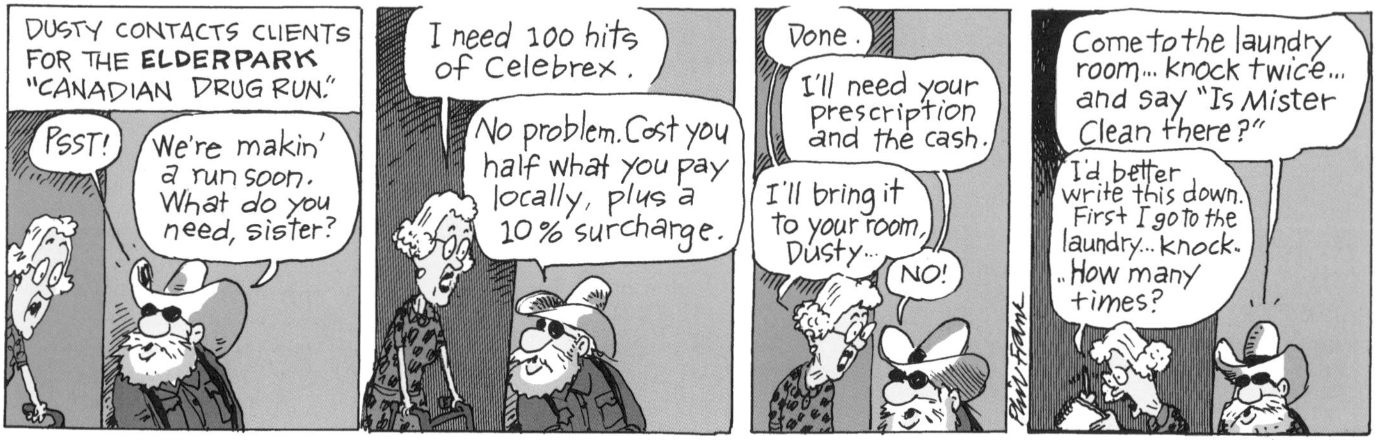
DUSTY CONTACTS CLIENTS FOR THE ELDERPARK "CANADIAN DRUG RUN."
PSST!
We're makin' a run soon. What do you need, sister?
I need 100 hits of Celebrex.
No problem. Cost you half what you pay locally, plus a 10% surcharge.
Done.
I'll need your prescription and the cash.
I'll bring it to your room, Dusty...
NO!
Come to the laundry room... knock twice... and say "Is Mister Clean there?"
I'd better write this down. First I go to the laundry... knock... ..How many times?

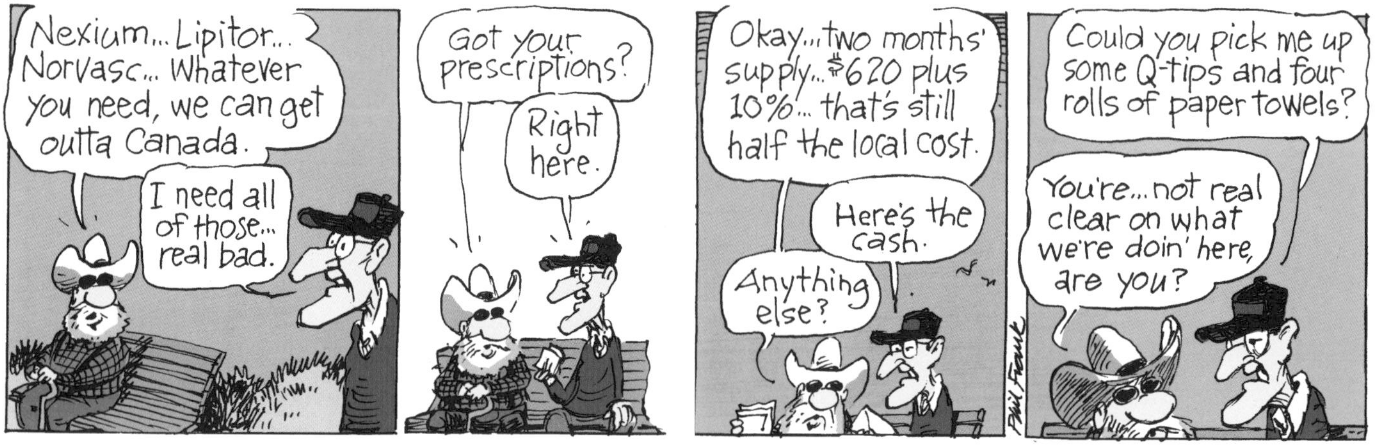
Nexium... Lipitor... Norvasc... Whatever you need, we can get outta Canada.
I need all of those... real bad.
Got your prescriptions?
Right here.
Okay... two months' supply... $620 plus 10%... that's still half the local cost.
Here's the cash.
Anything else?
Could you pick me up some Q-tips and four rolls of paper towels?
You're... not real clear on what we're doin' here, are you?

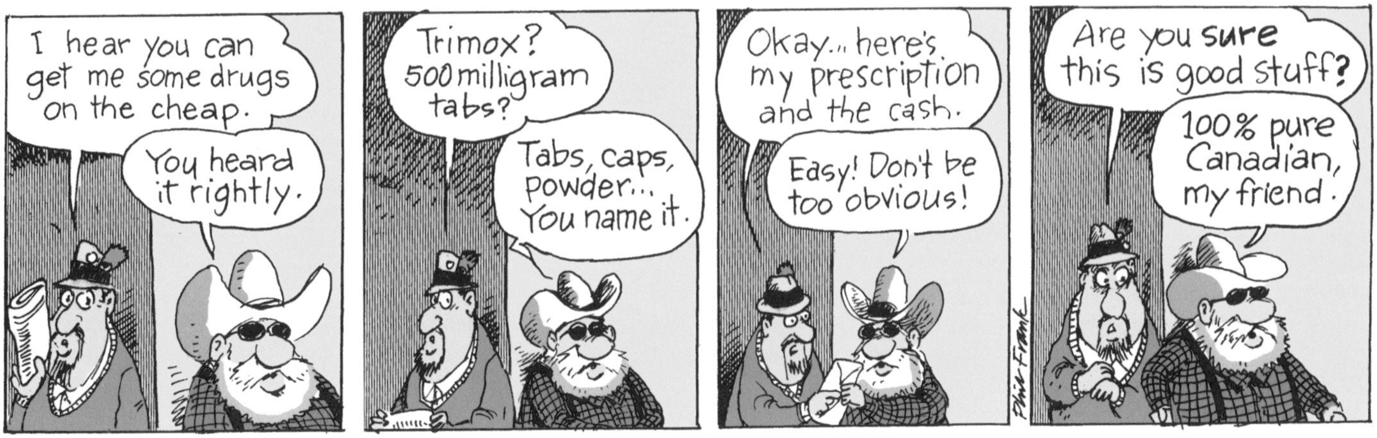
I hear you can get me some drugs on the cheap.
You heard it rightly.
Trimox? 500 milligram tabs?
Tabs, caps, powder... You name it.
Okay... here's my prescription and the cash.
Easy! Don't be too obvious!
Are you **sure** this is good stuff?
100% pure Canadian, my friend.

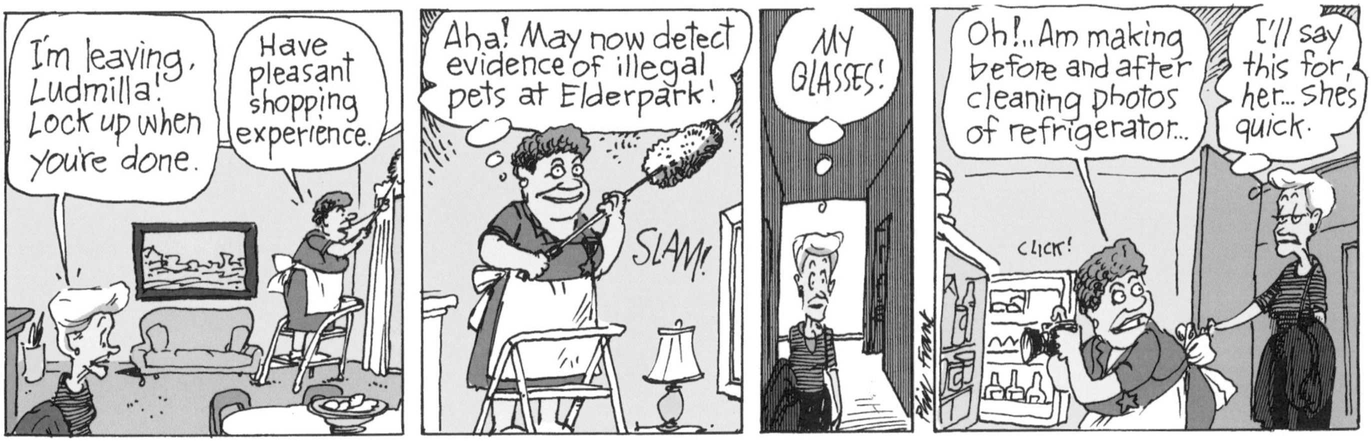
I'm leaving, Ludmilla! Lock up when you're done.
Have pleasant shopping experience.
Aha! May now detect evidence of illegal pets at Elderpark!
SLAM!
MY GLASSES!
Oh!.. Am making before and after cleaning photos of refrigerator...
Click!
I'll say this for her... She's quick.

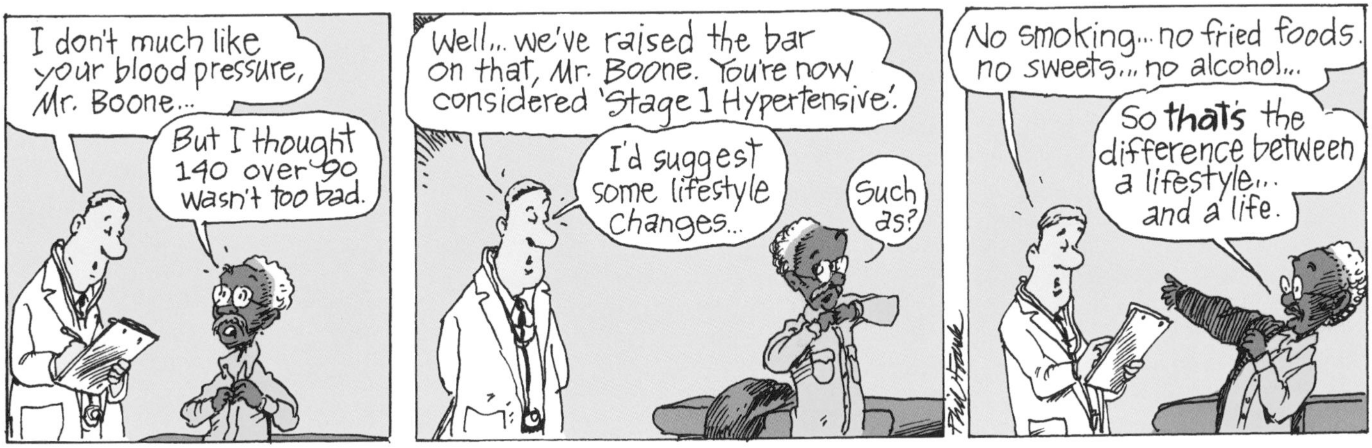
I don't much like your blood pressure, Mr. Boone...
But I thought 140 over 90 wasn't too bad.
Well... we've raised the bar on that, Mr. Boone. You're now considered 'Stage 1 Hypertensive'.
I'd suggest some lifestyle changes...
Such as?
No smoking... no fried foods. no sweets... no alcohol...
So **that's** the difference between a lifestyle... and a life.

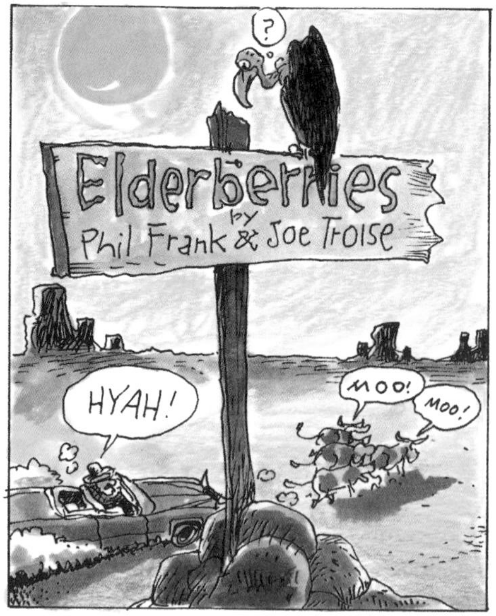
?
Elderberries
by
Phil Frank & Joe Troise
HYAH!
MOO!
MOO!

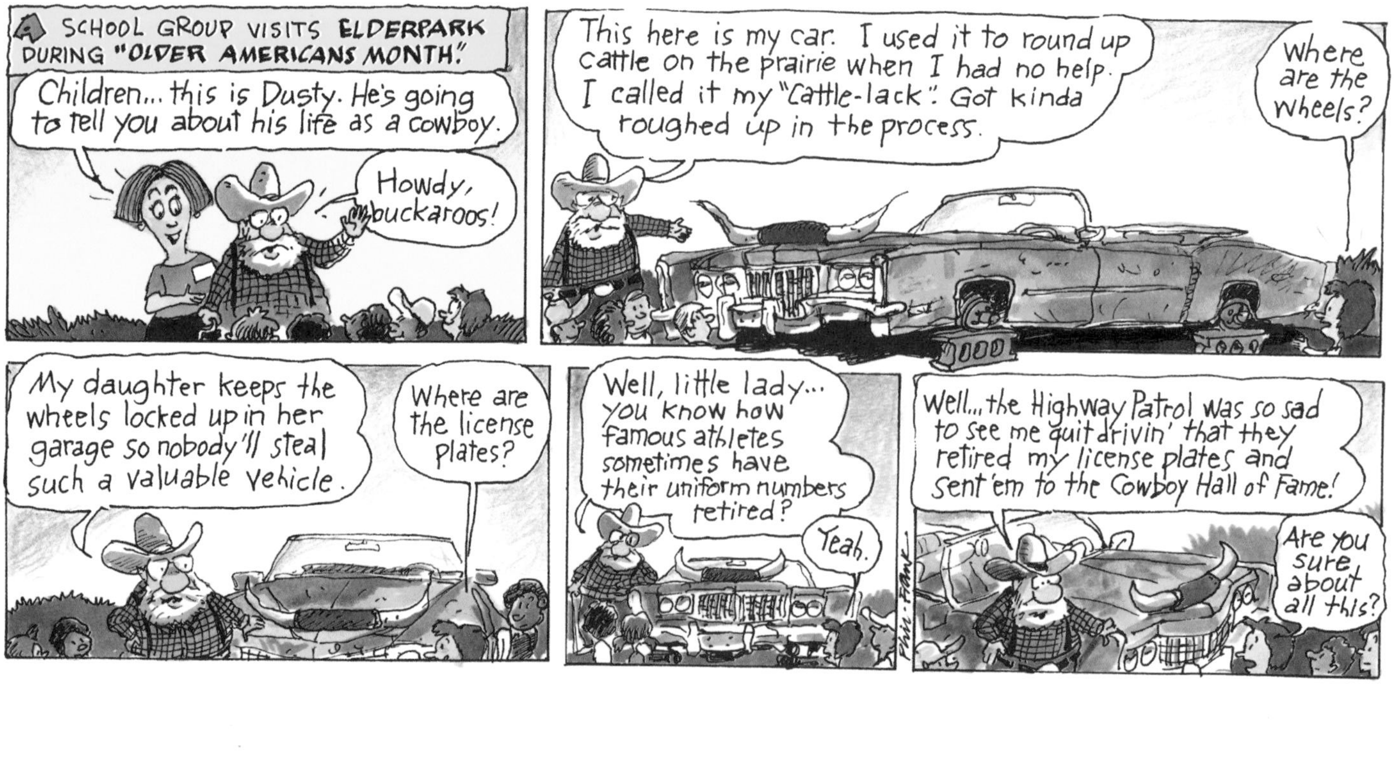
A SCHOOL GROUP VISITS ELDERPARK DURING "OLDER AMERICANS MONTH."
Children... this is Dusty. He's going to tell you about his life as a cowboy.
Howdy, buckaroos!
This here is my car. I used it to round up cattle on the prairie when I had no help. I called it my "Cattle-lack". Got kinda roughed up in the process.
Where are the wheels?
My daughter keeps the wheels locked up in her garage so nobody'll steal such a valuable vehicle.
Where are the license plates?
Well, little lady... you know how famous athletes sometimes have their uniform numbers retired?
Yeah.
Well... the Highway Patrol was so sad to see me quit drivin' that they retired my license plates and sent 'em to the Cowboy Hall of Fame!
Are you sure about all this?

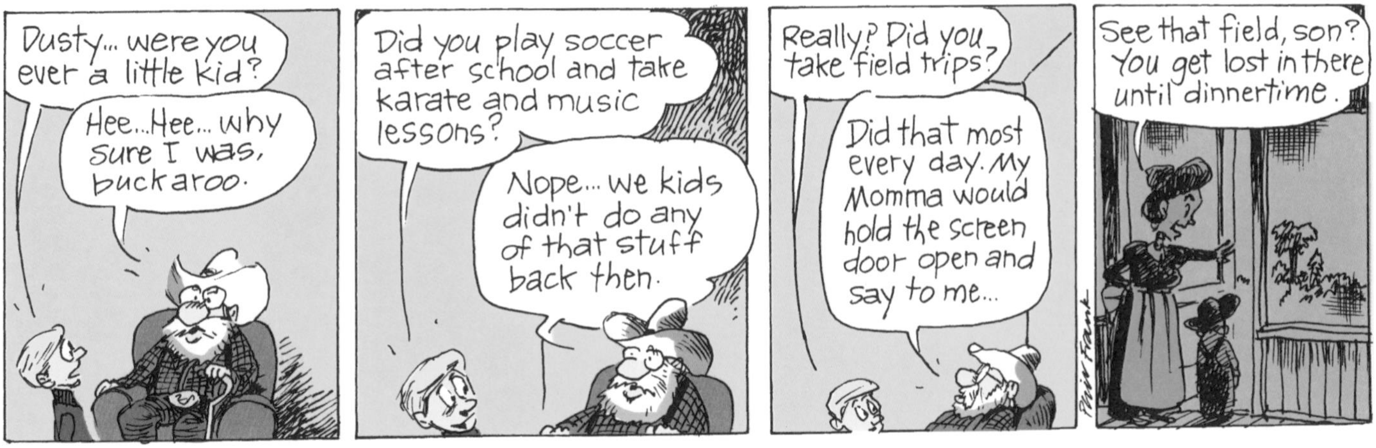
Dusty... were you ever a little kid?
Hee...Hee... why sure I was, buckaroo.
Did you play soccer after school and take karate and music lessons?
Nope... we kids didn't do any of that stuff back then.
Really? Did you take field trips?
Did that most every day. My Momma would hold the screen door open and say to me...
See that field, son? You get lost in there until dinnertime.

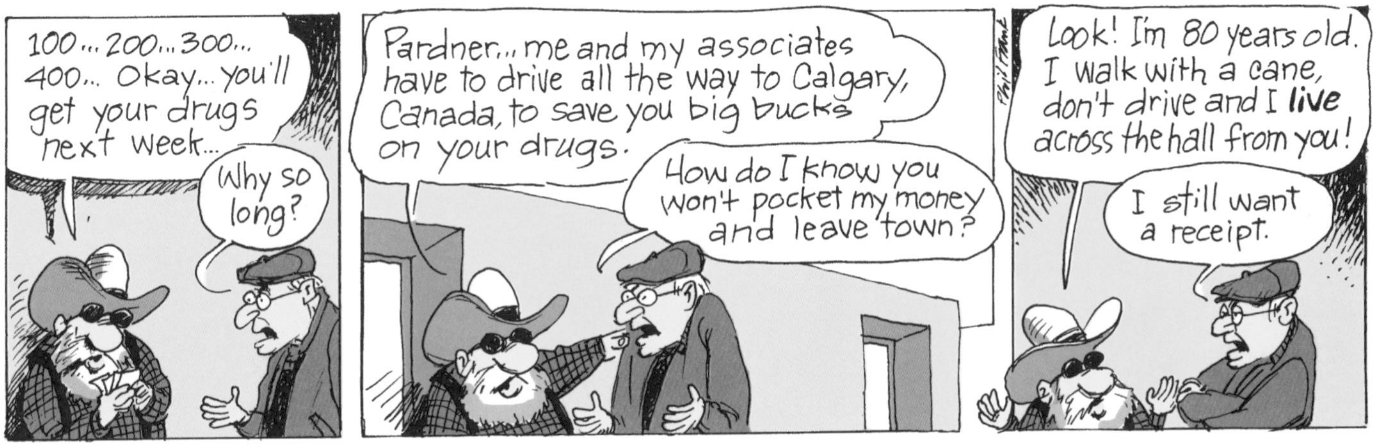
100... 200... 300... 400... Okay... you'll get your drugs next week...
Why so long?
Pardner... me and my associates have to drive all the way to Calgary, Canada, to save you big bucks on your drugs.
How do I know you won't pocket my money and leave town?
Look! I'm 80 years old. I walk with a cane, don't drive and I **live** across the hall from you!
I still want a receipt.

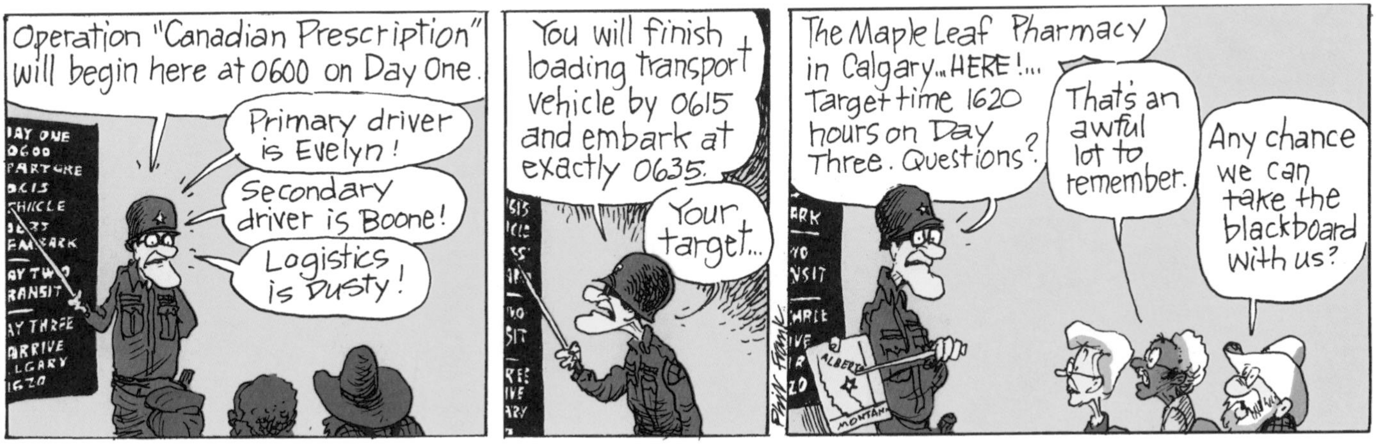
Operation "Canadian Prescription" will begin here at 0600 on Day One.
Primary driver is Evelyn!
Secondary driver is Boone!
Logistics is Dusty!
You will finish loading transport vehicle by 0615 and embark at exactly 0635.
Your target...
The Maple Leaf Pharmacy in Calgary... HERE!... Target time 1620 hours on Day Three. Questions?
That's an awful lot to remember.
Any chance we can take the blackboard with us?

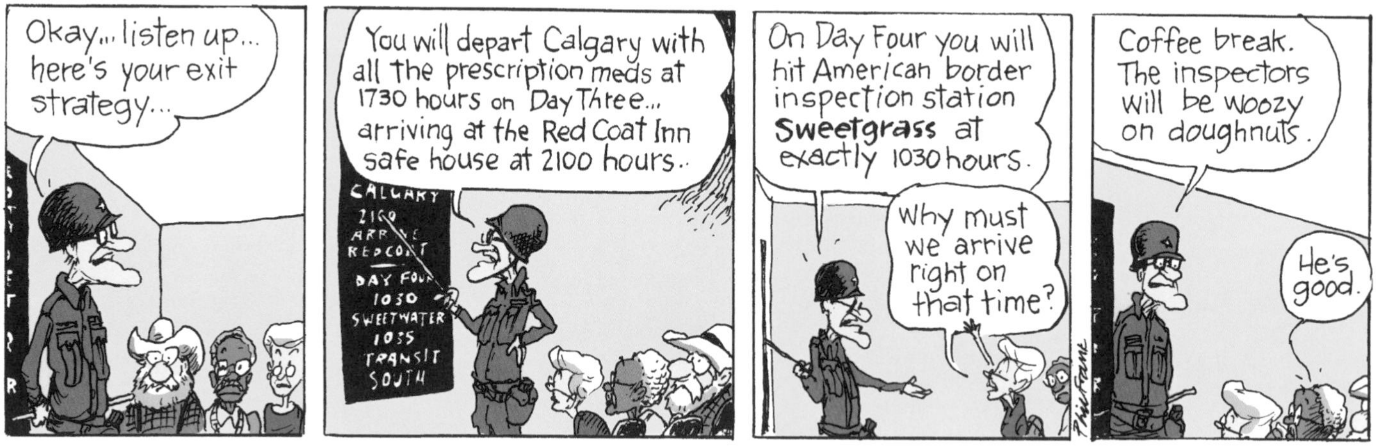
Okay... listen up... here's your exit strategy...
You will depart Calgary with all the prescription meds at 1730 hours on Day Three... arriving at the Red Coat Inn safe house at 2100 hours..
CALGARY
2100
DAY FOUR
1030
SWEETWATER
1035
TRANSIT
SOUTH
On Day Four you will hit American border inspection station **Sweetgrass** at exactly 1030 hours.
Why must we arrive right on that time?
Coffee break. The inspectors will be woozy on doughnuts.
He's good.

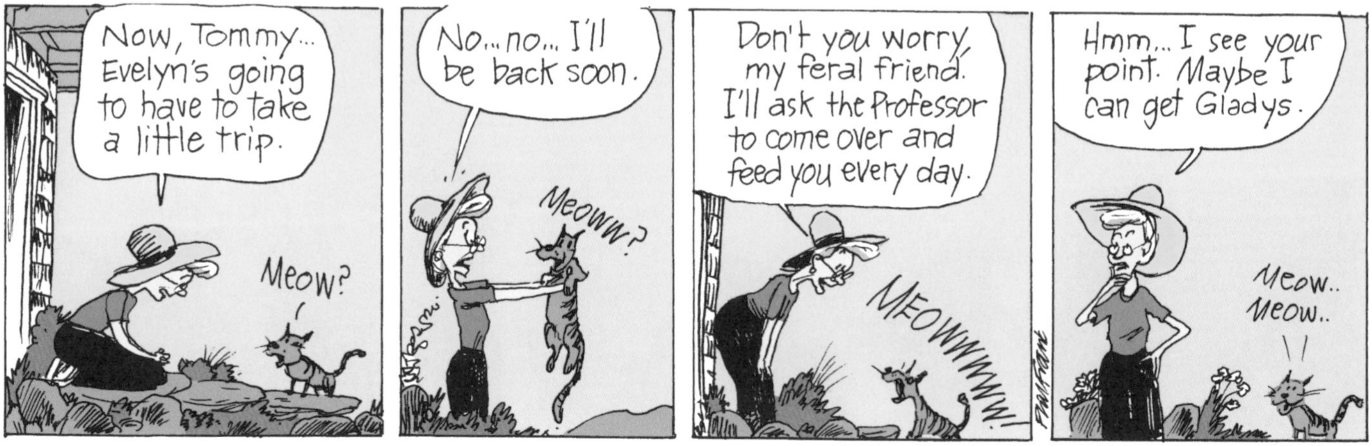
Now, Tommy... Evelyn's going to have to take a little trip.
Meow?
No... no... I'll be back soon.
Meoww?
Don't you worry, my feral friend. I'll ask the Professor to come over and feed you every day.
MEOWWWWW!
Hmm... I see your point. Maybe I can get Gladys.
Meow.. Meow..

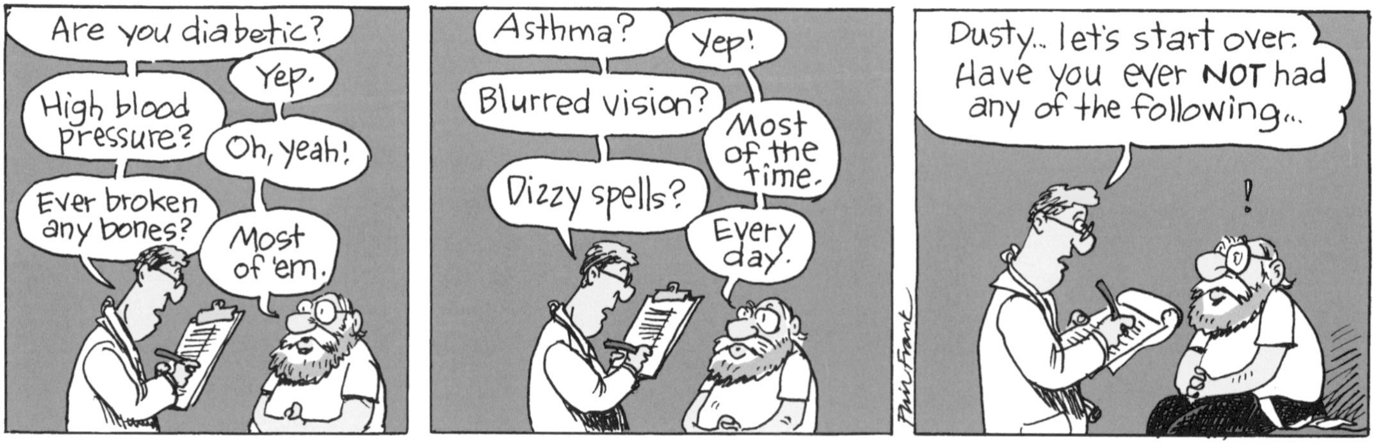
Are you diabetic?
Yep.
High blood pressure?
Oh, yeah!
Ever broken any bones?
Most of 'em.
Asthma?
Yep!
Blurred vision?
Most of the time.
Dizzy spells?
Every day.
Dusty.. let's start over. Have you ever **NOT** had any of the following...
!

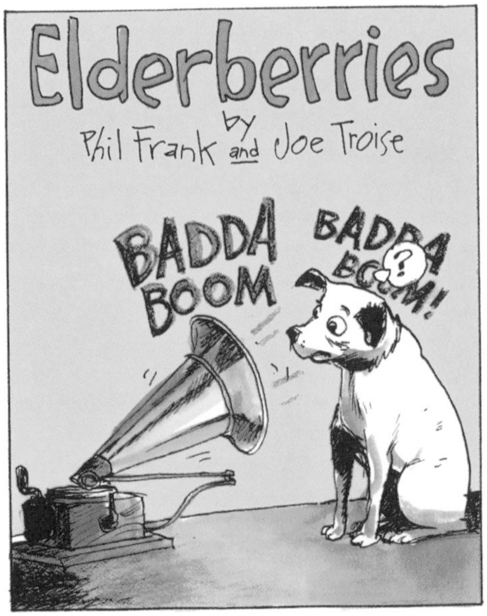

Elderberries
by Phil Frank and Joe Troise
BADDA BOOM
BADDA BOOM!
?

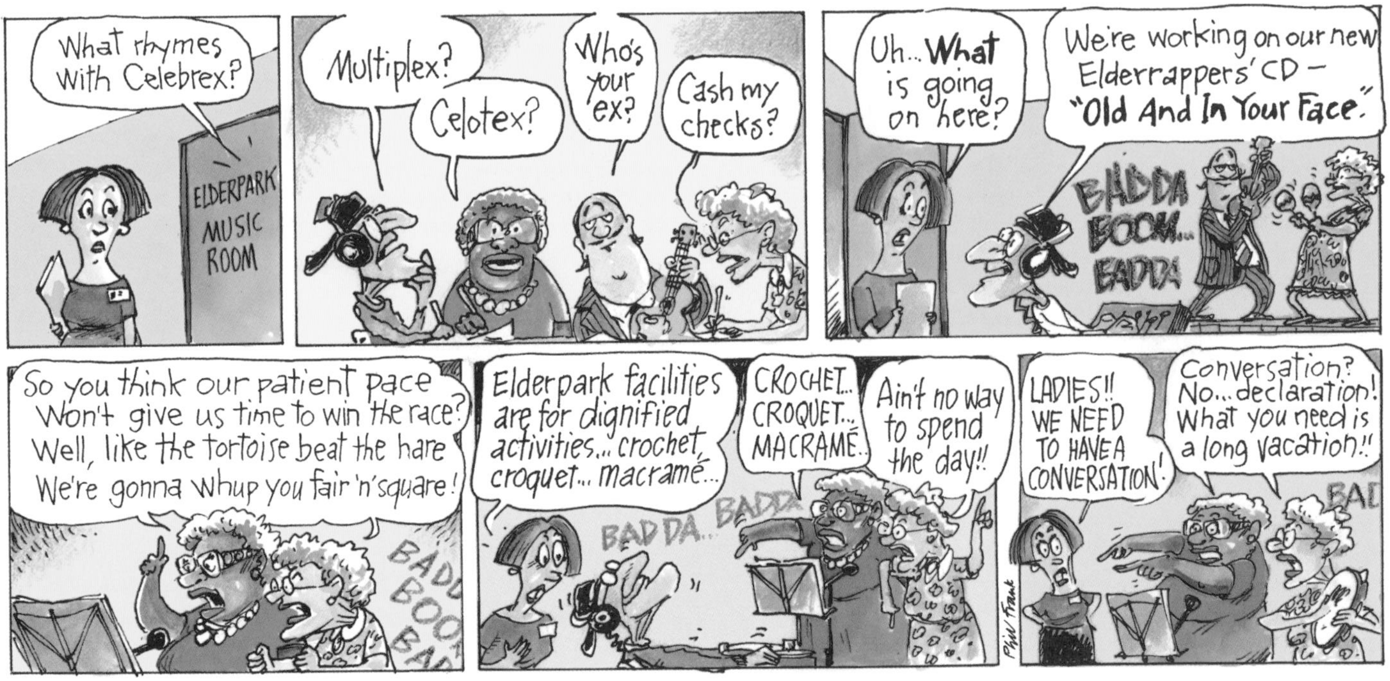

What rhymes with Celebrex?
ELDERPARK MUSIC ROOM
Multiplex?
Celotex?
Who's your ex?
Cash my checks?
Uh... What is going on here?
We're working on our new Elderrappers' CD – "Old And In Your Face."
BADDA BOOM... BADDA
So you think our patient pace Won't give us time to win the race? Well, like the tortoise beat the hare We're gonna whup you fair 'n' square!
Elderpark facilities are for dignified activities... crochet, croquet... macramé...
BADDA... BADDA
CROCHET... CROQUET... MACRAMÉ...
Ain't no way to spend the day!!
LADIES!! WE NEED TO HAVE A CONVERSATION!
Conversation? No... declaration! What you need is a long vacation!!
Phil Frank

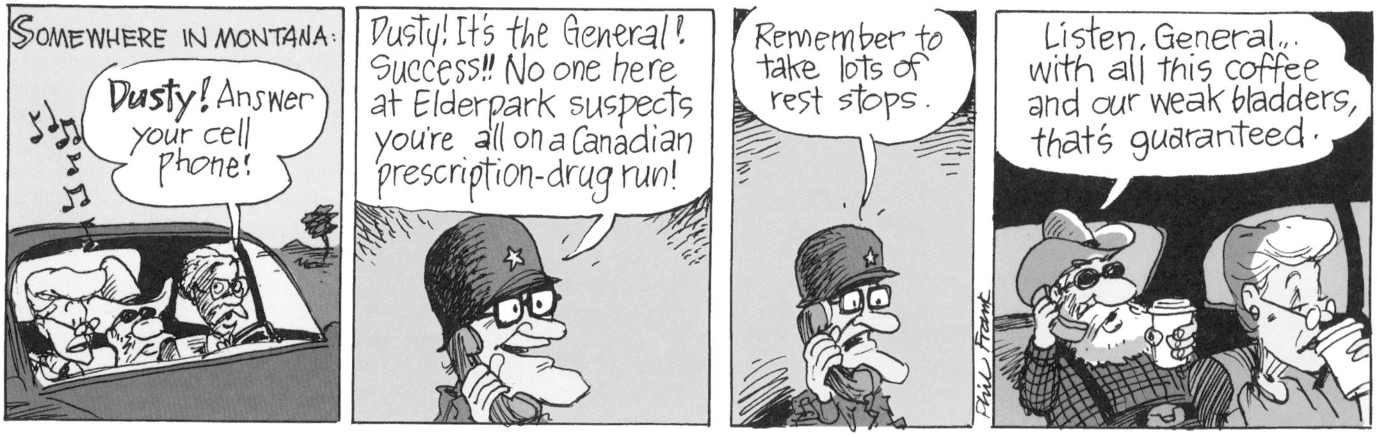
SOMEWHERE IN MONTANA:
Dusty! Answer your cell phone!
Dusty! It's the General! Success!! No one here at Elderpark suspects you're all on a Canadian prescription-drug run!
Remember to take lots of rest stops.
Listen, General... with all this coffee and our weak bladders, that's guaranteed.

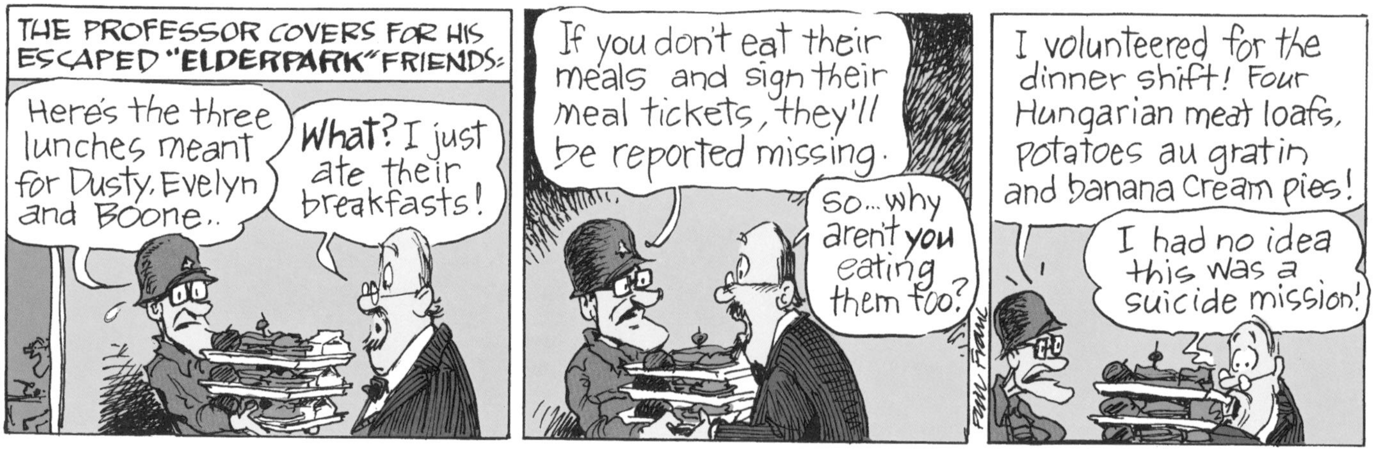
THE PROFESSOR COVERS FOR HIS ESCAPED "ELDERPARK" FRIENDS:
Here's the three lunches meant for Dusty, Evelyn and Boone..
What? I just ate their breakfasts!
If you don't eat their meals and sign their meal tickets, they'll be reported missing.
So... why aren't you eating them too?
I volunteered for the dinner shift! Four Hungarian meat loafs, potatoes au gratin and banana cream pies!
I had no idea this was a suicide mission!

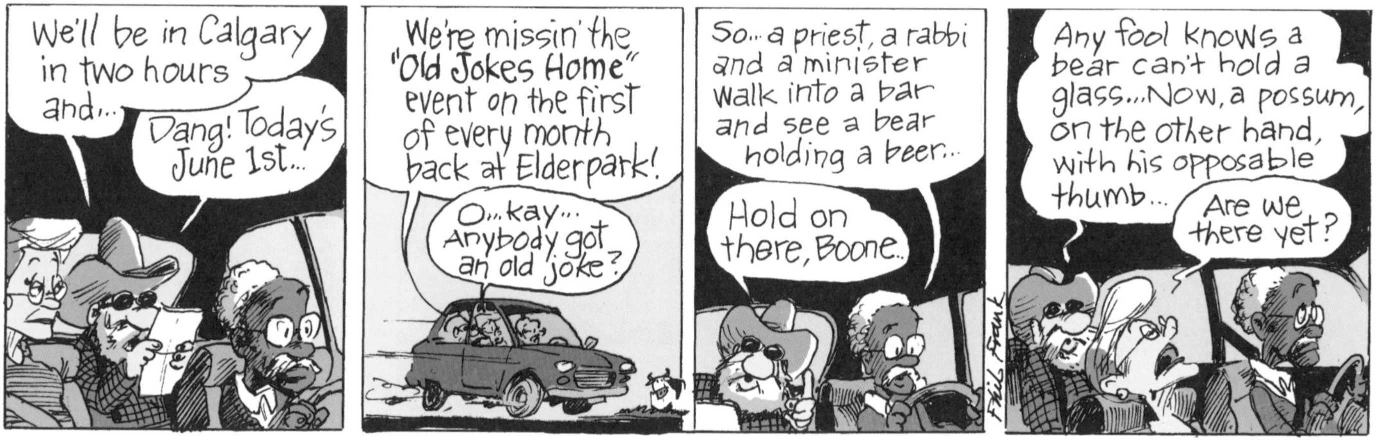
We'll be in Calgary in two hours and...
Dang! Today's June 1st...
We're missin' the "Old Jokes Home" event on the first of every month back at Elderpark!
O...kay... Anybody got an old joke?
So... a priest, a rabbi and a minister walk into a bar and see a bear holding a beer...
Hold on there, Boone..
Any fool knows a bear can't hold a glass... Now, a possum, on the other hand, with his opposable thumb...
Are we there yet?

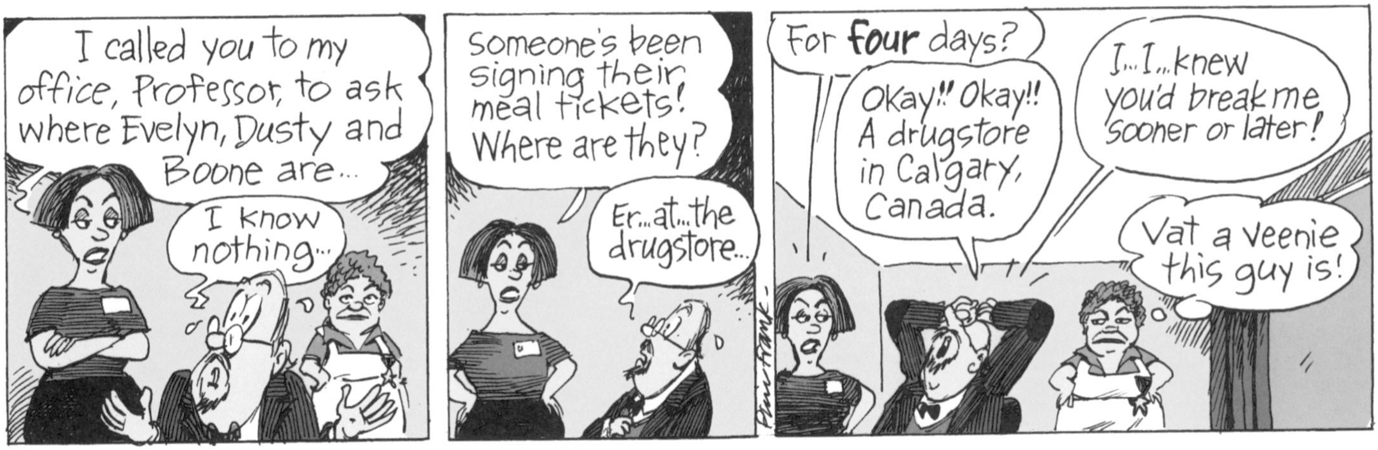
I called you to my office, Professor, to ask where Evelyn, Dusty and Boone are...
I know nothing...
Someone's been signing their meal tickets! Where are they?
Er...at...the drugstore...
For four days?
Okay!! Okay!! A drugstore in Calgary, Canada.
I...I...knew you'd break me sooner or later!
Vat a veenie this guy is!

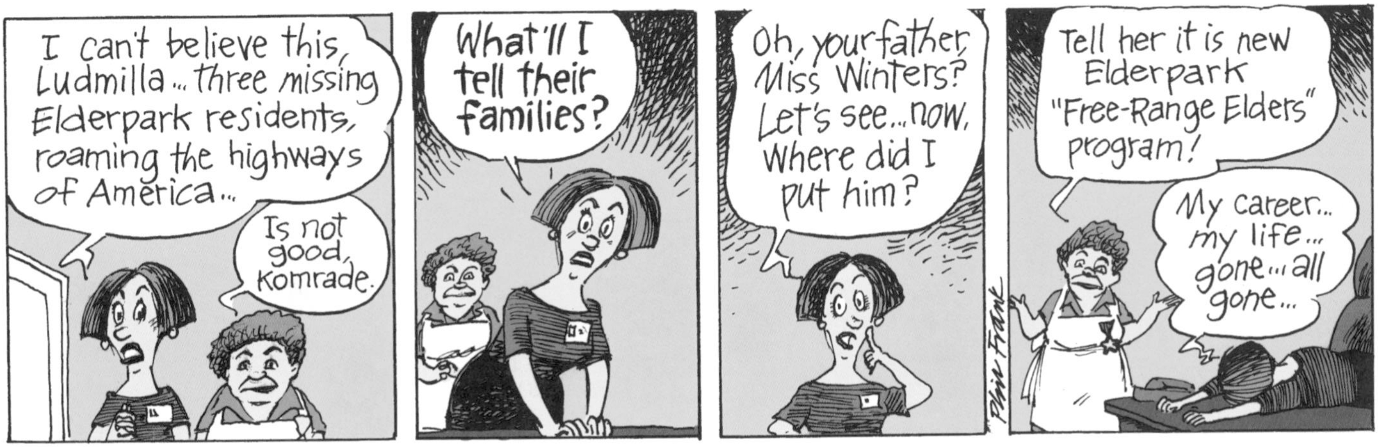
I can't believe this, Ludmilla... three missing Elderpark residents, roaming the highways of America...
Is not good, Komrade.
What'll I tell their families?
Oh, your father, Miss Winters? Let's see...now, Where did I put him?
Tell her it is new Elderpark "Free-Range Elders" program!
My career... my life... gone...all gone...

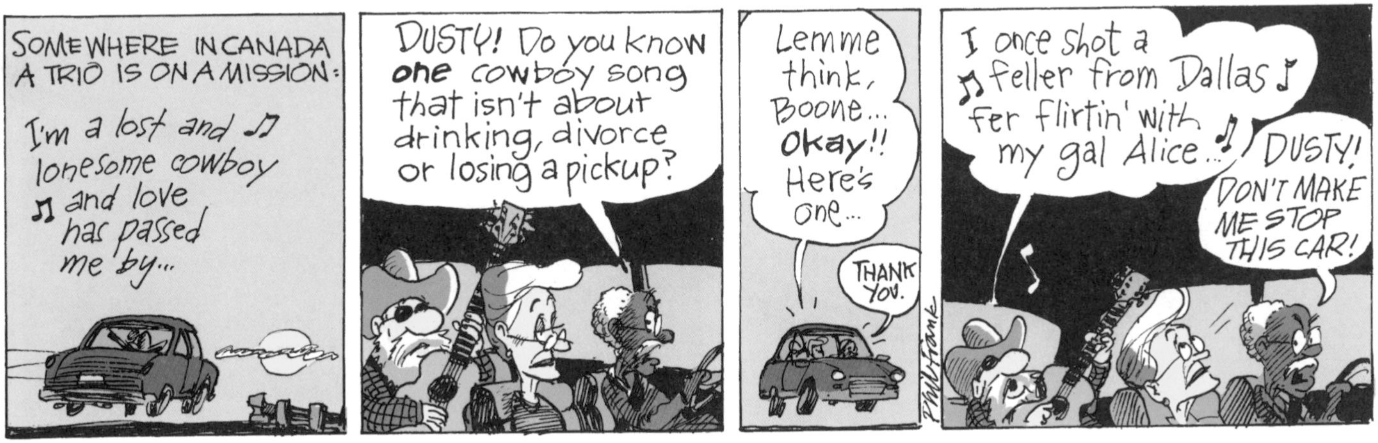
SOMEWHERE IN CANADA A TRIO IS ON A MISSION:
I'm a lost and ♫ lonesome cowboy ♫ and love has passed me by...
DUSTY! Do you know one cowboy song that isn't about drinking, divorce or losing a pickup?
Lemme think, Boone... Okay!! Here's one...
THANK YOU.
I once shot a ♫ feller from Dallas ♫ fer flirtin' with my gal Alice... ♫
DUSTY! DON'T MAKE ME STOP THIS CAR!

Elderberries
by Phil Frank and Joe Troise
San Ardo
Avenal
Parkfield
Adelaida
Whitley Gardens
Shandon
Creston
SAN LUIS OBISPO
Morro Bay
Los Osos
Santa Margarita
Pozo
California Valley
Los Padres
Nat'l. Forest
PANZA RANGE
Avila Beach
Shell Beach
Pismo Beach
Grover City
Arroyo Grande
Oceano
Nipomo
Guadalupe
Edna

So, Dusty... where are you dreaming about taking your rig on this sunny Sunday?
I'm thinkin' Pismo Beach! We could get a big bucket of clam chowder and some cold beers.
Then we could drive down to the beach.
We could all take off our shirts and grab a nap in the sand.
You do that, boys, and for sure someone is going to call the Beached Sea Mammal Rescue Squad!
PHIL FRANK

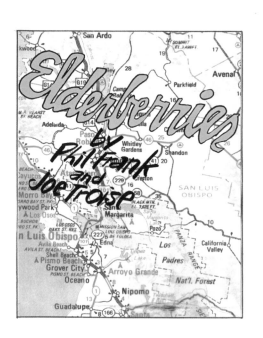

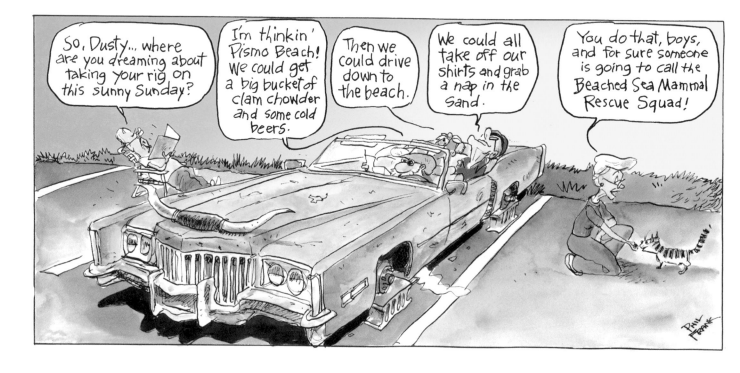

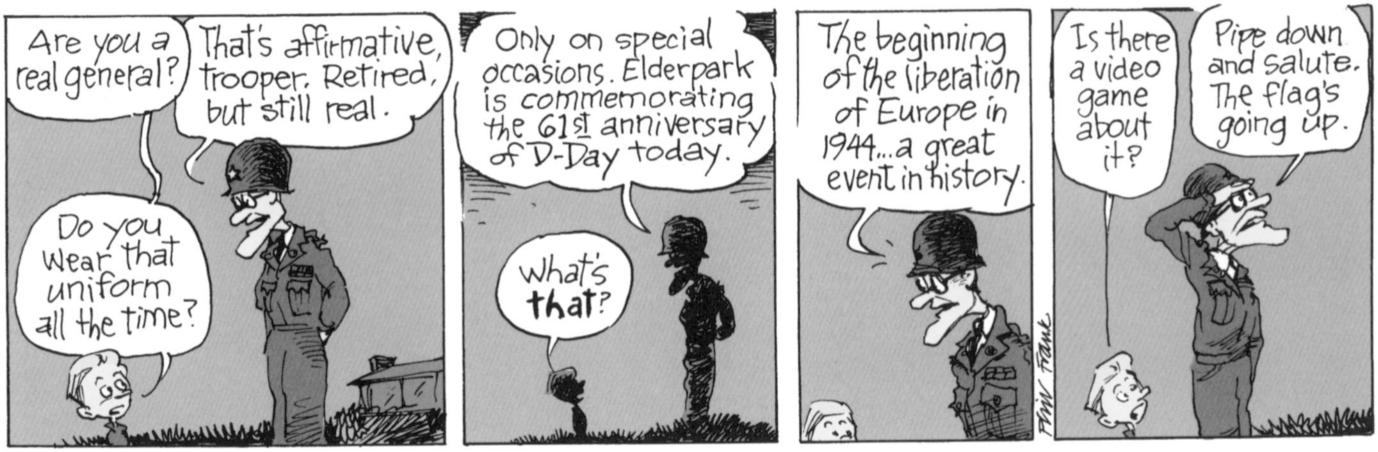
Are you a real general?
That's affirmative, trooper. Retired, but still real.
Do you wear that uniform all the time?
Only on special occasions. Elderpark is commemorating the 61st anniversary of D-Day today.
What's **that**?
The beginning of the liberation of Europe in 1944...a great event in history.
Is there a video game about it?
Pipe down and salute. The flag's going up.

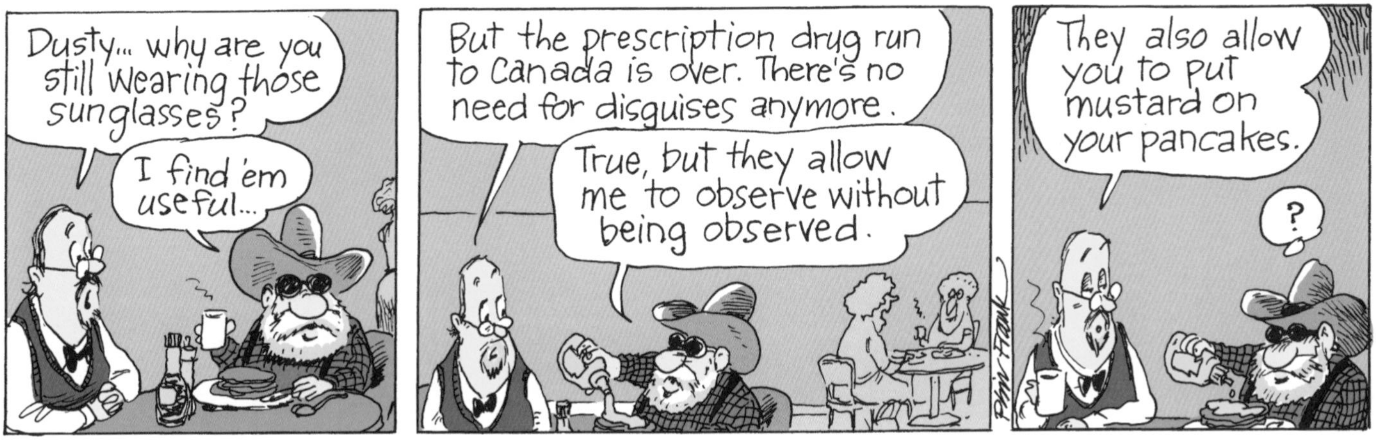
Dusty... why are you still wearing those sunglasses?
I find 'em useful...
But the prescription drug run to Canada is over. There's no need for disguises anymore.
True, but they allow me to observe without being observed.
They also allow you to put mustard on your pancakes.
?

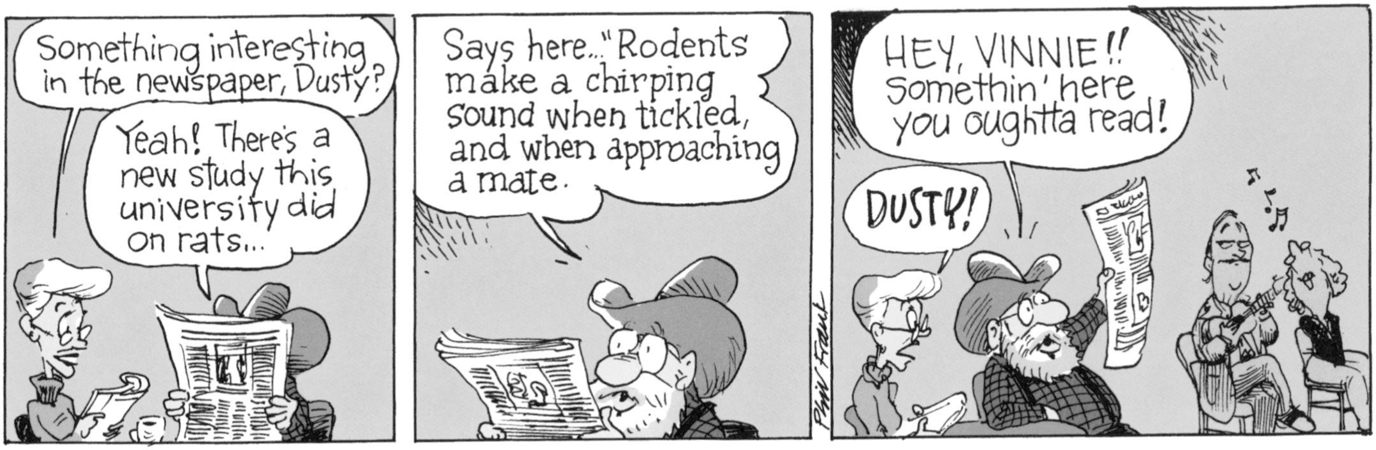
Something interesting in the newspaper, Dusty?
Yeah! There's a new study this university did on rats...
Says here..."Rodents make a chirping sound when tickled, and when approaching a mate.
HEY, VINNIE!! Somethin' here you oughtta read!
DUSTY!

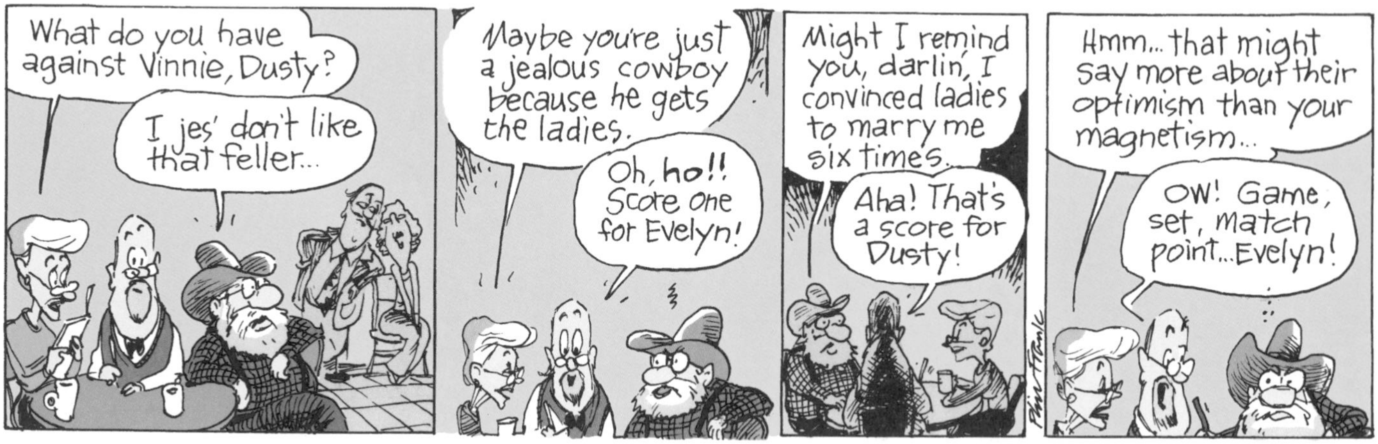
What do you have against Vinnie, Dusty?
I jes' don't like that feller...
Maybe you're just a jealous cowboy because he gets the ladies.
Oh, **ho!!** Score one for Evelyn!
Might I remind you, darlin', I convinced ladies to marry me six times.
Aha! That's a score for Dusty!
Hmm... that might say more about their optimism than your magnetism...
OW! Game, set, match point...Evelyn!
Phil Frank

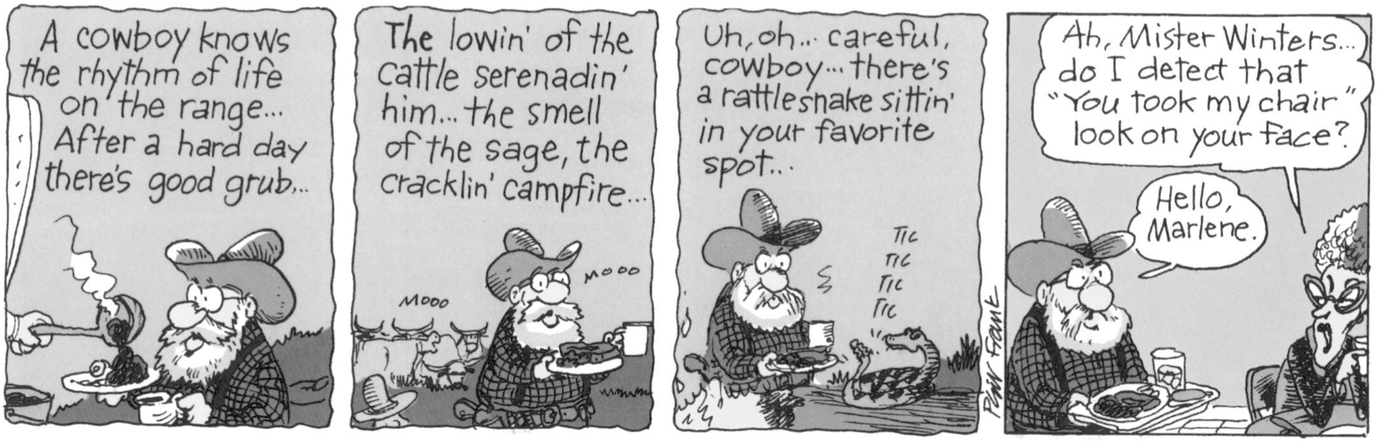
A cowboy knows the rhythm of life on the range... After a hard day there's good grub...
The lowin' of the cattle serenadin' him... the smell of the sage, the cracklin' campfire...
MOOO
MOOO
Uh, oh... careful, cowboy... there's a rattlesnake sittin' in your favorite spot...
TIC TIC TIC TIC
Phil Frank
Ah, Mister Winters... do I detect that "You took my chair" look on your face?
Hello, Marlene.

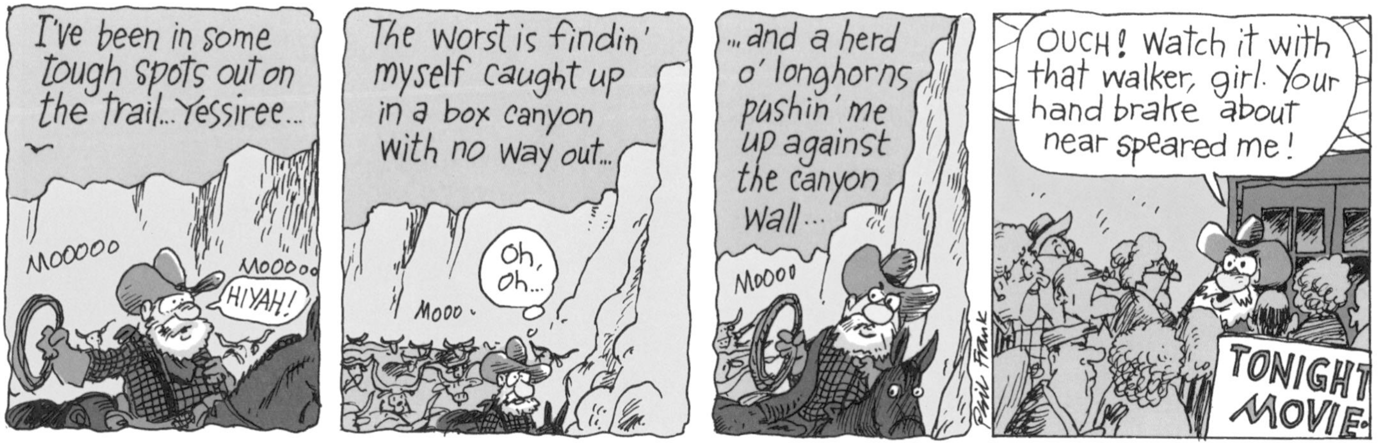
I've been in some tough spots out on the trail... Yessiree...
MOOOOO
MOOOOO
HIYAH!
The worst is findin' myself caught up in a box canyon with no way out...
Oh, oh...
MOOO
...and a herd o' longhorns pushin' me up against the canyon wall...
MOOOO
Phil Frank
OUCH! Watch it with that walker, girl. Your hand brake about near speared me!
TONIGHT MOVIE

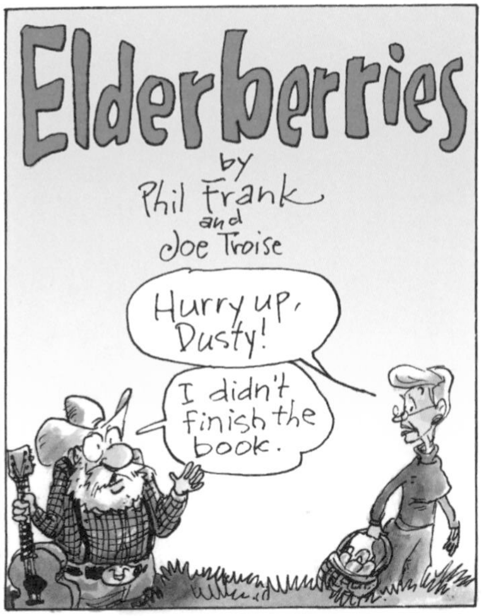
Elderberries
by
Phil Frank
and
Joe Troise
Hurry up, Dusty!
I didn't finish the book.

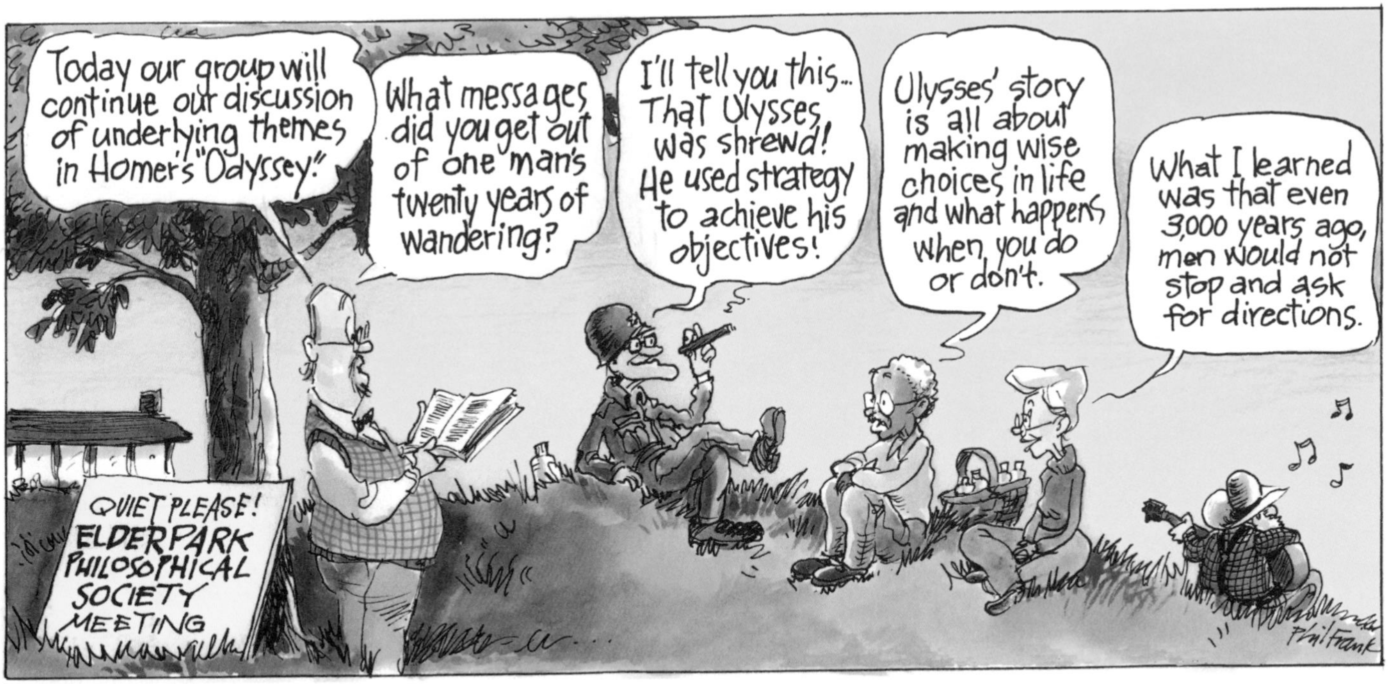
Today our group will continue our discussion of underlying themes in Homer's "Odyssey."
What messages did you get out of one man's twenty years of wandering?
I'll tell you this... That Ulysses was shrewd! He used strategy to achieve his objectives!
Ulysses' story is all about making wise choices in life and what happens when you do or don't.
What I learned was that even 3,000 years ago, men would not stop and ask for directions.
QUIET PLEASE! ELDERPARK PHILOSOPHICAL SOCIETY MEETING
Phil Frank

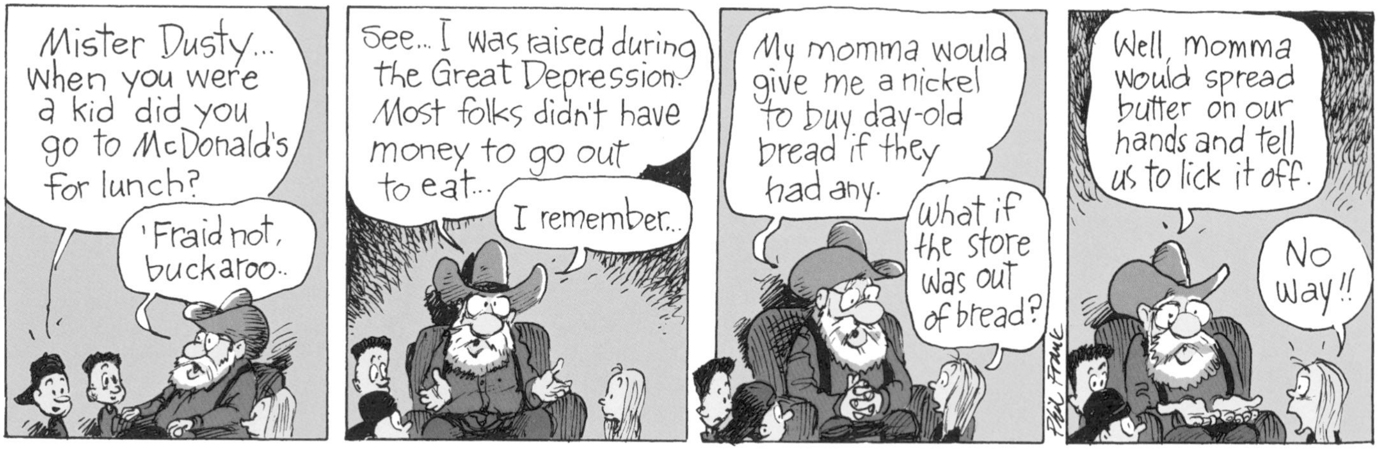
Mister Dusty... when you were a kid did you go to McDonald's for lunch?
'Fraid not, buckaroo..
See... I was raised during the Great Depression. Most folks didn't have money to go out to eat...
I remember...
My momma would give me a nickel to buy day-old bread if they had any.
What if the store was out of bread?
Well, momma would spread butter on our hands and tell us to lick it off.
No way!!

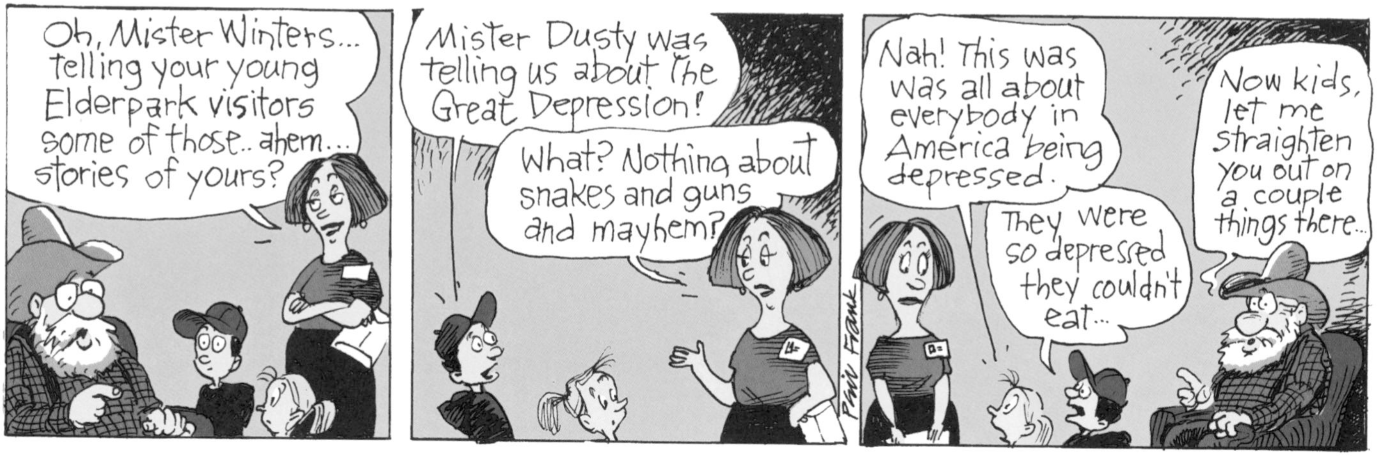
Oh, Mister Winters... telling your young Elderpark visitors some of those.. ahem... stories of yours?
Mister Dusty was telling us about the Great Depression!
What? Nothing about snakes and guns and mayhem?
Nah! This was was all about everybody in America being depressed.
They were so depressed they couldn't eat...
Now kids, let me straighten you out on a couple things there...

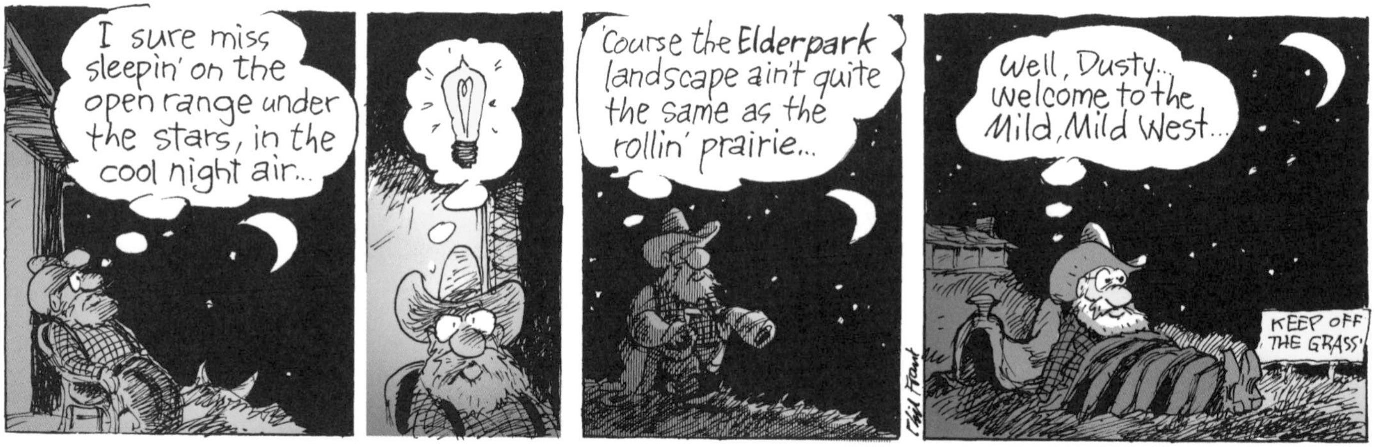
I sure miss sleepin' on the open range under the stars, in the cool night air...
'Course the Elderpark landscape ain't quite the same as the rollin' prairie...
Well, Dusty... welcome to the Mild, Mild West...
KEEP OFF THE GRASS!

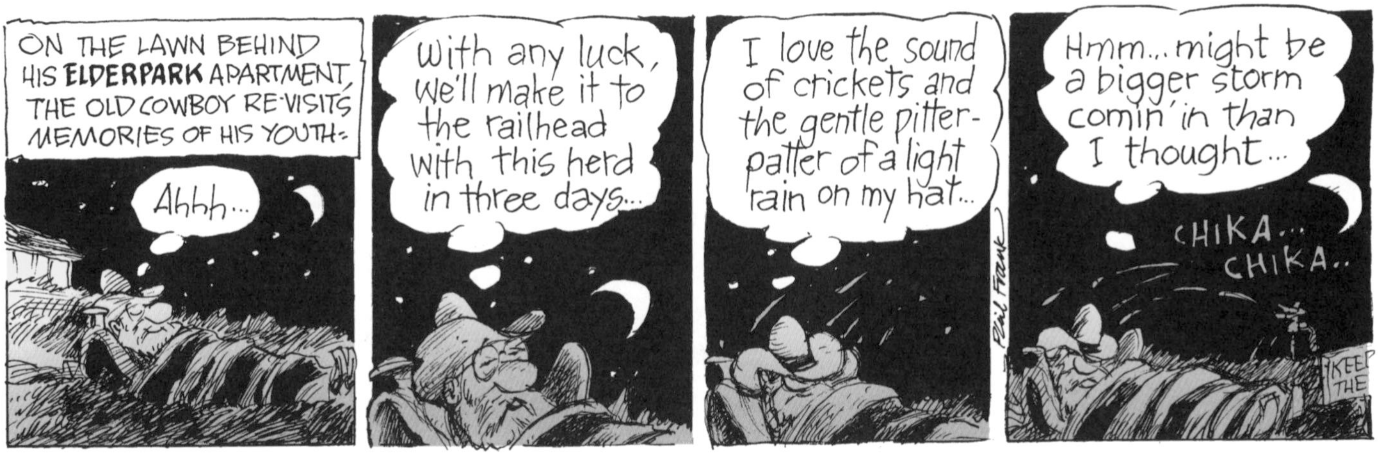
ON THE LAWN BEHIND HIS ELDERPARK APARTMENT, THE OLD COWBOY RE-VISITS MEMORIES OF HIS YOUTH-
Ahhh...
With any luck, we'll make it to the railhead with this herd in three days...
I love the sound of crickets and the gentle pitter-patter of a light rain on my hat...
Hmm... might be a bigger storm comin' in than I thought...
CHIKA... CHIKA...
KEEP THE

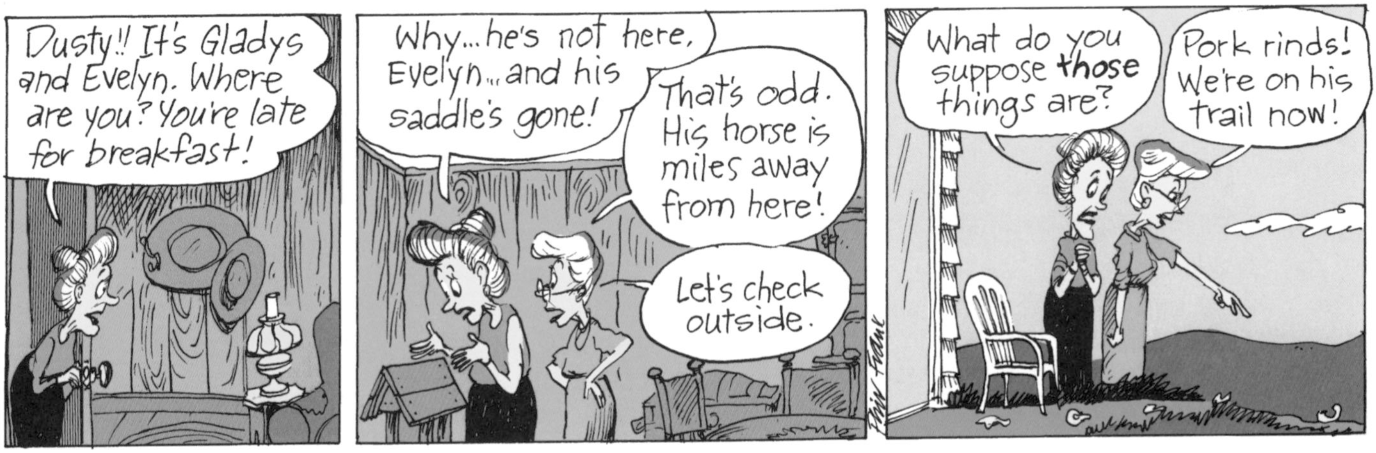
Dusty!! It's Gladys and Evelyn. Where are you? You're late for breakfast!
Why... he's not here, Evelyn... and his saddle's gone!
That's odd. His horse is miles away from here!
Let's check outside.
What do you suppose those things are?
Pork rinds! We're on his trail now!

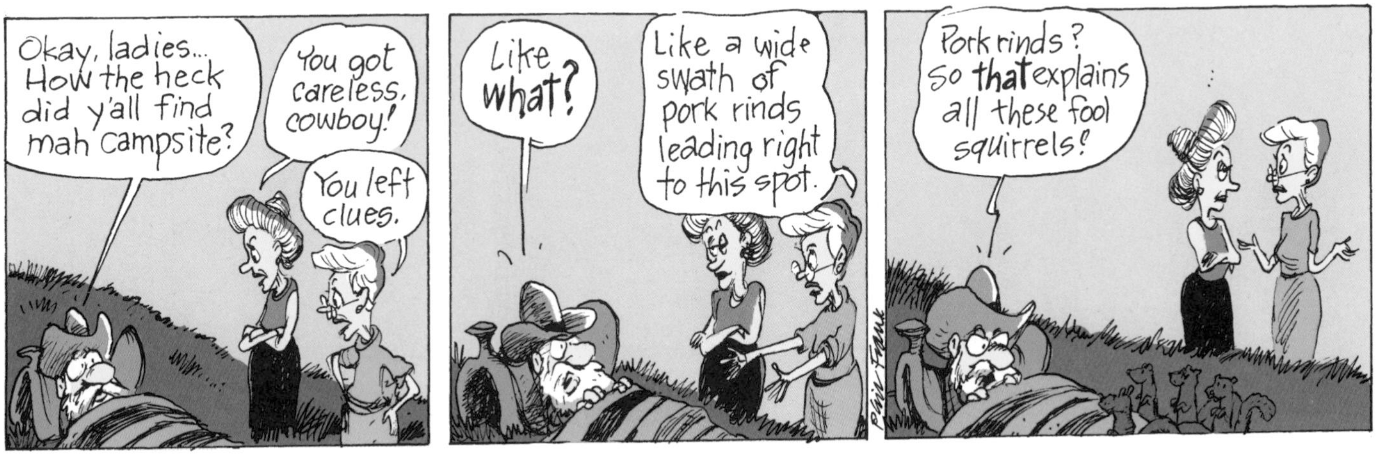
Okay, ladies... How the heck did y'all find mah campsite?
You got careless, cowboy!
You left clues.
Like what?
Like a wide swath of pork rinds leading right to this spot.
Pork rinds? So that explains all these fool squirrels?

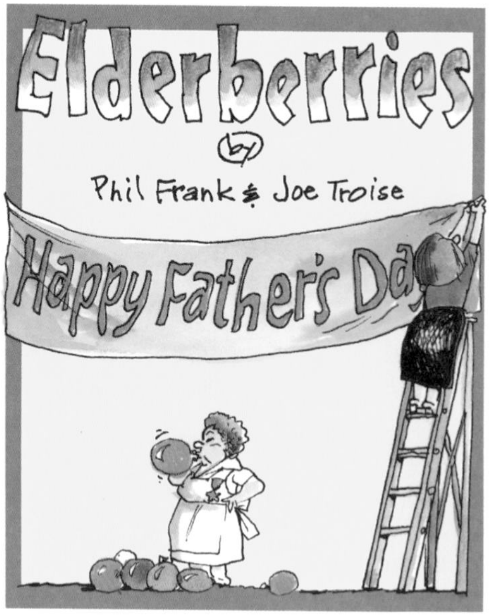
Elderberries
by
Phil Frank & Joe Troise
Happy Father's Da

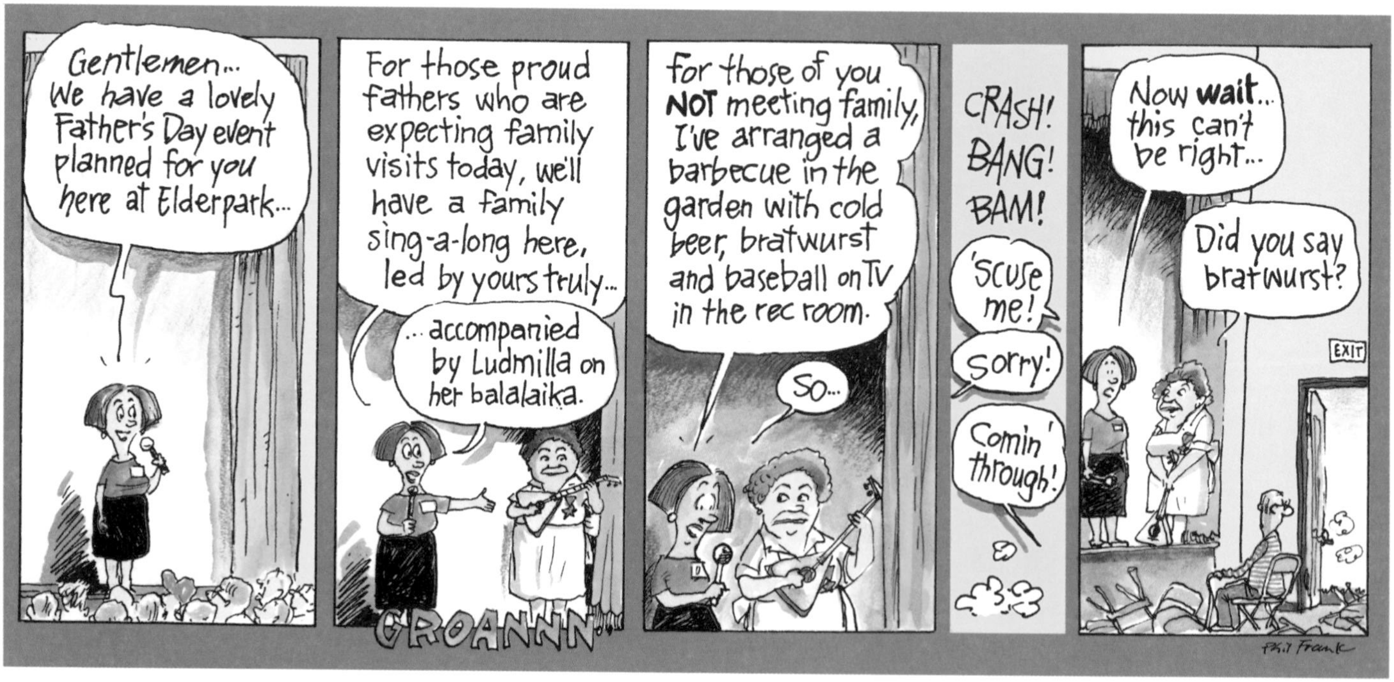
Gentlemen... We have a lovely Father's Day event planned for you here at Elderpark...
For those proud fathers who are expecting family visits today, we'll have a family sing-a-long here, led by yours truly...
...accompanied by Ludmilla on her balalaika.
GROANNN
For those of you NOT meeting family, I've arranged a barbecue in the garden with cold beer, bratwurst and baseball on TV in the rec room.
So...
CRASH! BANG! BAM!
'Scuse me!
Sorry!
Comin' through!
Now wait... this can't be right...
Did you say bratwurst?
EXIT
Phil Frank

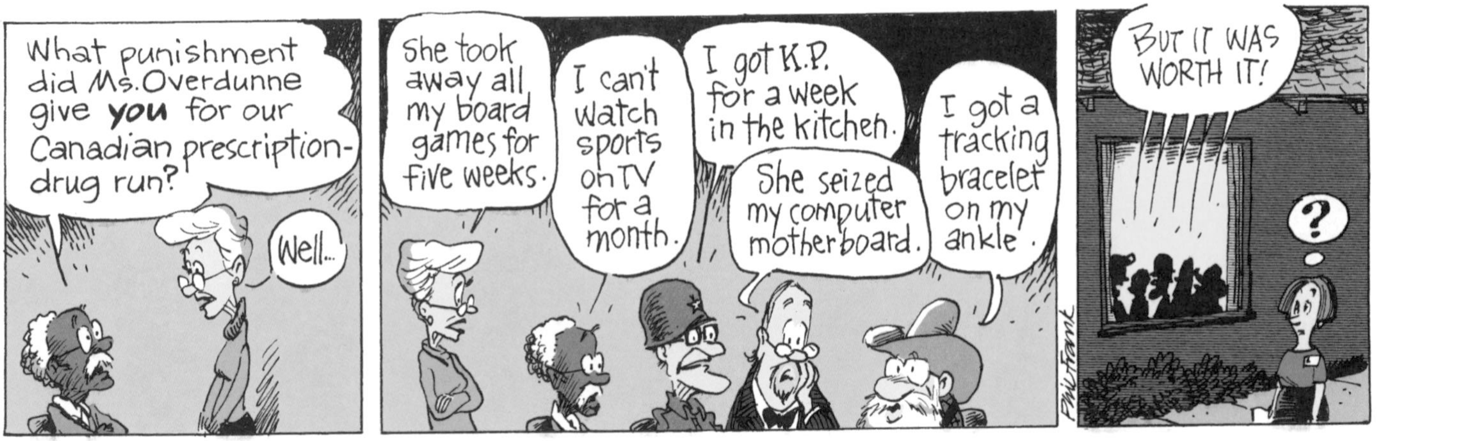
What punishment did Ms. Overdunne give **you** for our Canadian prescription-drug run?
Well...
She took away all my board games for five weeks.
I can't watch sports on TV for a month.
I got K.P. for a week in the kitchen.
She seized my computer motherboard.
I got a tracking bracelet on my ankle.
BUT IT WAS WORTH IT!
?

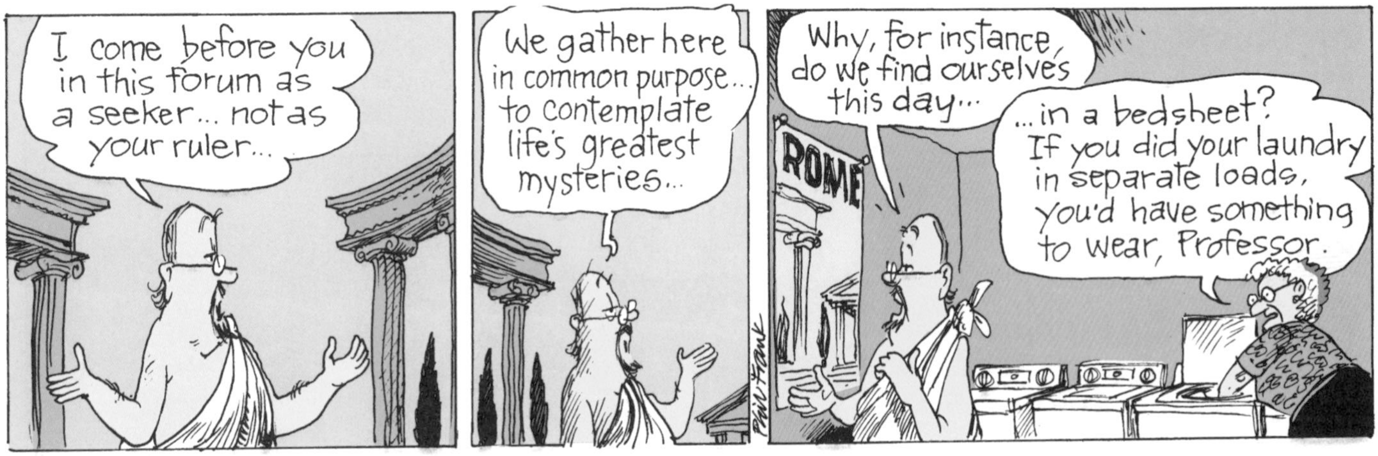
I come before you in this forum as a seeker... not as your ruler...
We gather here in common purpose... to contemplate life's greatest mysteries...
Why, for instance, do we find ourselves this day...
...in a bedsheet? If you did your laundry in separate loads, you'd have something to wear, Professor.
ROME

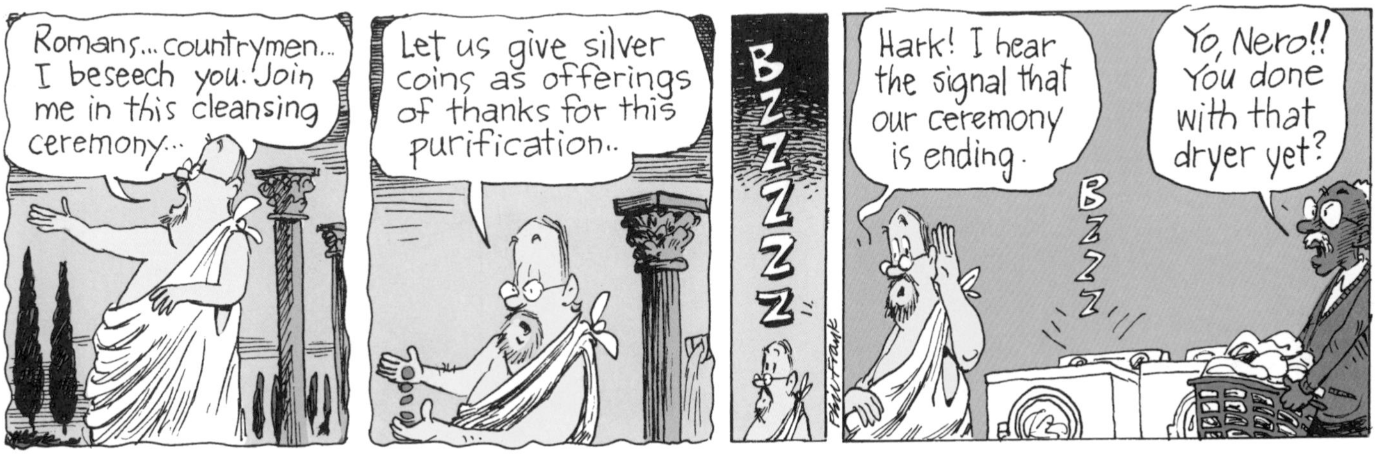
Romans... countrymen... I beseech you. Join me in this cleansing ceremony...
Let us give silver coins as offerings of thanks for this purification..
BZZZZ
Hark! I hear the signal that our ceremony is ending.
BZZZ
Yo, Nero!! You done with that dryer yet?

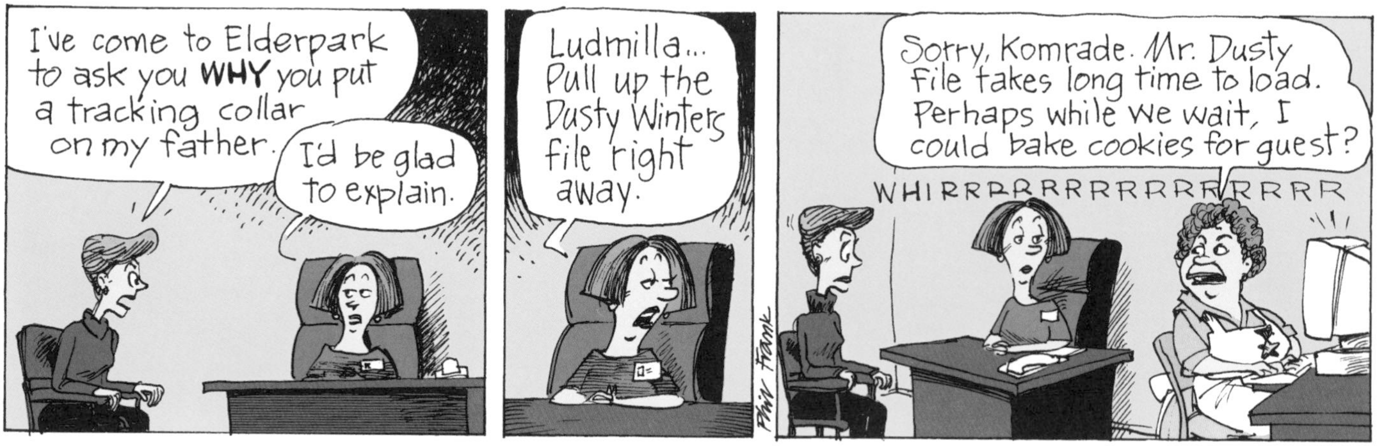
I've come to Elderpark to ask you **WHY** you put a tracking collar on my father.
I'd be glad to explain.
Ludmilla... Pull up the Dusty Winters file right away.
Sorry, Komrade. Mr. Dusty file takes long time to load. Perhaps while we wait, I could bake cookies for guest?
WHIRRRRRRRRRRRRRRRR
Phil Frank

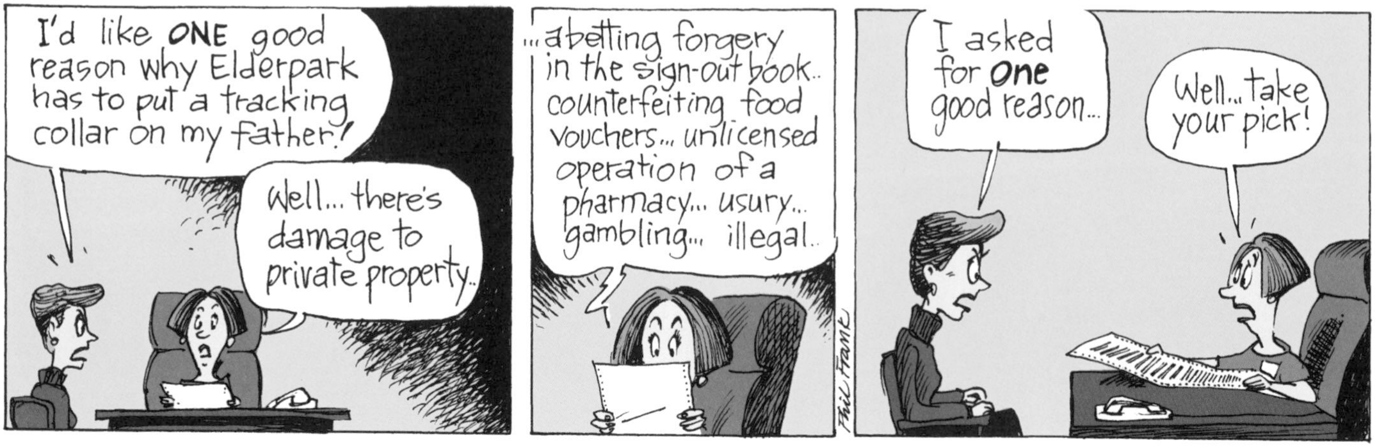
I'd like **ONE** good reason why Elderpark has to put a tracking collar on my father!
Well... there's damage to private property..
...abetting forgery in the sign-out book.. counterfeiting food vouchers... unlicensed operation of a pharmacy... usury... gambling... illegal..
Phil Frank
I asked for **One** good reason...
Well... take your pick!

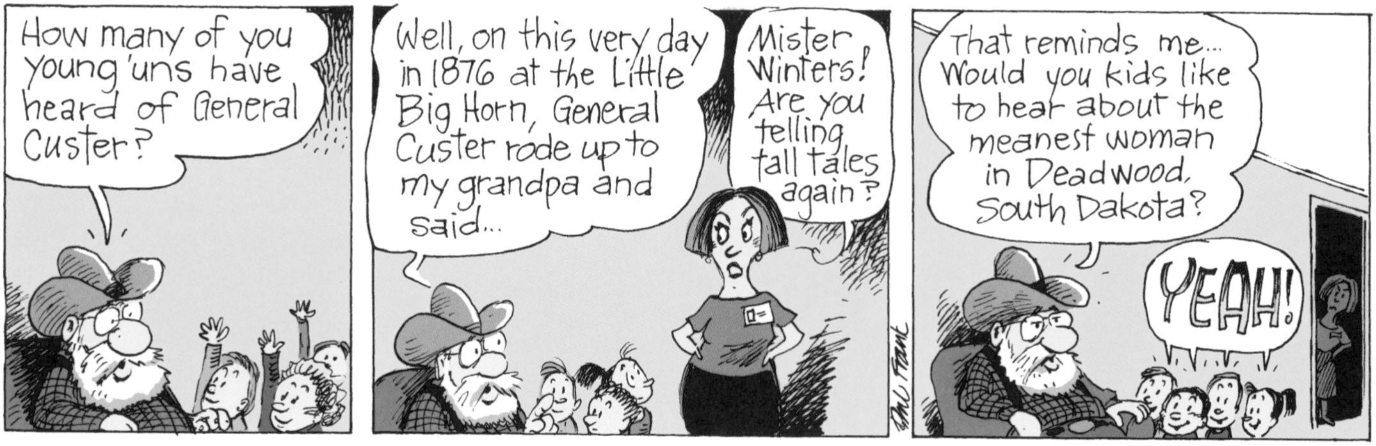
How many of you young 'uns have heard of General Custer?
Well, on this very day in 1876 at the Little Big Horn, General Custer rode up to my grandpa and said...
Mister Winters! Are you telling tall tales again?
Phil Frank
That reminds me... Would you kids like to hear about the meanest woman in Deadwood, South Dakota?
YEAH!

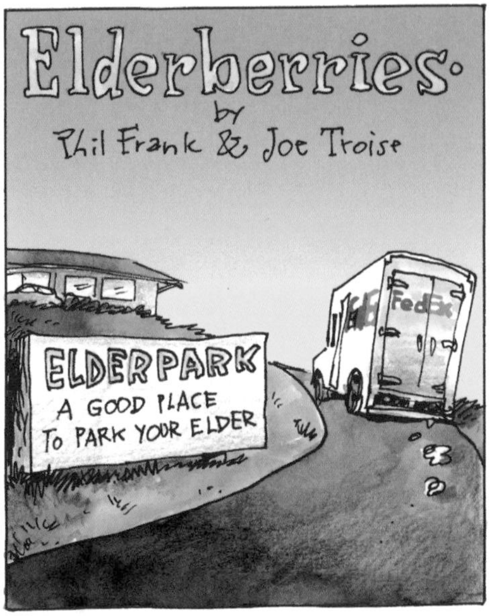
Elderberries
by
Phil Frank & Joe Troise
ELDER PARK
A GOOD PLACE TO PARK YOUR ELDER
FedEx

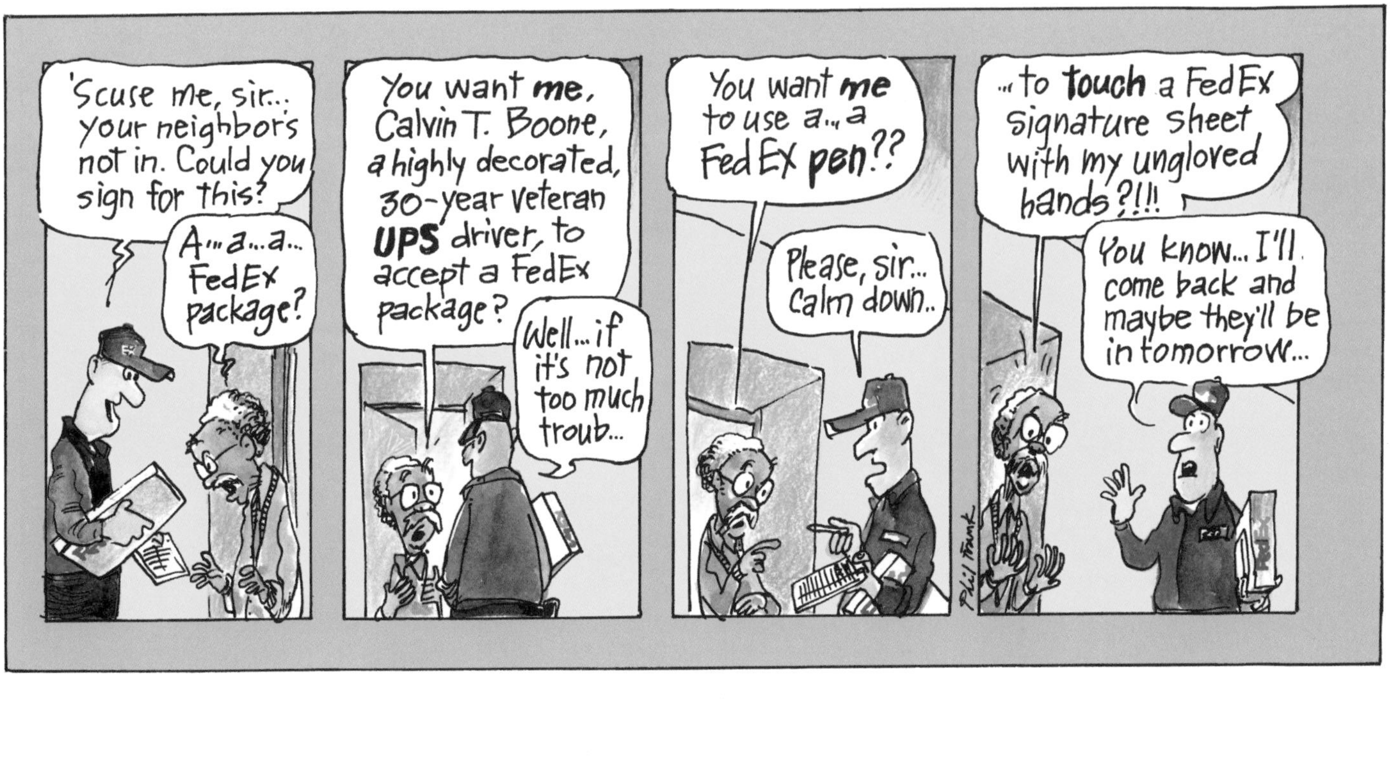
'Scuse me, sir... your neighbor's not in. Could you sign for this?
A... a... a... FedEx package?
You want me, Calvin T. Boone, a highly decorated, 30-year veteran UPS driver, to accept a FedEx package?
Well... if it's not too much troub...
You want me to use a... a FedEx pen??
Please, sir... calm down..
...to touch a FedEx signature sheet with my ungloved hands?!!!
You know... I'll come back and maybe they'll be in tomorrow...
Phil Frank

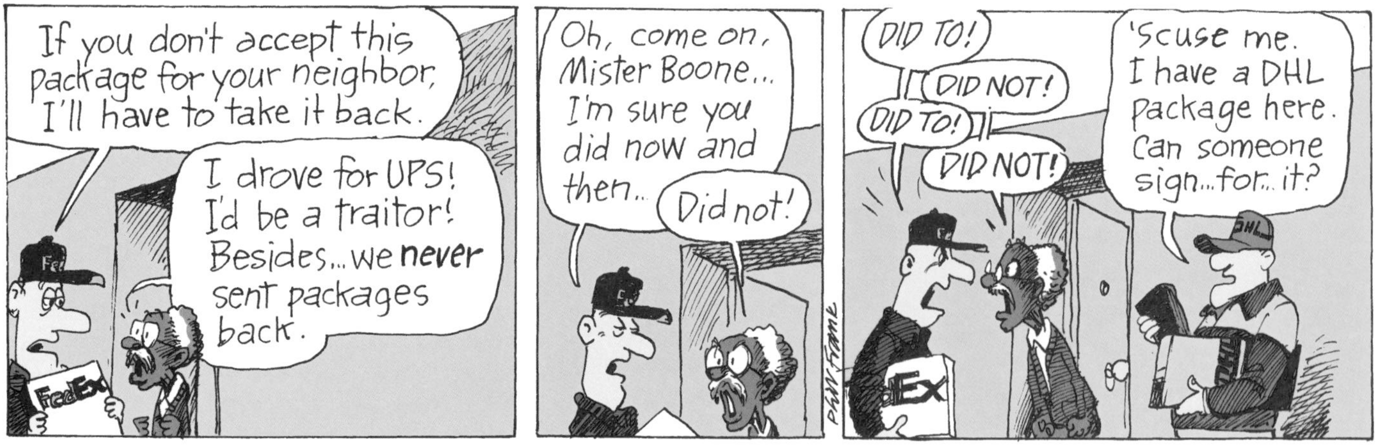
If you don't accept this package for your neighbor, I'll have to take it back.
I drove for UPS! I'd be a traitor! Besides... we **never** sent packages back.
FedEx
Oh, come on, Mister Boone... I'm sure you did now and then..
Did not!
DID TO!
DID NOT!
DID TO!
DID NOT!
'Scuse me. I have a DHL package here. Can someone sign...for...it?
DHL
FedEx

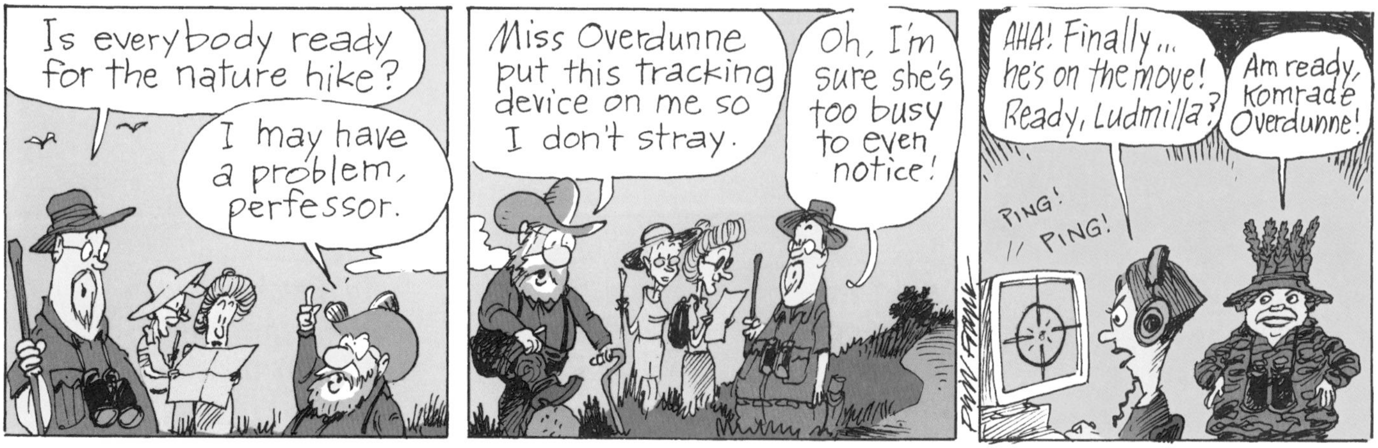
Is everybody ready for the nature hike?
I may have a problem, perfessor.
Miss Overdunne put this tracking device on me so I don't stray.
Oh, I'm sure she's too busy to even notice!
AHA! Finally... he's on the move! Ready, Ludmilla?
Am ready, Komrade Overdunne!
PING! PING!

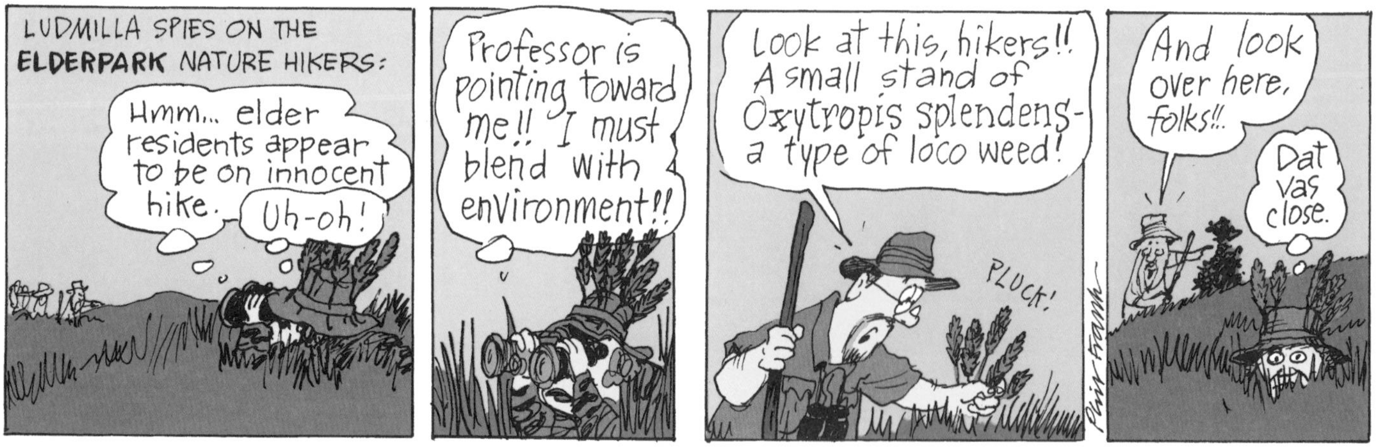
LUDMILLA SPIES ON THE **ELDERPARK** NATURE HIKERS:
Hmm... elder residents appear to be on innocent hike.
Uh-oh!
Professor is pointing toward me!! I must blend with environment!!
Look at this, hikers!! A small stand of Oxytropis splendens- a type of loco weed!
PLUCK!
And look over here, folks!!
Dat vas close.

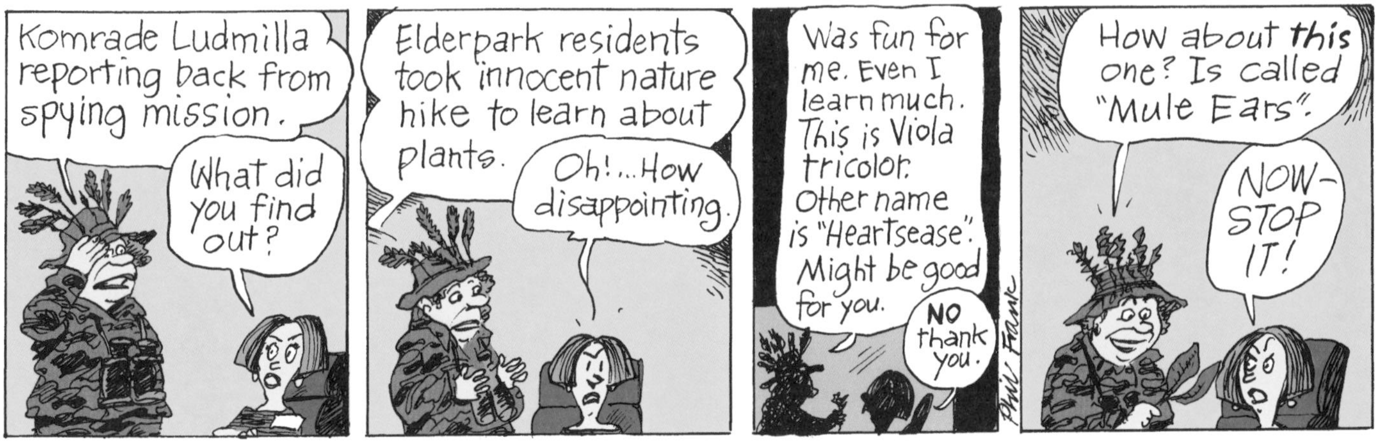
Komrade Ludmilla reporting back from spying mission.
What did you find out?
Elderpark residents took innocent nature hike to learn about plants.
Oh!...How disappointing.
Was fun for me. Even I learn much. This is Viola tricolor. Other name is "Heartsease". Might be good for you.
NO thank you.
How about this one? Is called "Mule Ears".
NOW-STOP IT!

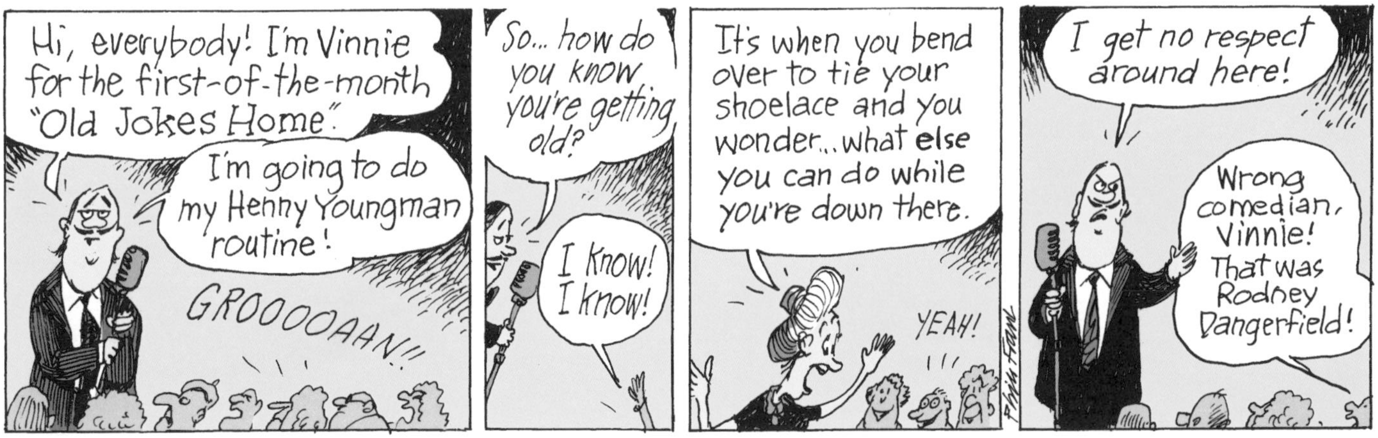
Hi, everybody! I'm Vinnie for the first-of-the-month "Old Jokes Home".
I'm going to do my Henny Youngman routine!
GROOOOAAN!!
So... how do you know you're getting old?
I know! I know!
It's when you bend over to tie your shoelace and you wonder... what else you can do while you're down there.
YEAH!
I get no respect around here!
Wrong comedian, Vinnie! That was Rodney Dangerfield!

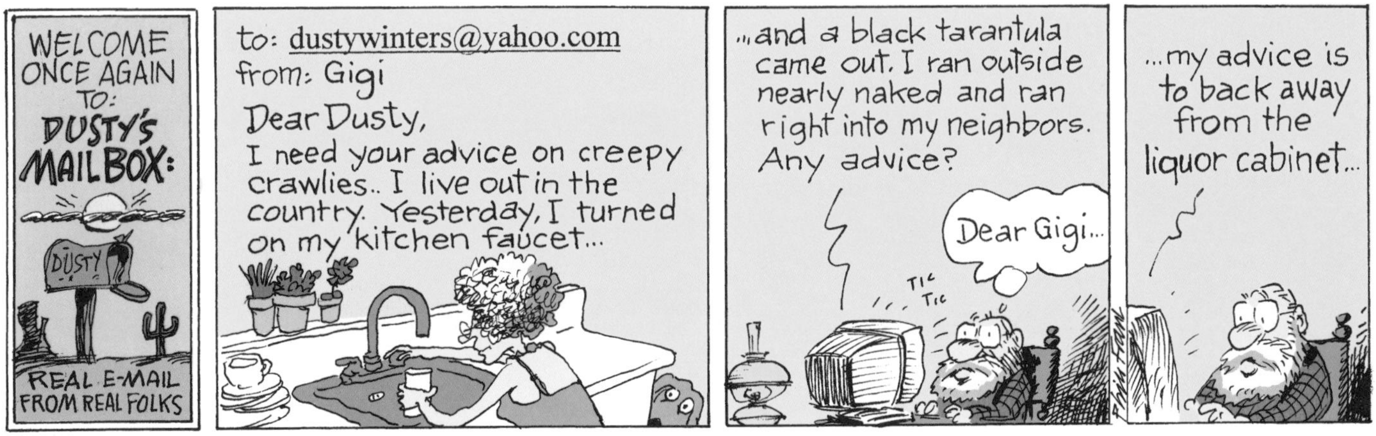
WELCOME ONCE AGAIN TO: DUSTY'S MAILBOX:
DUSTY
REAL E-MAIL FROM REAL FOLKS
to: dustywinters@yahoo.com
from: Gigi
Dear Dusty,
I need your advice on creepy crawlies.. I live out in the country. Yesterday, I turned on my kitchen faucet...
...and a black tarantula came out. I ran outside nearly naked and ran right into my neighbors. Any advice?
Dear Gigi...
TIC TIC
...my advice is to back away from the liquor cabinet...

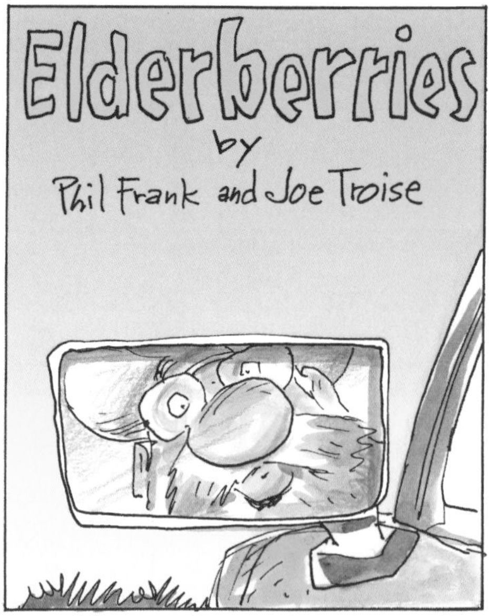
Elderberries
by
Phil Frank and Joe Troise

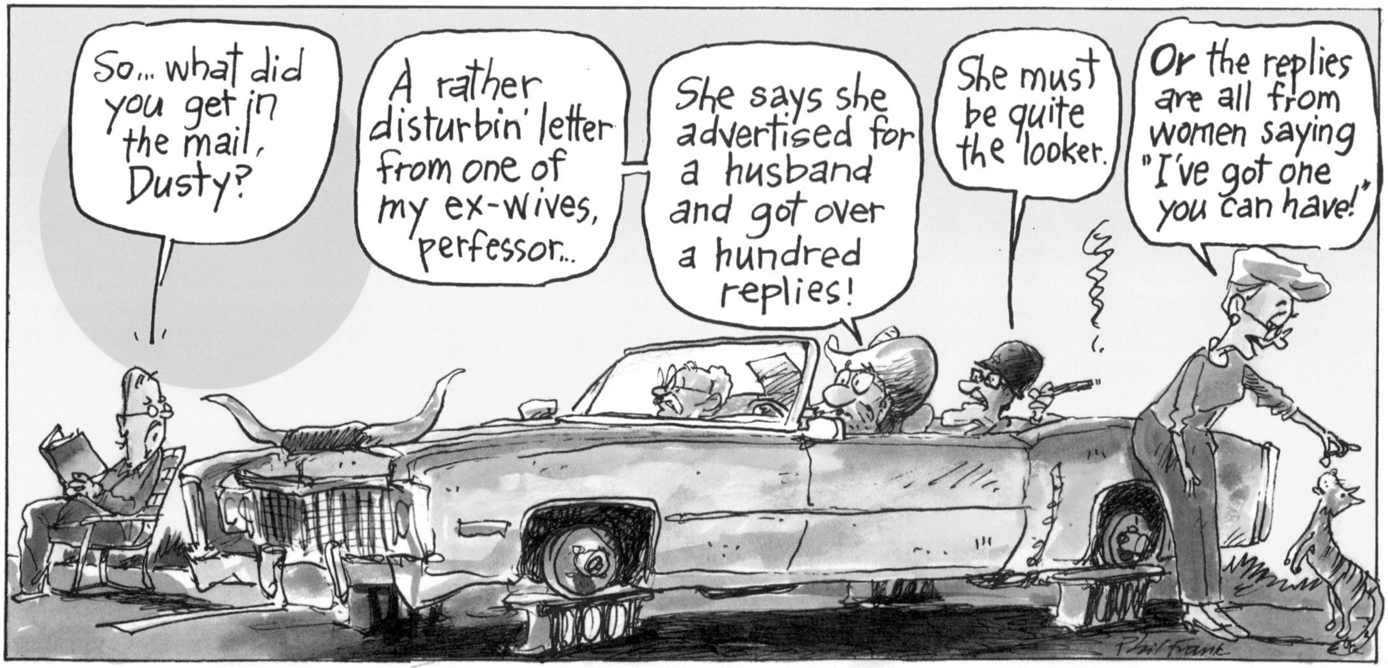
So... what did you get in the mail, Dusty?
A rather disturbin' letter from one of my ex-wives, perfessor...
She says she advertised for a husband and got over a hundred replies!
She must be quite the looker.
Or the replies are all from women saying "I've got one you can have!"
Phil Frank

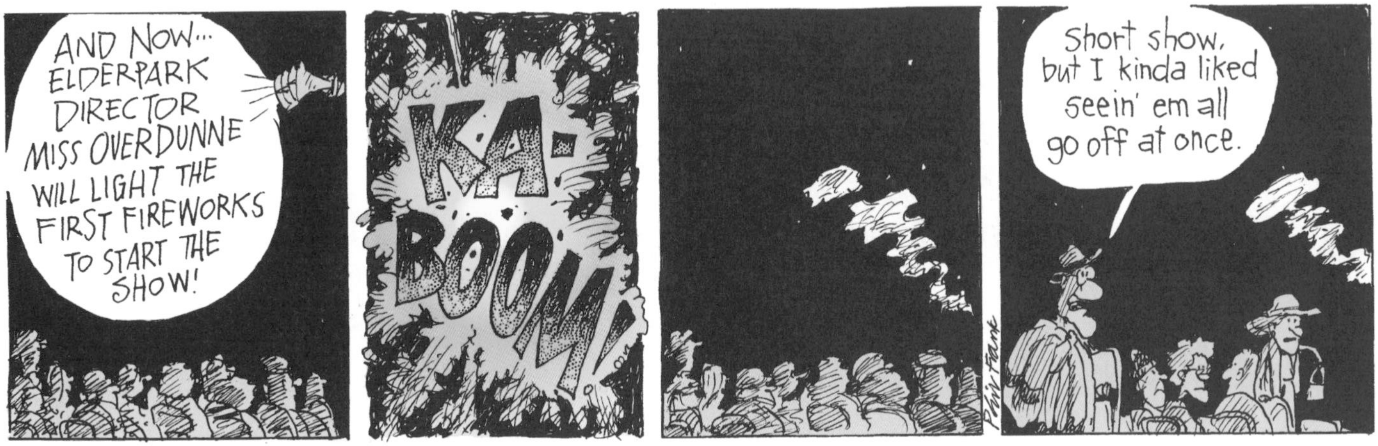
AND NOW... ELDERPARK DIRECTOR MISS OVERDUNNE WILL LIGHT THE FIRST FIREWORKS TO START THE SHOW!
KA-BOOM!
Short show, but I kinda liked seein' em all go off at once.

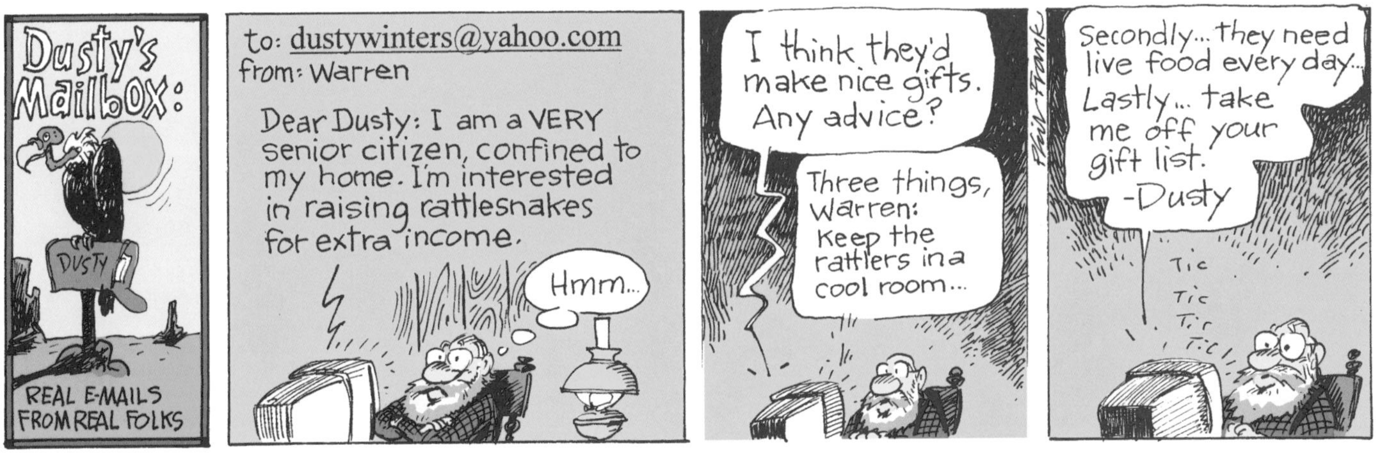
Dusty's Mailbox:
DUSTY
REAL E-MAILS FROM REAL FOLKS
to: dustywinters@yahoo.com
from: Warren
Dear Dusty: I am a VERY senior citizen, confined to my home. I'm interested in raising rattlesnakes for extra income.
Hmm...
I think they'd make nice gifts. Any advice?
Three things, Warren: Keep the rattlers in a cool room...
Secondly... they need live food every day... Lastly... take me off your gift list. -Dusty
Tic
Tic

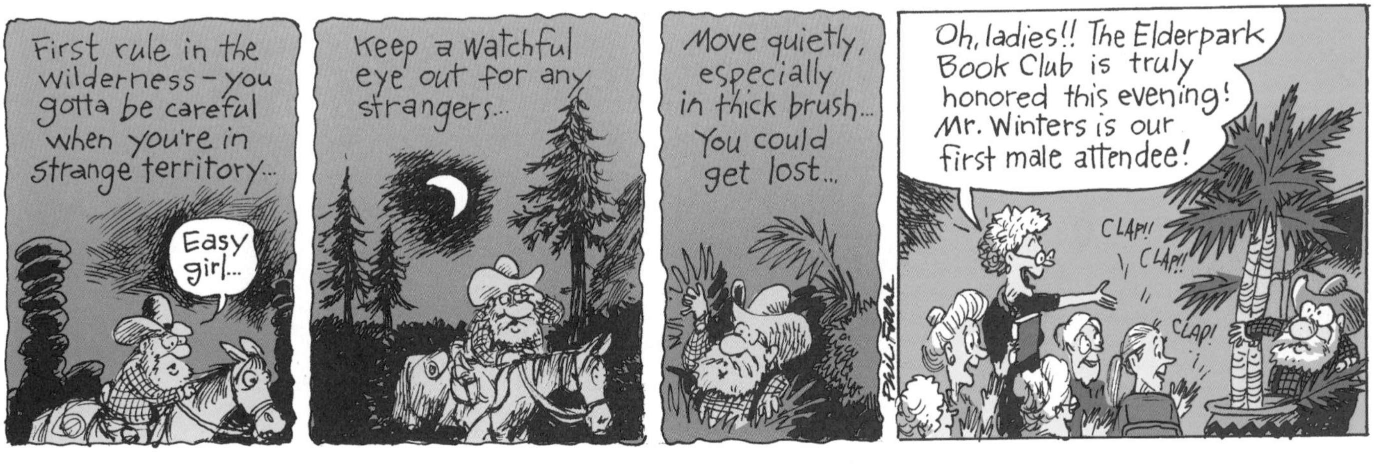
First rule in the wilderness - you gotta be careful when you're in strange territory...
Easy girl...
Keep a watchful eye out for any strangers...
Move quietly, especially in thick brush... You could get lost...
Oh, ladies!! The Elderpark Book Club is truly honored this evening! Mr. Winters is our first male attendee!
CLAP!!
CLAP!!
CLAP!

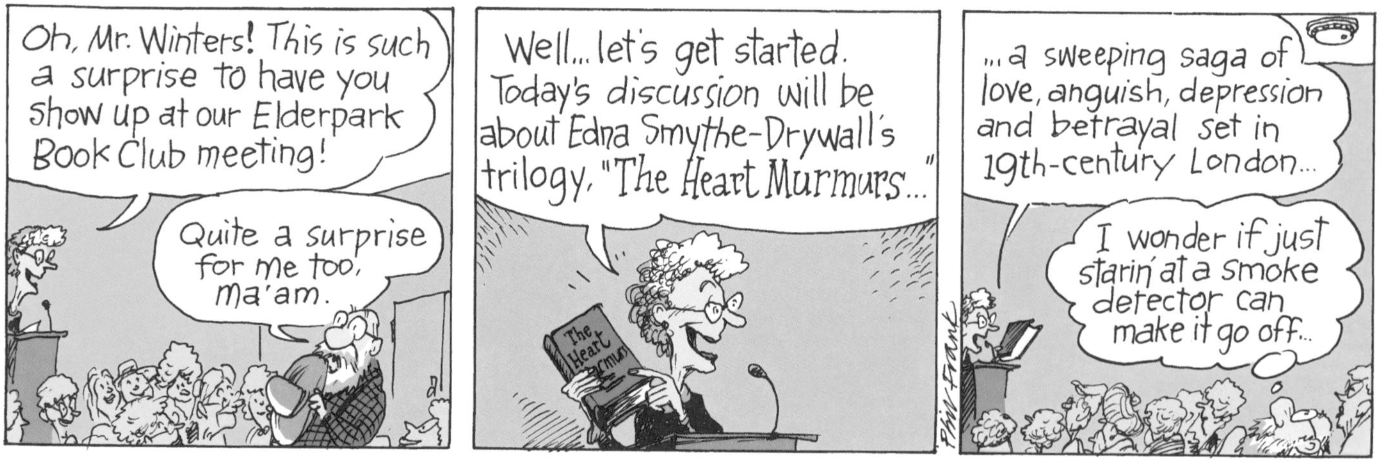
Oh, Mr. Winters! This is such a surprise to have you show up at our Elderpark Book Club meeting!
Quite a surprise for me too, ma'am.
Well... let's get started. Today's discussion will be about Edna Smythe-Drywall's trilogy, "The Heart Murmurs..."
...a sweeping saga of love, anguish, depression and betrayal set in 19th-century London...
I wonder if just starin' at a smoke detector can make it go off...

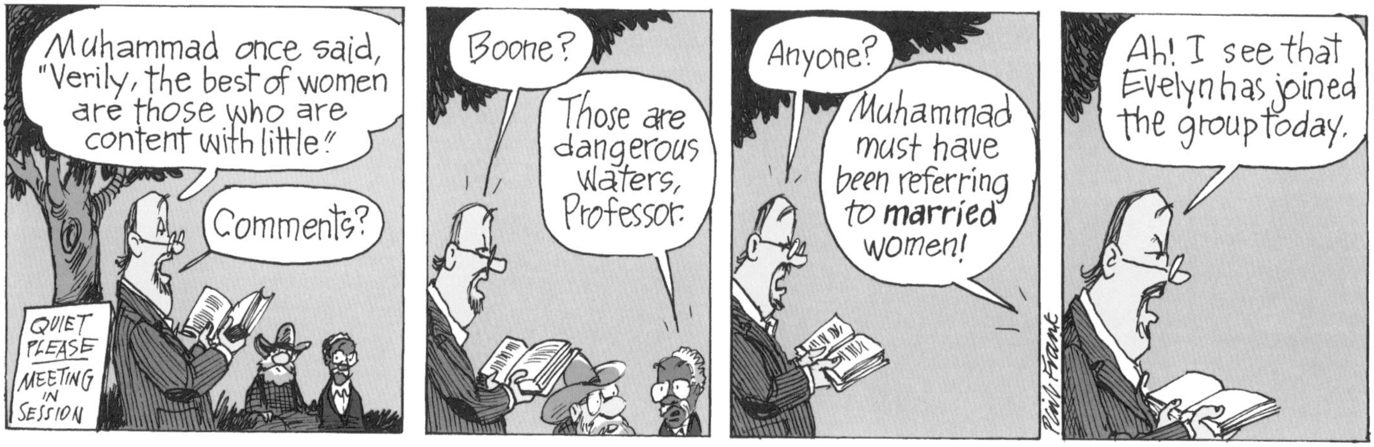
Muhammad once said, "Verily, the best of women are those who are content with little."
Comments?
QUIET PLEASE MEETING IN SESSION
Boone?
Those are dangerous waters, Professor.
Anyone?
Muhammad must have been referring to **married** women!
Ah! I see that Evelyn has joined the group today.

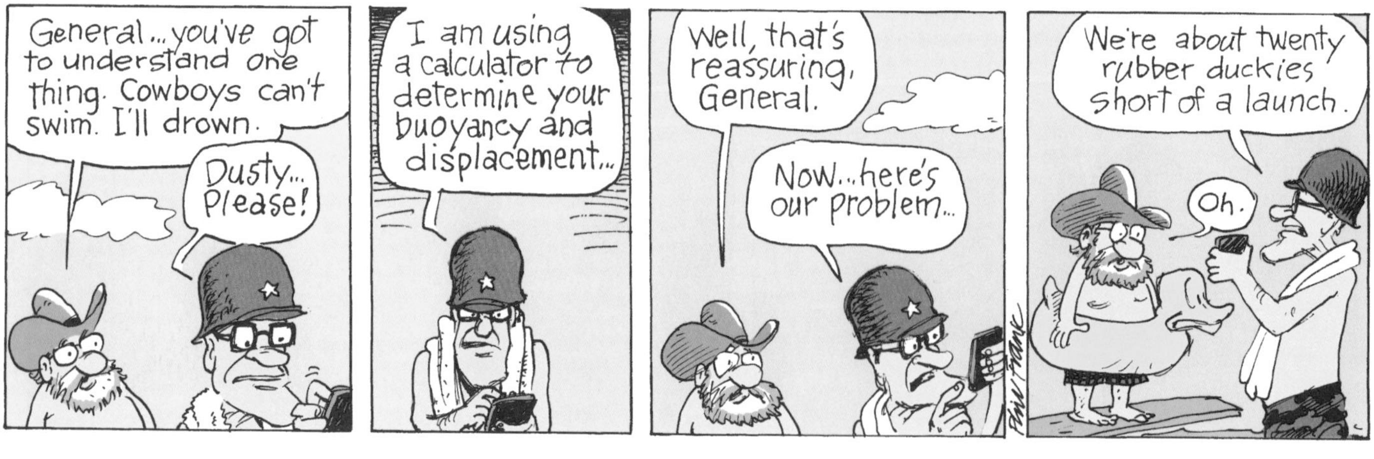
General... you've got to understand one thing. Cowboys can't swim. I'll drown.
Dusty... Please!
I am using a calculator to determine your buoyancy and displacement...
Well, that's reassuring, General.
Now... here's our problem...
We're about twenty rubber duckies short of a launch.
Oh.

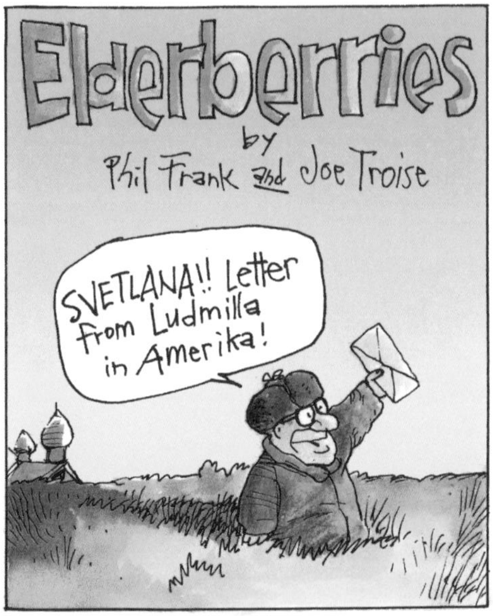
Elderberries
by
Phil Frank and Joe Troise
SVETLANA!! Letter from Ludmilla in Amerika!

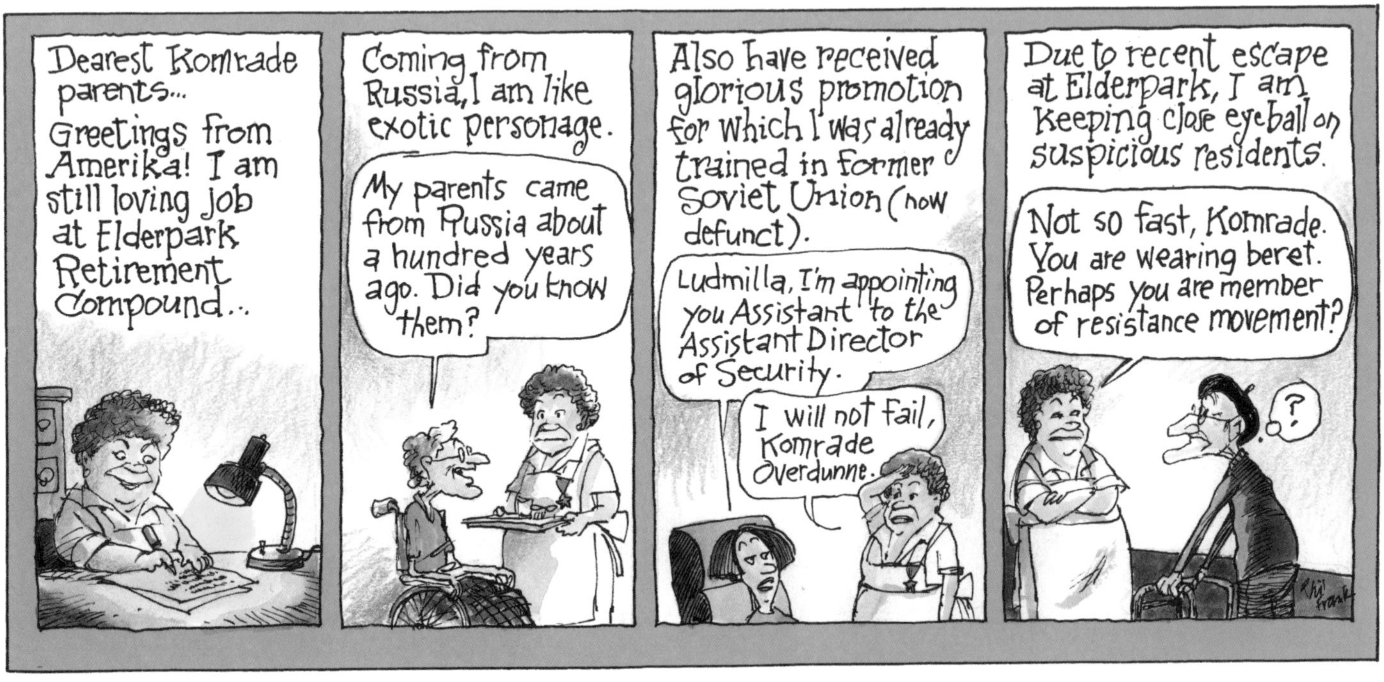
Dearest Komrade parents...
Greetings from Amerika! I am still loving job at Elderpark Retirement Compound...
Coming from Russia, I am like exotic personage.
My parents came from Russia about a hundred years ago. Did you know them?
Also have received glorious promotion for which I was already trained in former Soviet Union (now defunct).
Ludmilla, I'm appointing you Assistant to the Assistant Director of Security.
I will not fail, Komrade Overdunne.
Due to recent escape at Elderpark, I am keeping close eyeball on suspicious residents.
Not so fast, Komrade. You are wearing beret. Perhaps you are member of resistance movement?
?
Phil Frank

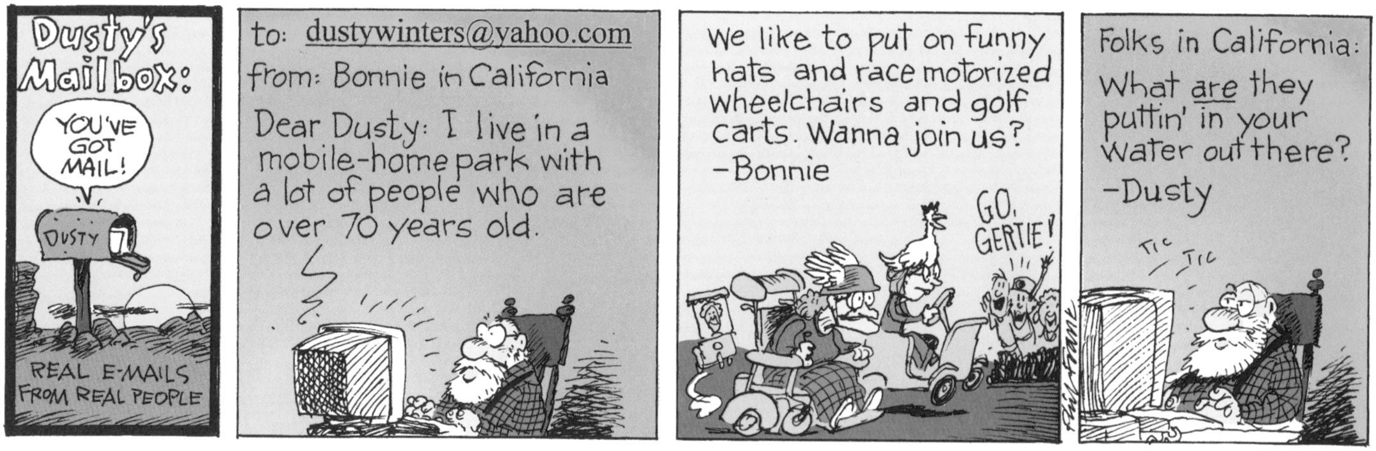
Dusty's Mailbox:
YOU'VE GOT MAIL!
DUSTY
REAL E-MAILS FROM REAL PEOPLE
to: dustywinters@yahoo.com
from: Bonnie in California
Dear Dusty: I live in a mobile-home park with a lot of people who are over 70 years old.
We like to put on funny hats and race motorized wheelchairs and golf carts. Wanna join us? -Bonnie
GO, GERTIE!
Folks in California:
What are they puttin' in your water out there?
-Dusty
TIC TIC

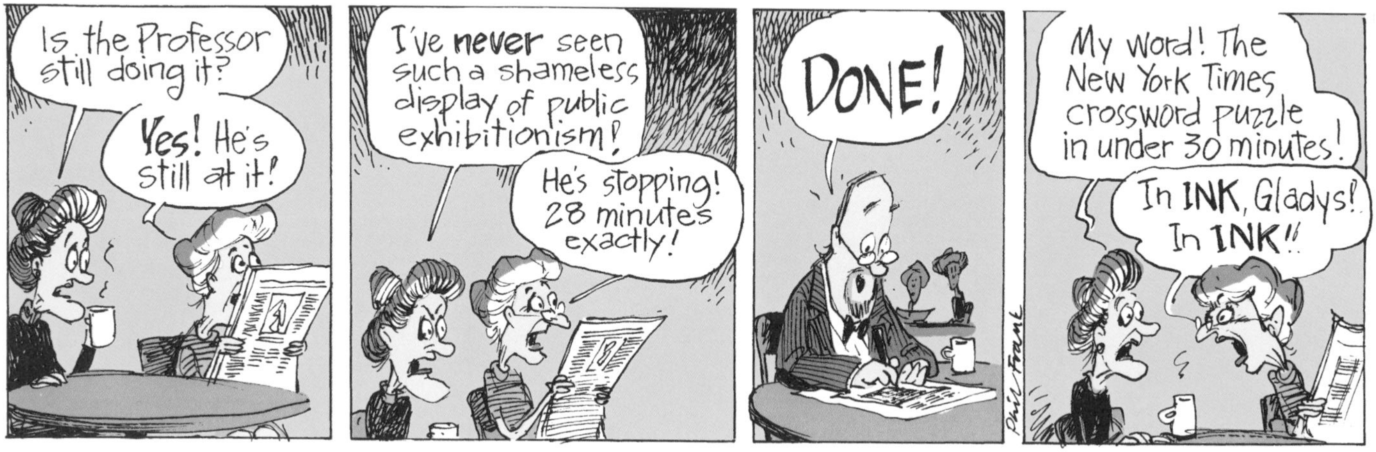
Is the Professor still doing it?
Yes! He's still at it!
I've never seen such a shameless display of public exhibitionism!
He's stopping! 28 minutes exactly!
DONE!
My word! The New York Times crossword puzzle in under 30 minutes!
In INK, Gladys! In INK!!

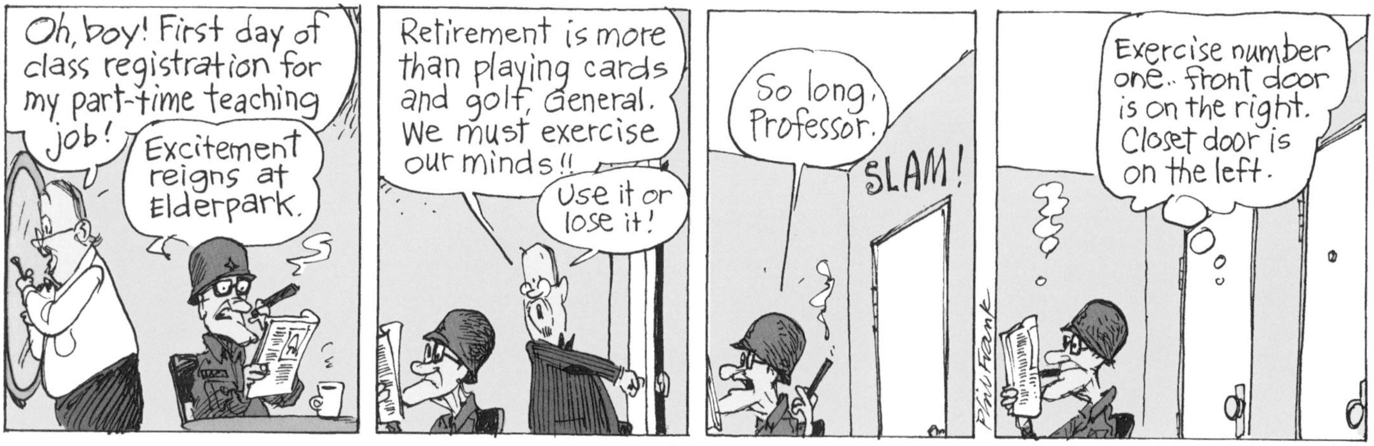
Oh, boy! First day of class registration for my part-time teaching job!
Excitement reigns at Elderpark.
Retirement is more than playing cards and golf, General. We must exercise our minds!!
Use it or lose it!
So long, Professor.
SLAM!
Exercise number one.. front door is on the right. Closet door is on the left.

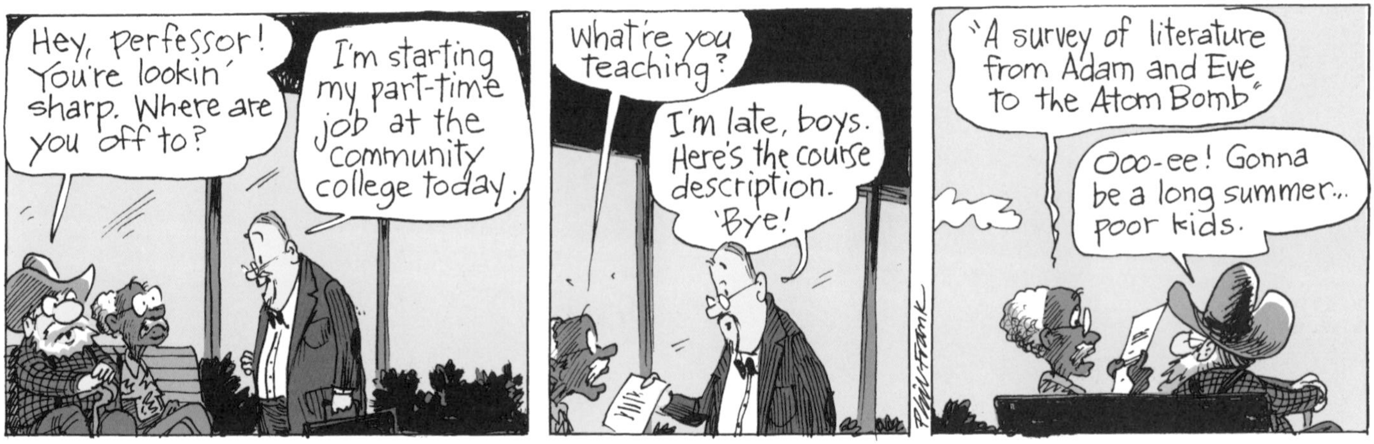
Hey, perfessor! You're lookin' sharp. Where are you off to?
I'm starting my part-time job at the community college today.
What're you teaching?
I'm late, boys. Here's the course description. 'Bye!
"A survey of literature from Adam and Eve to the Atom Bomb"
Ooo-ee! Gonna be a long summer... poor kids.

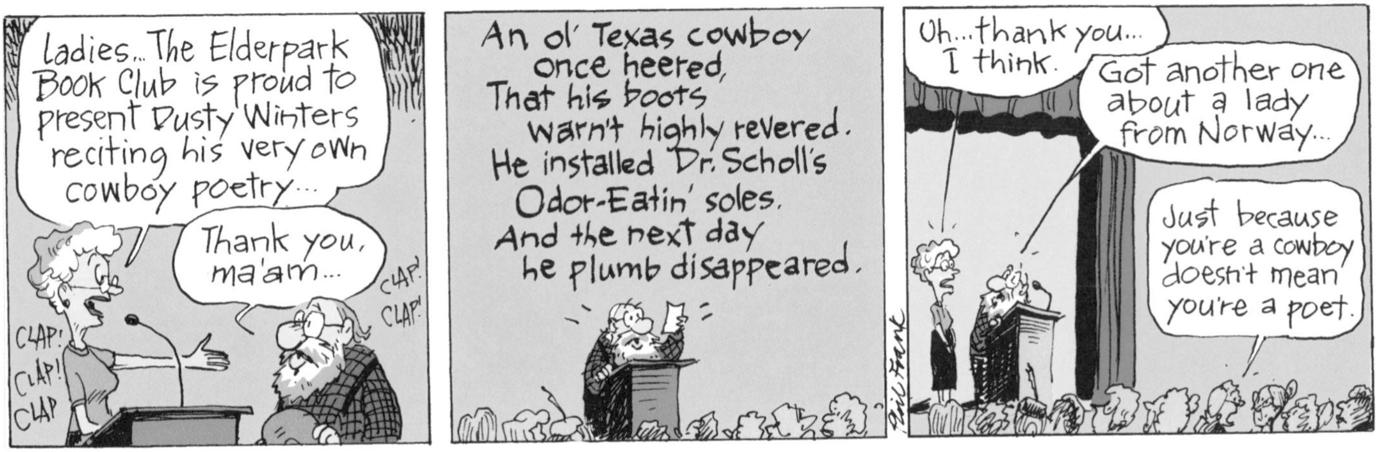
Ladies... The Elderpark Book Club is proud to present Dusty Winters reciting his very own cowboy poetry...
Thank you, ma'am...
CLAP! CLAP! CLAP
CLAP! CLAP!
An ol' Texas cowboy once heered, That his boots warn't highly revered. He installed Dr. Scholl's Odor-Eatin' soles. And the next day he plumb disappeared.
Oh... thank you... I think.
Got another one about a lady from Norway...
Just because you're a cowboy doesn't mean you're a poet.

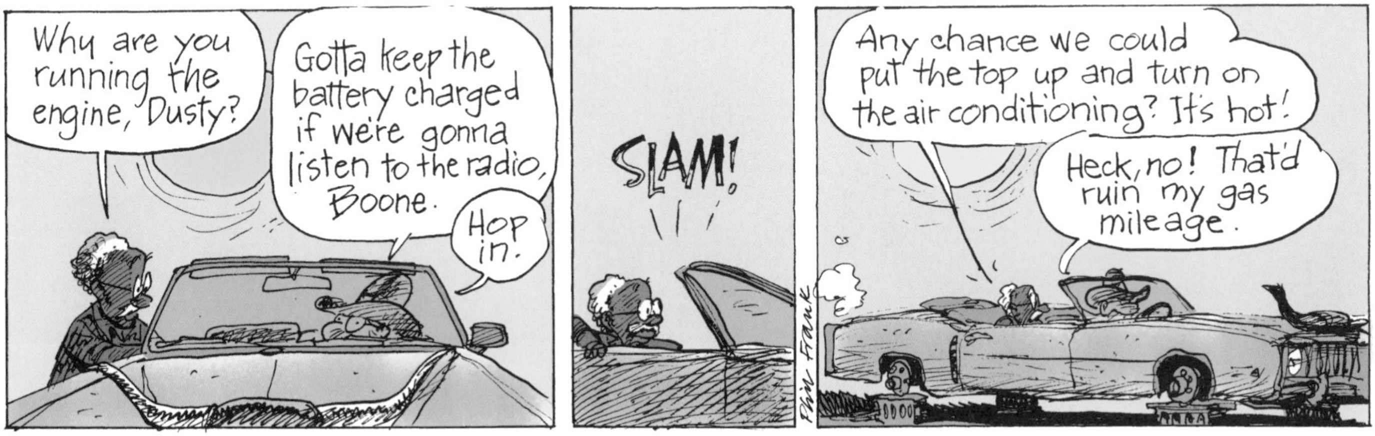
Why are you running the engine, Dusty?
Gotta keep the battery charged if we're gonna listen to the radio, Boone.
Hop in.
SLAM!
Any chance we could put the top up and turn on the air conditioning? It's hot!
Heck, no! That'd ruin my gas mileage.

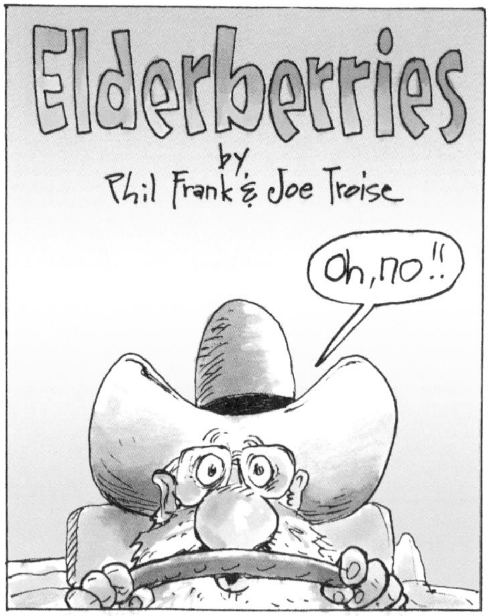
Elderberries
by
Phil Frank & Joe Troise
Oh, no!!

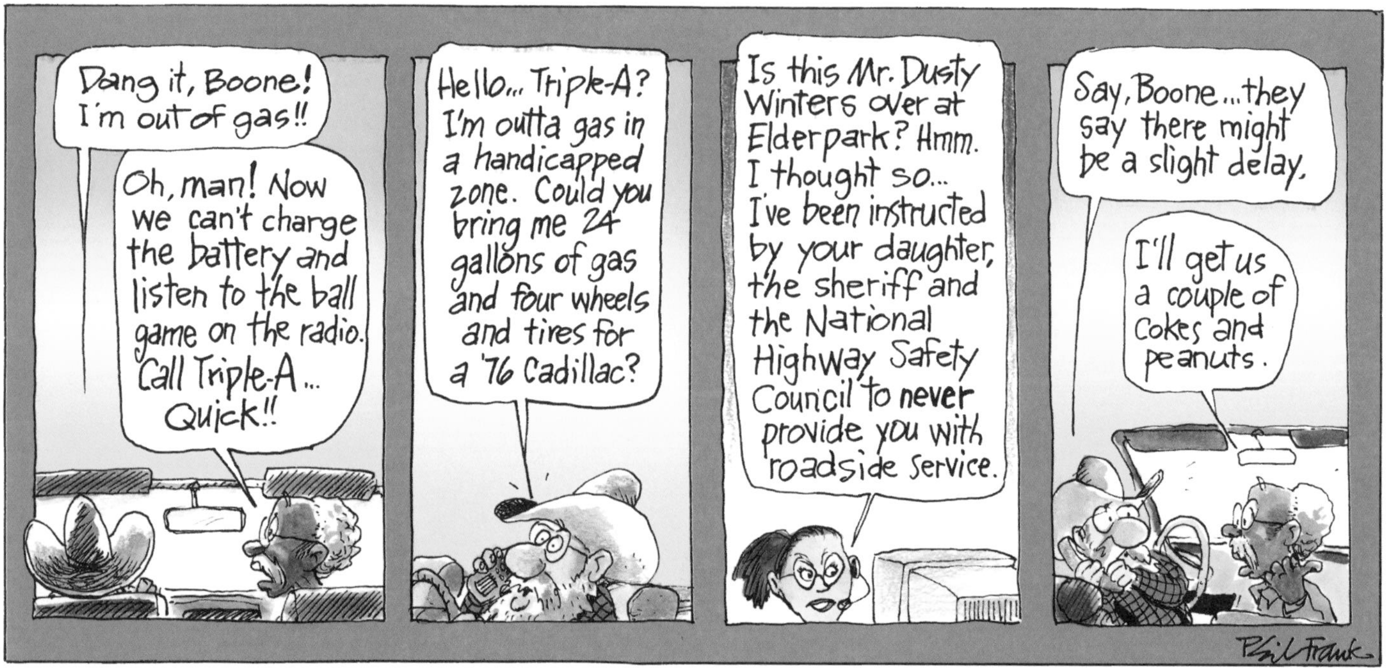
Dang it, Boone! I'm out of gas!!
Oh, man! Now we can't charge the battery and listen to the ball game on the radio. Call Triple-A... Quick!!
Hello... Triple-A? I'm outta gas in a handicapped zone. Could you bring me 24 gallons of gas and four wheels and tires for a '76 Cadillac?
Is this Mr. Dusty Winters over at Elderpark? Hmm. I thought so... I've been instructed by your daughter, the sheriff and the National Highway Safety Council to **never** provide you with roadside service.
Say, Boone... they say there might be a slight delay.
I'll get us a couple of Cokes and peanuts.
Phil Frank

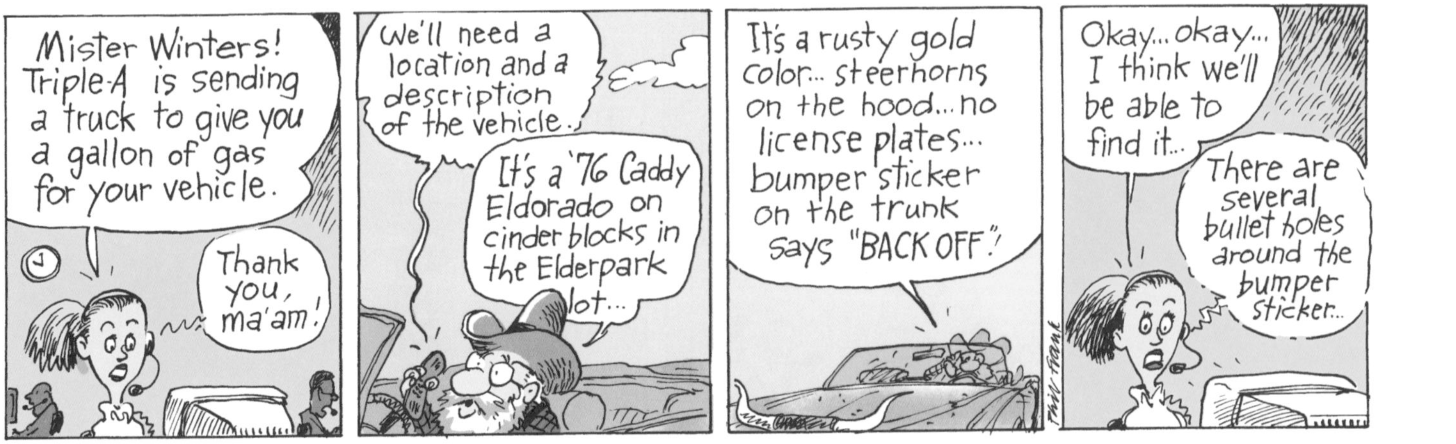
Mister Winters! Triple-A is sending a truck to give you a gallon of gas for your vehicle.
Thank you, ma'am!
We'll need a location and a description of the vehicle.
It's a '76 Caddy Eldorado on cinder blocks in the Elderpark lot...
It's a rusty gold color... steerhorns on the hood... no license plates... bumper sticker on the trunk says "BACK OFF".
Phil Frank
Okay... okay... I think we'll be able to find it...
There are several bullet holes around the bumper sticker...

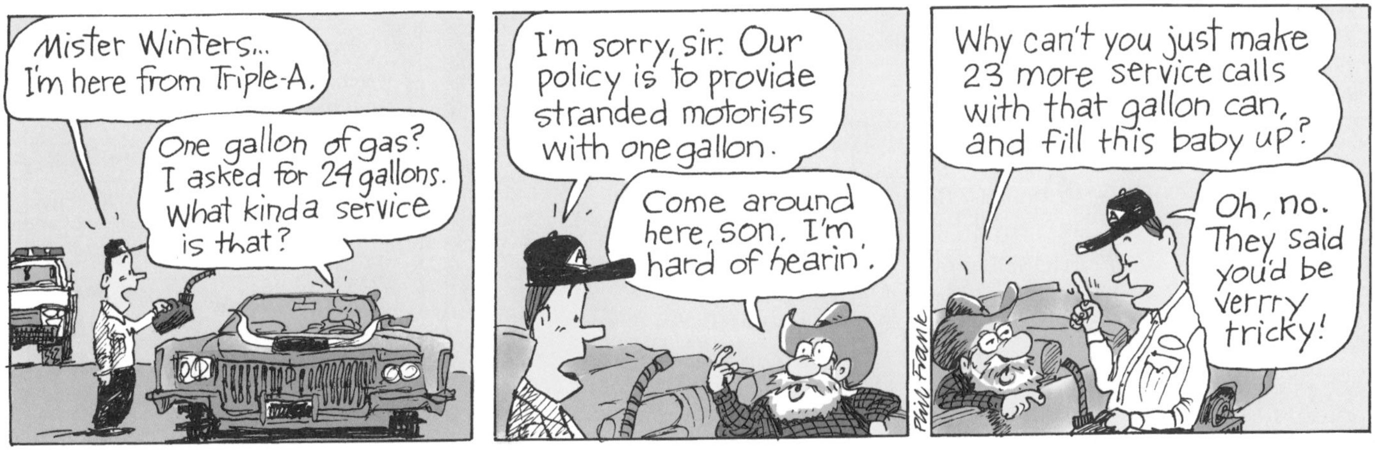
Mister Winters... I'm here from Triple-A.
One gallon of gas? I asked for 24 gallons. What kinda service is that?
I'm sorry, sir. Our policy is to provide stranded motorists with one gallon.
Come around here, son. I'm hard of hearin'.
Phil Frank
Why can't you just make 23 more service calls with that gallon can, and fill this baby up?
Oh, no. They said you'd be verrry tricky!

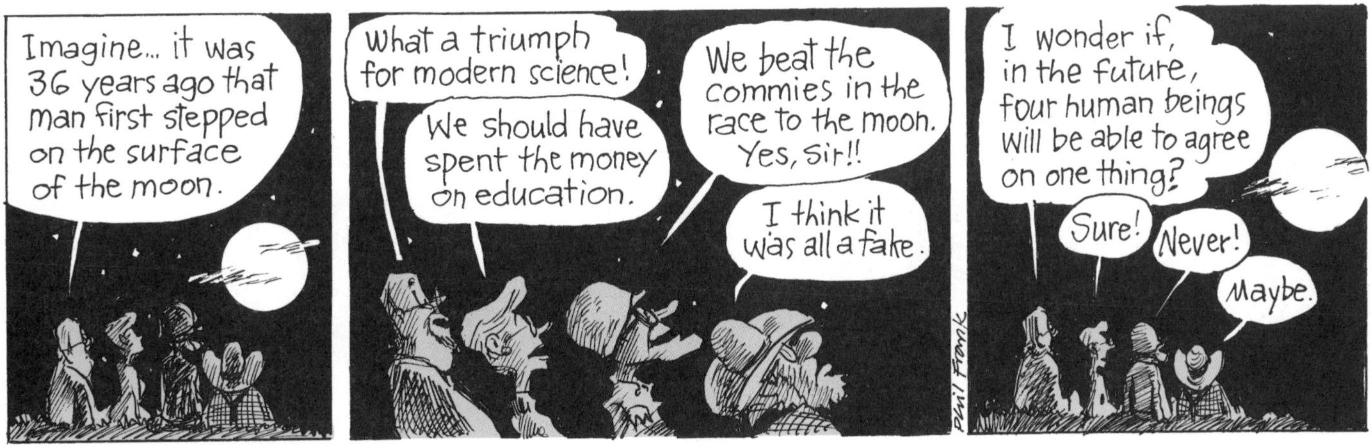
Imagine... it was 36 years ago that man first stepped on the surface of the moon.
What a triumph for modern science!
We should have spent the money on education.
We beat the commies in the race to the moon. Yes, sir!!
I think it was all a fake.
Phil Frank
I wonder if, in the future, four human beings will be able to agree on one thing?
Sure!
Never!
Maybe.

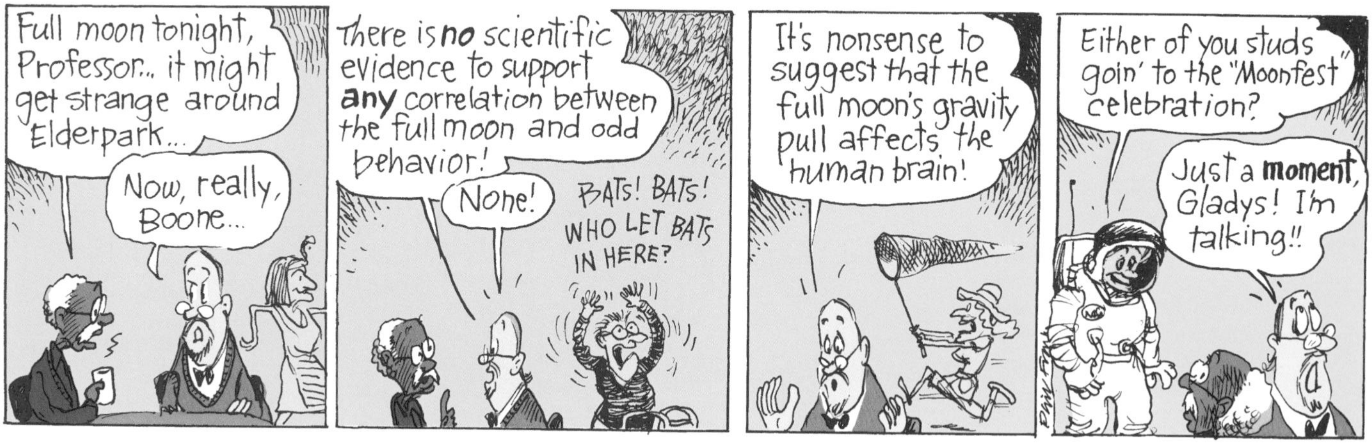
Full moon tonight, Professor... it might get strange around Elderpark...
Now, really, Boone...
There is **no** scientific evidence to support **any** correlation between the full moon and odd behavior!
None!
BATS! BATS! WHO LET BATS IN HERE?
It's nonsense to suggest that the full moon's gravity pull affects the human brain!
Either of you studs goin' to the "Moonfest" celebration?
Just a **moment**, Gladys! I'm talking!!

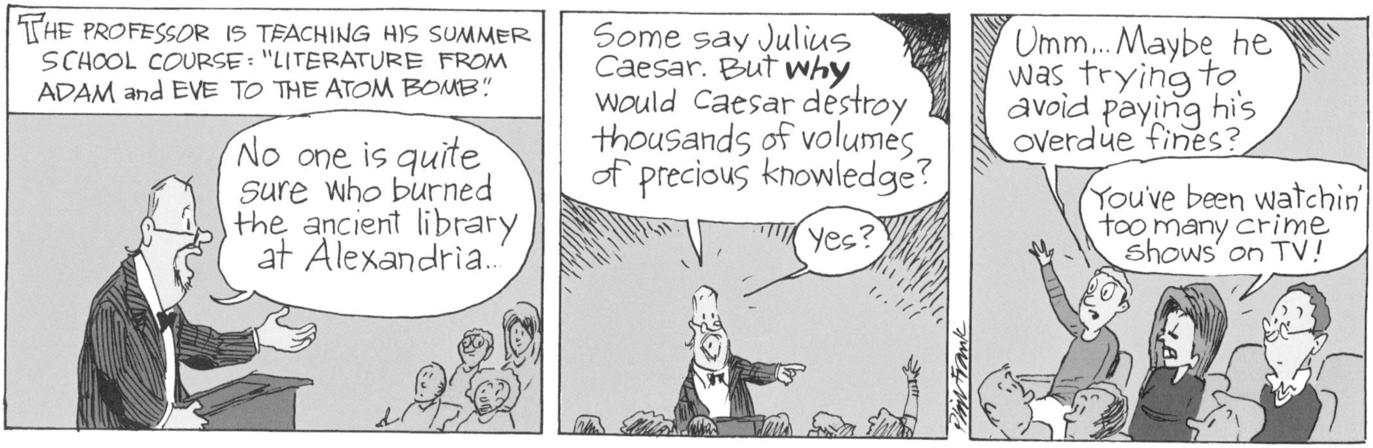
THE PROFESSOR IS TEACHING HIS SUMMER SCHOOL COURSE: "LITERATURE FROM ADAM and EVE TO THE ATOM BOMB."
No one is quite sure who burned the ancient library at Alexandria...
Some say Julius Caesar. But **why** would Caesar destroy thousands of volumes of precious knowledge?
Yes?
Umm... Maybe he was trying to avoid paying his overdue fines?
You've been watchin' too many crime shows on TV!

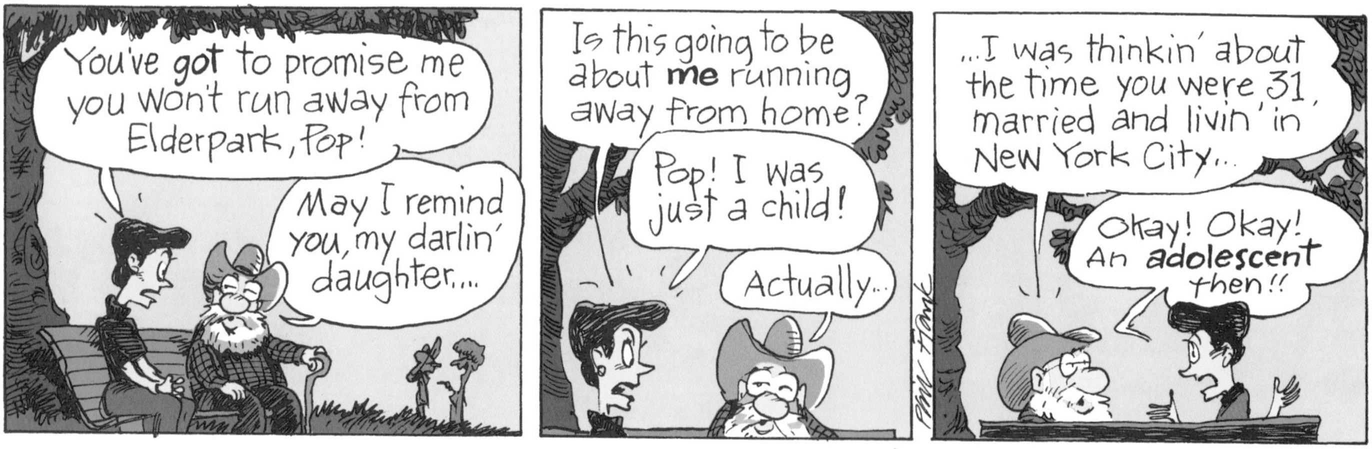
You've **got** to promise me you won't run away from Elderpark, Pop!
May I remind you, my darlin' daughter....
Is this going to be about **me** running away from home?
Pop! I was just a child!
Actually...
...I was thinkin' about the time you were 31, married and livin' in New York City...
Okay! Okay! An **adolescent** then!!

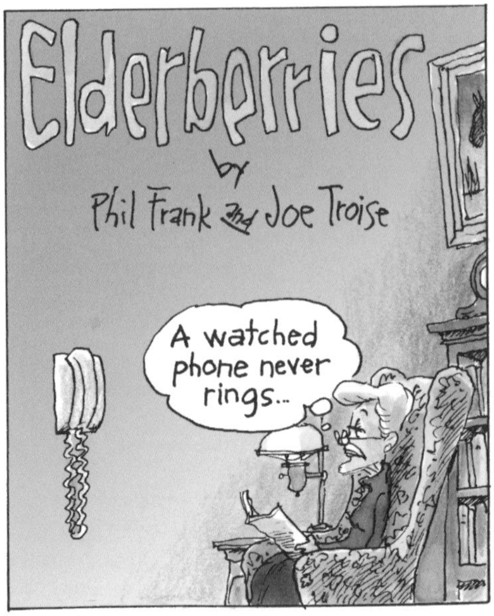
Elderberries
by
Phil Frank and Joe Troise
A watched phone never rings...

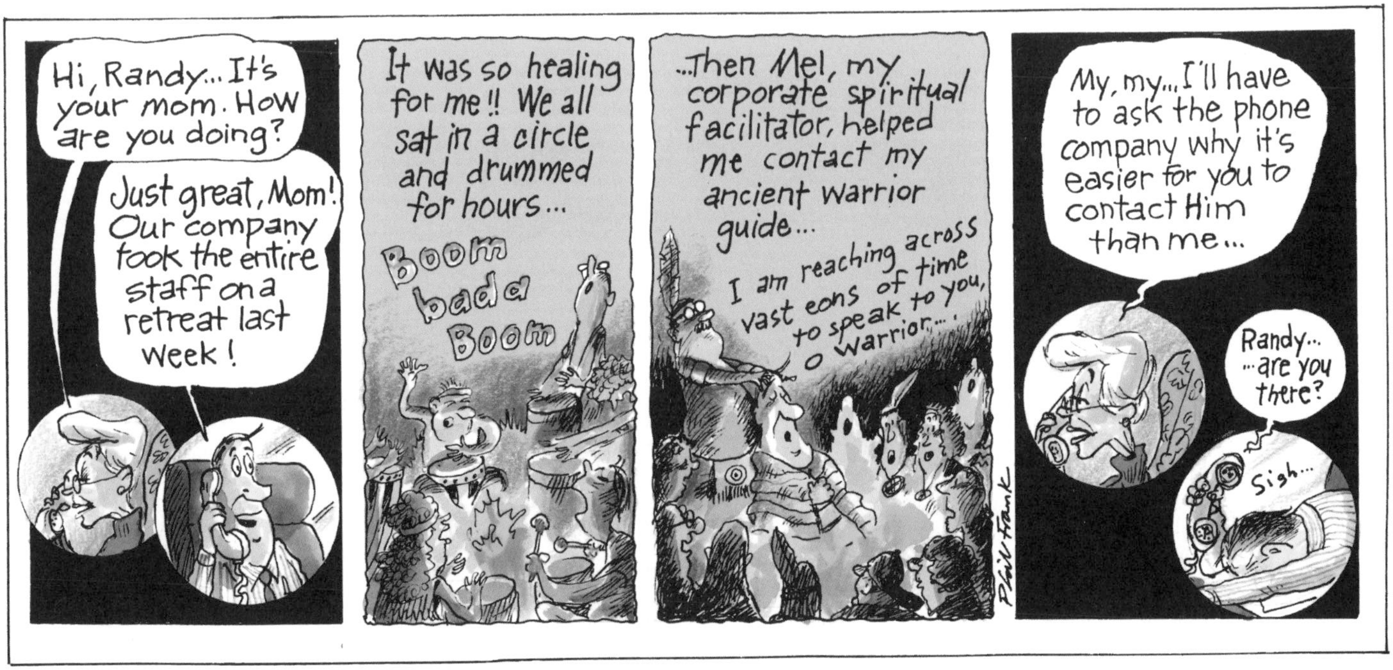
Hi, Randy... It's your mom. How are you doing?
Just great, Mom! Our company took the entire staff on a retreat last week!
It was so healing for me!! We all sat in a circle and drummed for hours...
Boom bada Boom
...Then Mel, my corporate spiritual facilitator, helped me contact my ancient warrior guide...
I am reaching across vast eons of time to speak to you, o warrior...
Phil Frank
My, my... I'll have to ask the phone company why it's easier for you to contact Him than me...
Randy... ...are you there?
Sigh...

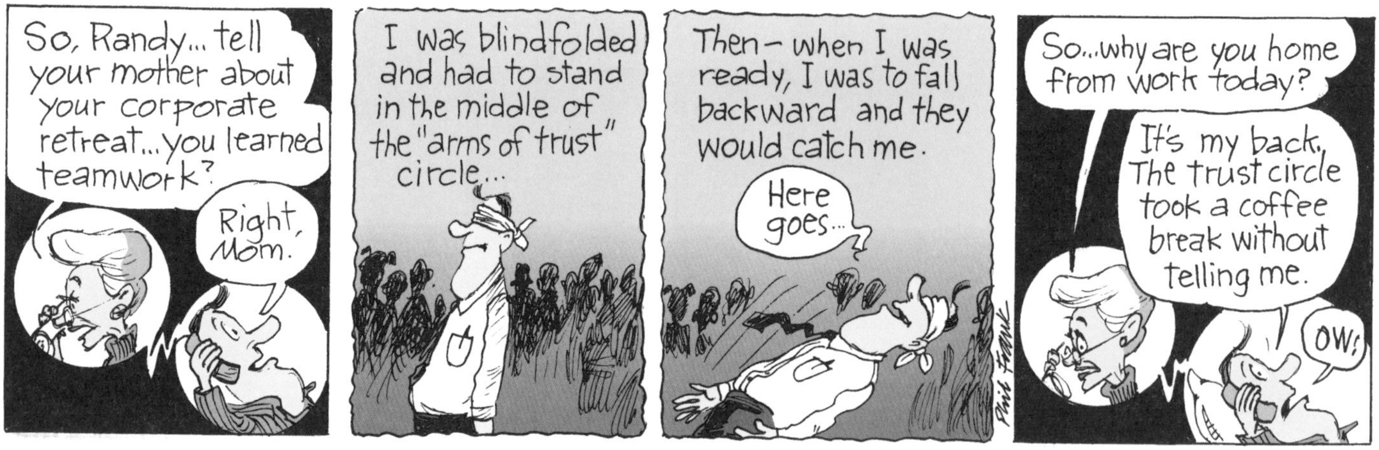
So, Randy... tell your mother about your corporate retreat... you learned teamwork?
Right, Mom.
I was blindfolded and had to stand in the middle of the "arms of trust" circle...
Then – when I was ready, I was to fall backward and they would catch me.
Here goes...
Phil Frank
So... why are you home from work today?
It's my back. The trust circle took a coffee break without telling me.
OW!

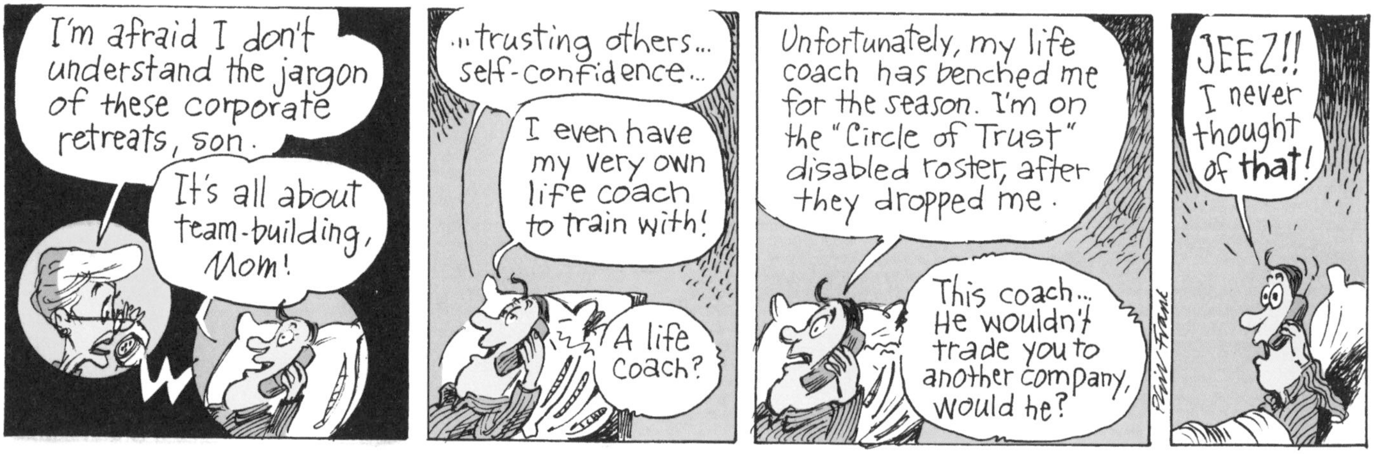
I'm afraid I don't understand the jargon of these corporate retreats, son.
It's all about team-building, Mom!
... trusting others... self-confidence...
I even have my very own life coach to train with!
A life coach?
Unfortunately, my life coach has benched me for the season. I'm on the "Circle of Trust" disabled roster, after they dropped me.
This coach... He wouldn't trade you to another company, would he?
Phil Frank
JEEZ!! I never thought of that!

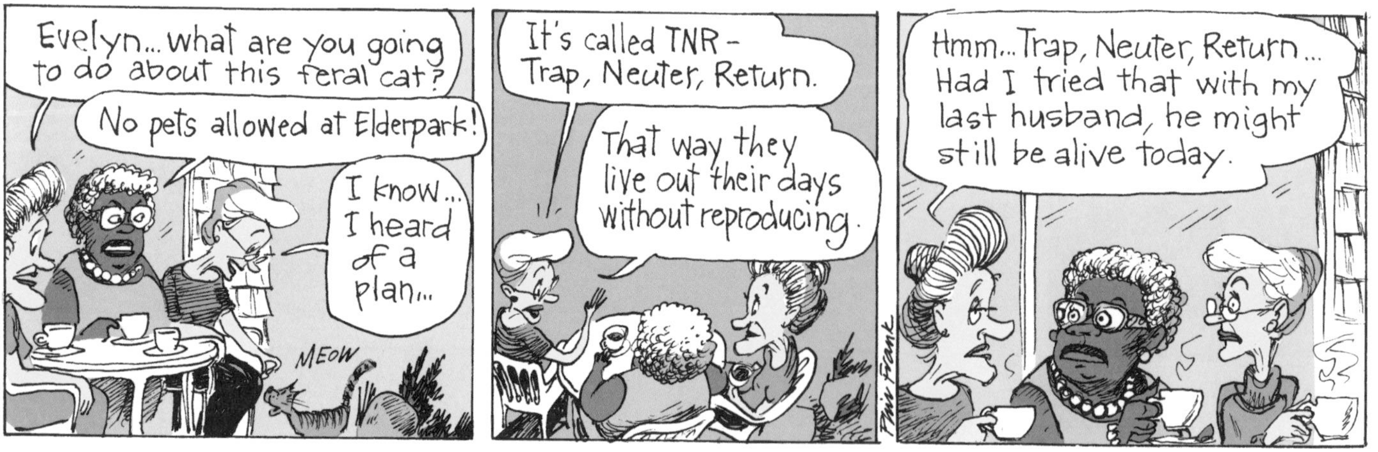
Evelyn... what are you going to do about this feral cat?
No pets allowed at Elderpark!
I know... I heard of a plan...
MEOW
It's called TNR – Trap, Neuter, Return.
That way they live out their days without reproducing.
Phil Frank
Hmm... Trap, Neuter, Return... Had I tried that with my last husband, he might still be alive today.

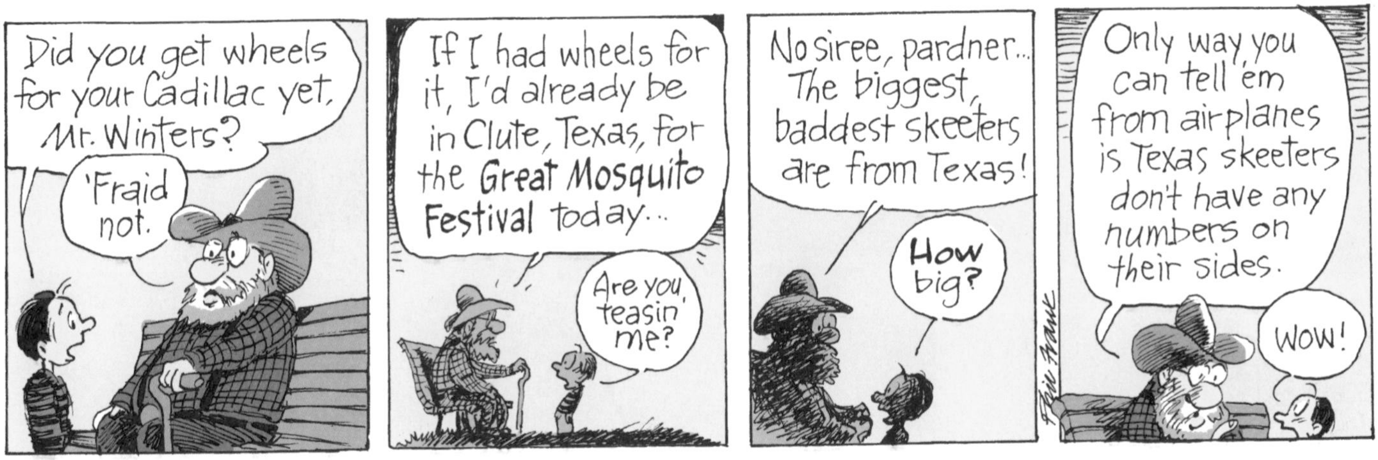
Did you get wheels for your Cadillac yet, Mr. Winters?
'Fraid not.
If I had wheels for it, I'd already be in Clute, Texas, for the **Great Mosquito Festival** today...
Are you teasin' me?
No siree, pardner... The biggest, baddest skeeters are from Texas!
How big?
Only way you can tell 'em from airplanes is Texas skeeters don't have any numbers on their sides.
WOW!

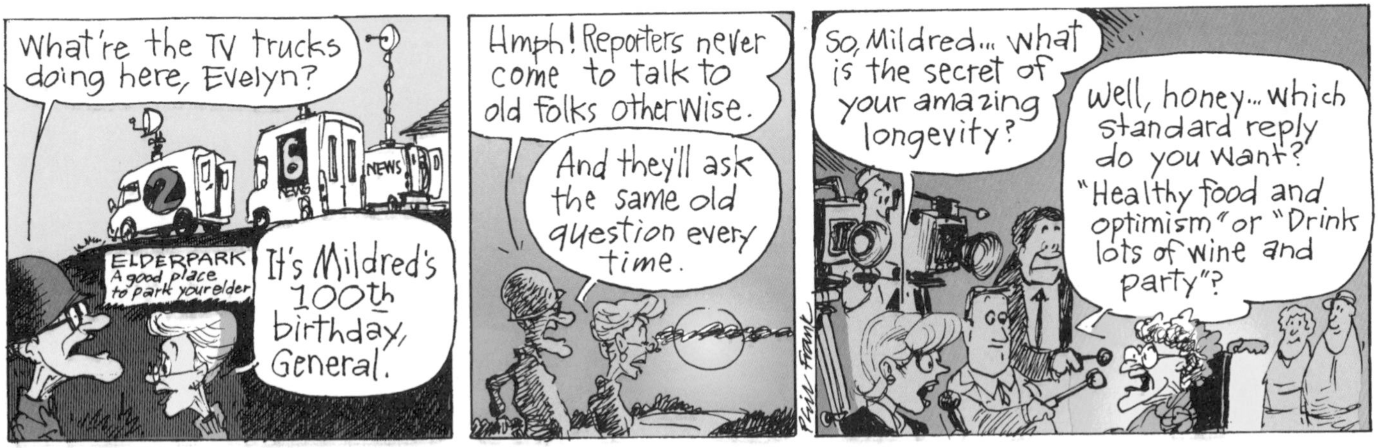
What're the TV trucks doing here, Evelyn?
NEWS
ELDERPARK A good place to park your elder
It's Mildred's 100th birthday, General.
Hmph! Reporters never come to talk to old folks otherwise.
And they'll ask the same old question every time.
So, Mildred... what is the secret of your amazing longevity?
Well, honey... which standard reply do you want? "Healthy food and optimism" or "Drink lots of wine and party"?

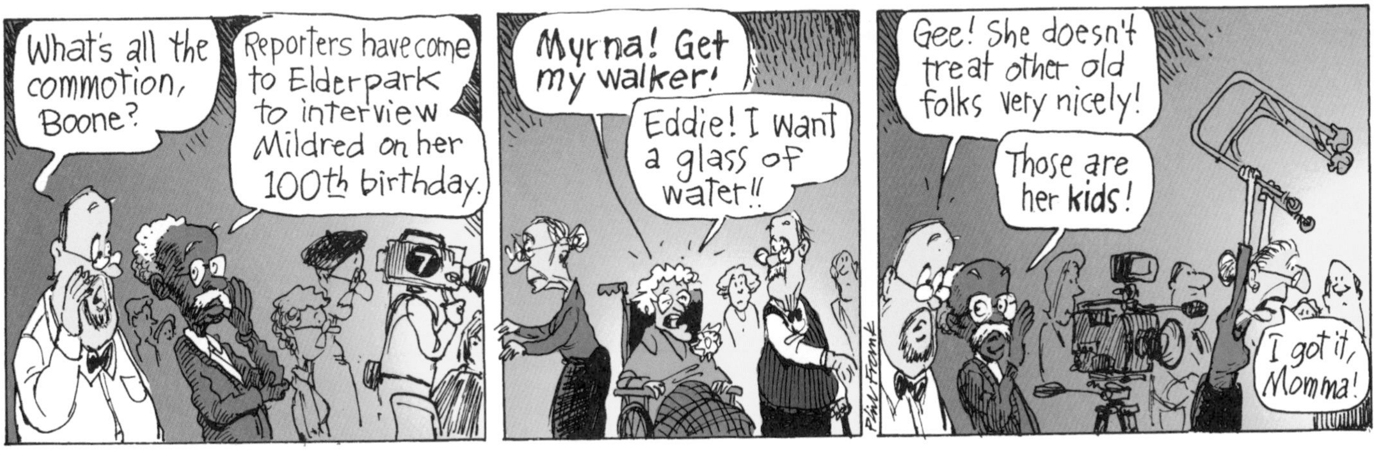
What's all the commotion, Boone?
Reporters have come to Elderpark to interview Mildred on her 100th birthday.
Myrna! Get my walker!
Eddie! I want a glass of water!!
Gee! She doesn't treat other old folks very nicely!
Those are her **kids**!
I got it, Momma!

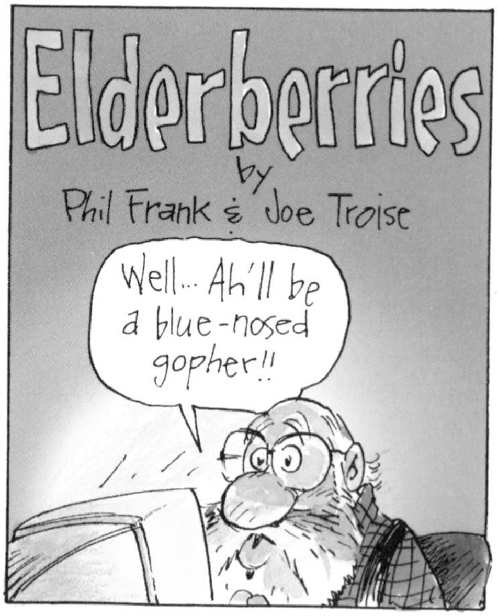
Elderberries
by
Phil Frank & Joe Troise
Well... Ah'll be a blue-nosed gopher!!

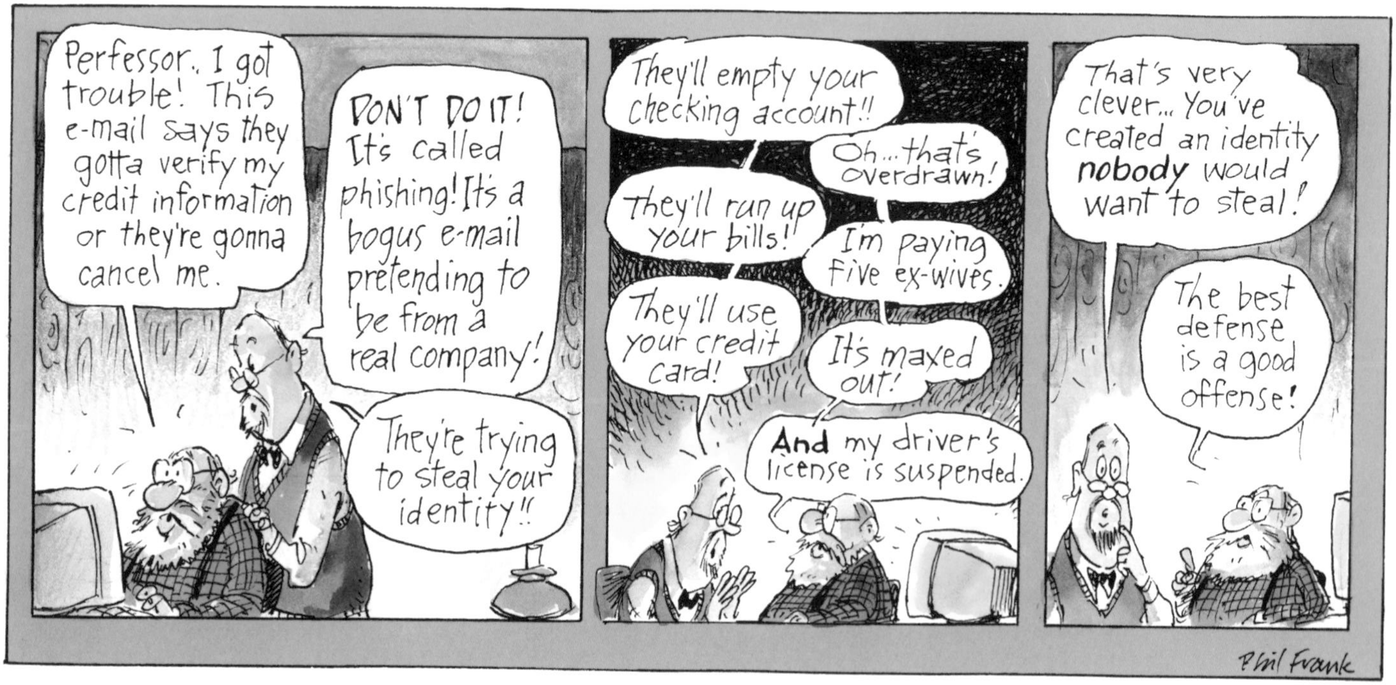
Perfessor.. I got trouble! This e-mail says they gotta verify my credit information or they're gonna cancel me.
DON'T DO IT! It's called phishing! It's a bogus e-mail pretending to be from a real company!
They're trying to steal your identity!!
They'll empty your checking account!!
Oh... that's overdrawn!
They'll run up your bills!
I'm paying five ex-wives.
They'll use your credit card!
It's maxed out!
And my driver's license is suspended.
That's very clever... You've created an identity nobody would want to steal!
The best defense is a good offense!
Phil Frank

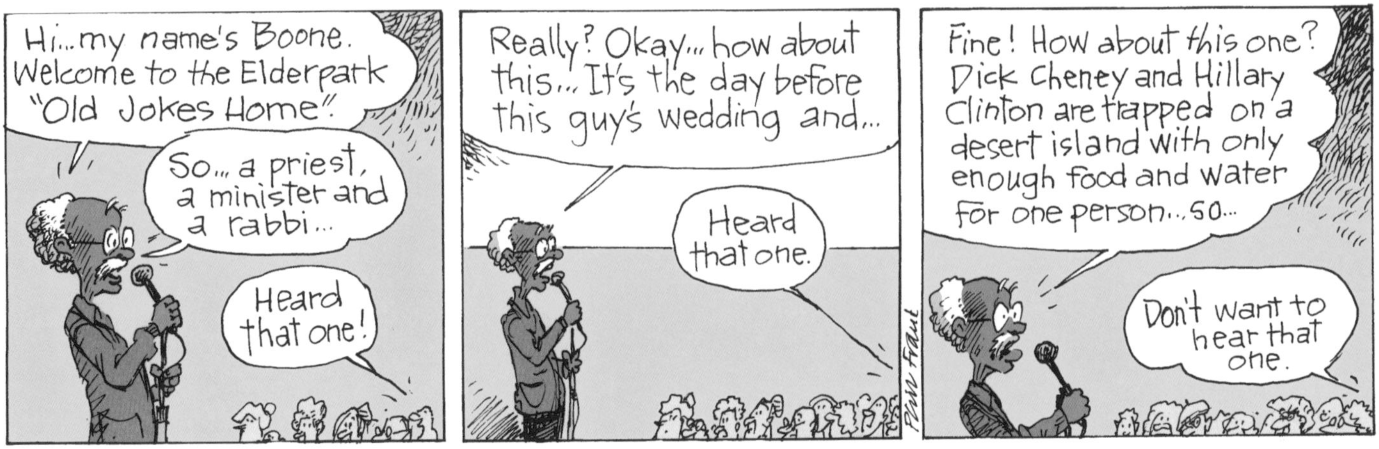

Hi...my name's Boone. Welcome to the Elderpark "Old Jokes Home".
So... a priest, a minister and a rabbi...
Heard that one!
Really? Okay... how about this... It's the day before this guy's wedding and...
Heard that one.
Fine! How about this one? Dick Cheney and Hillary Clinton are trapped on a desert island with only enough food and water for one person...so...
Don't want to hear that one.

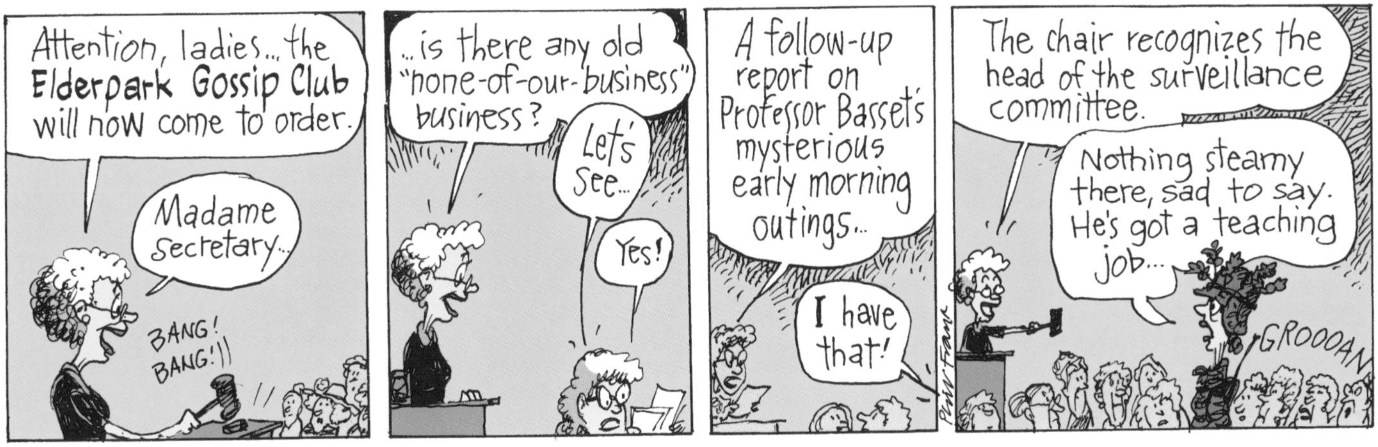

Attention, ladies... the Elderpark Gossip Club will now come to order.
Madame Secretary...
BANG! BANG!
...is there any old "none-of-our-business" business?
Let's See...
Yes!
A follow-up report on Professor Basset's mysterious early morning outings...
I have that!
The chair recognizes the head of the surveillance committee.
Nothing steamy there, sad to say. He's got a teaching job...
GROOOAN

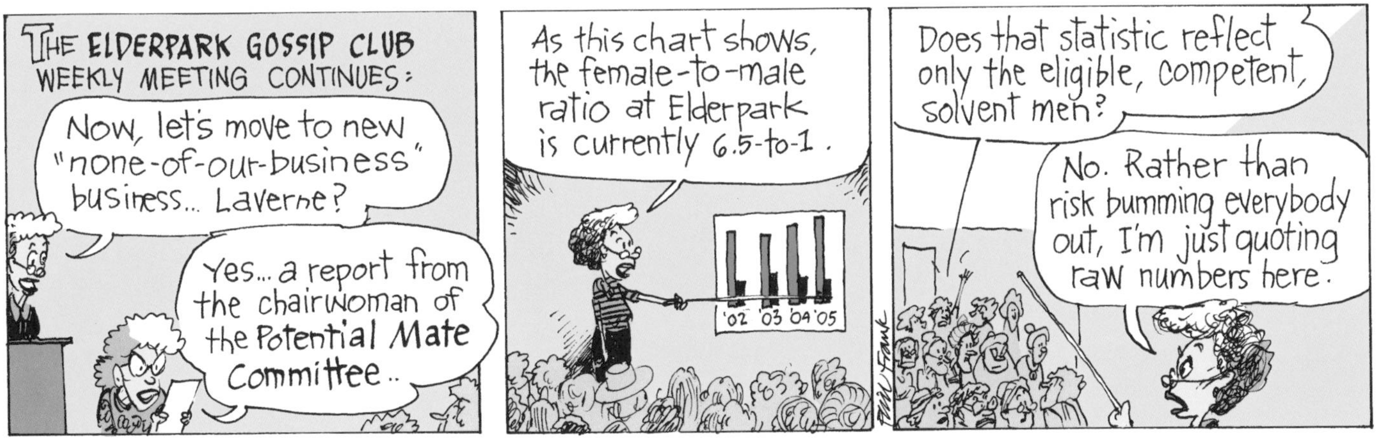

THE ELDERPARK GOSSIP CLUB WEEKLY MEETING CONTINUES:
Now, let's move to new "none-of-our-business" business... Laverne?
Yes... a report from the chairwoman of the Potential Mate Committee...
As this chart shows, the female-to-male ratio at Elderpark is currently 6.5-to-1.
'02 '03 '04 '05
Does that statistic reflect only the eligible, competent, solvent men?
No. Rather than risk bumming everybody out, I'm just quoting raw numbers here.

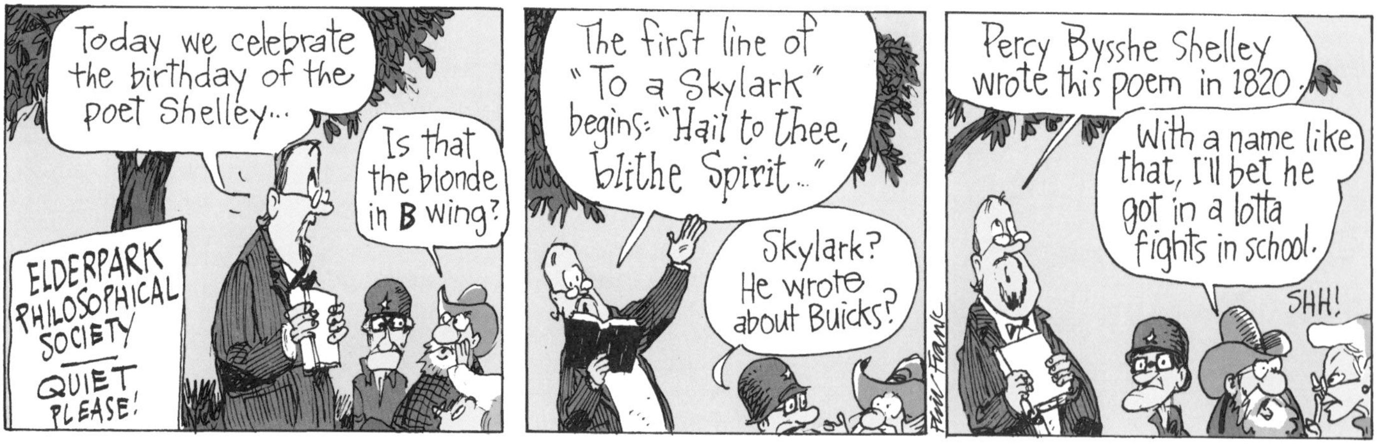
Today we celebrate the birthday of the poet Shelley...
Is that the blonde in B wing?
ELDERPARK PHILOSOPHICAL SOCIETY
QUIET PLEASE!
The first line of "To a Skylark" begins: "Hail to thee, blithe Spirit..."
Skylark? He wrote about Buicks?
Percy Bysshe Shelley wrote this poem in 1820.
With a name like that, I'll bet he got in a lotta fights in school.
SHH!

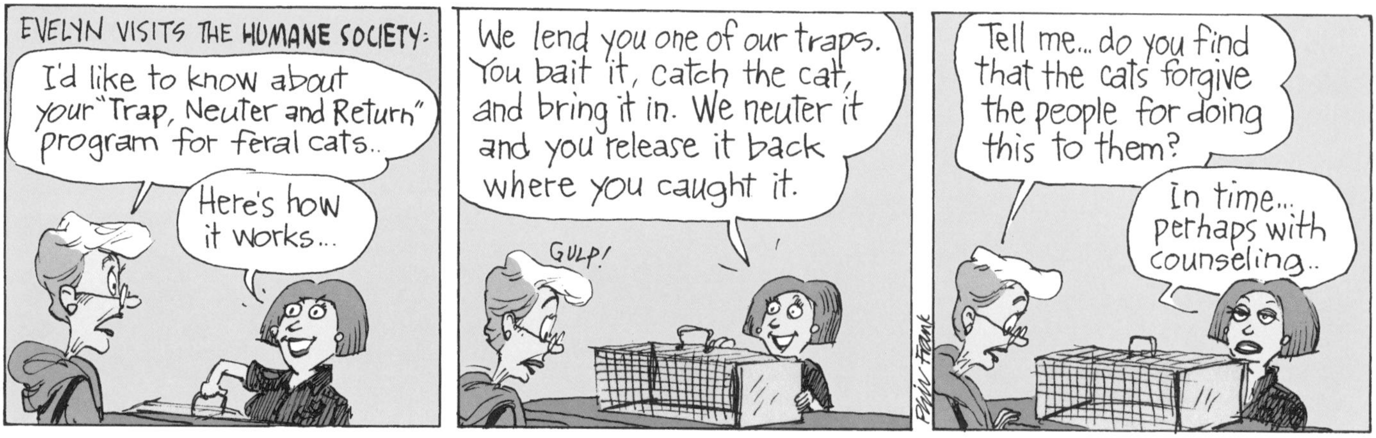
EVELYN VISITS THE HUMANE SOCIETY:
I'd like to know about your "Trap, Neuter and Return" program for feral cats..
Here's how it works...
We lend you one of our traps. You bait it, catch the cat, and bring it in. We neuter it and you release it back where you caught it.
GULP!
Tell me... do you find that the cats forgive the people for doing this to them?
In time... perhaps with counseling..

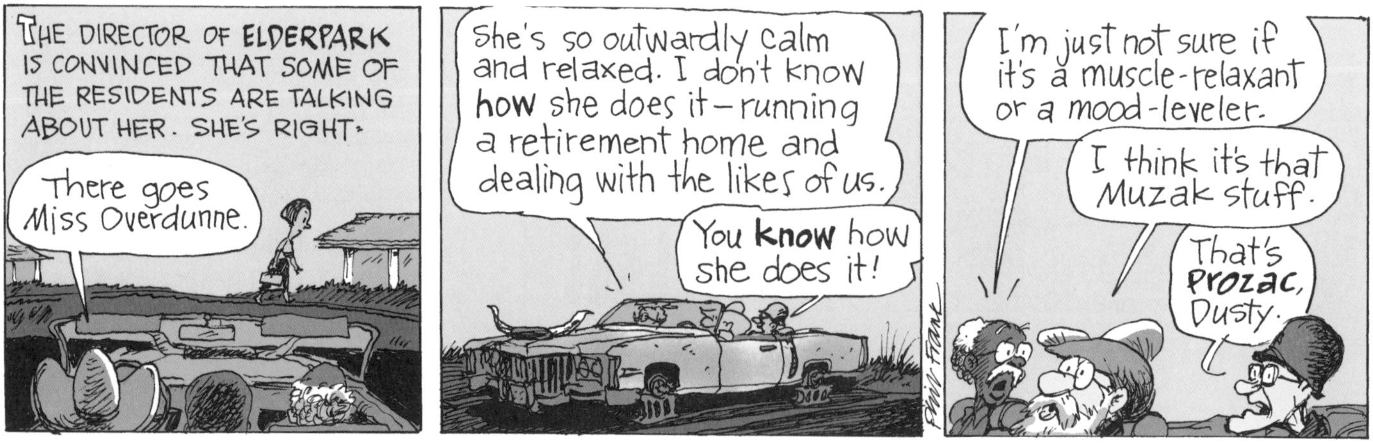
THE DIRECTOR OF ELDERPARK IS CONVINCED THAT SOME OF THE RESIDENTS ARE TALKING ABOUT HER. SHE'S RIGHT:
There goes Miss Overdunne.
She's so outwardly calm and relaxed. I don't know how she does it—running a retirement home and dealing with the likes of us.
You know how she does it!
I'm just not sure if it's a muscle-relaxant or a mood-leveler.
I think it's that Muzak stuff.
That's Prozac, Dusty.

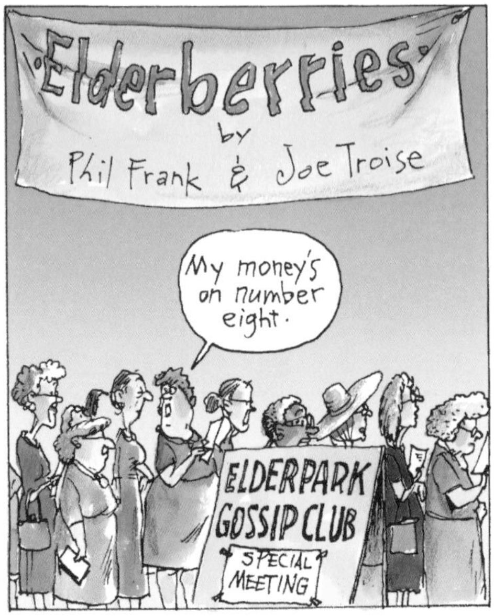
Elderberries
by
Phil Frank & Joe Troise
My money's on number eight.
ELDERPARK GOSSIP CLUB
SPECIAL MEETING

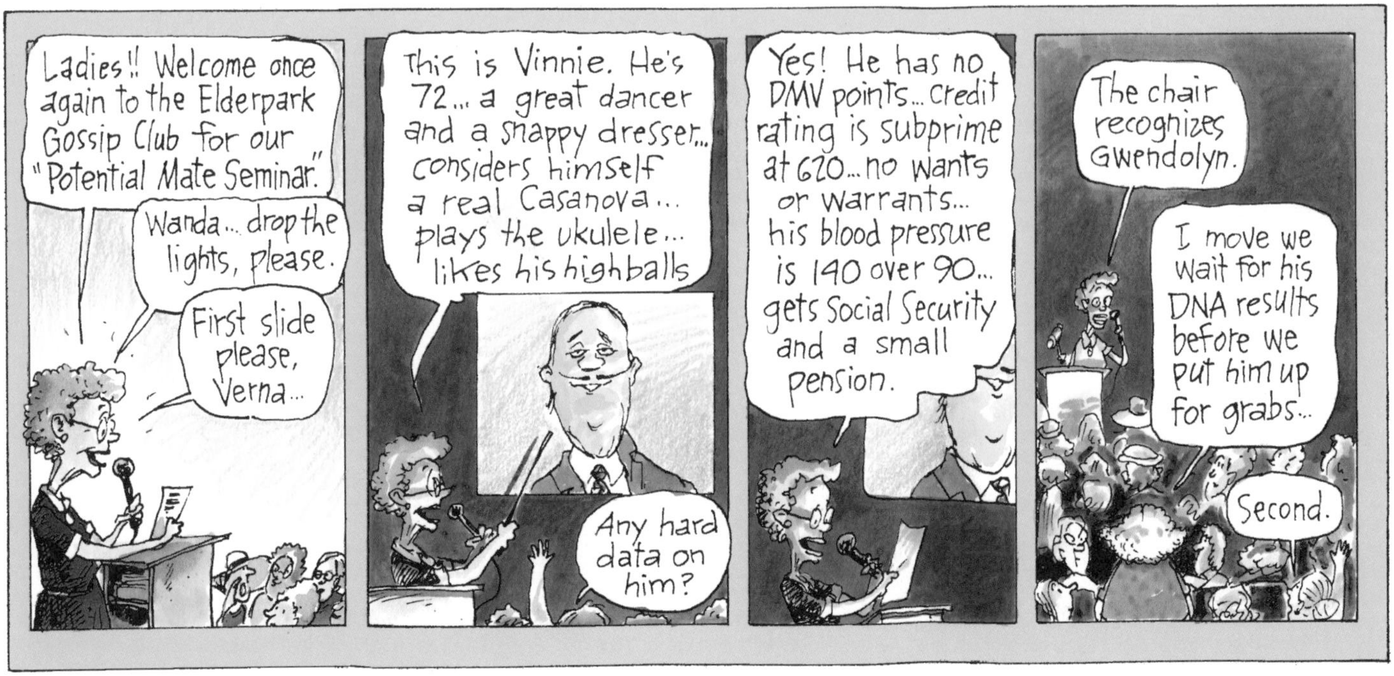
Ladies!! Welcome once again to the Elderpark Gossip Club for our "Potential Mate Seminar."
Wanda... drop the lights, please.
First slide please, Verna...
This is Vinnie. He's 72... a great dancer and a snappy dresser... considers himself a real Casanova... plays the ukulele... likes his highballs
Any hard data on him?
Yes! He has no DMV points... credit rating is subprime at 620... no wants or warrants... his blood pressure is 140 over 90... gets Social Security and a small pension.
The chair recognizes Gwendolyn.
I move we wait for his DNA results before we put him up for grabs...
Second.

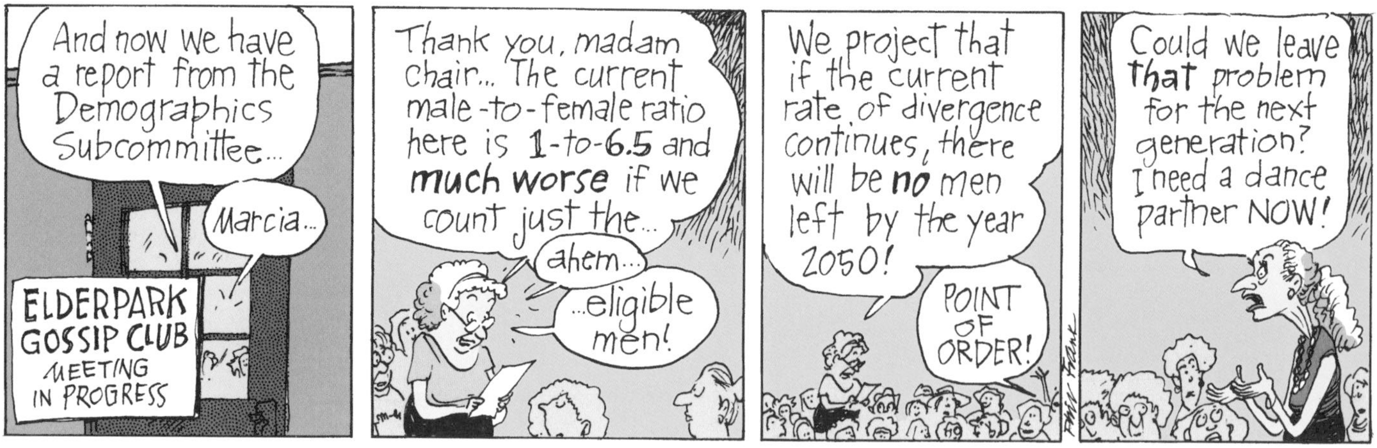
And now we have a report from the Demographics Subcommittee...
Marcia...
ELDERPARK GOSSIP CLUB MEETING IN PROGRESS
Thank you, madam chair... The current male-to-female ratio here is **1-to-6.5** and **much worse** if we count just the...
ahem...
...eligible men!
We project that if the current rate of divergence continues, there will be **no** men left by the year 2050!
POINT OF ORDER!
Could we leave **that** problem for the next generation? I need a dance partner NOW!

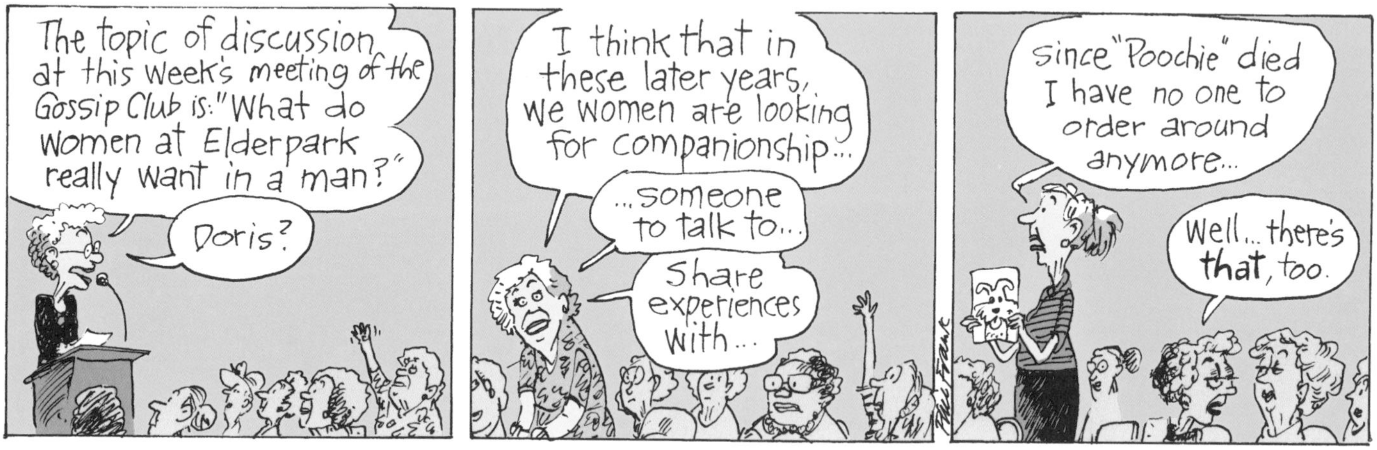
The topic of discussion at this week's meeting of the Gossip Club is: "What do women at Elderpark really want in a man?"
Doris?
I think that in these later years, we women are looking for companionship...
...someone to talk to...
Share experiences with...
Since "Poochie" died I have no one to order around anymore...
Well... there's **that**, too.

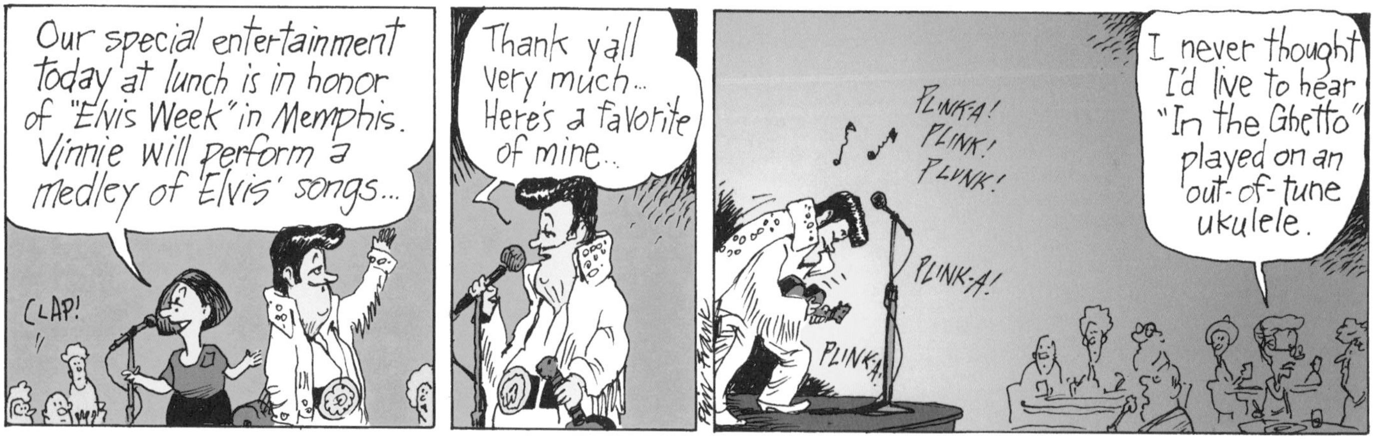
Our special entertainment today at lunch is in honor of "Elvis Week" in Memphis. Vinnie will perform a medley of Elvis' songs...
CLAP!
Thank y'all very much... Here's a favorite of mine...
PLINK-A!
PLINK!
PLUNK!
PLINK-A!
PLINK-A!
I never thought I'd live to hear "In the Ghetto" played on an out-of-tune ukulele.

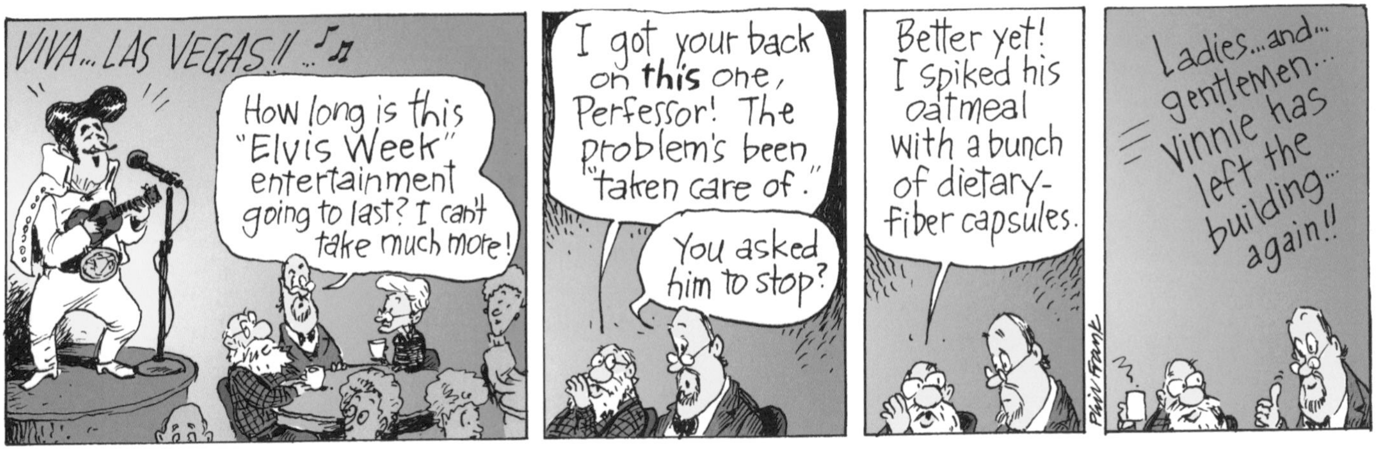
VIVA... LAS VEGAS!!
How long is this "Elvis Week" entertainment going to last? I can't take much more!
I got your back on **this** one, Perfessor! The problem's been "taken care of."
You asked him to stop?
Better yet! I spiked his oatmeal with a bunch of dietary-fiber capsules.
Ladies... and... gentlemen... Vinnie has left the building... again!!

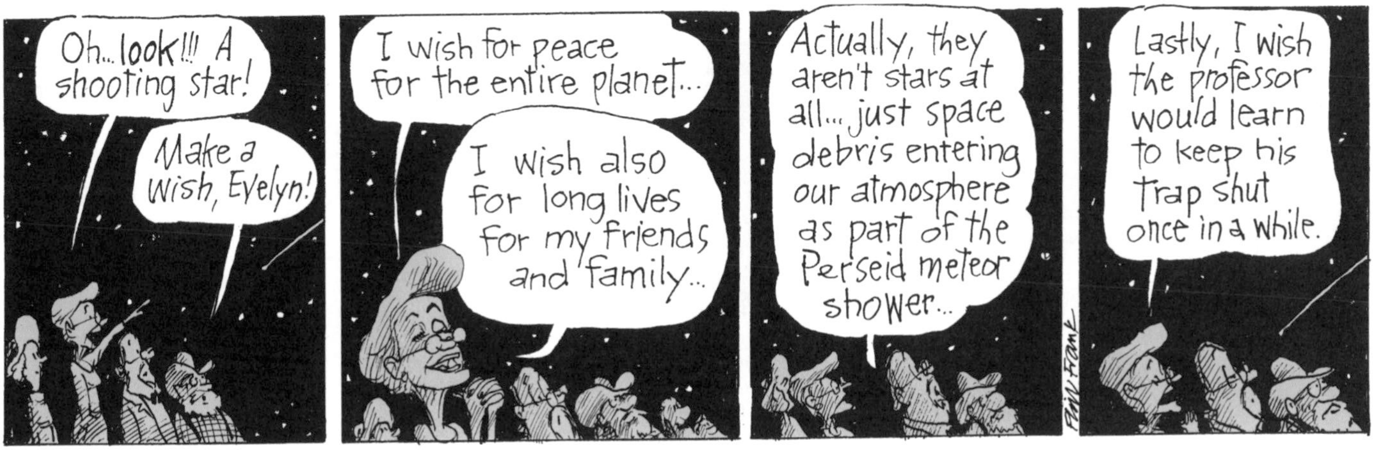
Oh... **look**!!! A shooting star!
Make a wish, Evelyn!
I wish for peace for the entire planet...
I wish also for long lives for my friends and family...
Actually, they aren't stars at all... just space debris entering our atmosphere as part of the Perseid meteor shower...
Lastly, I wish the professor would learn to keep his trap shut once in a while.

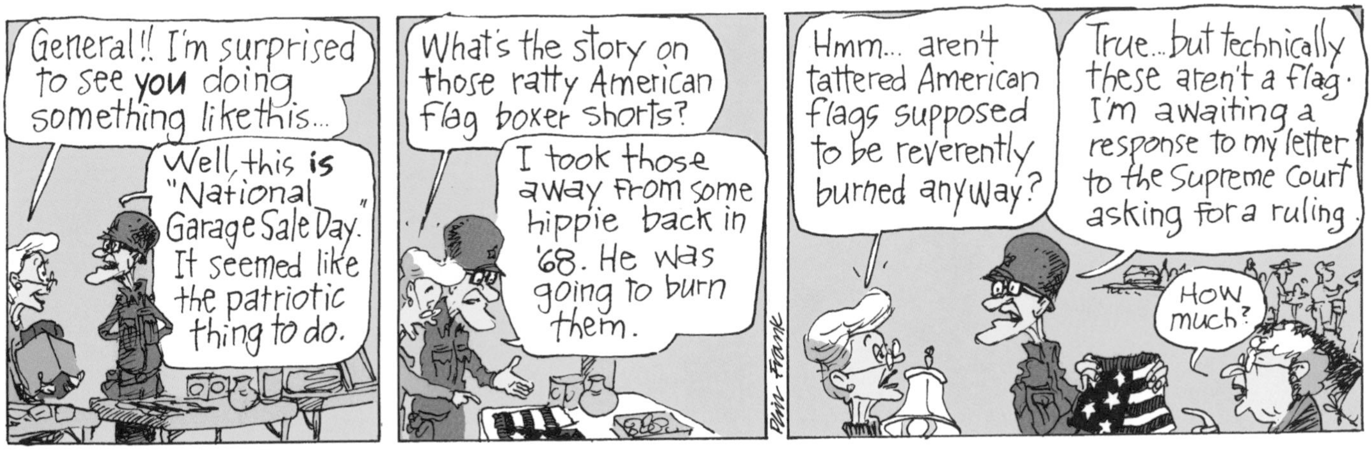
General!! I'm surprised to see **you** doing something like this...
Well, this **is** "National Garage Sale Day." It seemed like the patriotic thing to do.
What's the story on those ratty American flag boxer shorts?
I took those away from some hippie back in '68. He was going to burn them.
Hmm... aren't tattered American flags supposed to be reverently burned anyway?
True... but technically these aren't a flag. I'm awaiting a response to my letter to the Supreme Court asking for a ruling.
How much?

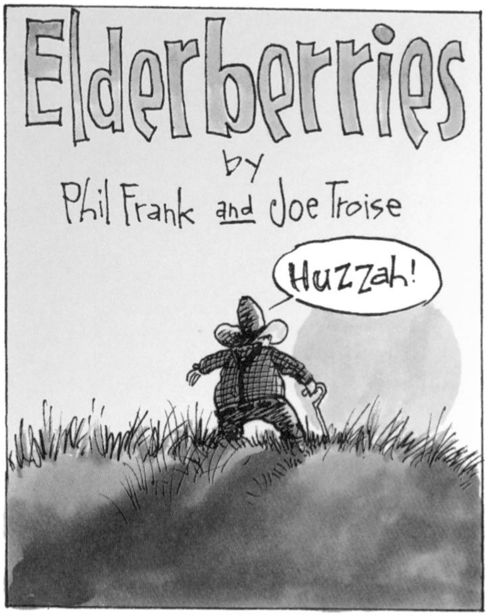
Elderberries
by
Phil Frank and Joe Troise
Huzzah!

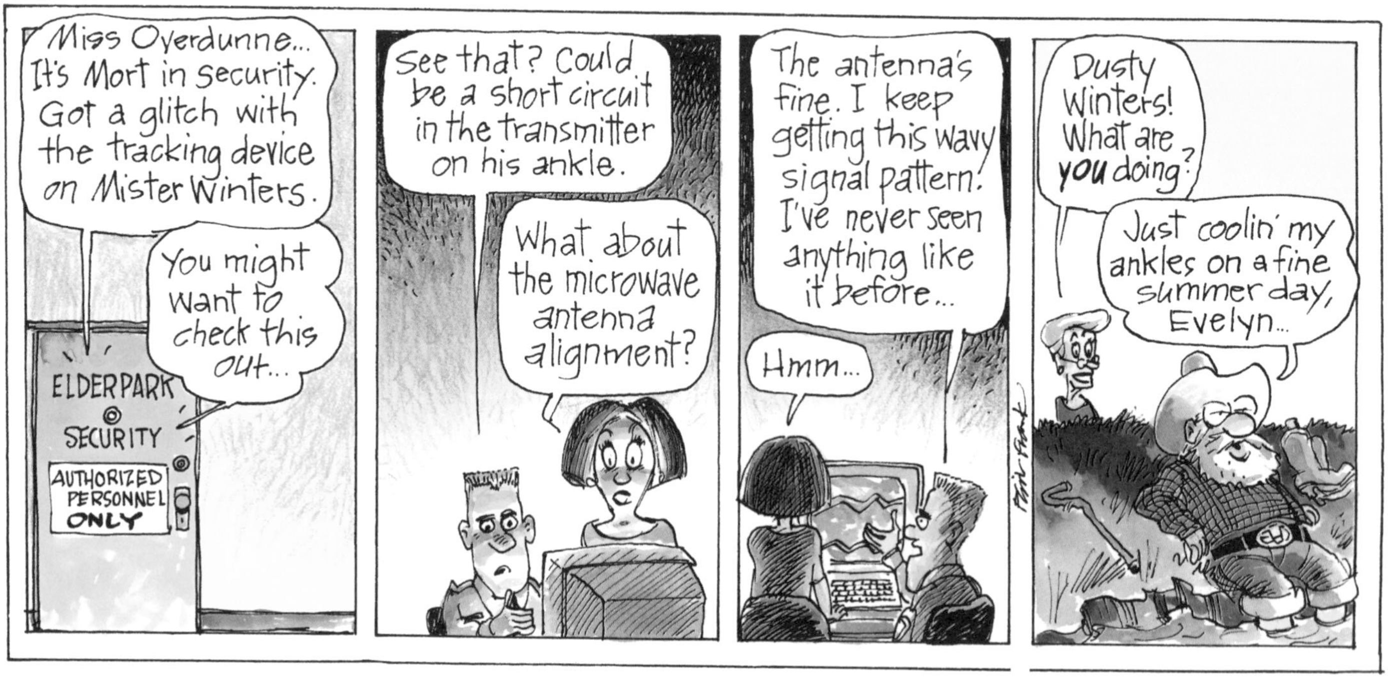
Miss Overdunne... It's Mort in security. Got a glitch with the tracking device on Mister Winters.
You might want to check this out...
ELDERPARK SECURITY
AUTHORIZED PERSONNEL ONLY
See that? Could be a short circuit in the transmitter on his ankle.
What about the microwave antenna alignment?
The antenna's fine. I keep getting this wavy signal pattern! I've never seen anything like it before...
Hmm...
Dusty Winters! What are **YOU** doing?
Just coolin' my ankles on a fine summer day, Evelyn...

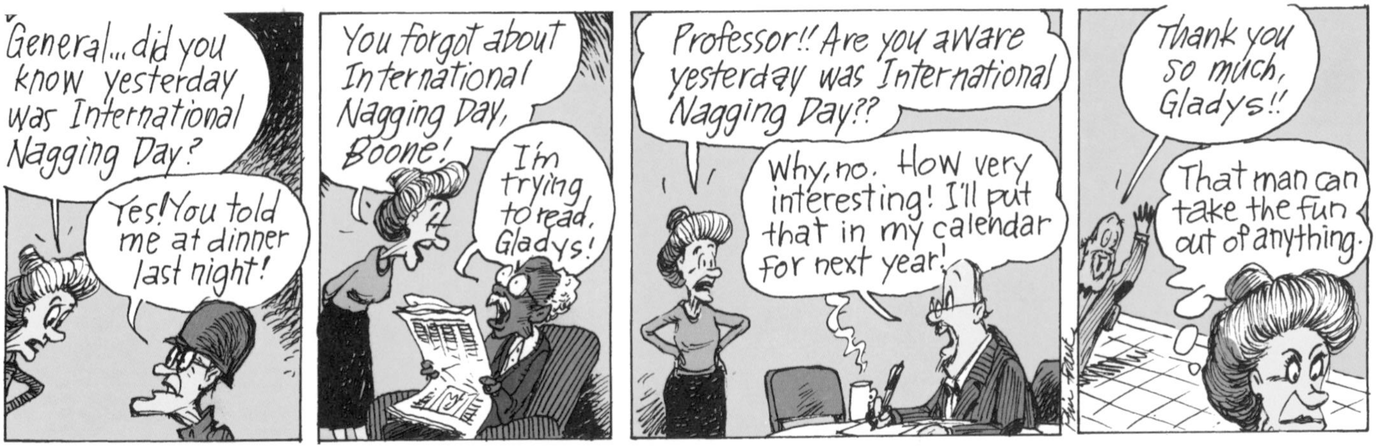
General... did you know yesterday was International Nagging Day?
Yes! You told me at dinner last night!
You forgot about International Nagging Day, Boone!
I'm trying to read, Gladys!
Professor!! Are you aware yesterday was International Nagging Day??
Why, no. How very interesting! I'll put that in my calendar for next year!
Thank you so much, Gladys!!
That man can take the fun out of anything.

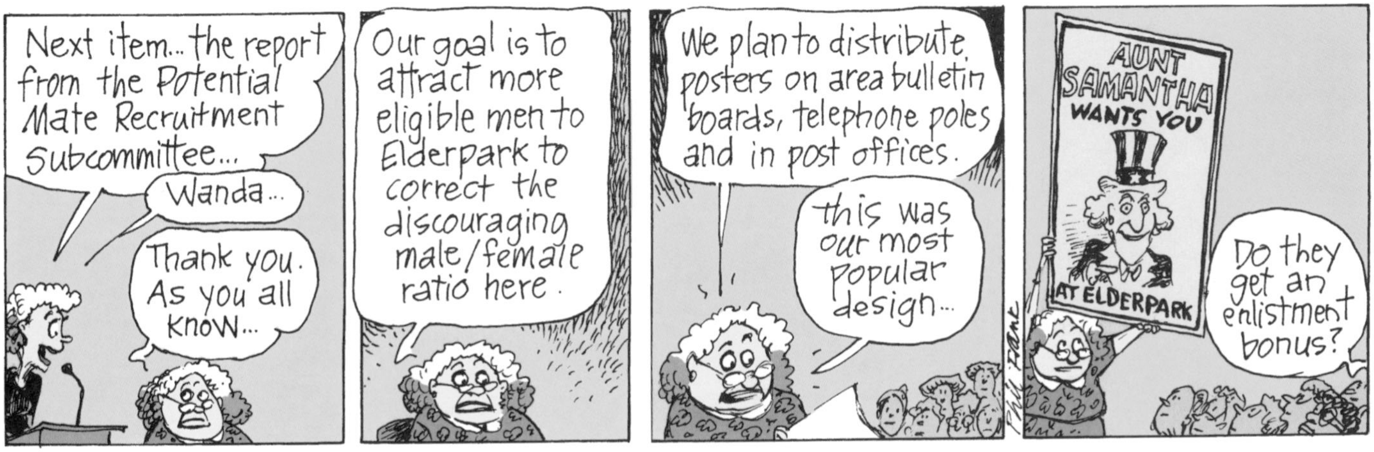
Next item... the report from the Potential Mate Recruitment Subcommittee...
Wanda...
Thank you. As you all know...
Our goal is to attract more eligible men to Elderpark to correct the discouraging male/female ratio here.
We plan to distribute posters on area bulletin boards, telephone poles and in post offices.
this was our most popular design...
AUNT SAMANTHA WANTS YOU AT ELDERPARK
Do they get an enlistment bonus?

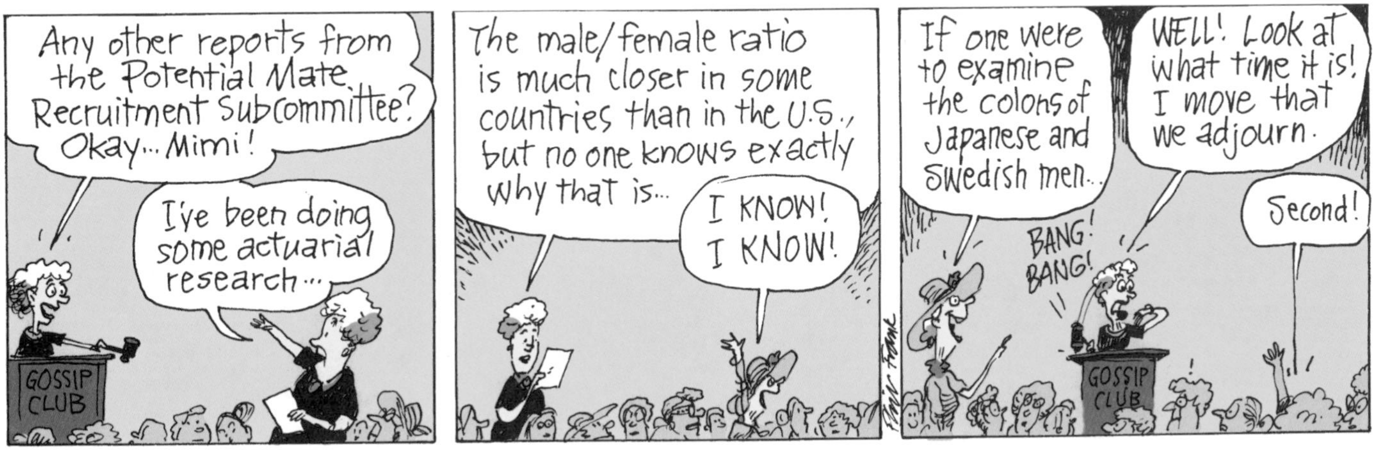
Any other reports from the Potential Mate Recruitment Subcommittee? Okay... Mimi!
I've been doing some actuarial research...
GOSSIP CLUB
The male/female ratio is much closer in some countries than in the U.S., but no one knows exactly why that is...
I KNOW! I KNOW!
If one were to examine the colons of Japanese and Swedish men...
BANG! BANG!
WELL! Look at what time it is! I move that we adjourn.
Second!
GOSSIP CLUB

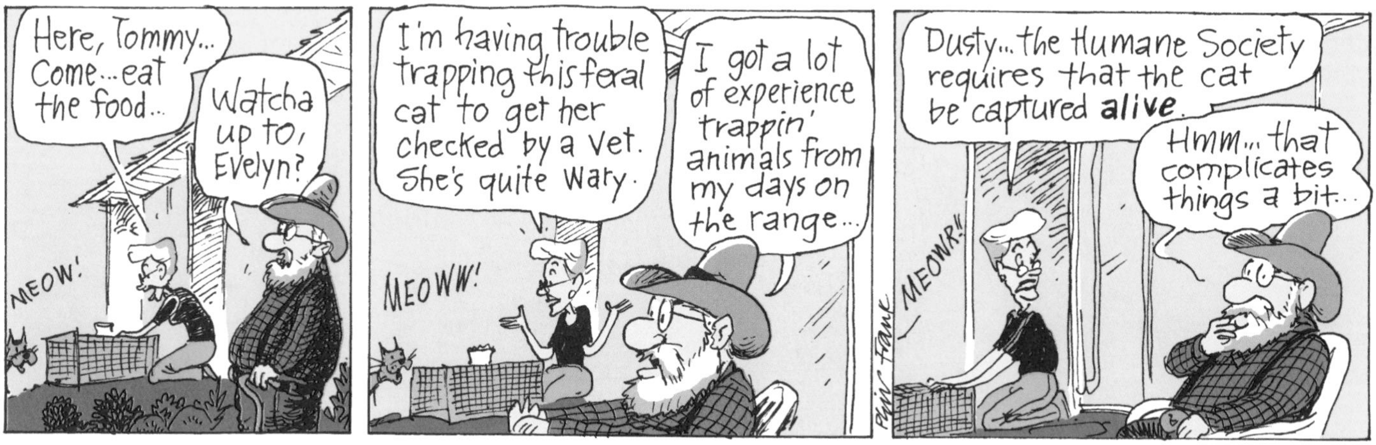
Here, Tommy... Come... eat the food...
Watcha up to, Evelyn?
MEOW!
I'm having trouble trapping this feral cat to get her checked by a vet. She's quite wary.
MEOWW!
I got a lot of experience trappin' animals from my days on the range...
Dusty... the Humane Society requires that the cat be captured **alive**.
MEOWR!!
Hmm... that complicates things a bit...

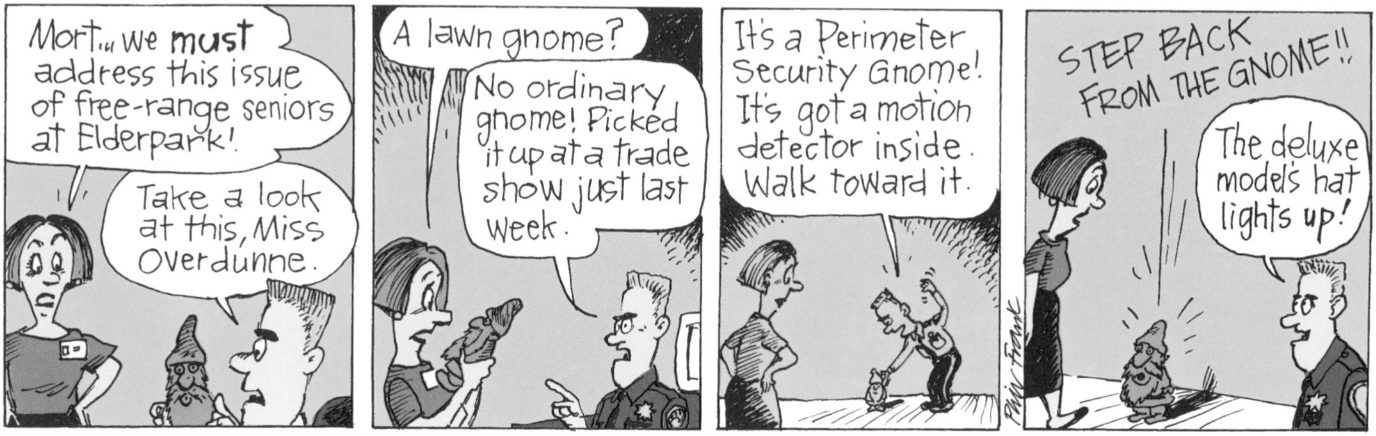
Mort... we **must** address this issue of free-range seniors at Elderpark!
Take a look at this, Miss Overdunne.
A lawn gnome?
No ordinary gnome! Picked it up at a trade show just last week.
It's a Perimeter Security Gnome! It's got a motion detector inside. Walk toward it.
STEP BACK FROM THE GNOME!!
The deluxe model's hat lights **up**!

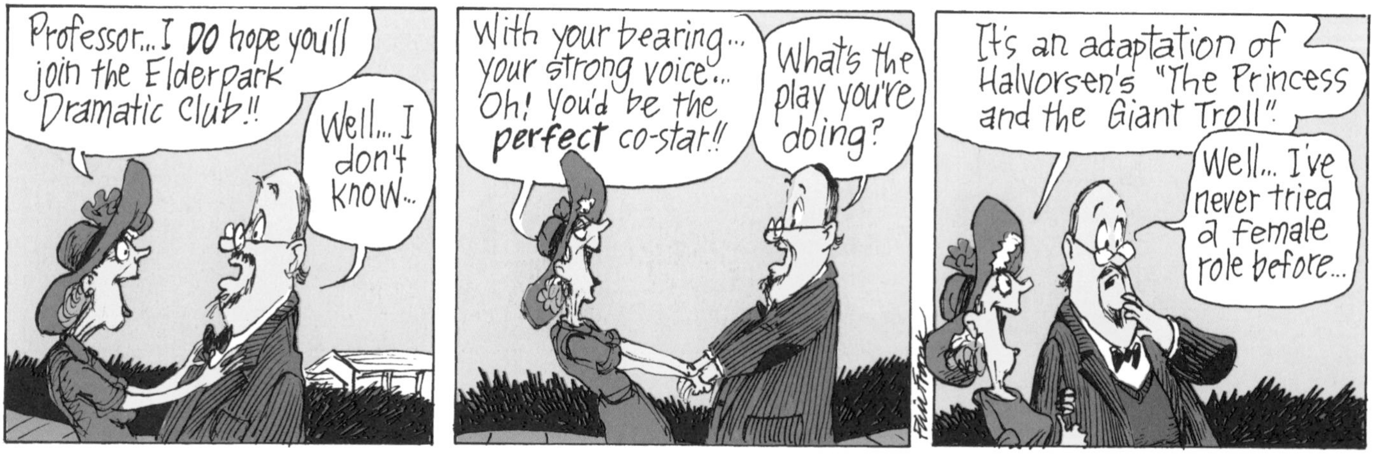
Professor... I **DO** hope you'll join the Elderpark Dramatic Club!!
Well... I don't know...
With your bearing... your strong voice... Oh! You'd be the **perfect** co-star!!
What's the play you're doing?
It's an adaptation of Halvorsen's "The Princess and the Giant Troll".
Well... I've never tried a female role before...

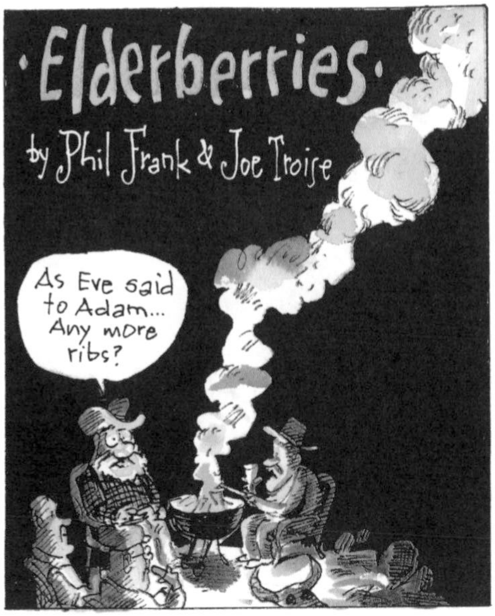
Elderberries
by Phil Frank & Joe Troise
As Eve said to Adam... Any more ribs?

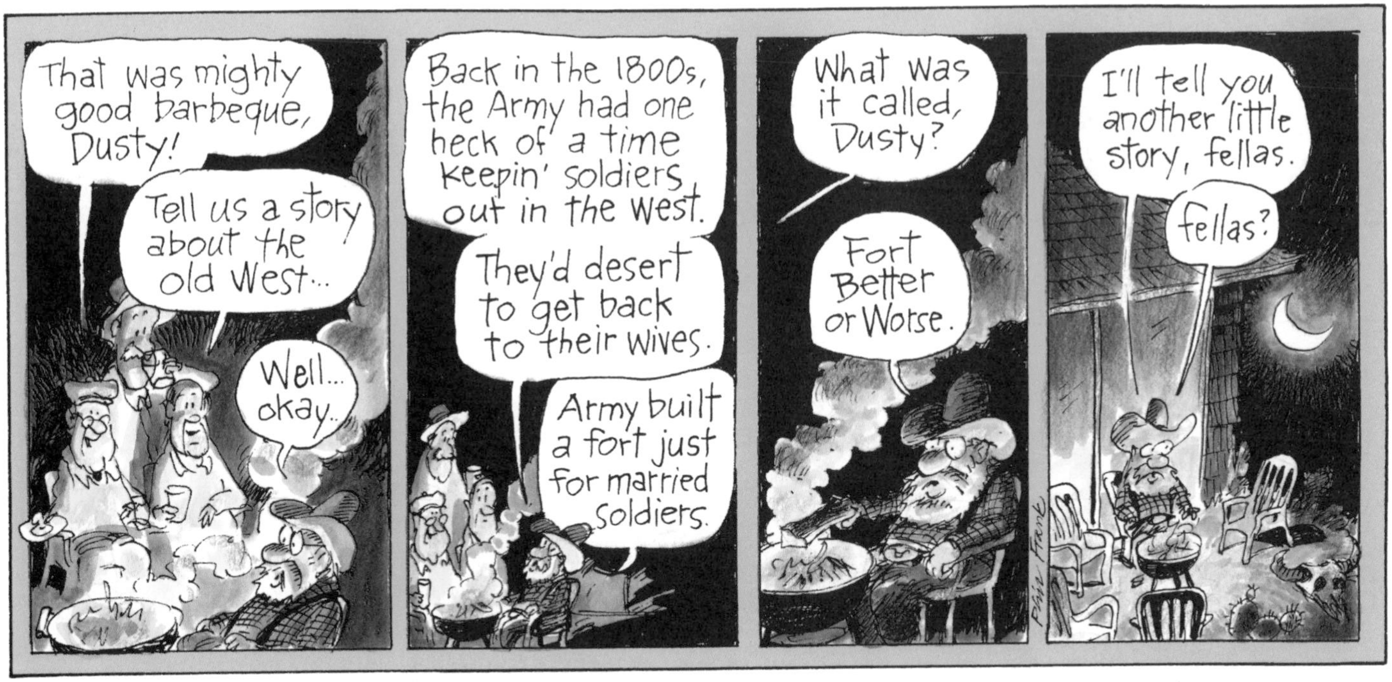
That was mighty good barbeque, Dusty!
Tell us a story about the old West...
Well... okay..
Back in the 1800s, the Army had one heck of a time keepin' soldiers out in the West.
They'd desert to get back to their wives.
Army built a fort just for married soldiers.
What was it called, Dusty?
Fort Better or Worse.
I'll tell you another little story, fellas.
fellas?
Phil Frank

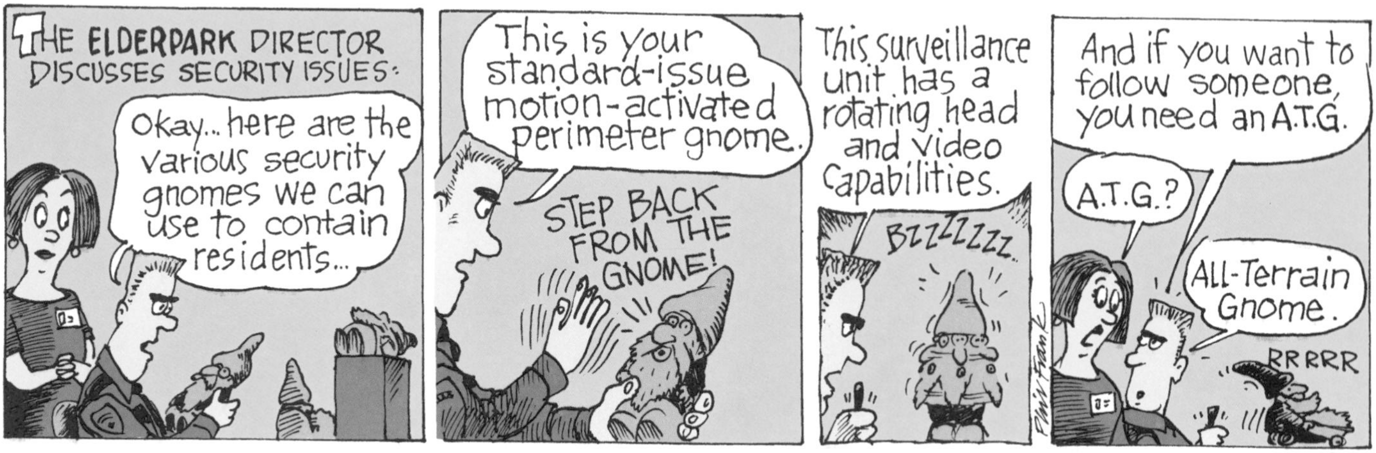
THE ELDERPARK DIRECTOR DISCUSSES SECURITY ISSUES:
Okay... here are the various security gnomes we can use to contain residents...
This is your standard-issue motion-activated perimeter gnome.
STEP BACK FROM THE GNOME!
This surveillance unit has a rotating head and video capabilities.
BZZZZZZ..
And if you want to follow someone, you need an A.T.G.
A.T.G.?
All-Terrain Gnome.
RRRRR

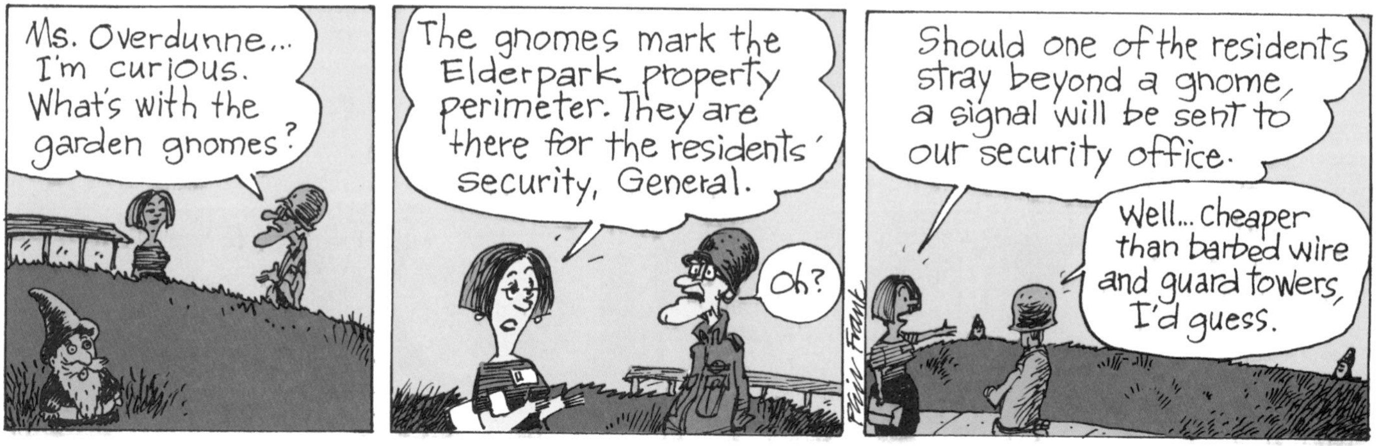
Ms. Overdunne... I'm curious. What's with the garden gnomes?
The gnomes mark the Elderpark property perimeter. They are there for the residents' security, General.
Oh?
Should one of the residents stray beyond a gnome, a signal will be sent to our security office.
Well... cheaper than barbed wire and guard towers, I'd guess.

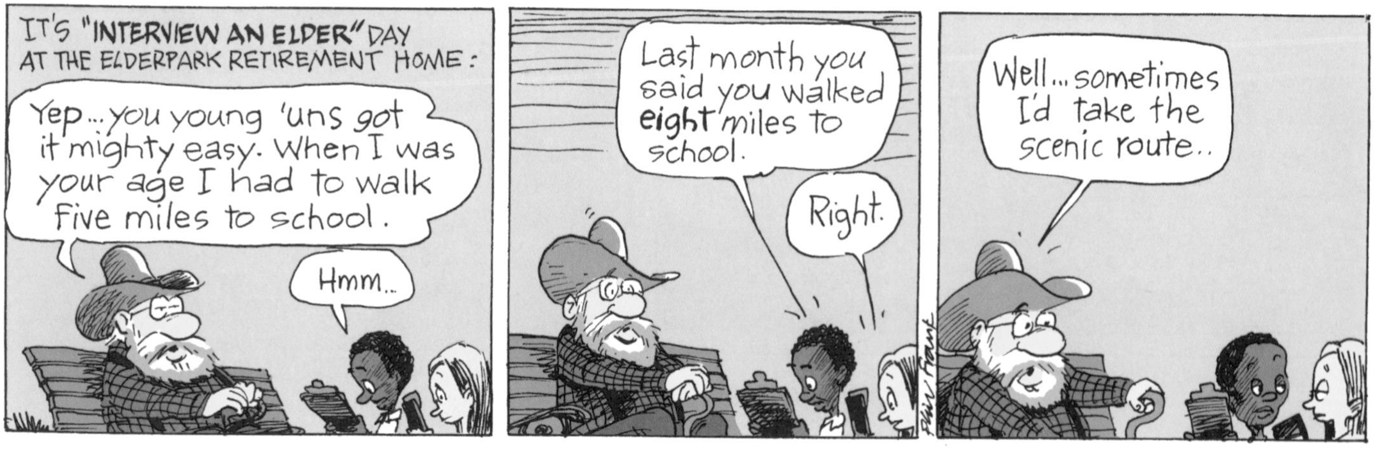
IT'S "INTERVIEW AN ELDER" DAY AT THE ELDERPARK RETIREMENT HOME:
Yep... you young 'uns got it mighty easy. When I was your age I had to walk five miles to school.
Hmm...
Last month you said you walked eight miles to school.
Right.
Well... sometimes I'd take the scenic route..

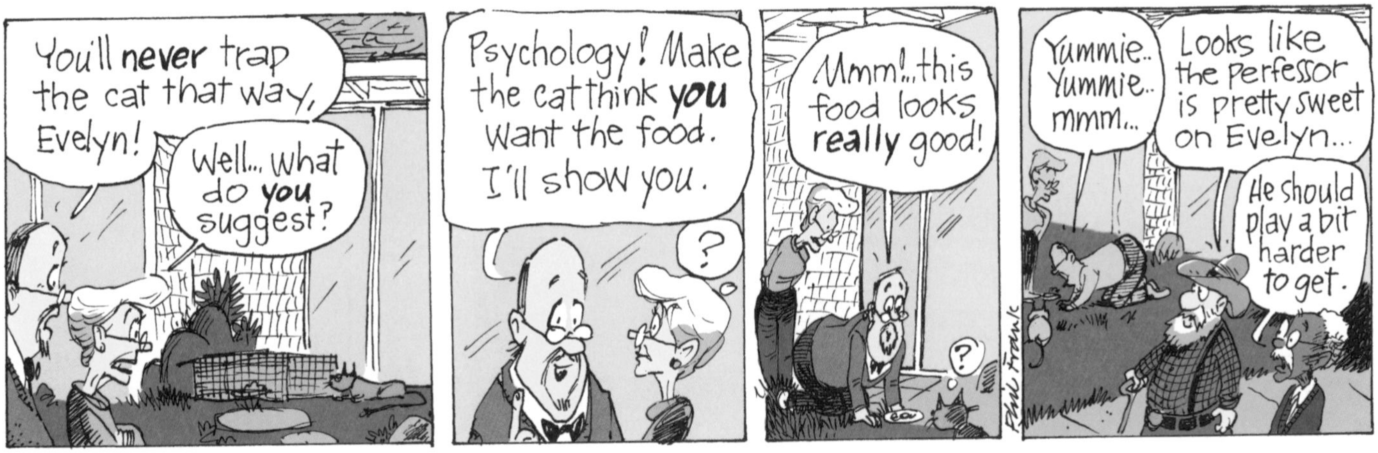
You'll **never** trap the cat that way, Evelyn!
Well... what do **you** suggest?
Psychology! Make the cat think **you** want the food. I'll show you.
?
Mmm!.. this food looks **really** good!
?
Yummie.. Yummie.. mmm...
Looks like the perfessor is pretty sweet on Evelyn...
He should play a bit harder to get.

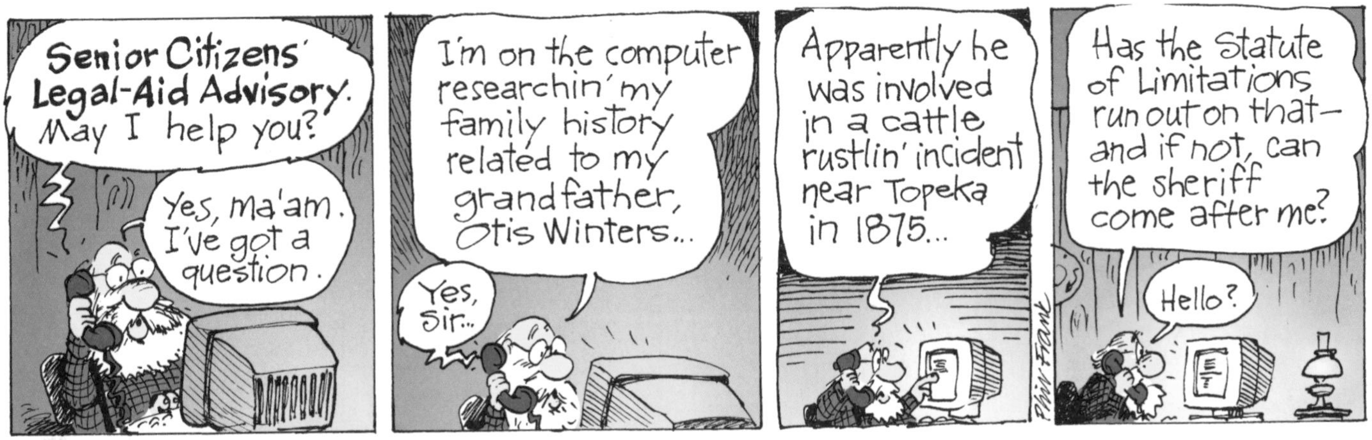
Senior Citizens' Legal-Aid Advisory. May I help you?
Yes, ma'am. I've got a question.
I'm on the computer researchin' my family history related to my grandfather, Otis Winters...
Yes, sir...
Apparently he was involved in a cattle rustlin' incident near Topeka in 1875...
Has the Statute of Limitations run out on that— and if not, can the sheriff come after me?
Hello?

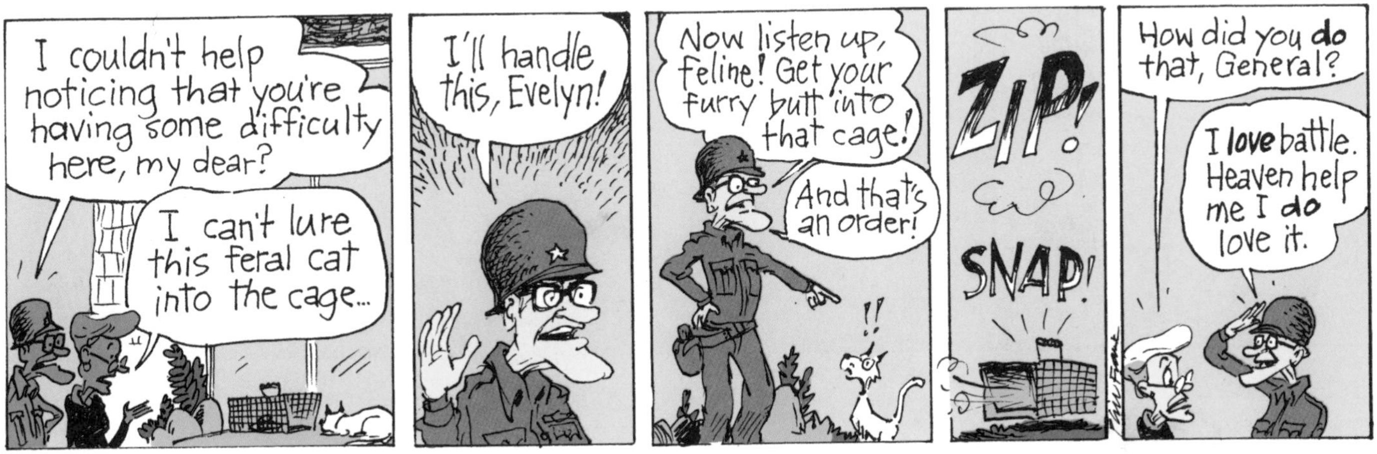
I couldn't help noticing that you're having some difficulty here, my dear?
I can't lure this feral cat into the cage...
I'll handle this, Evelyn!
Now listen up, Feline! Get your furry butt into that cage!
And that's an order!
!!
ZIP!
SNAP!
How did you **do** that, General?
I **love** battle. Heaven help me I **do** love it.

Elderberries
by Phil Frank and Joe Troise
Mom... is that you?

I like our visits, Randy. It gives me a chance to catch up with my boy's life.
Suddenly... the jungle grew strangely quiet... Randy Adams sensed danger...
I heard your brother-in-law's medical practice is growing by leaps and bounds.
Without any warning... THWACK! ...the poison dart hit him in the neck...
And your wife's pay increase... how great!! She must be making more than you now...
THWACK! ...a second dart strikes home... Randy feels the paralysis creep over him...
Randy!! Are you listening to me?
The tall Amazon warrior stands over her quarry as he slips mercifully... ...into... unconscious... ...ness...
Phil Frank

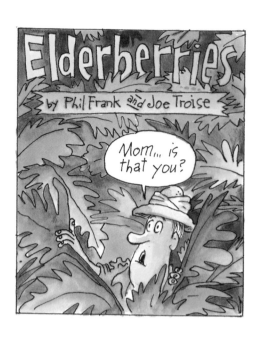

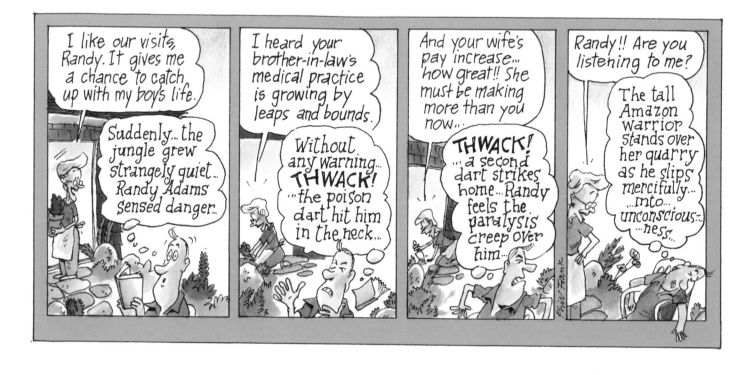

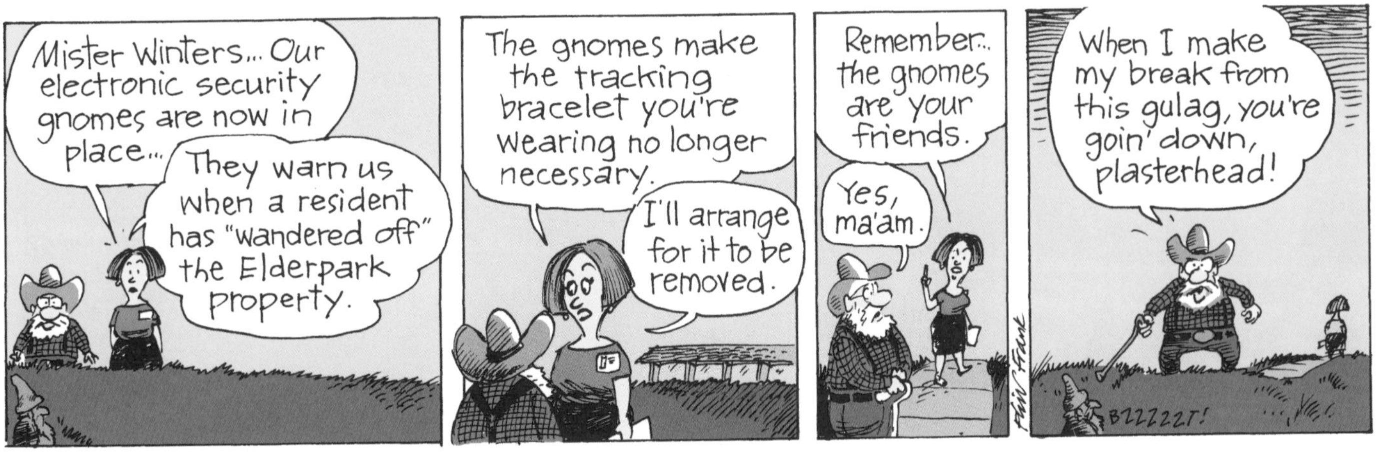
Mister Winters... Our electronic security gnomes are now in place...
They warn us when a resident has "wandered off" the Elderpark property.
The gnomes make the tracking bracelet you're wearing no longer necessary.
I'll arrange for it to be removed.
Remember... the gnomes are your friends.
Yes, ma'am.
When I make my break from this gulag, you're goin' down, plasterhead!
BZZZZZT!

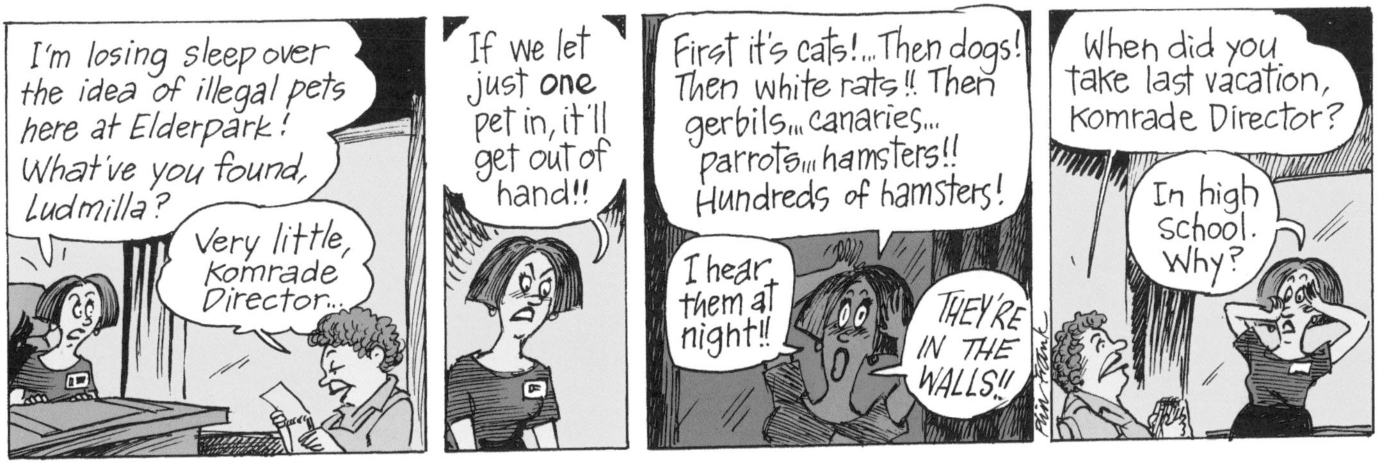
I'm losing sleep over the idea of illegal pets here at Elderpark! What've you found, Ludmilla?
Very little, Komrade Director...
If we let just **one** pet in, it'll get out of hand!!
First it's cats!... Then dogs! Then white rats!! Then gerbils... canaries... parrots... hamsters!! Hundreds of hamsters!
I hear them at night!!
THEY'RE IN THE WALLS!!
When did you take last vacation, Komrade Director?
In high school. Why?

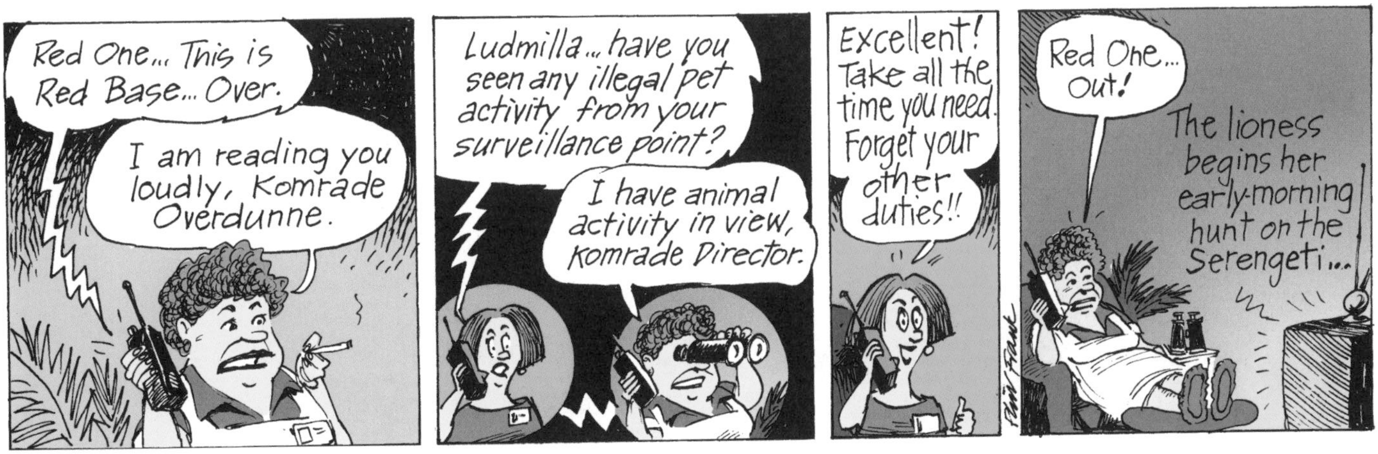
Red One... This is Red Base... Over.
I am reading you loudly, Komrade Overdunne.
Ludmilla... have you seen any illegal pet activity from your surveillance point?
I have animal activity in view, Komrade Director.
Excellent! Take all the time you need. Forget your other duties!!
Red One... Out!
The lioness begins her early-morning hunt on the Serengeti...

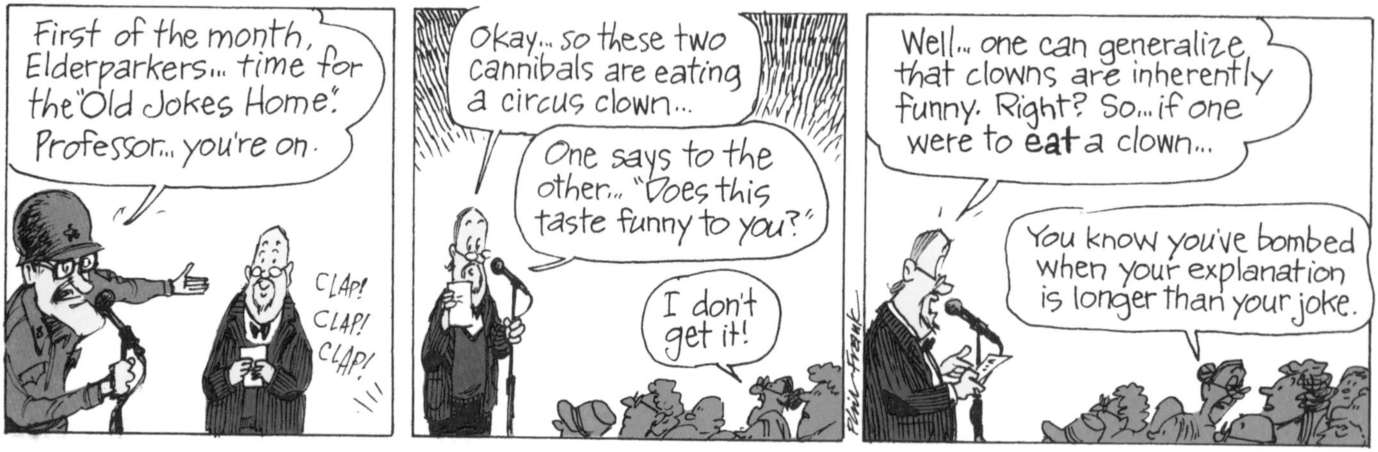
First of the month, Elderparkers... time for the "Old Jokes Home". Professor... you're on.
CLAP! CLAP! CLAP!
Okay... so these two cannibals are eating a circus clown...
One says to the other... "Does this taste funny to you?"
I don't get it!
Phil Frank
Well... one can generalize that clowns are inherently funny. Right? So... if one were to **eat** a clown...
You know you've bombed when your explanation is longer than your joke.

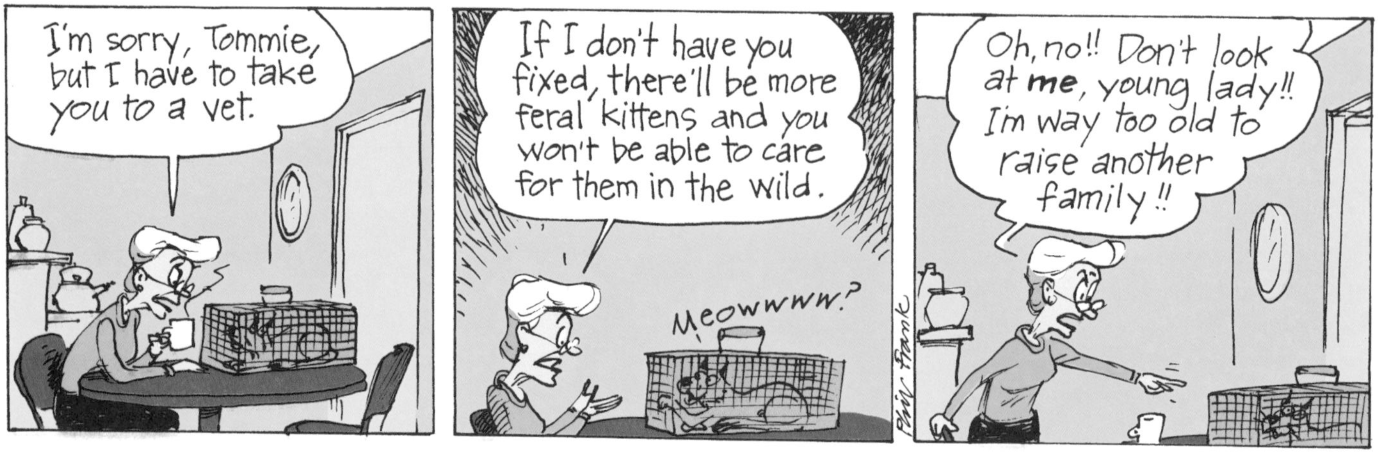
I'm sorry, Tommie, but I have to take you to a vet.
If I don't have you fixed, there'll be more feral kittens and you won't be able to care for them in the wild.
MEOWWWW?
Phil Frank
Oh, no!! Don't look at **me**, young lady!! I'm way too old to raise another family!!

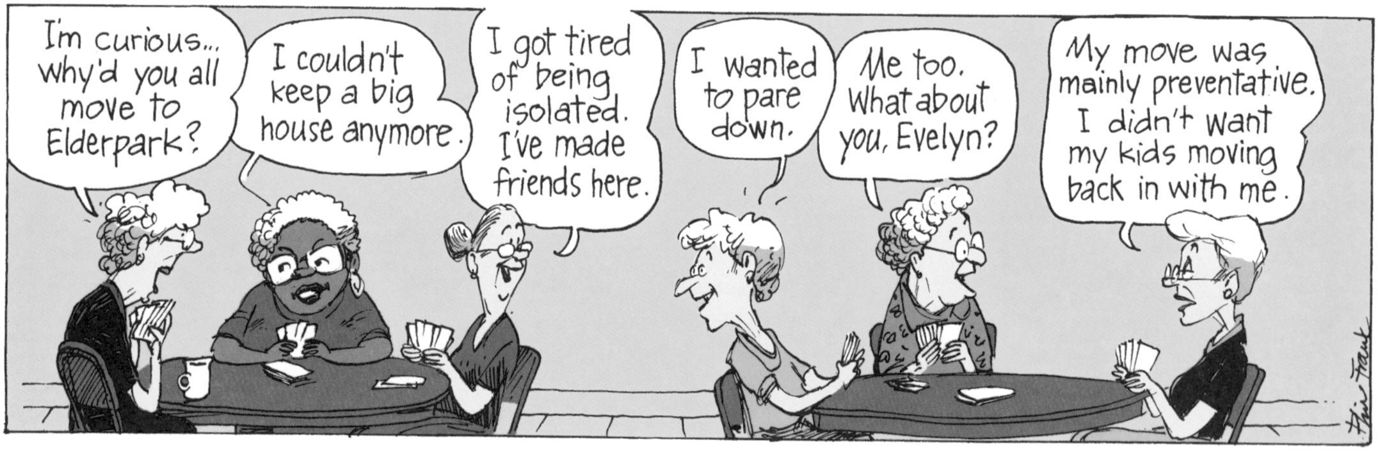
I'm curious... why'd you all move to Elderpark?
I couldn't keep a big house anymore.
I got tired of being isolated. I've made friends here.
I wanted to pare down.
Me too. What about you, Evelyn?
My move was mainly preventative. I didn't want my kids moving back in with me.
Phil Frank

Elderberries
by Phil Frank & Joe Troise
BREAK A LIMB, DUSTY!

Ladies and gentlemen... I proudly present the "Elderpark Players" in... "Salute to Labor Day."
I am the tireless American worker... Industrious... loyal... never a shirker.
I build your boats and planes and cars... And even rockets sent to Mars.
I build your highways – Straight and true. Your bridges, tunnels and houses too!
My leafy boughs will shade your lawn... Upon my branches fruit are borne. I shelter creatures great and small, Like squirrels, birds and...
PSSST!! Dusty! Labor Day. Not Arbor Day!
?
Phil Frank

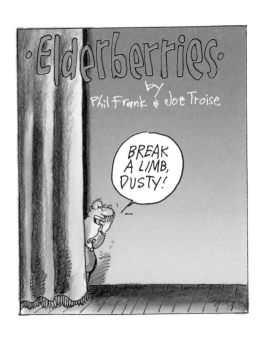

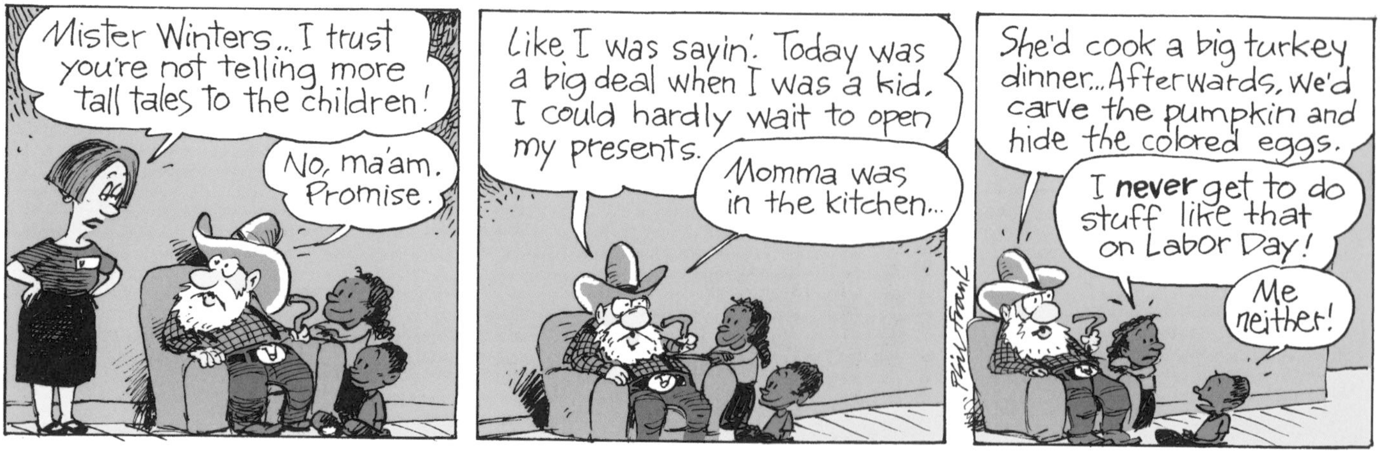
Mister Winters... I trust you're not telling more tall tales to the children!
No, ma'am. Promise.
Like I was sayin'. Today was a big deal when I was a kid. I could hardly wait to open my presents.
Momma was in the kitchen...
She'd cook a big turkey dinner... Afterwards, we'd carve the pumpkin and hide the colored eggs.
I **never** get to do stuff like that on Labor Day!
Me neither!

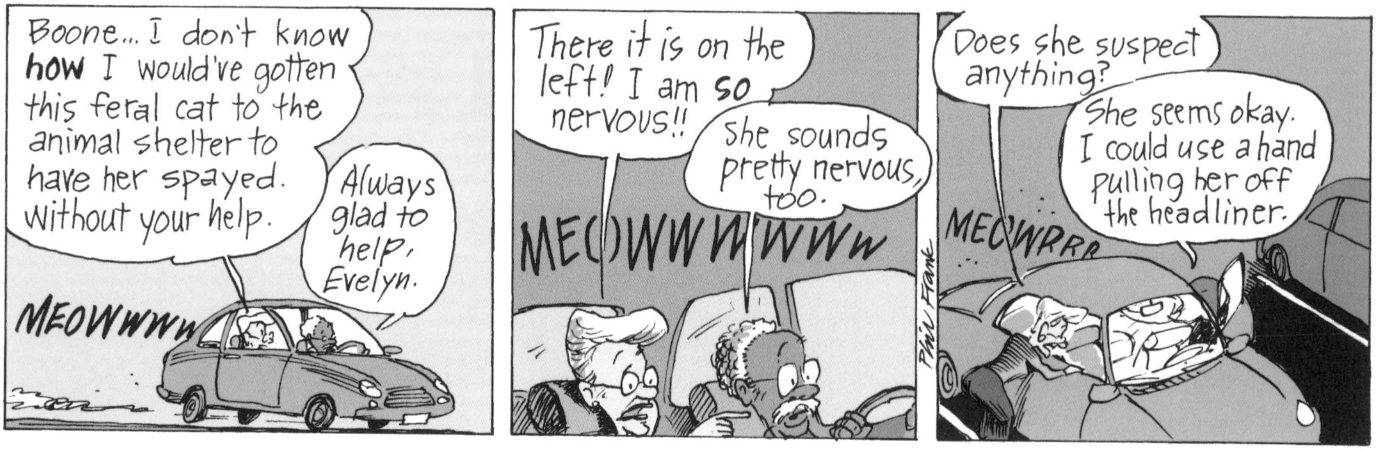
Boone... I don't know **how** I would've gotten this feral cat to the animal shelter to have her spayed. without your help.
Always glad to help, Evelyn.
MEOWWWW
There it is on the left! I am **so** nervous!!
She sounds pretty nervous, too.
MEOWWWWWWW
Does she suspect anything?
She seems okay. I could use a hand pulling her off the headliner.
MEOWRRR

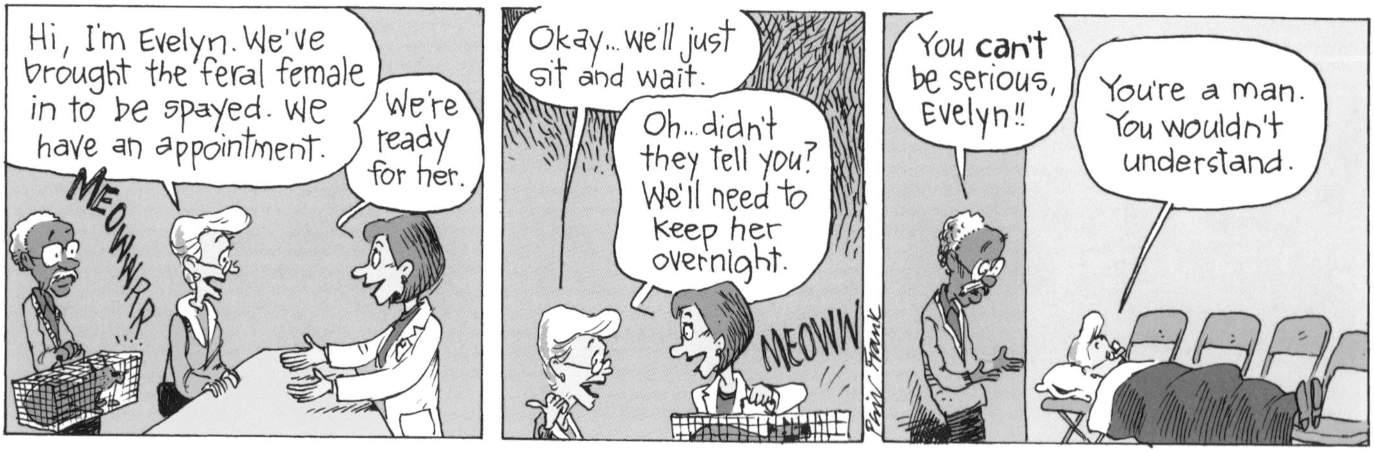
Hi, I'm Evelyn. We've brought the feral female in to be spayed. We have an appointment.
We're ready for her.
MEOWWRR
Okay... we'll just sit and wait.
Oh... didn't they tell you? We'll need to keep her overnight.
MEOWW
You **can't** be serious, Evelyn!!
You're a man. You wouldn't understand.

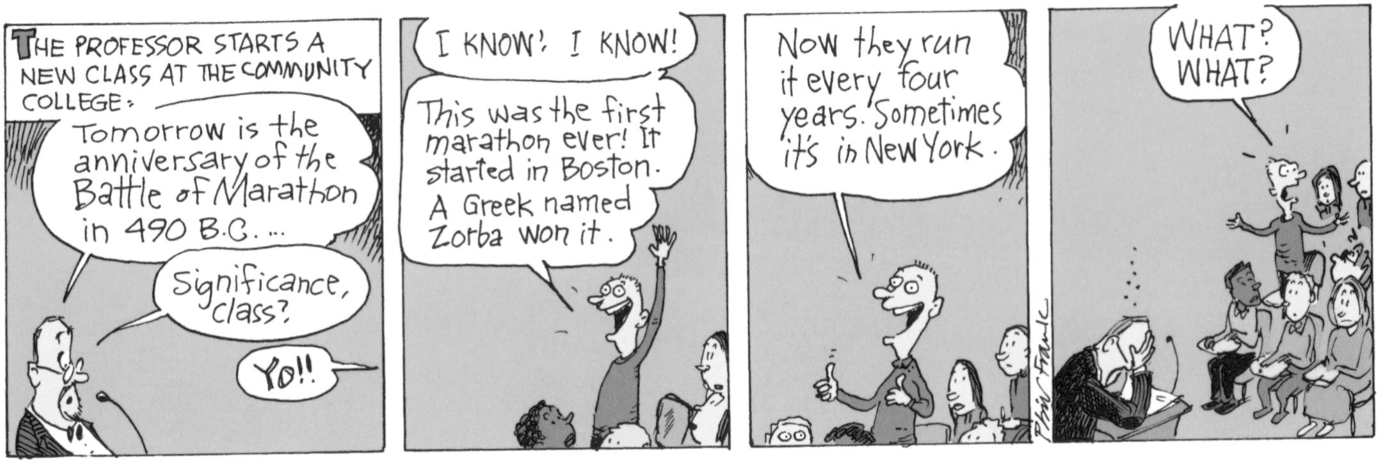
THE PROFESSOR STARTS A NEW CLASS AT THE COMMUNITY COLLEGE:
Tomorrow is the anniversary of the Battle of Marathon in 490 B.C. ...
Significance, class?
YO!!
I KNOW! I KNOW!
This was the first marathon ever! It started in Boston. A Greek named Zorba won it.
Now they run it every four years. Sometimes it's in New York.
WHAT? WHAT?

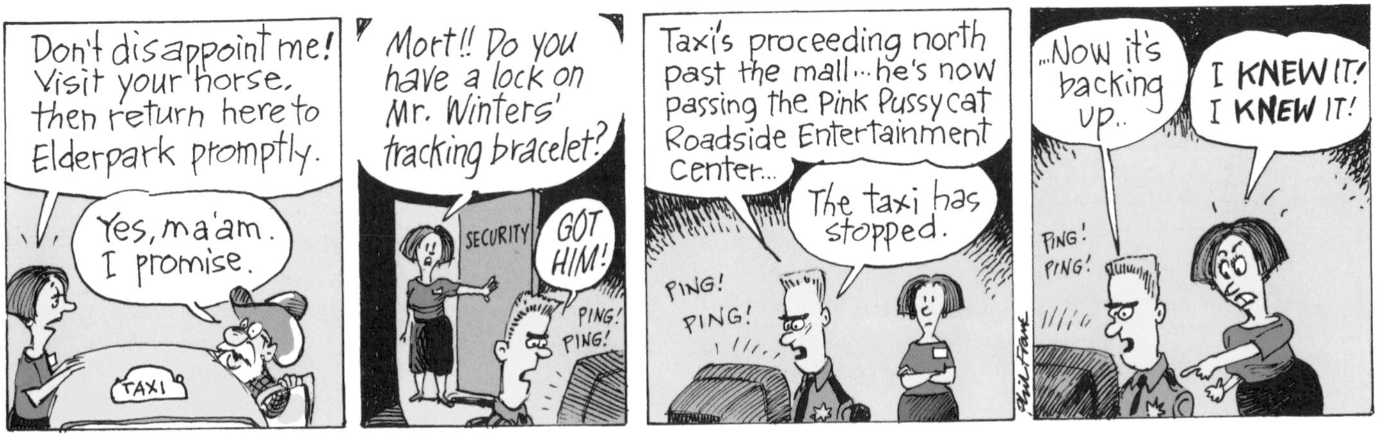
Don't disappoint me! Visit your horse, then return here to Elderpark promptly.
Yes, ma'am. I promise.
TAXI
Mort!! Do you have a lock on Mr. Winters' tracking bracelet?
SECURITY
GOT HIM!
PING! PING!
Taxi's proceeding north past the mall... he's now passing the Pink Pussycat Roadside Entertainment Center...
The taxi has stopped.
PING! PING!
...Now it's backing up..
I KNEW IT! I KNEW IT!
PING! PING!

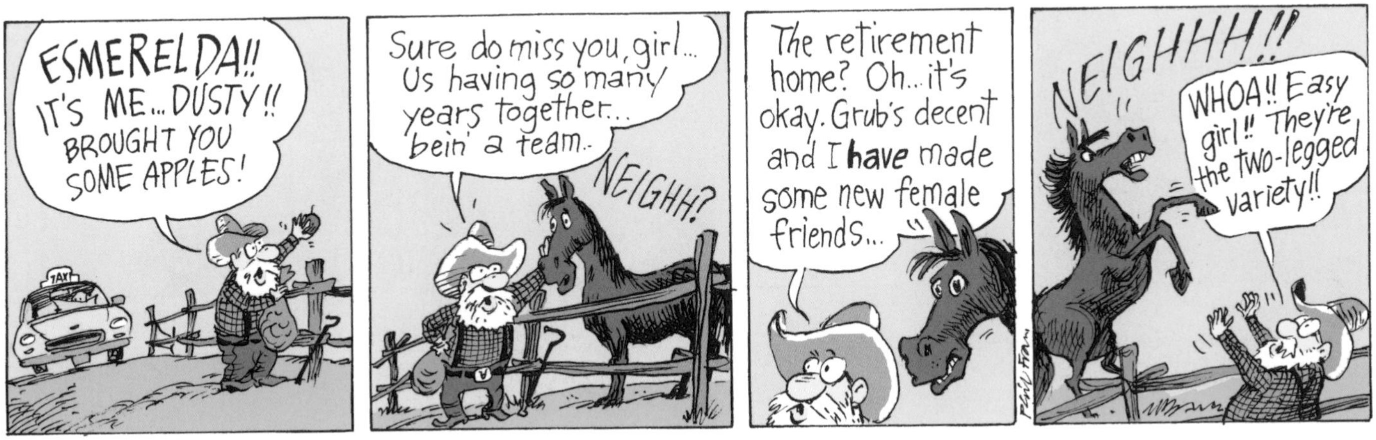
ESMERELDA!! IT'S ME... DUSTY!! BROUGHT YOU SOME APPLES!
TAXI
Sure do miss you, girl... Us having so many years together... bein' a team..
NEIGHH?
The retirement home? Oh... it's okay. Grub's decent and I have made some new female friends...
NEIGHHH!!
WHOA!! Easy girl!! They're the two-legged variety!!

Elderberries
by
Phil Frank & Joe Troise
Just be another minute, pardner.
TAXI

I ken still remember the very first time I rode you in a rodeo, back in our salad days, Esmerelda...
TAXI
Why... you could accelerate like nobody's business. Ain't no way you was gonna git outrun, girl!
You rode like a dream and turned on a dime...
...'course, the brakes were a little touchy.
INCOMING!

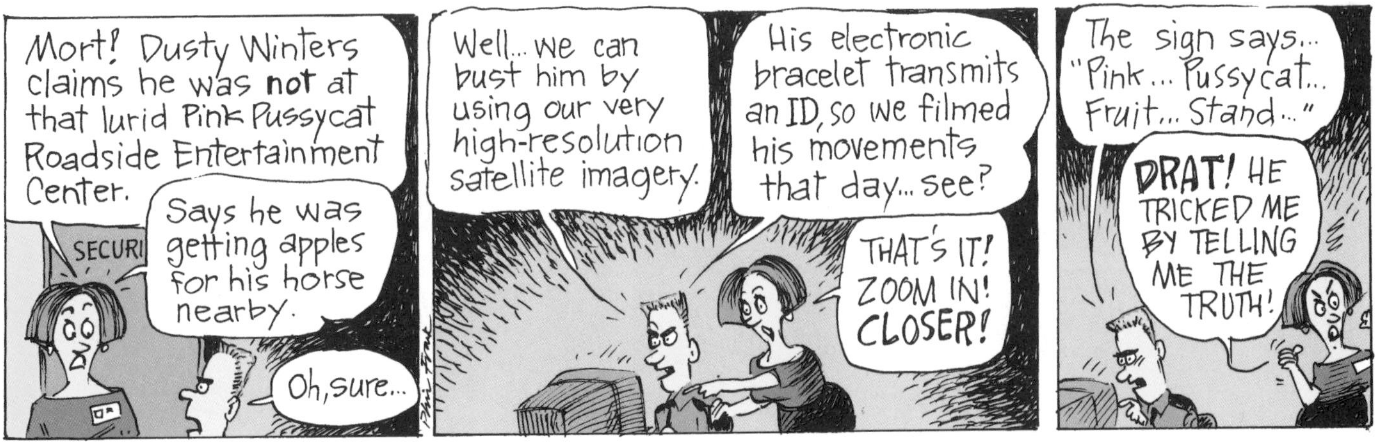
Mort! Dusty Winters claims he was **not** at that lurid Pink Pussycat Roadside Entertainment Center.
SECURI
Says he was getting apples for his horse nearby.
Oh, sure...
Well... we can bust him by using our very high-resolution satellite imagery.
His electronic bracelet transmits an ID, so we filmed his movements that day... see?
THAT'S IT! ZOOM IN! **CLOSER!**
The sign says... "Pink... Pussycat... Fruit... Stand..."
DRAT! HE TRICKED ME BY TELLING ME THE TRUTH!

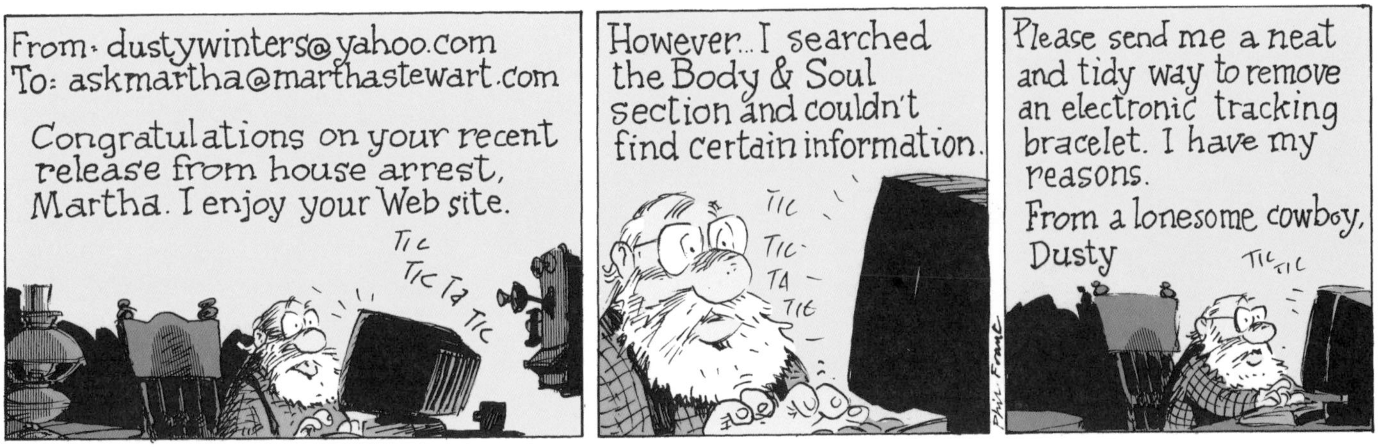
From: dustywinters@yahoo.com
To: askmartha@marthastewart.com
Congratulations on your recent release from house arrest, Martha. I enjoy your Web site.
TIC TIC TA TIC
However... I searched the Body & Soul section and couldn't find certain information.
TIC TIC TA TIC
Please send me a neat and tidy way to remove an electronic tracking bracelet. I have my reasons.
From a lonesome cowboy, Dusty
TIC TIC

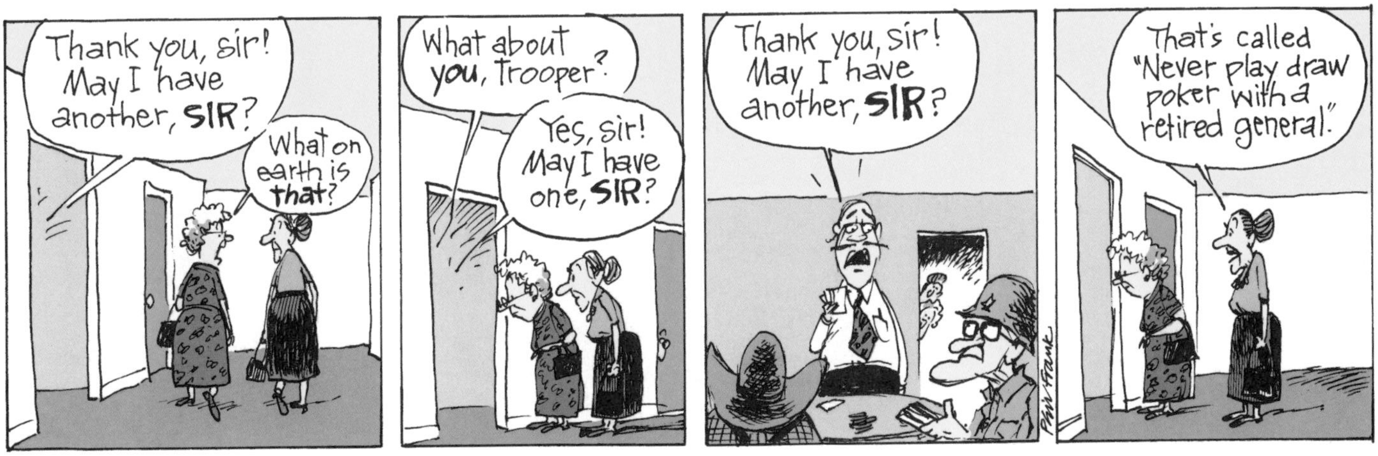
Thank you, sir! May I have another, **SIR**?
What on earth is **that**?
What about **you**, Trooper?
Yes, sir! May I have one, **SIR**?
Thank you, sir! May I have another, **SIR**?
That's called "Never play draw poker with a retired general."

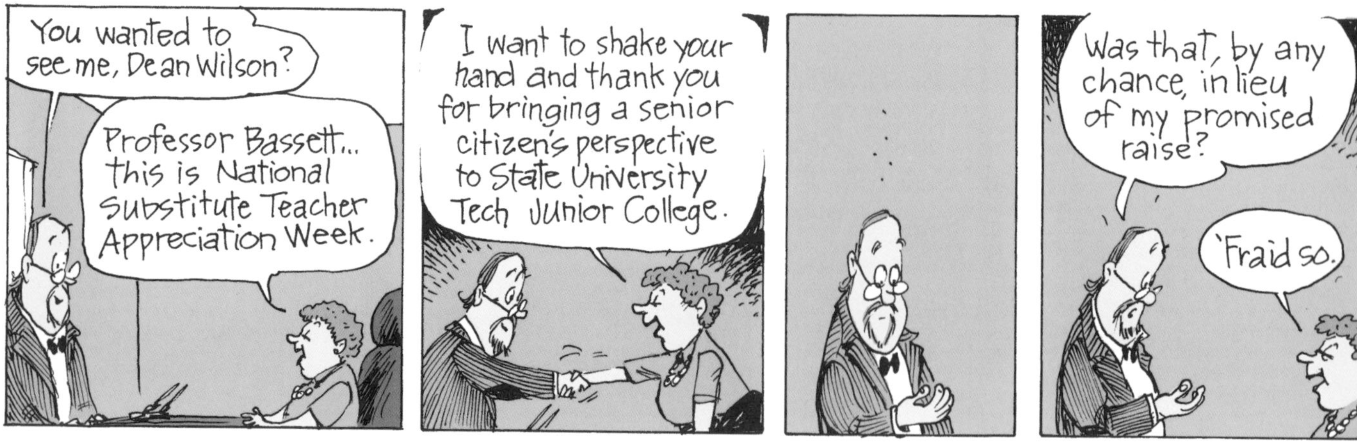
You wanted to see me, Dean Wilson?
Professor Bassett... this is National Substitute Teacher Appreciation Week.
I want to shake your hand and thank you for bringing a senior citizen's perspective to State University Tech Junior College.
Was that, by any chance, in lieu of my promised raise?
'Fraid so.

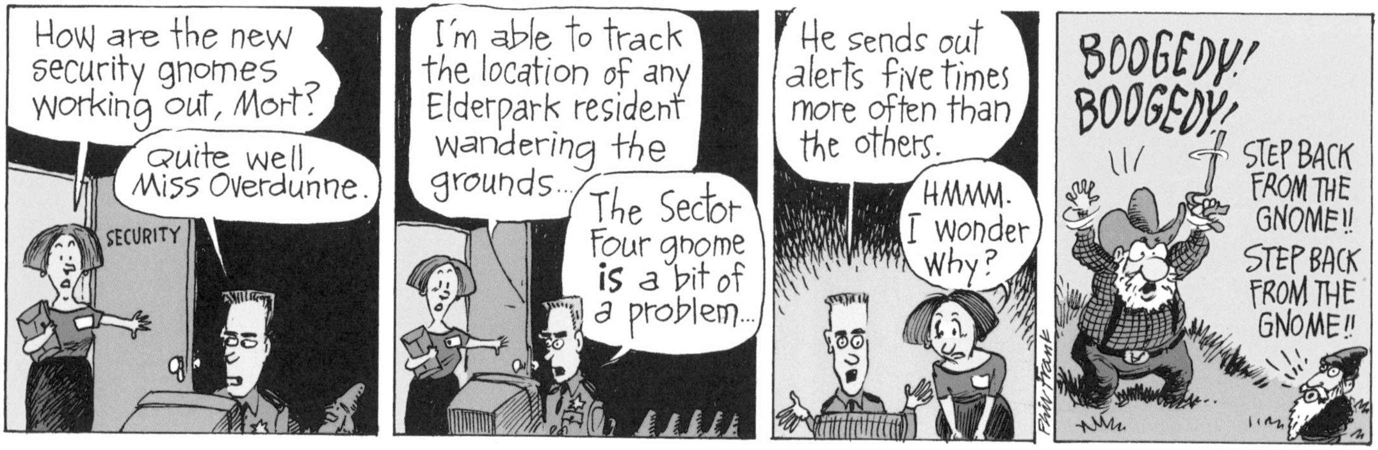
How are the new security gnomes working out, Mort?
Quite well, Miss Overdunne.
SECURITY
I'm able to track the location of any Elderpark resident wandering the grounds...
The Sector Four gnome **is** a bit of a problem...
He sends out alerts five times more often than the others.
HMMM. I wonder why?
Phil Frank
BOOGEDY! BOOGEDY!
STEP BACK FROM THE GNOME!! STEP BACK FROM THE GNOME!!

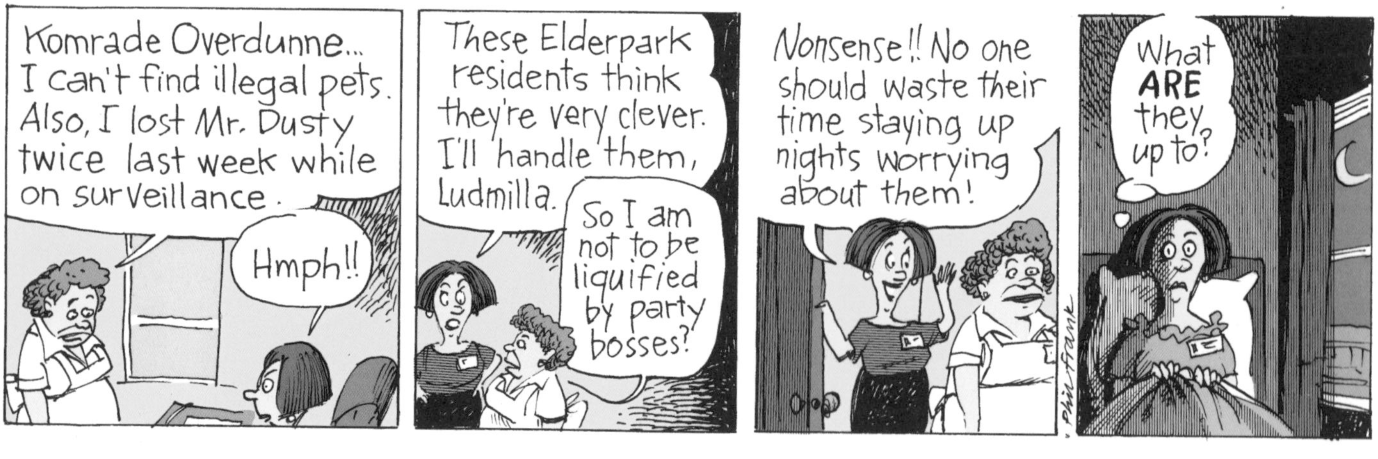
Komrade Overdunne... I can't find illegal pets. Also, I lost Mr. Dusty twice last week while on surveillance.
Hmph!!
These Elderpark residents think they're very clever. I'll handle them, Ludmilla.
So I am not to be liquified by party bosses?
Nonsense!! No one should waste their time staying up nights worrying about them!
Phil Frank
What **ARE** they up to?